A SHORT HISTORY
OF WORLD WAR II

A SHORT HISTORY OF WORLD WAR II

JAMES L. STOKESBURY

William Morrow and Company, Inc.
New York   1980

Library of Congress Cataloging in Publication Data

Stokesbury, James L.
  A short history of World War II.

  Bibliography: p.
  Includes index.
  1. World War, 1939-1945.   I. Title.
D743.S67   940.53   79-20896
ISBN 0-688-03587-6
ISBN 0-688-08587-3 pbk.

Printed in the United States of America.

First Edition

1   2   3   4   5   6   7   8   9   10

Soon after Pearl Harbor, my father enlisted in the army, where he served until 1945 as a sergeant in the 338th Infantry, 85th Division, in the Italian campaign. My mother went to work in a defense plant in Connecticut. I would like to think that this book is a small thank-you for what they did during those years of war.

Acknowledgments

IT IS A PLEASURE for me to acknowledge the assistance, direct and indirect, of many friends who have helped in the preparation of this work. The staffs of the Acadia University Library, the Dalhousie University Library, and the Cambridge Military Library, Halifax, have been uniformly helpful. All my colleagues in the Department of History, Acadia University, have been unfailingly supportive; special thanks must go to Dr. A. H. MacLean, Head of the Department, and to Dr. Martin Blumenson and Dr. Thaddeus V. Tuleja, both holders of the Visiting Professorship of Military and Strategic Studies, for their encyclopedic knowledge of World War II. Miss Debbie Bradley typed the entire manuscript with a most encouraging enthusiasm. A more general word of thanks is due to my students in my course on World War II for their interest and inquisitiveness over the years, which did much to prompt this study. I must add the cautionary note that any errors of fact or interpretation are mine, and not to be attributed to anyone else. My final, and most heartfelt, thanks go to my wife, who has been my kindest and most patient critic.

JAMES L. STOKESBURY

Contents

CONTENTS

PART III: "THE HOUR WHEN EARTH'S FOUNDATIONS FLED. . . ."

PART IV: TOWARD THE ELUSIVE VICTORY

PART I: PROLOGUE

1. Peace and Rearmament

WORLD WAR II BEGAN in Europe at dawn on September 1, 1939, as units of the German Wehrmacht crossed the Polish border. Britain and France, honoring their pledge to Poland made earlier in the year, declared war on Germany on September 3. The war lasted nearly six years, and by the time it was over, much of the civilized world lay in ruins, something more than thirty million people had been killed, great empires had been destroyed, and weapons of new and hitherto unimagined potential had been unleashed upon the world.

Such a result could not have stemmed from a border dispute between Germany and Poland. The powder train that led to the outbreak of war went back far beyond the immediate causes of it. Without stretching historical continuity too far, the causes of World War II can be taken back at least into the nineteenth century. For practical purposes, however, World Wars I and II can be considered part of one large struggle—the struggle of united Germany to claim its place as the dominant power on the European continent—and the causes of World War II can be traced from the immediate aftermath of World War I.

In 1919, a series of treaties was made between the victorious Allies and the various defeated powers. All of these were punitive in nature. They consisted of the Peace of Versailles with Germany, the Peace of Saint-Germain-en-Laye with Austria, the Peace of Neuilly with Bulgaria, the Peace of the Trianon with Hungary, and the Peace of Sèvres with Turkey, later modified by the Peace of Lausanne. The fact that all of the original treaties were signed in the suburbs of Paris and bore their names was indicative of the place still occupied by the French in the world of diplomacy and power. Though she had virtually ruined herself, in the present and for the future, France had proved that she was still the major power of Europe. All of the peace treaties, though they did put the burden of the war on the defeated Central Powers, also contained the provision that the vanquished might subsequently be admitted to the League of Nations, that much maligned brainchild of President Woodrow Wilson. The League, its supporters hoped, with its provisions for collective security, would provide alternatives to war in the future.

The five years after the establishment of the "Versailles system" have been called "the period of settlement." Assorted border disputes left over from the war and the collapse of the eastern European empires—Russia, the Hapsburgs, and Turkey—were settled, and diplomatic groupings were made and unmade. The Greeks fought the Turks; the Poles fought the Russians; Italians and Yugoslavs quarreled over the head of the Adriatic. France, Britain, and the United States negotiated a defensive alliance that promised to protect France from Germany. On the basis of that, the French modified their demands against Germany. The United States Senate then refused to ratify the alliance treaty, as it did also the Versailles treaty. The French were then disposed to meddle ineffectually in German politics, trying to foster a breakaway Rhenish republic, occupying the industrial Ruhr district, and engaging in activities that made the Americans, at least, believe that the French could not have been trusted anyway.

Nonetheless, by 1924, it looked as if some degree of stability were returning to Europe, and the late twenties were the nearest to a period of peace and prosperity that post-World War I Europe got. In 1924, assorted member-states of the League of Nations attempted to overcome some of the security deficiencies of the League by drafting treaties of compulsory arbitration. None of these developed, largely because the United States, Germany, and Russia were not members, and because the British dominions were unwilling to commit themselves to minding distant neighbors' houses.

The unsuccessful discussions did lead, though, to a conference held at Locarno in Switzerland in 1925. This produced another series of agreements, known as the "Locarno system," which effectively updated the Versailles system. In the first of these, France, Great Britain, Belgium, Germany, and Italy guaranteed the Franco-German and the Belgo-German borders. Next, Germany signed an arbitration treaty with Poland, and one with Czechoslovakia. Then Germany signed a similar treaty with France and one with Belgium. Theoretically, these treaties removed any likelihood of German aggression in the future. In spite of that, France then proceeded to develop further her mutual defense treaty with Poland, in which one agreed to come to the rescue if the other were attacked by Germany. France then went on and signed the same kind of treaty with Czechoslovakia.

Locarno was hailed as a milestone in European diplomacy, and for a while the "spirit of Locarno" and the "Locarno honeymoon" were phrases widely used by the newspapers. A later outgrowth of it was the famous Kellogg-Briand Pact, signed between the United States Secretary of State and the French Foreign Minister; this pact was rather like the Holy Alliance of Tsar Alexander in 1815, which Metternich called a "high-sounding nothing." All the states that eventually adhered to it renounced the use of aggressive warfare as an instrument of policy. There was, however, an opting-out clause, and there was no provision for any enforcing of the pact. Like Locarno, it looked good on paper.

It was Germany's neighbors who had most to fear, or thought they had, and it was they, particularly France, who soon discovered the cracks beneath all this paper. France had after all been twice invaded by Germany in recent memory, in the Franco-Prussian War of 1870-71 and again in 1914-18, and she was not disposed to put her faith in someone else's expression of good intent. Even in the early twenties then, the French began creating their own private alliance-system against Germany.

France and Poland had signed a defensive alliance in 1921. At that time the newly resurrected Poland was busy fighting with Russia; just as in the eighteenth century, she proved no match for the Russians—though at one point the Poles did threaten Moscow —and now as then she turned to France for help. A French military mission helped the Poles keep the Russians away from Warsaw, and the two states signed an alliance in which both looked fearfully east: the Poles to Moscow, and the French to Berlin.

There were also assorted mini-systems in central and eastern Europe. In 1920, Yugoslavia and Czechoslovakia signed an alliance that became known as the "Little Entente." Poland allied with Rumania in 1921, and Rumania then joined in with the Little Entente. After Locarno, France realized that her various alliances did not prevent German aggression directed toward the east and the south. She therefore reaffirmed her alliance with Poland, and she also joined the Little Entente, extending her ties to the southeast. Theoretically, she had created a diplomatic barrier against potential German aggression in any direction. Actually, she had now made it extremely likely that, if Germany developed any expansionist tendencies at all, the French would be dragged into another war—exactly what the alliances were all supposed to avoid. None of the treaties could disguise the basic fact of European life— a united Germany was potentially the strongest power on the Continent. France began to rearm.

Less than a decade after the end of the war to end all wars, and after all the talk of peace settlements, guarantees, mutual-defense systems, alliances, and treaties, the countries of Europe were faced once again with the old problem of military force. A concomitant to the bankruptcy of diplomacy was the even worse failure of the movement for disarmament.

At the signing of the military armistice in November of 1918, and more definitively in the Peace of Versailles, Germany had been effectively disarmed. She had been limited to an army of 100,000 men, which made the French happy. Her navy had been held to no more than thirty-six combat vessels, including no submarines and no modern battleships, and that made the British happy. She was not allowed to have an air force, and she was not permitted any military installations within fifty kilometers of the east bank of the Rhine River—the famous "demilitarization of the Rhine."

All of these provisions were systematically circumvented by the German government, often unwittingly aided by the Allied Control Commissions set up to oversee them. The army, for example, had been envisaged by the peacemakers as an internal police force. But the German General Staff, officially broken up at the end of the war, actually reformed and disguised as a troop-organization office, built up an army in which every man was to be a potential officer or noncommissioned officer. The 100,000-man *Reichswehr* thus became the skeleton of a larger army, to be fleshed out when the occasion arose. The Allied control officers, all serving professional soldiers rather than internal-security specialists, allowed and in some cases encouraged the Germans to set up organizations capable of dealing with armored cars which would one day become tanks, and heavy infantry weapons and artillery pieces.

Denied an air force, the Germans developed a great interest in sport gliding. That was in the thirties, after Hitler came to power, and he would soon spring a full-grown air force on the world. Before Hitler, there was liaison between the Germans and the other European outcasts of the twenties, Bolshevik Russia; substantial numbers of Germans trained troops of the Soviet army and air force, and were in turn trained by them. The navy perhaps lagged behind, as 1940 would show, but it too kept up on technical developments, and when it did start rebuilding, it was in the forefront of naval design.

The disarmament of Germany was predicated on the idea that there would be a general disarmament after World War I. The prewar arms race was widely regarded as one of the major contributing causes to the Great War, and there was a strong movement to get rid of arms and armaments manufacturers—the "merchants of death"—after the war ended. This movement resulted in the usual series of conferences.

The most famous of these was probably the Washington Conference of 1922. Most of the disarmament movement came to be concentrated on naval strengths. This was ironic, because the mythology of militarism tends to regard navies as defensive and democratic, and armies as offensive and autocratic. Perhaps because ships are more visible than tanks, perhaps because they are more readily countable, more likely because the leaders of the movement were the British and the Americans, both naval powers, the conferences generally dealt with naval strengths first.

The Washington Conference was held essentially because the British could not afford a naval race with the United States. The American government, before it got involved in World War I, had launched a massive naval-building program. During the war this had been shelved, and the United States built escort vessels rather than battleships to beat the submarine menace. After the war, the big-ship building program was dusted off, and work on the battleships was begun again. The British protested vehemently; they had not defeated Germany only to end up playing second fiddle to the United States. Finally, a conference was convened at Washington, to which all the major naval powers were invited.

Some small progress was made. The conference agreed to the famous 5:5:3 ratio for capital-ship tonnage—the United States and Britain being 5, the Japanese 3. France and Italy both came out as 1.75; neither liked the idea. There was also an agreement that the United States would not fortify its holdings in the Pacific west of Hawaii, nor the British east of Singapore, a concession to Japanese pride and the British and American taxpayer that would be paid for in 1942.

In 1927, the Allied Control Commission stopped overseeing Germany. Another naval conference was held at London in 1930. The idea at this one was to extend the 5:5:3 ratio to other classes of vessels, but not much was accomplished. The British, Americans, and Japanese all had different imperial requirements, and wanted different classes and types of ships to meet them. Some watered-down provisions were accepted. The Russian delegation, led by Maxim Litvinov, proposed complete and immediate disarmament for everybody; this was rejected out of hand as a Bolshevik trick.

In 1932, a commission of the League of Nations produced a preparatory draft for a general scheme of disarmament. The proposal, however, left untouched all previous treaties that dealt with arms limitations. Among these, the French insisted on including the Versailles treaty, with its provisions about German strengths. This meant there could be no German rearmament; that meant there could be no equality of arms, and that in turn, by the convoluted logic of politics, meant there could be no disarmament.

There was another try in 1935, but by then Hitler was in power in Germany, and the talk was more of the need for rearmament, rather than disarmament. For practical purposes the movement was dead. Strengths and weapons-systems would now increase instead of decrease. How far this would go, and what direction it might take in any given state depended upon a variety of factors: geographical, economic, and political. For in pre-World War II Europe, each state had its own particular problems and its own particular ideas of how they should be dealt with.

2. The European Democracies

IN ANY DISCUSSION of World War II, the first question that arises is why the democracies of Europe did not stop Germany before it was too late. In a sense, this question is no more than the usual Monday-morning quarterbacking. One answer must obviously be that if the democracies knew what lay ahead, and if they knew that they could have stopped Hitler, then of course they would have done so. They knew neither of these things at the time, though perhaps they should have. Hitler had spelled out his program for all the world, provided anyone were sufficiently persevering to wade through *Mein Kampf*; but like most political testaments, it was not taken seriously until its author was in a position to carry it out. We now have sufficient evidence not only that Hitler could have been stopped, but also that the Western Powers knew he could have been stopped, had they had the will to do it when it could be done short of war. They remained, however, resolutely preoccupied with their own difficulties, of either a general or a specific nature.

In general terms, it is fair to say that the victors of World War I were as demoralized by their victory as the losers were by their defeats. They may even have been more demoralized—they, after all, had won; then they discovered how little their victory had brought them. The costs of winning were enormous, both in material terms and in manpower, and the truth was that relatively few of the great powers of 1914 were able to sustain them.

At the start of the Great War, the myth of the "Russian steamroller" was still alive and well. It was German fear of the increasing power of Russia that had been one of the factors in her decision for war in 1914. Yet by 1916, not only had the steamroller failed to materialize, but Russia was on the verge of collapse, a collapse that occurred dramatically but not surprisingly in 1917. Both Germany and the Austro-Hungarian Empire followed in 1918 at the end of the war. Though Italy was spared outright military defeat, her

political institutions were so strained by war that they did not out-
last the immediate aftermath of it. France had neared the edge of
the precipice in 1917 when her army mutinied, and when the
United States entered the war in the same year, Great Britain was six
weeks away from starvation at the hands of the U-boats and even
closer to financial bankruptcy. The fact that France and Britain did
go on to win the war preserved their great-power status, but to a
very considerable extent they were great powers by default, and
their appearance of strength and solidity was no more than an
illusion.

This was particularly true of France. In 1919, Russia was in
revolution, Germany was in anarchy, and the Austro-Hungarian
Empire had finally split up into its component parts. The British
went back to insisting they were not a continental power. France
therefore reclaimed the position she had held from 1648 to 1870,
of being the pre-eminent power on the Continent, which had been
challenged by the Germans after the unification of Germany and
the Franco-Prussian War. It was a position that France was not
really entitled to in a modern industrial world. France's iron and
steel production was below that of her neighbors, her coal output
was lower, her financial base was less secure, and her birthrate was
declining.

Aware though they might be of the grim outlook presented by
these basic statistics, Frenchmen were reluctant to recognize the
logical conclusion to be drawn from them: that France was well on
the way to becoming a second-class power. The official view was
that as long as Germany could be kept down, France would retain
her primacy. The French therefore became the most obstinate supporters of the status quo as enacted at Versailles. It was they who
supported Rhenish separatism, they who occupied the Ruhr Valley
in 1923 when Germany fell behind in her war reparations. This
backfired, as did most of the measures of the period. The French
insisted on their reparations payments; the German government
responded by printing paper, thereby paying off its bills in useless
currency. The French nonetheless continued to insist on receiving
their payments and it was they, even up to the mid-thirties, who
were the most resolute against any revision of the Versailles treaty
and any equality of status for Germany.

This was about the only item on which French governments
were resolute. As a nation they were impoverished, enfeebled, and
enervated by war. The stereotype personification of the Frenchman
before the war was of a vigorous officer winning bits of empire for

la civilisation française. After the war it was of an old man, slump-shouldered, bowed down by his cares and his past, making his annual pilgrimage along the *voie sacrée* to the Armistice Day ceremonies at Verdun. If little things give away a country's sense of itself, it is significant that French subway cars still reserve rush-hour seats for *"les grands mutilés de la guerre"*—the multiple amputees of World War I.

Politically, the French argued their causes passionately and developed deep divisions between the right and the left. The divisions went so deep that the French Republic got lost somewhere in the middle.

Governments of the twenties and thirties rose and fell with alarming regularity. Even more alarming was the fact that they were the same old governments. Coalition after coalition of tired politicians played musical chairs and swapped ministries and made their back-room deals. The real problems of the republic—finance, industry, social reform, education—all were held in abeyance while the politicians talked. Words were the only surplus item in interwar France.

Of all the problems they failed to solve, the military one would become the most crucial, at least from the viewpoint of World War II. It was, indeed, a complex problem.

The first difficulty was the matter of manpower. The French had had military conscription, in one form or another, for some centuries. It had become regularized and modernized in the latter part of the nineteenth century, after the Franco-Prussian War had demonstrated, apparently conclusively, that a big short-service army was better than a small long-service one. This conclusion was probably wrong, but it was nevertheless the one all the experts drew from the war. France had rebuilt her army after 1871 with large numbers of conscripts on the German model. Her problem was that in the twentieth century she lacked the basic bodies to conscript. Before World War I her birthrate declined to the point where she had to keep her conscripts with the colors a year longer than the Germans did just to keep her numbers up. Every man-year in the army was an unproductive one from the point of view of the national economy, and equally from the point of view of marriage, parenthood, and the production of future potential conscripts. Add to this already existing difficulty the enormous wastage of World War I—1,654,000 deaths, most of them presumably of potential parents—and the demographic problems of filling up the ranks become readily apparent. During the thirties the French government would respond to its financial problems by reducing the length of military service, but that only further aggravated the difficulties of an army committed to large masses of citizen-soldiers.

For the army itself it was not just a problem of numbers, but of what to do with them. The whole question of the French inter-war military doctrine is crucial to what happened in 1939 and 1940. Had they made different decisions, there might well have been no World War II.

The major question was, what sort of military posture should France adopt? The man most responsible for the answer was Henri Philippe Pétain, hero of Verdun, Marshal of France. He was to France in the period what Wellington had been to Britain after Waterloo, or what Eisenhower would be to the United States after World War II. He had saved Verdun, he had restored the French Army after the 1917 mutinies, he had won through to victory in 1918. His stock was immeasurably high; it had not always been so.

Pétain had been the maverick of the pre-World War I army. At that time the French had sought to overcome their material deficiencies by developing the idea that the defensive strategy employed in the Franco-Prussian War was unsuited to the French temperament. The French were used to attacking. Writers conjured up visions of the *furia francese* of the French invasions of Italy during the Renaissance, of the glorious attacks of Murat's cavalry during the Napoleonic wars. French élan would carry all before it; their battle cry was *Toujours l'audace!*

The only thing wrong with this doctrine, which had a fatal attraction for a nation behind materially, was that it would not work. All the daring in the world produced only enormous casualty lists when tried against German machine guns. It was Pétain who realized this fatal flaw. A dour, phlegmatic man, cold and aloof, he produced his own response to the idea of the unlimited attack. He said simply, *"Le feu tue."* "Fire kills." It was a douche of cold water on the heads of the theorists. They responded by making him virtually an outcast in the army. He and his supporters found themselves at the bottom of the promotion lists. Always quoted of Pétain is the remark one of his early commanders made on his annual fitness report: "If this man rises above the rank of major, it will be a national disaster for France."

But now World War I had come and gone, and fire had indeed killed; it had killed more than one and a half million Frenchmen, and the man who had said it would do so was the saviour of France. Where his opponents had said "attack" he had said "defend," and he had been right. Now in his seventies—a Marshal of France did not retire—still vigorous, still commanding, he saw no reason to change his mind. He had been a heretic in 1910, but he had been right. He was the citadel of orthodoxy in 1925, and he was still right—or so he thought.

There were not too many people who argued with him, though there were some. Basically, the French Army commanders tied their thinking to the idea of the defensive. Key men in a nation that prided itself on its logic, they carried this idea to a logical conclusion. If hastily prepared field fortifications had been the war winner of 1914-18, how much stronger therefore would be fully prepared fortifications, dug in, cemented, casemated at leisure, with carefully tended fields of fire, amenities for the troops, modern communications and control systems. The French embarked on the building of a great belt of fortifications on the German frontier. They named it after their Minister of War, significantly a *"grand mutilé"* of the Great War, a man named André Maginot.

The Maginot Line was begun after Locarno, and it eventually grew to be a series of steel-and-concrete emplacements that ran from almost the Swiss border north along the west bank of the Rhine as far as Montmédy at the southeastern extremity of Belgium. It was billed as impenetrable, and it probably was.

The French have been accused of monumental national stupidity in that they built half a fortress and left the other half of their country completely vulnerable to an end-run around their fortified belt. In reality it was not that simple. First of all, the cost of the Maginot Line was enormous, and though the Franco-German border portion of it was pretty well finished by the late twenties, the Depression hit France before any more of it was done. More vital than money, however, was the problem of allies. In 1914, Belgium had been neutral, her status guaranteed by a treaty going back to the 1830's—this was Kaiser Wilhelm's "scrap of paper" over which Great Britain went to war. Throughout the war the Belgians had fought valiantly alongside the French and British; it had been their country that had been invaded by Germany in the famous Schlieffen Plan. After the war, Belgium had reasserted her neutrality and had not aligned herself with France.

Theoretically then, the French had no obligation to consider the Belgians in their defense planning. They could, had they chosen to do so, have continued the Maginot Line along the Belgian frontier to the sea. But for one thing they could not afford it; for another, it would mean abandoning a likely ally. It would also mean running the line through heavily built up and highly industrialized territory, and that was undesirable. Finally, it would mean, in the event of another German war and a replay of the Schlieffen Plan, letting the Germans come in through Belgium, and therefore fighting the war on French soil rather than on Belgian soil.

None of these was especially appealing, so the French decided on other alternatives. In the event of another war, they would leave Luxembourg and Belgium open and fight the war there. The Maginot Line was not seen anyway as an absolutely impervious barrier. It was instead a way of conserving troops; a relatively few men manning the fortifications would be able to withstand heavy numbers. This would leave the mobile masses of the French Army free to maneuver on the Belgian frontier. The Line would also have the effect of channeling a German attack into Belgium, where the French would be ready to meet them. The French therefore would not fortify the dense Ardennes region of southeastern Belgium, which they considered unsuitable country for mobile operations, and they would not fortify along the Belgian frontier. This was where they would fight their war.

There were two problems with this. One was that it required a certain degree of German agreement on how the war would be fought and where; the Germans would have to accept the French assessment of the Maginot Line and its role, and of the Ardennes and its impassability. They would have to agree to fight World War I over again. When the time came they nearly did.

The second problem was that, having built an immensely expensive fortification so that they could free a large part of their army for mobile operations, the French then lacked the money and the disposition to make the army mobile. Throughout the thirties, though they produced many fine weapons and armored vehicles in prototype, they seldom put them into production. Their military doctrine was not sufficiently well formed for them to proceed on the basis of it and produce the necessary weaponry. Basically dominated by the ideas of the defensive, paying only lip service to the idea of mobility, they were uncertain what to do about the technology that would restore mobility to war. In effect, their weapons technology was the victim of their flawed or inconsistent strategic and tactical doctrine.

The difficulty here was that 1914-18, which provided the mental set of the French high command in the years after the war, had been a predominantly defensive war. In fact, it had hardly been even that, and more than anything else it had been a siege on a gigantic scale, essentially a static war. Both sides had sought a way out of this impasse; neither had found it. Artillery, barbed wire, and the machine gun had combined to deny movement to the participants on the battlefield. This was true even in the vast stretches of the Eastern Front; it was particularly the case on the Western Front.

The weapons, or vehicles, that would restore mobility to warfare were of course used, but not in a visibly significant sense. The tank was introduced by the Allies; it was a simple concept: mount a weapon on a caterpillar tread and you can break through a defensive line. Military conservatism militates against the use of simple innovations, however, and it was not until 1918 that the tank was produced and used in numbers sufficient to demonstrate its potential as an infantry-support weapon. That it might become more than that was an idea left to a few visionaries. The Germans, thought to be the most innovative of military thinkers, virtually ignored the tank until the end of the war. Their first experience of it had shown that it was probably useless. After it appeared in numbers, they could not see how to counter it, so they tried to forget it. They also lost the war.

When the French considered the problem of the tank between the wars, they took an essentially conservative view of it. It would not be much more than it had been in 1918. This idea was challenged by a whole series of theoretical writers. In Britain, B. H. Liddell Hart and J. F. C. Fuller were developing the ideas that would make the linear trench systems of 1914-18 obsolete. Instead of distributing tanks to the infantry, they ought to be used en masse, as armored spearheads. Like the cavalry of old, they could break the enemy's line and then go on the rampage in his rear areas, disrupting communications and the passage of reserves. This was Liddell Hart's theory of "the expanding torrent." The tank would become the dominant weapon, and the infantry would just move in and occupy ground after the tanks had taken it. These ideas were picked up by some German students, notably Guderian and Manstein, and they were also paralleled by those of French thinkers, especially General Estienne, the father of the French tank force. In the thirties, they were adopted by a Colonel Charles de Gaulle, who wrote a book called *Vers l'armée du metier*. The book had little influence and was largely a rehashing of Fuller and Liddell

Hart. What de Gaulle advocated was a small, mobile, professional army. Ironically, he was asking for the kind of army that Versailles had forced on the Germans.

What the French high command wanted, and got, was the large, slow, mass army of World War I. With their fixation on linear defense-systems, they were not disposed to listen favorably to ideas of armored spearheads that could break lines. They stuck to tanks as an infantry-support weapon. This in turn led them to neglect speed, maneuverability, and especially tank-to-tank communication. Therefore, even when they did finally organize fully armored formations, their tanks, the best in the world for infantry cooperation, were deficient for armored combinations.

The worth of the airplane was recognized, but since both sides had it, it had achieved nothing decisive either. It was useful for artillery spotting and reconnaissance and for shooting down the other side's artillery spotters and reconnaissance. A few people, British officers in the Royal Flying Corps, conceived the idea that airplanes could do more, that they might be capable of long-distance bombing and some strategic results. What little they accomplished was enough to convince the visionaries of the value of their vision; most observers remained skeptical.

Unfortunately, by the time either the tank or the airplane did anything of real note, the Germans were cracking anyway. Professional military minds were therefore able to reassure themselves that, while these new inventions might be valuable adjuncts to warfare, they were not and never would be anything more than that. Until 1939, an officer could still make his career in the horse cavalry. The French, having won the war by conventional methods, were not disposed to introduce unconventional ones.

What they did produce during the interwar years was a very respectable navy. It had new and modern units that were certainly able to dominate the Mediterranean in a potential conflict with the other Mediterranean power, Italy. The spirit and the equipment of the French navy in the thirties was probably higher than it had been since the days of Choiseul in the mid-eighteenth century. The navy had a notable place in the French imperial scheme of things. Unhappily, it would not be of much immediate value in another Franco-German war.

The upshot of the whole thing was that France, wracked by internal crisis and the strain of maintaining its image as a great power, staggered uncertainly into the decade of the Depression. Her military forces were basically strong, but the doctrines that infused them were inconsistent at best and faulty at worst. The weapons technology that flowed from those doctrines was partially flawed. By the time she needed it, her strength was already crippled by self-inflicted wounds.

Though they were reluctant to admit it, the French believed their security ultimately depended upon their relation with Great Britain. The British themselves were far less certain about this. British policy had traditionally been directed toward maintaining the balance of power on the Continent, and this had led her, from about 1689 on, into a series of anti-French coalitions. After 1870, it was no longer the French who threatened to achieve a hegemony over Europe, and therefore the British had gravitated, almost unknowingly, into the anti-German coalition that fought the First World War. Yet old ideas died hard. In terms of national stereotypes, even though the British and French fought World War I together, they did not really *like* each other. The alliance always had divergent ends, and ideas of means to achieve them; it was Marshal Foch in 1918 who remarked that after his experience with coalitions, he had less respect for Napoleon than he used to have.

The British had also resented the kind of war they had had to fight. Their policy was always to use their navy to great advantage, and to employ a small army, beefed up by subsidized allies whom they bought among the continental powers. In 1914, they found that that would no longer work; they had been forced to field a large army, and had watched for four years while it slowly sank into the Flanders mud. Several times at crisis points the Anglo-French alliance threatened to come apart at the seams.

At the end of the war the French and British views parted company. France wanted to ruin Germany permanently; Britain was not so sure. Germany was a threat, but she was also Britain's largest prewar customer. The British backed off from any long-term commitment to France, glad of the excuse given them by the Americans, and they preferred to put their hopes on the League of Nations. Somewhat paradoxically, the British became the major backer of the League, a backing that was always ineffective because they were conscious of lacking the support of the United States.

In addition to casting a disapproving eye on French policies toward the Germans, the British had their own difficulties. The war had created enormous social dislocation; there was unemployment, unrest, and a wave of strikes through the twenties. New York had replaced London as the world's financial capital. Though some historians say the war was good for Britain, as unleashing hitherto dormant or unproductive energies, most regard it as an unmitigated disaster. There were major problems with the empire as well: Ireland finally broke away, there were riots in South Africa, there was a massacre in India, Gandhi began his campaigns of nonviolent resistance, the white dominions loosened the ties of empire even further, to the point of invisibility. The new territories gained by Britain after the war, mandated to her by the League of Nations, proved to be no bargain. Her conflicting wartime deals with assorted factions in the Middle East came home to roost, and though stout-hearted colonels might take comfort from the large splotches of the map still colored British, the color was fading fast.

With the Channel between them and the Continent, and secure in the knowledge that the Royal Navy was still supreme, the British were able to take a more benevolent view of their late enemies than the French were. As the twenties rolled on, Britain came to the view that the Germans had indeed been harshly treated at Versailles. The punitive peace was predicated on conditions that did not develop, or turned out not to apply. Therefore, Britain became at least mildly revisionist in her views about Germany. Even before the term "appeasement" was coined, the British were conceding that Germany might be better treated than was the case. It was this view that led them, in 1935, into signing the Anglo-German Naval Agreement.

The agreement was a major setback for the Western Powers, though it did not look like it at the time. Britain agreed that Germany might build up her naval strength to a point where it was one third that of the Royal Navy. They further agreed to Anglo-German parity in submarine tonnage. That might seem incredible in view of what the British had gone through in 1914-18, but they had after all defeated the submarine in the end, so they were not disposed to take it as seriously in 1935 as they had been in 1915. In the larger sense, the agreement was a slap in the face to France, since it was undertaken unilaterally by Britain, without reference to France, who was also a signatory to the Versailles treaty which was now being thrown out the window. Hitler had already repudiated the disarmament clauses of Versailles, so the agreement had the further effect of retrospectively legitimizing Herr Hitler's actions. The French were not pleased, and the British did not care.

In the mid-thirties, there was not a great deal the British could have done about Hitler, even had they chosen not to go along with him. As soon as the war ended they demobilized their large army and reverted to the traditional policy of dependence upon the navy. Even that lost ground, however. It was Britain's financial situation that led her into considering the naval limitations of the Washington Conference and its successors. Her strength at sea was in many ways nearly as illusory as was France's on land. The old Royal Navy of the days of sail had been capable of dominating the water of any area of the world for a time. Now British supremacy included a tacit recognition of the local command of the United States Navy over the western Atlantic and most of the Pacific, and the dominance of Japan over east Asian waters. France and Italy could challenge her hold on the Mediterranean, and the two of them combined could have held the Mediterranean against her. Relatively speaking, the British were weaker in the thirties than they had been before 1914. They resolved this problem by adopting the infamous "ten-year rule," a government prediction that as there was no war on the horizon for ten years, weakness was permissible. They were still using the formula in 1935.

Britain was weaker in another way, too. In 1914, the Channel had been a barrier that was nearly impassable. Once during the Napoleonic Wars Earl St. Vincent as First Lord of the Admiralty was asked about the possibility of a French invasion; his reply was, "Gentlemen, I do not say that the enemy cannot come; I say only that they cannot come by sea." That sublime confidence was still justified in 1914. But by 1935, it was possible that the enemy might come by air.

Before 1914, France had led the world in aircraft development, what there was of it. Britain and Germany had both equaled her as a result of the demands of the war. Both had gone even further in the direction of producing long-range heavy bombers and the British, alone of the great powers, had brought in an independent air force at the end of the war.

They had then succumbed to the visionaries. Through the twenties, a group of theorists, the most famous of whom was Giulio Douhet of Italy, had produced ideas that strategic bombers, in and of themselves, would determine the course of future wars. A country needed no more for its defense than a heavy-bomber force. If invaded, it would launch its bombers against the enemy at home, against his means of production and transport. Massive destruction would follow, the invading forces would either be withdrawn for home defense or would wither from lack of supplies. Civilian demands for protection would paralyze the enemy's war effort. The best civil defense would be a bomber force that would carry the war to the enemy; there was no need for fighter protection, because "the bomber would always get through." Strategic heavy bombers were the ultimate terror weapon of the twenties and thirties.

The British agreed with this, or at least the leading lights of the infant Royal Air Force did. Arthur Harris, who would lead R. A. F. Bomber Command in World War II, and was known to the public as "Bomber" Harris; Sir Hugh Trenchard, who commanded the R. A. F. in its early days, and others were men looking for a role for their service, and they found it in the ideas of Douhet. Air defense was subordinated to the idea of long-distance strategic bombing. Unfortunately, the aircraft technology of the time could not fulfill the promises of the theorists, and the primary effect of these ideas was to downgrade the British fighter force and defense forces. It was not until about 1937 that the British began to put more effort into fighter-aircraft production and development. They were just barely in time.

If Britain and France were weak during the interwar period, it was partly because of the effects of World War I, but only partly. They had, after all, come out of the war better than the Germans or the Russians. Their basic weakness stemmed not from the war, but from the attitudes of their governments, and even more fundamentally, of their citizens. People eventually get the government they want, and the French and British taxpayer chose to support governments whose policies led to military weakness rather than strength. Of course, it was not the fault of the civilian politicians if the money they did allocate to their military advisors and experts was misspent, as it generally was. But the populace of both countries, on the whole, was neither inclined to vote much money for military force, nor to examine too closely the question of what ought to be done with it. At bottom, their basic problem was a lack of national will.

Among the dictatorships, there was no such problem.

3. The Revisionist States

ITALY WAS THE FIRST of the World War I victors to go. She had been the weakest of the great powers in 1914, and her democratic institutions had been the most fragile. Measured in terms of industrial potential and productive capacity, she was a great power only on sufferance.

In 1914, Italy had been allied with Germany and Austria-Hungary as a member of the Triple Alliance. This was a defensive alliance, and when war broke out the Italians stood on the letter of their treaty; as Germany was technically the aggressor, the deliverer of the ultimata that began the war, Italy was not obligated to enter it, and she announced her neutrality. Through the next year both sides angled for Italian support. Most of the territory Italy coveted belonged to the Central Powers—either Austria or Turkey—so in 1915 she entered the war on the side of the Allies.

Through the war, the Italians and the Austrians fought thirteen battles of the Isonzo River before the Germans intervened and beat Italy at Caporetto. Nevertheless, with belated help from France and Britain, Italy survived the war and emerged officially one of the victors in 1918, at cost of 1,180,000 war dead.

The Italians then appeared at Versailles and presented their bill. They could point not only to their one million war dead, but also to a disproportionately large number of blinded and assorted other head wounds, the price of fighting in the rocks and mountains where it was impossible to dig in properly. They found that many of the things that had been used as bait to lure Italy into the war had now been promised to other states as well, or simply outpaced by the tumble of events in the Balkans at the end of the war. Having fought the war not as an ideological crusade, but as a straight nineteenth-century territorial and diplomatic deal, the Italians now felt cheated and went home from the peace talks the least happy of all the winners.

As it did in every other country, the war caused great social and economic dislocation and distress in Italy. Through 1919 and 1920, there was a wave of strikes, lockouts, and riots. Communists and Socialists threatened to take over the country. Action, as usual, bred reaction. Out of the chaos there gradually emerged a dominant group, right wing and authoritarian. It started out as a veterans' organization, the *Fascio di combattimento*, or Fascists for short, and its leader, a lantern-jawed orator and writer named Benito Mussolini, became the man of the hour in Italy.

In this terribly confused period it was a measure of the times that Mussolini was the type who could dominate events. Born in 1883, the son of a blacksmith, he had been a teacher in his early years. Moving into left-wing politics and journalism, he was for a time before the war the editor of the Socialist newspaper *Avanti*. He broke with socialism over the war which, as did so many others, he supported wholeheartedly as a national purging. After serving in the army—it failed to cure him—he began to edit a rightist paper, *Popolo d'Italia*, and he gravitated from there to fascism. His veterans met the Communists with their own medicine—violence—and he formed groups of toughs who joined in the riots, wearing their distinctive black shirts. Their opportunity lay in disruption and unrest, and they often fomented riots so that they could then put them down. Gradually, it appeared that only the Fascists could save Italy from complete disaster. In 1922, in Naples at a Fascist conference, Mussolini demanded full political power and began the famous "March on Rome." The march itself went only from the Fascists' meeting hall to the railway station; they actually went on trains the rest of the way, and Mussolini ended up as the premier of Italy.

Italy became a one-party state. Opposition was driven underground, or imprisoned, sometimes tortured, occasionally murdered. It was, according to Mussolini, a necessary price for efficiency and stability. There were rewards: marshes were drained, malarial swamps cleaned out, industry fostered. As well-disposed English tourists never tired of remarking, the trains ran on time. In the general climate of interwar Europe, many people thought Mussolini was "a good thing."

It was in foreign affairs that he began to make himself a nuisance. His weakest spot was a grandiose vision of Italy's power, potential, and rightful place in the world, a vision he was determined to realize. Part of it was harmless; Italian planes made long-distance flights and world records, Italian ships were fast, well designed, and a visible reminder of the new Italy. When he referred to the Mediterranean as *"mare nostrum,"* "our sea," he could either be forgiven for pardonable pride or ignored as a comic-opera heavy. But then he began trying to make it work.

In 1923, Italian officers engaged in settling a boundary dispute between Greece and Albania were assassinated. Mussolini responded by sending in troops, bombarding and occupying the island of Corfu, on the Greek side of the mouth of the Adriatic. Greece appealed to the League of Nations, which settled the issue, largely in favor of Italy, and the Italian forces evacuated the island a bit sheepishly, looking as if they had barked before they were kicked.

The policies of internal reorganization and external assertion went on simultaneously. Yugoslavia ceded Fiume to Italy, the Socialist leader Giacomo Matteotti was murdered, there was tension with Germany over a policy of Italianization of the Tyrol, an Irish lady named Violet Gibson tried to assassinate Mussolini, but succeeded only in shooting him in the nose. It was still difficult to know if he should be taken seriously.

Yet gradually, by the mid-twenties, it became obvious that Mussolini was setting out on a policy of allying with and dominating all the revisionist states, those dissatisfied with the conditions after Versailles and wanting to do something about them. In 1925, there was a treaty of friendship with Spain and a virtual takeover of Albania. In 1927, there was a treaty with Hungary, in 1930, with Austria.

The Depression slowed Mussolini down a bit, as it did everything else. It brought Hitler to power too, and gave Mussolini a potential right-wing bedfellow. Mussolini was not initially impressed with Hitler. Hitler admired Mussolini; Mussolini regarded Hitler as an upstart, a flattering but not too successful imitator. In those early years of fascism, Mussolini was definitely the senior. It was largely his intervention that thwarted Hitler's first attempt to take over Austria. Only slowly did the demonic power of Hitler and the real potential of Germany overtake the perhaps illusory power of Italy.

Meanwhile, there were foreign adventures, which had the effect of sounding the death knell of the League of Nations and of collective security and which made Mussolini appear rather less of a clown and more of a villain. In 1935, Italian forces operating out of their territories on the Red Sea coast invaded Ethiopia.

The Italians had tried to take over Ethiopia (Abyssinia as it was then called), in the 1890's. Their army had been ambushed and destroyed at Adowa in 1896, and they had never gotten over it. Not even the takeover of Libya in 1911 had assuaged their humiliation, so now Mussolini tried again. The Ethiopian emperor, Haile Selassie, protested to the League of Nations, which found itself caught in a bind. Eventually, the League voted economic sanctions against Italy and cut off supplies of everything except those things, especially oil, which she needed to win her war. The British did not close the Suez Canal, which was the lifeline of the Italian war effort. Haile Selassie protested in vain.

The problem was that Britain and France wanted Italian support against the growing power of Hitler, and though they could not condone his takeover of Ethiopia, they did not wish to antagonize him any more than was absolutely necessary. They did not dare fight to stop him, as they were all too conscious of their own weakness. Italy had oil reserves for no more than a couple of days' steaming for her fleet. The British did not know that; all they knew was that their own Mediterranean fleet had ammunition in its lockers for fifteen minutes' firing. Anxious to offend no one, the Western Powers inevitably ended by alienating everyone. Haile Selassie lost his country, the League lost its credibility, assorted French and British politicians who tried to make deals with Mussolini lost office, Britain and France lost both prestige and the friendship of Italy.

The whole sorry story ended with Mussolini on his balcony proclaiming to a cheering crowd—a few of whom cared—that King Victor Emmanuel III was now "Emperor of Ethiopia" as well as King of Italy. Muscular, virile fascism, with the aid of tanks, bombers, and poison gas against tribesmen with antiquated rifles and a touching belief in the sincerity of the League of Nations, had fulfilled its destiny.

Conquest awaits those who are ready for it. Two months after the Ethiopian War ended, civil war broke out in Spain. In 1931, a republic had been set up in Spain, on the collapse of the monarchy of King Alfonso XIII. The new regime was too radical for the conservative forces in Spain—the landowners, army, and Church —and not radical enough for the masses—the urban poor and the landless peasants. There were constant risings and attempted coups from both right and left. In 1936, army officers in Spanish Morocco rose up against the leftist government, and the country burst into a full-scale civil war. Liberals and leftists not only in Spain but around the world rallied to the republic. Russia supported the

Communists and, to a much lesser extent, the official Republican forces. Volunteers from Britain, France, the United States, Canada, and elsewhere went to Spain to fight. The rightist governments of the world supported the generals, or the Nationalists as they called themselves. Mussolini was the chief intervener. Italy eventually sent more than 50,000 troops to Spain. They were called volunteers, but they volunteered with their tanks, aircraft, and artillery.

The war became the great ideological battle of the thirties, not unlike the Vietnam War for the United States in the sixties. The western democracies refused to get involved and set up embargoes, nonintervention agreements, and neutrality patrols. The Russians were the main prop of the republic, though their selective support of only its Communist element may have done as much harm as good. The Italians and later the Germans were the chief support of General Franco and the Nationalists. The Italian contribution was probably greater, but as was by now coming to be normal, the Germans stole the limelight. It was they who tested their tactical concepts, by bombing undefended towns such as Guernica, and perfected some of the material they would use later and more profitably elsewhere. Eventually, they intervened on both sides; while overtly supporting Franco, they gave surreptitious aid to the Republicans to keep the war going, so that Mussolini would still be busy in Spain while they took over Austria.

While the civil war ground down to a Franco victory, Italy came more and more into the German orbit. Mussolini joined the Anti-Communist Pact with Germany and Japan in 1937 and withdrew from the League of Nations. He meddled around the fringes of the Munich crisis in 1938. He took over Albania openly in 1939, and in May of that year he signed a political and military alliance with Germany. The master had by now been thoroughly upstaged by the pupil; Italy had become the tail of the Fascist kite.

Germany tried democracy from 1919 to 1933, and nearly made it work. Kaiser Wilhelm, who did so much to bring about his own destruction, abdicated in November of 1918. A republic was proclaimed, a constitutional convention met in early 1919 at the university town of Weimar, and the Weimar Republic was launched on its hopeful but ill-fated journey. From the beginning it was hampered by burdens imposed by others.

The members of the Weimar government, for one thing, had to bear the stigma, in German eyes, of having signed the Versailles peace, the humiliating "Diktat" against which German politicians and demagogues raged so profitably for the next decade. The German Army very cleverly and successfully passed off the fiction that it had not been defeated "in the field," but that it had been stabbed in the back by insidious and cowardly politicians, who were now, of course, running the country. The republic also had to bear the weight of Allied reparations payments, and although it can be argued that these were no real burden, that in fact the German government made more from American loans than it paid to the Allies in reparations, nonetheless, reparations became a major bone of contention in Germany and were a chief factor in the Germans' ruining their own economy by bringing about massive inflation.

At bottom, however, the root of the whole matter was that there were simply not enough people in Germany committed to parliamentary forms and the idea of democracy. The essence of that, ultimately, is compromise, and the Germans could not quite make it work. The president of the republic himself, for most of its existence, Marshal Paul von Hindenburg, the "wooden titan," was a heartfelt monarchist and hoped someday to see the Kaiser restored to power. His views were shared by substantial groups of right-wing politicians and agitators, who, if they did not necessarily want a return to monarchy, wanted some form of one-party authoritarian state. Equally strong on the other side were the left-wing radicals, especially the Communists, who also wanted their own form of authoritarian state. The republic was caught in the middle.

A regime which lacked broad popular support could hardly hope to deal with the social and economic problems left by the war. Happily for Germany, the war had not been fought on her soil; she had not therefore suffered the kind of property damage that France and Belgium had. But she had incurred damages of another kind. The Allied blockade had eventually taken its toll by the end of the war, and thousands of Germans had suffered from malnutrition and deprivation of one kind or another. Germany had had nearly two million war dead, she had lost millions more in the great influenza epidemic at the end of the war—as had indeed everyone else—the Allied blockade had been kept up until mid-1919 after the signing of the Versailles treaty, and the country's institutions lay in chaos by then.

The government was beset by attempts on its life from both sides. In January of 1919, the extreme left, Communists known as Spartacists, led by Karl Liebknecht and Rosa Luxemburg, broke out in revolt. They were finally put down after bitter fighting by the provisional government and troops of the regular army. Later in the spring, a Soviet government was established in Bavaria; it too was crushed by the regular troops. Early in 1920, there was a rightist coup. Organized veterans' groups known as the *Freikorps* led by a nonentity named Dr. Kapp temporarily occupied Berlin. This time, when called upon to put them down, the army commander, General Hans von Seeckt, refused, saying, "Troops do not fire on troops." Fortunately, the Kapp Putsch collapsed of its own ineptitude, helped by a massive general strike of German workers. At the same time there was a Spartacist rising in the Ruhr; the troops put this down too, apparently unaware that there was a certain degree of selectivity about their willingness to support the government.

Next, as a result of vast amounts of paper being printed to pay off reparations, the mark collapsed. The French and Belgians occupied the Ruhr and seized German industry. The government responded with an unsuccessful policy of passive resistance. The Allies took over various German territories; assorted others were lost to breakaway movements among minority groups on the frontiers. Even some of the major states threatened to go their own way, negating the work of Bismarck in his unification of Germany a generation ago. The French supported a Rhenish republic. Bavaria was a hotbed of intrigue and separatism. Against this background an unknown but enterprising politician named Adolf Hitler made his own bid for power.

One of the myriad of mini-parties spawned by postwar Germany was a small group known as the National Socialist German Workers' Party. Initially, it consisted of no more than half a dozen cronies. Hitler joined it in 1920, ironically as a paid informer for the army, to keep watch on potentially dangerous political groups.

Born an Austrian in 1889, Hitler had had a totally undistinguished career to this point. Destined to follow his father into the lower ranks of the civil service, Hitler saw himself instead as a great artist. He failed, however, to pass the exams to get into art school in Vienna. From 1904 to 1913 he lived, or existed, on part-time jobs in Vienna, selling not very good postcards, living in flophouses, engaging in passionate arguments about politics, and doing nothing very successfully. All he managed to do was develop a hatred of the Jews—anti-Semitism was a swelling current in central Europe in the years before the Great War—and an equal distaste for the system that was refusing to recognize his own genius.

In 1913, he left Austria and went to Munich in Bavaria, and he has actually been identified in a photo of a cheering crowd listening to the declaration of war in 1914. Hitler enlisted in a Bavarian regiment, fought on the Western Front, and was promoted to corporal. At the collapse of Germany he was lying in a hospital, temporarily blinded by gas. He drifted through the period immediately after the armistice and ended up in low-level political intelligence work for the army, a nonentity.

He soon came to dominate the little party of which he had become a member, and it was he who gave it its name and what program it had, a mixture of radicalism, contempt for the politicians, provincialism, and resentment of Versailles. Slowly, profitting by the currents of dissatisfaction and despair throughout Bavaria, the party grew.

Its most illustrious recruit was General Erich von Ludendorff, Germany's second soldier and Marshal von Hindenburg's alter ego. Ludendorff was becoming more and more radically anti-Semitic, anti-Jesuit, anti-Freemasons; he would eventually become totally immersed in the delights of Norse mythology. He was a natural for Hitler.

By 1923, the NSDAP, or Nazis, as they called themselves, were ready to act. In November, they tried to seize the government of Bavaria, in what came to be known as the Beer-Hall Putsch, named after the place where the idea was concocted. Supported by their Brownshirts—Mussolini had pre-empted black—they marched through the streets of Munich. They thought they had a deal with the police, but instead the police machine-gunned the column, and that was the end of the Putsch. Ludendorff was arrested, tried, and acquitted of treason; another recruit, a famous air ace named Hermann Goering, was badly wounded. Hitler himself was arrested, and sentenced to five years in jail. He served a triumphal nine months during which he wrote his political statement for all the world to see. He called it *Mein Kampf* or *My Struggle*. Turgid and wordy, but full of venom, it was nicknamed by the few who bothered to read it, *Mein Krampf*, or *My Diarrhoea*. As soon as he was released, he returned to politics.

Meanwhile, however, Germany was beginning to pull herself together. Foreign loans, the American Dawes Plan which poured money into Germany, a firm government in which the outstanding figure was Gustav Stresemann, finally put Germany on the road to recovery. The five years from 1924 to 1929 were the best Germany had between wars. They were lean years for Hitler; good

times for everyone else were bad times for the Nazis. As a national party, they could muster only twelve out of 491 seats in the Reichstag in 1928.

But in 1929, the world's bubble burst. The Depression began with the failure of Austrian banks and rapidly spread throughout the world. American loans stopped coming in, the world economy ground to a halt, unemployment rose, and with it Hitler's hopes.

There was an election to the Reichstag in 1930. The Nazis went all out, damning the government, the Western Powers, the capitalists, the Jews. In the desperate masses of Germany they found willing listeners. They returned from the elections with 107 seats, more than the Communists, and just less than the majority Socialists. Nazism was a force in Germany, and Hitler a major contender for power.

The next couple of years were bad ones. The country was run by successive coalition governments, who went through the same process: formation of a coalition, attempt to solve the country's difficulties, government by decree, setting aside of the regular parliamentary system, collapse. By 1932, it was really the army that kept governments afloat, or sank them, by granting or withholding its willingness to back any given combination. The army leaders did this while steadfastly denying that they were interested in politics. What they really wanted was a leader acceptable to them. Their first choice was Franz von Papen, a fellow officer and politician. He could not square the circle, so they then turned to Kurt von Schleicher; he too proved unable to master the German scene.

The irony of Hitler was that he was nobody's first choice, but most people's second or third. The men who really counted in Germany—the soldiers, the businessmen, the established politicians— kept making their deals and shutting him out. His followers urged him to carry out a coup d'état, but he insisted on waiting. He moderated his tone and promised all things to whatever group he was talking to. He told the generals he would give them what they wanted, which was true enough; he said the same to big business, which was also true. Finally, they all thought they could use him, and on January 30, 1933, Adolf Hitler, ex-artist, ex-corporal in the Linz Regiment, took office as Chancellor of the German Republic.

Hitler then carried out what has come to be called the Nazi Revolution. In effect, he used the organs of parliamentary government to destroy parliamentary government. The state governments of Germany were stripped of their powers. All public positions were restricted to Aryans, that is, non-Jews. The judicial system was overhauled and a series of People's Courts set up; summary execution and the concentration camp made their appearance in German life. The National Socialist Party was declared the one legal party in the state. Racial laws were passed against Jews; the churches in Germany were nationalized; in industry, strikes and lockouts were forbidden. From now on, Germans would march forth together—and they would all be in step.

Of all the factions in Germany which had to be satisfied, or eliminated, the army was the most important. Ostensibly shunning politics, it was in reality the one force in the country whose support a would-be politician must have. Hitler was highly conscious of this, and his early moves were calculated to assuage the army's misgivings, just as his later ones would be to destroy the army's independence. In October of 1933, he withdrew from the League disarmament talks and then topped that by walking out of the League itself.

The most important step in his affair with the army, however, was one that satisfied both the soldiers and Hitler himself. Now that he was securely in power it was necessary that he rid himself of the more unsavory elements in the Nazi Party. Some of these were radical in their social and political ideas, some were just bully boys from the street-fighting days of the Depression, some of them with their "storm troopers" had ambitions to form a private army, even to take over the regular forces. On the night of June 30, 1934, Hitler carried out what came to be called the Great Blood Purge or the "night of the long knives." The Sturmabteilung (SA) or party army, prominent party men, and potential rivals to Hitler were rounded up and summarily shot. Big names in the party disappeared: Ernst Roehm, leader of the SA; Gregor Strasser, one of the most radical leaders. There was a bit of overzealousness. General von Schleicher, the former Chancellor, and his wife were taken out and shot, but by and large Hitler could now tell the army he was clear of the kind of radical they found distasteful.

In August, Hindenburg died, and Hitler combined the roles of head of government with head of state. Having cleaned his house to the satisfaction of the generals, he now presented his bill. It did not look too heavy; it was an oath:

> I swear by God this sacred oath, that I will render unconditional obedience to Adolf Hitler, the Fuehrer of the German Reich and people, Supreme Commander of the Armed Forces, and will be ready as a brave soldier to risk my life at any time for this oath.

That simple formula may have produced more misery and more shame than any set of words of equivalent length in human history.

The next year was a good one for professional military men in Germany. In March, Hitler decreed universal military conscription, and in June the Anglo-German Naval Agreement was signed. The keel of the *Bismarck* was laid at the Blom und Voss yard in Hamburg, and the roads of Germany were filled with young marching men. Hitler was soon ready to move.

His generals were less certain of events. Nothing is more upsetting to soldiers than war; it disrupts their training routines, and few professional soldiers are really ever ready to go. When Hitler called his generals in and said it was time to move back into the demilitarized Rhineland, they were terrified; France had the strongest army in the world, while they still had very little with which to work. Hitler pushed, and on March 7, 1936, German troops moved back into the Rhineland. They could manage to move only a division, and they could support it with a mere two squadrons of the newly founded Luftwaffe. Only three battalions crossed to the west bank of the Rhine. Orders were not to fight, but to retreat at the first sign of resistance.

There was no such sign. Britain and France hastily consulted. The British urged inaction; the French generals pointed out that their army was aligned solely for defensive measures, and that if the government wanted it to move forward, it would probably entail full national mobilization; they could perhaps advance in several weeks. In the end, Britain, France, Belgium, and Italy combined to register a protest. The League of Nations recognized that there had been a violation of the Locarno treaties. Hitler was delighted; his generals, though they felt a bit foolish at their misjudgment, were delighted too.

Hitler had still further designs, both in foreign affairs and more importantly, for the moment, on the army. He was not content that he and it should be equal partners in Germany's rehabilitation. In early 1938, he brought the officers corps to heel by purging the high command. The Minister of War, General von Blomberg, and the Commander-in-Chief of the Army, General von Fritsch, were both sacked. It was a particularly sordid business, designed not only to replace the commanders, but also to strike at the army's sense of self. Blomberg was a widower; he made a second marriage, to his secretary; it turned out she had once been arrested for prostitution. The misalliance was sufficiently shocking, in the social context of the German officer class and 1938, to cause Blomberg's fall. Von

Fritsch, next in line, was accused of homosexuality. The matter was allowed to drag on for some weeks. While the army fumed and fretted about its honor, Hitler made a clean sweep of the upper echelons. He also annexed Austria, so that his personal stock skyrocketed. By the time von Fritsch was cleared, the Army High Command was now dominated by Hitler's representative, Keitel, and its Commander-in-Chief was General von Brauchitsch. Twist and turn as it might from then on to escape, the army was securely in Hitler's pocket. As for Fritsch, a colonel-general leading an artillery regiment, he was killed by a Polish machine gun in September of 1939.

In the words of the slogan, Germany was now truly, *Ein Reich, ein Volk, ein Fuehrer* ("One state, one people, one leader"). Hitler was ready to roll.

Clouds were gathering in Asia as well as in Europe. Like Italy, Japan had been an Allied power and one of the victors in World War I. She had not been invited in, but had insisted on joining, and the Japanese had used war as an opportunity to take over the scattered but useful German imperial holdings in the north Pacific and on the Chinese mainland. Japanese expansion went back actually before World War I, to the Sino-Japanese War of 1894-95 and the Russo-Japanese War of 1904-05. She was interested especially in the Korean Peninsula, the Yellow Sea, and the great underdeveloped hinterland of Manchuria. Her ambitions had brought conflict with China, and then with Russia, both of whom she was in the process of displacing. World War I led to a boom in the Japanese economy and unrest after it ended. Overpopulated and overproductive, the Japanese believed they needed room for economic exploitation and for territorial expansion.

Like most of the secondary powers, they left Versailles dissatisfied. Japan wanted to insert in the League Covenant a statement on racial equality, but the other powers refused this. In 1920, Japan took over as formal mandates the islands granted to her by the League—the Carolines, Marshalls, and Marianas—mere names on the map at that time, and not nearly as much as Japan wanted. The country felt humiliated at being only three to five of the United States and Britain in the naval treaties, and further offended by the American policy in the twenties of exclusion of Japanese immigration on the West Coast.

By the late twenties a short era of liberalism in Japan was coming to an end. Emperor Hirohito acceded to the throne in 1926, marking the beginning of the Showa period. The population was increasing by more than a million a year, to more than sixty million by 1930. In a desperate search for solutions to their national problems, the Japanese turned increasingly to militarism and the manly virtues that so strongly infused the national character anyway. Army men were coming more and more to the forefront, as seems to be a norm in a crisis period.

In 1931, soldiers of the Kwangtung Army were involved in the "Mukden incident." This army, garrisoning the Liaotung Peninsula and Port Arthur, fruit of the Russo-Japanese War, was the most militaristic of all the forces of Japan. When several soldiers on night maneuvers were hurt in an explosion, the Japanese used it as an excuse to invade the Chinese-held territories of Manchuria. The weak Chinese forces were able to offer no resistance and withdrew to the south, toward China proper. The Chinese responded with a boycott on Japanese imports, but the army went ahead, and by early 1932 had occupied most of Manchuria. In February of 1932, Japan announced the independence of a new puppet state, Manchukuo. The United States refused to recognize it, and the League of Nations, after sending an investigatory commission, withheld recognition and gently chided Japan. The Japanese delegation later walked out of the League; in Manchukuo, Japanese soldiers advanced south into Chinese territory and were soon butting up against the Great Wall of China.

If that were not enough, the Japanese decided to force China into abandoning her boycott by direct action. In late January of 1932, 70,000 Japanese troops landed at Shanghai in China, and drove the Chinese Army out of the city. There was great consternation among the Powers as they tried to protect their international settlements in Shanghai. Finally, the Japanese found they had bitten off more than they could manage. The Chinese fought back, the diplomats went to work, and the Japanese pulled out in May, after China had given up the boycott.

The army was not satisfied yet, however. Reactionaries assassinated the Premier at home, soldiers moved to the fore in the cabinet, and in 1934, Japan announced a virtual protectorate over Chinese foreign relations. Two years later, young officers attempted a coup; though several were executed, they succeeded in getting rid of most of the civilian ministers of the government. Japan joined Germany in the Anti-Communist Pact that came to be known as the "Axis."

Finally, in July of 1937, what is known in Japanese history as

"the China Incident" began. Once again it was precipitated by soldiers on night maneuvers. This time there was an exchange of shots
near the Marco Polo Bridge north of Peking. Chinese troops were
alleged to have fired on Japanese units. The Japanese Army responded with a full-scale invasion of China. Fighting spread rapidly
along the entire length of the China-Manchukuo border. Before the
month was out, the Japanese had taken the ancient Chinese capital
of Peking, as well as the port city of Tientsin. In the late summer,
they attacked Shanghai and, after fierce resistance by the Chinese,
took the city. They then advanced up the Yangtze River valley,
driving the Chinese before them, resorting to heavy bombing and
machine-gunning of refugees to clear the way. They imposed a
naval blockade on the coasts of the rest of China. In December,
they attacked British and American ships and sank the United
States river gunboat *Panay*. The second Chinese capital, Nanking,
fell before Christmas. The rest of the world watched in dismay and
horror, and in this part of the globe, although it never was declared,
World War II had already begun.

4. The Unknown Quantities

HITLER HAD ASSESSED Great Britain and France as weak; they were not disposed to challenge his reassertion of German power. Mussolini followed suit. In the Far East, Japan had taken the line that she, and she alone, would dominate the affairs of east Asia; the imperial powers were decadent and they were far away. Neither Germany and Italy on the one hand, nor Japan on the other, paid a great deal of attention to the two potential giants, Russia and the United States.

Hitler especially was a European politician, continental in his outlook, understanding little of the sea, and extraordinarily ignorant of the United States. More surprising, in view of his anti-Slav and anti-Communist views, was his ignorance of Russia. Perhaps the difficulty lay less in ignorance than in the fact that, in the thirties, both Russia and the United States were free-floating variables as far as world affairs went. The potential was there; what either might do with it was nearly impossible to assess.

Russia was the more immediate of the two. It was impossible even to look at a map of Europe without sensing something of the immensity of Russia. Yet so little was known in the rest of the world of Russia's strength and attitudes that she remained an unknown element. That was equally true of her government.

The old Tsarist government of the Romanovs had made great contributions to the Allied victory in World War I. Time and again through the war, they had launched offensives at the behest of the western states, and in accordance with the Allies' timetables rather than their own. Imperial Russia had virtually destroyed itself for its allies, though indeed it was probably rotten enough to go anyway; Trotsky later wrote that without the enthusiasm for the war and the dynasty, the Russian Revolution would have broken out before it did.

47

After the abdication of the Tsar in 1917, the provisional government tried to remain in the war, faithful to its obligations. It may well be that that, more than any one other decision, killed parliamentary government in Russia. The democratic slogan of "on with the war" was no match for the Communist, Bolshevik cry, "Peace, land, bread." When the Bolsheviks seized power later in 1917, overthrowing the provisional government, the country broke up in civil war, which lasted until 1920. The Western Allied governments and Japan all intervened in Russia. They sent forces to Murmansk and Archangel, and to Vladivostok in the east, ostensibly to protect the war materials they had already sent Russia. Actually, they gave surreptitious and ineffective help to the counter-revolutionary movement, the Whites.

The Whites had little to offer except a return to the past, however, and they were finally defeated, partly by the genius of Trotsky as the organizer of the Red Army, partly by their own internecine squabbles. The White cause died. In 1920, there was a war with Poland, in which Poland tried to take over the Ukraine, which wanted to break away from Russia anyway. The Poles lost, and when the whole civil war period ended, three things were obvious: The Reds were firmly in power; they thoroughly distrusted the West; and the West already thoroughly distrusted them.

The policy that Lenin and later Stalin produced was as complete a dictatorship as any of those of the right wing; the only difference was that it masqueraded under a different set of slogans. A dictatorship of the proletariat was still a dictatorship, and the state did not wither away in the classic Marxist formula.

Karl Marx, laboring away in the British Museum in the nineteenth century, had discarded Russia as inappropriate for the kind of class revolution he prophesied. He may well have been right. When Lenin died in 1924, there was a power struggle for his mantle. The chief contenders were Leon Trotsky, brilliant, intellectually supple, a figure with a world view, and Joseph Stalin, once the bully-boy of the party, now its secretary, with a spider-like web through all the channels of command. Stalin ended up in control. Trotsky ended up in exile in Mexico City where an assassin buried a geology pick in the back of his head in 1940.

Whether communism might have developed differently had Lenin lived longer, or had Trotsky succeeded him, is impossible to say. Many authorities accuse Stalin of betraying the revolutionary cause, of being a Russian of the Russias, of succumbing to nationalism. He went his own way, he killed his millions, and he must therefore be accounted one of the great forces of the twentieth century.

In 1922, Russia and Germany had allied in the Treaty of Rapallo, the two pariahs of Europe getting together. It was this agreement that let Germany's officially nonexistent airmen train in Russia, among other things. Then Britain finally accorded diplomatic recognition to the Soviet Union in 1924, followed by most of the other European states; it was not until 1933 that the United States acknowledged her existence. Through the late twenties and the early thirties Russia signed nonaggression pacts and mutual-defense treaties with most of the central and east European states, and in 1934, she joined the League of Nations. She was always foremost in saying everyone ought to disarm; perhaps Russia said it too often, because few believed her. More than the Fascists, the Bolsheviks were the bogeymen of the interwar period.

Nonetheless, in 1935, France and Czechoslovakia signed an alliance with her. The timing was by no means accidental: Hitler denounced the disarmament clauses of Versailles in March; Britain, France, and Italy conferred in April; France, Russia, and Czechoslovakia signed their agreement in May. In July, the Third International, the voice of communism outside Russia, declared that Communists would support the democracies against fascism. Next year, Russia was the major prop of the Spanish Republicans against Franco in Spain.

Stalin had the same internal problems other dictators had, and he sought the same kind of solutions. Potential rivals accused of "Trotskyism" were put on trial late in 1936. Throughout the next year possible rivals were arrested and tried in a series of affairs that were called the "Purges." They reached their height in June when Marshal Michael Tukhachevski, the victor of the Polish War, was executed after a secret court-martial. He and other top officers were accused of plotting with the Germans and the Japanese. The purges eventually did away with most of the higher echelons of the civil, diplomatic, and military service—and most of the men who might have challenged Stalin for power. These affairs seriously discredited Russia abroad; they also politicized the army, which would really pay the price for them in 1940 and 1941.

They further added to the difficulty for western observers in assessing Russia, so that by the time Hitler was ready to move, Russia remained a question mark. Nobody knew what she was worth, or how much she might be counted upon. In central Europe there was an added complication; from the Baltic to the Balkans, they were as scared of the Russians as they were of the Germans.

No one, on the other hand, was scared of the United States. She was far away from the center of things viewed by European eyes, and except for her navy was practically unarmed. Americans spent about 1 percent of their annual budget on all their military forces. There was no conscription for the army and no independent air force. In 1936, the U. S. Army consisted of 110,000 men. The War Department believed it could mobilize for war and call up what reserves it possessed in a month. If it had done so, the force would have been short of trucks, tanks, scout cars, antiaircraft equipment, machine guns, and machine-gun ammunition. In short, the United States hardly had an army.

This was no more than the reflection of the recent past. The United States had probably been the one state to benefit unequivocally from World War I. She had successfully resisted pressure to join overtly in it until 1917. Before then the Americans had produced masses of military material for, and invested large amounts of money in, the Allied cause. In 1917, mostly because of German strategic mistakes about their ability to win the war with submarines, the United States had entered the war. American troops did not reach the front until late in 1917, and they did not fight in large numbers until 1918. The U. S. sustained 109,000 battle deaths, about the same as Bulgaria, and less than half those suffered by Belgium. In 1918, they arrived in France in a flood, and they and their wealth were enough to tip the balance, and give victory to the exhausted Allies.

There were paradoxes in this situation that would come home to haunt the next generation. The Americans believed they had won the war, and in a sense they were right: without the contribution they made, partly in manpower but more in matériel, the Allies almost certainly would have collapsed before Germany did. Yet the Americans had won the war only because Britain and France—and Russia—had fought so hard and so long. World War I was like a tag-team match in which all of the opponents were staggering on the ropes, some of them already beaten, when a fresh player leaped in at the last moment, knocked out the enemy, and then having done little of the work, threw up his hands and shouted, "I won!"

Having won, the Americans went home again.

This was all right as long as the euphoria of victory lasted.

Europeans were glad of American help, they recognized its significance, and after it was over, they were glad to have the Americans
out of the way so they could return to the traditional ways of man-
aging affairs. The Americans refused to enter into a long-term alliance with France and Britain, and they refused to sign the Treaty
of Versailles. In July of 1921, Congress simply passed a resolution,
declaring that the war with Germany was over. Most important of
all, they refused to join the League of Nations. Their absence told
against both the effectiveness of the League and Britain's leadership
of it.

Through the twenties the United States became increasingly
preoccupied with its own affairs. An extremely jaundiced view of
World War I and what it had been all about sprang up, and many
men—not just Americans—of the generation who had fought the
war, began to question what it had been about anyway. At a distance of ten years it looked less like a crusade for freedom and
democracy than a large confidence trick, foisted on a gullible public by crooked diplomats, arms manufacturers, and backroom politicians. The anti-war movement was in full cry, and a series of
great books painted an appalling picture of what the war had really
been like. There has always been a vision in the United States of
Europeans as a sordid bunch of petty-minded states, and the interwar debunkers did nothing to disabuse the public of it. Americans
were busy with their own affairs, foremost among them prohibition.
They limited immigration, especially of Asians, and they invoked
high tariffs to protect American industry. There was a great deal of
labor unrest, there were Communist scares, there were political
scandals, and there was unhappiness in the veterans' organizations.

The things that interested Americans internationally were not
such as to make them better disposed toward Europe. There was
the ongoing matter of disarmament talks that never seemed to
achieve anything solid. There was above all the question of reparations payments and war debts.

Germany at Versailles had agreed to pay war reparations, with
the cost to be filled in later. Meanwhile, all of the Allied governments had contracted immense debts to the United States. After
the end of the war the United States wanted to be repaid. The other
Allies tended to the view that the debts had been incurred in the
common cause, and perhaps ought to be canceled. Needless to say,
this did not appeal to the American taxpayer. The Allies then
proposed that the debtors repay the money, but that payment be
contingent upon their, in their turn, receiving reparations from

Germany. Since the Allied governments simply did not have the money—there was not enough money in the world to repay the debts—the Americans had to settle for this.

But Germany did not have the money either. She soon defaulted on her reparations, inflated the mark, and went officially bankrupt.

The solution arrived at was logical only to financiers and, presumably, voters. Under the Dawes Plan the United States loaned money to Germany. Germany thereupon paid war reparations to the Allies; they then repaid some of their war debts to the United States, who turned about and loaned more money to Germany. This circular cash flow lasted until the Depression, when everyone defaulted all along the line. The only state that fully paid off its war debt to the United States was the little Baltic state of Finland, independent of Russia after the 1917 revolution. Americans were left to conclude, not entirely accurately, but not entirely inaccurately either, that they had not only been tricked into the war, but had also been tricked into paying for it. Americans were not inclined to take a profound or particularly benevolent interest in Europe in the thirties.

They were mildly interested in the Far East. There has always tended to be an oscillation in American foreign interests, from Europe to East Asia; Russian foreign policy tends to swing, too, between central Europe and the Far East. American interests were upset by the forward Japanese policy in Manchuria, they were outraged by the intervention in China, and they delivered a constant series of protests to the Japanese government. They made it quite clear, however, that they were not going to war over China. If moral suasion would not make the Japanese behave, the United States would not go any farther. Indeed, given the state of its armed forces, the United States *could* not go any farther. Even if President Roosevelt had wished to pursue a more active foreign policy, there was no way he could have carried popular opinion and Congress with him. Between the end of the Depression and the New Deal social legislation, he was busy enough at home.

Rather than thinking of intervention, the United States thought more in terms of how to stay clear of the mess. In August of 1935, in February of 1936, and definitively in May of 1937, Congress passed a series of Neutrality Acts. They prohibited the export of arms and ammunition to belligerents. Strategic materials designated as such by the President had to be paid for in cash before leaving the United States, and they had to be carried in foreign ships, rather than U. S.-flag vessels. All other materials must be paid for in cash. No American citizen was to take passage on the ship of a belligerent, and there were to be no American loans to any state at war.

The acts illustrated graphically how the Americans thought they had been dragged into World War I, and even more important, how the United States had no intention of being led down the garden path a second time. If Adolf Hitler, out of ignorance, thought he could count the United States out, most Americans completely agreed with him. Once burned, twice shy.

5. The Prewar Series of Crises

BY EARLY 1938, Adolf Hitler had put the German house in order. He had assessed the opposition, internal and external, and found it weak and vacillating. He had retaken the Rhineland, and elicited no real response. He was now ready for greater things.

It is customary to look at the series of crises that preceded World War II, and blame them almost exclusively on Hitler and his ambitions. For nearly a generation after the war, the simplest explanation of why World War II happened was that Hitler caused it. It is only fair to point out that since the sixties there has been considerable challenge, and some revision, to this thesis. The challenge came with an intriguing book by the eminent British historian A. J. P. Taylor called *The Origins of the Second World War.* Taylor's argument, somewhat oversimplified, was that Hitler was doing what politicians are supposed to do, i.e., he was asserting the interests of his state. It was therefore the duty of the other European politicians, especially Prime Minister Chamberlain in Britain and Premier Daladier in France, to assert the claims of their states equally forcefully. Taking the view that politics is basically amoral, there was little difference between Hitler and the others, and the basic fault—and therefore the blame for causing World War II—lay not in Hitler's overassertion of Germany's status but in Daladier and Chamberlain's underassertion of France and Britain's status. Needless to say, this view was widely attacked in Britain, France, and the United States. It was rather more welcome in Germany. Its importance lay in the fact that it did spur a great deal of argument, ranging from table-thumping to the more philosophical proposition that there are moral ends to politics after all, and out of this argument came a perhaps more balanced view of the causes, and especially their complexity, of World War II. One can still assert that Hitler did cause the war, but no longer so dogmatically or so unqualifiedly. He has become *a* cause rather than *the* cause.

*   *   *

The first overt external act on the road to war was the takeover of Austria, the *Anschluss* of early 1938. The nation of Austria was a strange creation, with a rather bizarre history. In 1272, at the end of the Great Interregnum in German history, the crown of the German empire was given to an obscure Austrian nobleman, Rudolf of Hapsburg. He and his descendants built up a great medieval empire, a conglomeration of peoples and territories that lasted until 1806 when Napoleon tore it apart. At its greatest extent, under Emperor Charles V in the early sixteenth century, the Hapsburg Empire ruled all of the German states, Hungary and part of the Danube Valley, the Low Countries, Spain, Spain's territories in southern Italy, and the Spanish empire in the New World. By Napoleon's day it had considerably shrunk, and the ruling Hapsburg at the time ended up as emperor of Austria-Hungary, an ethnic hodgepodge in the Danube Basin and the Balkans. During the 1848 revolutions and after, even this was transformed, becoming the Dual Monarchy, Empire of Austria and Kingdom of Hungary, with the intriguing title prefix, *Kaiserlich und Koniglich* —Imperial and Royal. The Austrian part of it was German, and the Hungarian part was Slavic.

Through the mid-nineteenth century, Austria was too weak to unify Germany under her leadership, but too strong to let anyone else do it in spite of her. This dilemma was resolved by Bismarck, who defeated Austria in 1866 and went on to pull Germany together under Prussian domination. At the end of World War I the Dual Monarchy collapsed; all the ethnic minorities seceded, then Hungary broke away, and finally, in a sort of ultimate revulsion, the Austrians seceded from their own empire. Thus there was a small German state to the south of Germany proper. The peace treaties after World War I saddled Austria with all the sins of the old empire before the war and further declared that Austria and Germany should never be united.

Adolf Hitler had been born an Austrian, and it was part of his policy right from the beginning to incorporate Austria in the Greater Reich. Through the Depression the same currents ran in Austria as elsewhere—the crash that set off the Depression actually occurred there—and there was an Austrian branch of the Nazi party, just as there were branches in other neighbors with German-speaking portions in their populations. In 1932, the League of Nations gave Austria a loan of several million dollars in return for an agreement that the country would not enter any political or economic union with Germany until 1952. The government, led by Chancellor Englebert Dollfuss, was faced with riots and violence caused chiefly by the Austrian Nazis, but by other extremist groups as well. By early 1934, Dollfuss was ruling by decree, and had dissolved all the political parties except his own, permanently alienating especially the Socialists, the last, because the strongest, group that might have withstood a Nazi takeover.

In July, there was an attempted Nazi coup, badly bungled, in which a group of Nazis seized the radio station in Vienna. Before being rounded up all they really managed to do was assassinate Chancellor Dollfuss. His place was taken by a supporter, Kurt von Schuschnigg, who continued the same policies and may well have been working toward a restoration of the exiled Hapsburgs. For a couple of years, largely under the tutelage of Mussolini, who did not want the European boat rocked while he was busy in Ethiopia, Austria and Germany got along, but by 1937, as Schuschnigg became more overtly pro-Hapsburg, Hitler reapplied the pressure, and affairs heated up again.

In February of 1938, Hitler summoned Schuschnigg to his private retreat at Berchtesgaden in the Bavarian Alps. Under pressure the Austrian succumbed to Hitler's demands for better treatment for the Austrian Nazis and agreed to take one of their leaders, Arthur Seyss-Inquart, into the cabinet. Through the rest of the month Hitler kept up an intense form of psychological warfare, and the situation inside Austria became increasingly tense. The Nazis demanded union with Germany. In desperation, Schuschnigg called for a plebiscite on the question of Austrian independence, whereupon Hitler lost what little patience he possessed, delivered an ultimatum, and began concentrating his troops on the frontier. Austria was in chaos, with riots everywhere and the government completely unable to preserve order. On March 11, Schuschnigg resigned, Seyss-Inquart replaced him as Chancellor, and the next day German troops crossed the frontier. The day after that, Seyss-Inquart proclaimed union with Germany and on the 14th, Adolf Hitler rode in triumph through the streets where he had once lived in flophouses. The local boy had made good.

After a month of unrestrained violence against Jews and anyone else who dared speak against the Nazis or union with Germany, there was a plebiscite; 99.75 percent of the voters announced themselves in favor of union.

Britain and France lodged the obligatory formal protests, but they did no more. They were busy with the neutrality patrols around Spain and the complications arising therefrom, and the problems of what Japan was doing in Asia, and they were again unwilling to act. It was almost, if not quite, the height of the movement to "appease" the dictators, the theory being that if they were given everything they asked for, eventually they would run out of things for which to ask.

The big loser was Italy. Mussolini had several times taken Austria under his protection; it was no part of his plan to have a major power at the northern end of the Alpine passes. But he too was busy in Spain, and there was little he could do about affairs except put the best face he could muster on them. Il Duce sent his warmest congratulations to der Fuehrer.

The slightest look at the map would show that the next target had to be Czechoslovakia. With Austria now an integral part of Germany, the western part of Czechoslovakia was surrounded by German territory. The question was, would there be another target, or was Hitler satisfied? and if there was to be another one, could he take on the Czechs anyway? because Czechoslovakia was a different prospect from Austria.

The Czechs were one of the successor states of the Hapsburg Empire. The state had been formed out of the most valuable parts of the old empire and included basically, from west to east, the Sudetenland, which was the mountainous rim around the western end of the Bohemian basin; then there was Bohemia itself; then Moravia; and then Slovakia. Essentially, when the empire broke up, the South Slavs had taken the southern Slavic areas and formed Yugoslavia, and the Czechs had taken the rest of the Slavic areas to form Czechoslovakia. The population was about 15,000,000 including substantial numbers of non-Czech minorities, especially Germans in the Sudetenland, and some Poles and Magyars as well here and there.

In spite of its ethnic complexity, Czechoslovakia, under the leadership of its President and virtual founder, Jan Masaryk, was viewed as the most viable democratic state in central Europe. It was certainly the most prosperous and the most industrialized. There was substantial heavy industry, the most famous being the Skoda works which were the major military suppliers to the old empire, and in the interwar years produced some of the best weaponry in Europe.

The Czechs had fortified the Sudetenland, the mountainous western boundary. They had a good army, bigger than the German;

they were well supplied with tanks and artillery, and they had a useful little air force. They were allied with Rumania, Yugoslavia, and most important, France, and through France with Poland as well. They had an arbitration agreement with Germany, and in 1935 they signed a mutual-assistance pact with Russia, which obligated Russia to come to Czechoslovakia's aid if France did so. This agreement resulted from a pact France signed with Russia earlier in 1935, when she began to be even more worried than usual about Germany; the flaw in the treaty lay in the fact that Russia and Czechoslovakia had no contiguous territory, and to come to her aid, the Russians would need transit rights from her neighbors.

The Czechs nonetheless were buttressed by their own resources, as well as their allies. They were committed to western-style democracy and to their own independence.

Most of them.

The minorities presented a problem, and the biggest minority, and therefore the biggest problem, was the Sudeten Germans. For centuries German had dominated Slav, and the Sudetenlanders did not like being a minority among people they had customarily looked down on. There was, of course, a Sudeten Nazi Party, led by Konrad Henlein. The Czechs had tried to bolster Austrian independence, and this, and their deal with Russia, drew blasts from Hitler's minister of propaganda, Josef Goebbels, even before the Anschluss. Henlein's locals responded with riots and tales of outrage. The Sudetenland Germans rapidly became an "oppressed suffering minority," intolerable to German sensibilities.

The Czechs took a jaundiced view of all this nonsense, but the Anschluss changed the strategic situation immeasurably to their disadvantage. On the day Hitler paraded through Vienna, France and Russia both categorically restated their intention to stand behind Czechoslovakia. Whether they would do so or not remained to be seen; what was already certain was that geographically Czechoslovakia was caught between the upper and nether millstones.

In April, Henlein produced a series of demands known as the Carlsbad program; these would practically have turned the state over to the Nazis. France, and Britain as well, urged that they be accepted. The Czech government in Prague turned them down. Hitler fulminated, and there were riots in the Sudetenland. The Czechs replied by mobilizing 400,000 men. France and Britain therefore announced they would support her, and Hitler was constrained to back down. He was furious, but the "May crisis" was over.

This was in the spring. The summer was tortuous, with tension increasing daily, and negotiations seeming to get nowhere. Gradually through these negotiations the British moved to center stage.

British involvement happened in a curious way. Britain was not allied with the central European powers and she had hitherto played a somewhat detached role, generally seconding but not fully associating herself with France. However, the British Prime Minister, Neville Chamberlain, was anxious to assume a major role in foreign policy. He was a man about whom opinions still differ radically; some authorities see him as a great figure who deliberately sacrificed himself to gain precious time for Britain's rearmament; others see him as a meddling amateur who lied to his own Foreign Office, and who sacrificed not himself to his country but Czechoslovakia to his vanity. In either case, he was heaven-sent for France.

The dominant wish in France was that this cup might pass from them. They were re-equipping their army, slowly, and they were obsessed by their fears of Germany, whose propaganda claims they tended to accept uncritically. Though they were at this time far stronger than Germany, they believed—and that is what counts— that they were far weaker. What the French government of Premier Daladier really wanted was someone to get it off the hook. Chamberlain volunteered.

By the end of August tempers were short, and the crisis was reaching a flash point. For summer maneuvers the Germans called up 750,000 men. Hitler toured the new fortifications in the west of Germany. The Royal Navy for its summer tour did a practice mobilization, and then kept the fleet at war readiness. Henlein rejected proposed concessions by the Czech government; early in September, France called a million reservists to the colors. In a speech at Nuremberg, Hitler declared he would not tolerate the Czech oppression of the Sudetenland much longer. Europe teetered on the edge.

The result was not war, but a personal meeting between Chamberlain and Hitler. With the relieved concurrence of the French government the British Prime Minister suggested that he fly to Germany and talk to Hitler face to face. This was unprecedented "summit" diplomacy for those days. The Prime Minister had never even flown before. He believed the effort would demonstrate his willingness to go to any lengths to be reasonable, and the whole exercise was given that air in the western press. Hitler took it all as a sign of cowardliness and weakness.

The two met at Berchtesgaden on September 15. Hitler demanded annexation of the Sudetenland and said he was ready to fight. Chamberlain went home, met with the French in London on the 18th, and the two governments jointly advised the Czechs to accept. The Czechs suggested arbitration according to the Locarno treaty. Britain and France refused it; they had now put themselves in a position of doing Hitler's dirty work for him. Finally, on the 21st, the Czech government gave in. Poland and Hungary both sent in their demands for territory too.

On a winning streak, Hitler then upped his bid. He now demanded immediate cession of all the territory he claimed, no destruction or removal of military property, and the possibility of more territory to come. Chamberlain flew back to Germany, met him again at Bad Godesberg on September 22 and 23, and came home thinking that war was imminent.

Since everyone else thought the same thing, it is appropriate to examine the relative military strengths at this time. The British Army was virtually negligible, able to muster no more than four divisions. There was the navy, however, and there was for the period a respectable air force; rearmament was proceeding apace, if not fast enough to satisfy the service chiefs. The French Army consisted of more than a million men, with about sixty-odd divisions regularly formed. Statistics vary so much that it is difficult to be more precise. In tanks and aircraft France was stronger than Germany. The Czechoslovakian Army was 800,000 strong, organized in forty-some divisions. Its tanks and aircraft were good, and so was its morale. The Russians were an unknown quantity, and remained that way, partly because the other central European states announced they would not allow transit rights, and partly because the Western Powers seemed to have a major disinclination to consult with them.

The German Army consisted of forty-eight divisions, in various stages of training. Three were armored, four more motorized. Three would have to be left in East Prussia; that left forty-five to guard the western frontier and to overrun Czechoslovakia. Hitler proposed to keep only five regular divisions on the Western Front. His armored and motorized formations, the spearhead of his operation, had been rendered virtually helpless by breakdowns in their occupation of Austria, which had been absolutely unopposed. Even with the minimal forces he was going to leave in the west, he would be outnumbered by the Czechs alone.

As if this were not enough, his senior generals were plotting to overthrow him. Leading figures in the high command, such as General Ludwig Beck and General Wilhelm Adam, the commander-designate of the Western Front, tried desperately through August to convince him that he could not survive an attack on Czechoslovakia. When he refused to listen, other generals began plotting a coup. Led by Halder, Chief of the General Staff, they planned to seize Berlin and displace Hitler the moment conflict actually broke out. Not only did they plan to do it, they told the British they planned to do it. They sent General Ewald von Kleist-Schmenzin to London. He saw Winston Churchill, then no more than a leading anti-appeaser in the Commons, and officials at the Foreign Office. Later they sent Dr. Erich Kordt, *chef de cabinet* to the Foreign Minister, von Ribbentrop. He saw the British Foreign Secretary, Lord Halifax. All the generals asked was that Britain stand firm, and at the right moment, they would do the rest.

Instead, Chamberlain caved in. He and Daladier appealed to Hitler for a conference, so that the already-agreed-to cession might be done without force. Mussolini added his pleas, and even President Roosevelt sent a message. Hitler let himself be persuaded, and agreed to a meeting at Munich on September 29.

There Chamberlain and Daladier met with Hitler, Mussolini, and their two Foreign Ministers, von Ribbentrop and Count Ciano, Mussolini's son-in-law. While the Czech ministers, unconsulted, waited nervously in an anteroom, the Western Powers signed away everything Hitler wanted. The agreement was completed just after midnight of the 29th-30th, and during the course of that next long day the Czech government acceded to it.

In a physical sense, the agreement was carried through during the next few weeks. Germany got the Sudetenland and about three and a half million Czechoslovaks, most of whom were ethnic German. Subsequently, Poland took several hundred square miles and about a quarter of a million people, and Hungary got another million and about 5,000 square miles. Czechoslovakia became a truncated, indefensible piece of territory in the midst of a German-dominated central Europe.

The initial reception to the agreement was interesting. Chamberlain had been told by his military chiefs that he had to buy time; Britain simply could not fight. He came home convinced that he had won a great diplomatic victory; he stepped off the airplane, waving his umbrella and his little slip of paper, and assured the cheering crowds that he had achieved "peace in our time." Daladier had fewer illusions. He knew his country had suffered a crushing setback, and when he flew home to Paris, seeing masses awaiting him at the airport, he feared for his own safety. Instead of a lynch mob, he found a wildly jubilant and profoundly grateful crowd. So did Mussolini; he went home by train, and when he pulled into the first station on the Italian side of the frontier he too was met by cheering throngs. Disgusted with this lack of martial Fascist ardor, he turned to Ciano and said, "Look at that! The Italians need a good kick in the gut!"

Hitler was equally annoyed. From some deep welling need in his soul, he had wanted a war. Not knowing that his generals might have tried to overthrow him had he got it, he was disappointed. He returned to Berlin, got out the maps, and started looking at the next target.

Popular opinion on Munich soon began to veer, however. The Little Entente was now ruined, and France's carefully constructed diplomatic web in central Europe was torn to shreds. The Franco-Russian alliance of 1935 was also a dead letter; unconsulted and unconsidered, the Russians were left to draw their own conclusions about the value of alliances with the West. Within a couple of months the triumph of appeasement at Munich had turned to gall, and the names "Munich" and "appeasement" ever since have been synonymous with weakness and disaster.

As soon as the euphoria wore off, it became obvious that war was not far away. In the last frantic months of peace, there was a general scurrying about to tidy up affairs before the storm would come. Munich was like the gust before the hurricane; people ran around to get the garage doors and windows closed and to fasten down the shutters. For the next several months the gusts came more quickly, with varying intensity, until the storm broke.

Poland and Russia renewed their nonaggression pact. Italy turned on anti-French demonstrations and moved more overtly into the German orbit. In the Western Hemisphere the American republics passed the Lima Declaration, declaring their solidarity and opposition to foreign intervention. The United States pressed for stronger wording against totalitarianism but lost the argument. Britain and France did their best to re-equip their forces.

The initiative still lay with Hitler, and he did not wait long to use it. In March of 1939, he moved in and took over the rump of Czechoslovakia. There had been a Fascist-orientated separatist movement in Slovakia, led by the premier, Msgr. Tiso. When the Prague government deposed Tiso, he appealed to Hitler. Hitler summoned the Czech President, Hacha, to Berlin. The result was that he turned "the fate of the Czech people . . . trustingly" over to Hitler. On March 15, Bohemia and Moravia became German protectorates, and were occupied by German troops. The next day Slovakia also came under German protection, and Czechoslovakia was gone. Germany now surrounded Poland on three sides, as she had previously done with Czechoslovakia, and the southeastern-most point of her territory was within a hundred miles of the Rumanian oil fields—and within a hundred miles of Russia.

There was panic in central Europe, among governments and peoples both. Many Czechs fled for the frontiers, and there would be Czech units later in the French Army and the Royal Air Force. They were the lucky ones who got away. In the conquered country itself, the Germans immediately took measures against the Jews and prominent supporters of the former regime. Tortures, imprisonments, and executions became the order of the day. This was the first time the Germans had brought large numbers of "non-Aryans" under their control; if the savagery did not reach the systematic depths it would later achieve, that could be no consolation to the early victims of it.

At the same time that Czechoslovakia was taken over, Hitler put pressure on the Poles. They were next. Poland has no really defensible frontiers, which has given rise to the aphorism, "Poland has no history, only neighbors." In the Middle Ages, the Baltic shore of Poland was settled and taken over by a German crusading organization, the Teutonic Knights. This area became the state of Prussia, later dynastically united with Germany by the Hohenzollern rulers of Brandenburg, the last reigning incumbent of which was Kaiser Wilhelm II. It was an aim of German policy to unite Prussia with the main part of Germany, and in the late eighteenth century, Germany, Russia, and Austria between them partitioned Poland out of existence. At the end of World War I Poland re-emerged phoenix-like from the ashes, and was set up once again as an independent state. So that she might have access to the sea, her boundaries were extended to include the mouth of her main river, the Vistula. This "Polish Corridor" cut Prussia off from Germany once again. All of this was recognized at Versailles, and indeed, historically, it was perfectly just. As a concession to the Germans, the city of Danzig at the mouth of the Vistula was set up as a free city under League supervision.

Even before Czechoslovakia was digested, Hitler was demanding adjustment of the corridor and of the status of Danzig. He also annexed the city of Memel, at the eastern end of Prussia, between it and Lithuania. With the horrible example of Czechoslovakia before them as the fate of those who negotiated with Hitler, the Poles rejected his demands. Poland always had illusions about her own power and weight, and she was determined to stand firm. She also had an unconditional guarantee from Britain and France.

The scales had at last fallen from Chamberlain's eyes. Whatever else he was or was not, Chamberlain was an English gentleman. He had believed Hitler's protestations that all he was interested in was reclaiming those Germans unfortunate enough to live under the domination of foreigners. But when Hitler took over Slavic Bohemia, Moravia, and Slovakia, Chamberlain woke up with a start; Hitler, whatever else he was or was not, was not a gentleman. At the end of March, Britain and France gave Poland their guarantee that they would come to her aid if she were attacked.

This could hardly be expected to deter Hitler, since they had also said they would support Czechoslovakia; he could not know that this time they meant it. He continued his agitation and his demands, and through the summer of 1939 the situation became increasingly tense.

The big prize for the summer was not really Poland. To most people, war was now a foregone conclusion; the only remaining question was who would fight it and how. Once again it was a matter of geography. Poland had an army of about a million men, not too well equipped by the standards of the time, and a much less formidable force than the Czechs had been. If war broke out, they could hope only to hold on long enough and keep the Germans busy enough so that France and Britain could invade Germany and topple her from the west.

Unfortunately, France and Britain did not plan to invade Germany from the west. The British had no army that could do it, the French, who did have the army, planned to fight their next war in comfort behind the shelter of their fortified lines and their neighbors' frontiers. Who then, was going to bail out Poland? The answer could only be Russia, and that answer was, like the certainty of war, obvious to everyone but the Poles. They hated the Russians more than they feared the Germans.

Both sides angled for the support of Russia. On the surface,

France and Britain should have gotten it. The whole tenor of nazism, and its main stalking horse throughout its existence, had been hatred and fear of bolshevism. The two were avowed and inveterate enemies. Yet the skill with which Hitler courted Stalin was matched only by the ineptitude of the western nations. France sent a general and Britain sent an admiral, neither of them leading figures, by slow boat to Russia. Through the summer, negotiations dragged on; Russia wanted major commitments, a solid military alliance, a free hand in the Baltic states, and she also had to have the acquiescence of the Poles before she could come to their help. The Poles were extremely reluctant to give in, and neither France nor Britain pressed with any real sense of urgency. They too were gulled by the fact that an alternative arrangement seemed unthinkable.

But Hitler was not. Why not a temporary alliance with Russia? Even though he officially hated bolshevism, there was nothing to say he could not use Russia if that appeared desirable. Unlike the Allies, he pulled out all the stops. Instead of minor military figures, Russia got a full-scale visit from the German Foreign Minister, Joachim von Ribbentrop.

Agitation in Danzig and along the Corridor reached a crescendo in late August. With the world expecting war at any moment, Hitler and Stalin dropped their joint bomb. On August 21, it was announced that Germany and Russia were concluding a nonaggression pact; it was signed in Moscow two days later.

In the West this was regarded with horror as a typical example of Communist duplicity. From Stalin's point of view it was far different; he was faced with a simple either-or proposition: either he could ally with Britain and France, in which case there would be a war, a war that Russia was expected to fight while Britain and France sat and waited it out, after which, when Germany and Russia had destroyed each other, France and Britain would move in and pick up the pieces; or, he could make a deal with Hitler, they could divide Poland between them, Hitler would (probably) turn west, and Germany, France, and Britain would fight it out, after which Stalin would move in and pick up the pieces. However distressing the course of European history since 1939, Stalin can hardly be blamed for making the choice he did. Britain and France wanted to use him to gain time and to fight their war; he wanted to use Britain and France to gain time and to fight his war—and he did.

Not only that, but it is possible his deal enabled Russia to survive the ordeal that lay ahead. Part of the pact was a secret agreement that Poland would be partitioned between Russia and Germany. This was carried out, and it had the effect of moving the Russian frontier more than a hundred miles west into Poland. Some writers claim that without that extra hundred-mile cushion, the German offensive against Russia in 1941 would have succeeded, and Russia would have been destroyed. It may be, then, paradoxically, that the deal that enabled Hitler to defeat Poland cost him the war.

The diplomats were practically done now. Men in Feldgrau and khaki were moving to the forefront. Roosevelt made a general appeal to European leaders to negotiate, to conciliate, to wait, but it fell on deaf ears. In London, Parliament met and voted all but dictatorial powers to the government; the fleet put to sea. Poland called up her reserves; France manned the Maginot Line. The Wehrmacht massed troops in the borders of East Prussia and down in newly won Slovakia. On the 29th, Hitler delivered an ultimatum to the Polish government, with a twenty-four-hour time limit. It was a sham, and the movement orders had already been issued; the troops were ready to go, the Luftwaffe bombed up and waiting to pounce. The Polish government issued mobilization orders on August 30. Hitler sent a last demand and the telegraph wires were shut down before he could receive an answer. The German attack began at daylight on the first of September.

There was still a last-minute attempt to avoid the unavoidable. Britain and France, having guaranteed Poland their support if she were attacked, still tried to escape the snare. They mobilized but said they would negotiate if the Germans pulled back. There was a final flurry of notes, but while the Panzers raced across the Polish plains and the Luftwaffe swooped out of the skies, the hours, then minutes, ran out. At 11:15 on the morning of the 3rd, a tired Chamberlain announced to Great Britain that she was now at war. As he finished his short speech the air raid sirens began to wail. At 10:20, the French ambassador delivered France's ultimatum to von Ribbentrop. It expired at five that afternoon, and Daladier told the Chamber and the nation that France too was at war with Germany.

When the news of Britain and France's action was finally given to Hitler, he listened to his interpreter translate the phrases of diplomacy. He sat slumped down in his chair, silent for a few moments. He looked up, and said, "Well . . . what do we do now?" Europe slid over the edge of the cliff.

PART II: THE EXPANDING WAR

6. Blitzkrieg in Poland

THROUGH THE LAST, all-too-short summer of peace, both the Germans and Poles had prepared frantically for what was coming. If the diplomats and the civilians hoped against hope for peace, the soldiers knew that war could come at any time, and they were doing their best to get ready for it; through August there was a palpable girding of loins.

The high command of the Wehrmacht had been planning the invasion of Poland since March of 1939; immediately after the takeover of the remains of Czechoslovakia, Hitler had called his generals together, told them Poland was next on his list, and instructed them to work up an operational plan. The occupation of Bohemia, Moravia, and Slovakia meant that Poland was all but indefensible, just as Czechoslovakia had been after the Anschluss. Very roughly, Poland consisted of a large irregular triangle, with the Polish Corridor jutting up out of the western apex of it. On two sides of the triangle Poland was bordered by East Prussia, Germany proper, and the occupied territory of Czechoslovakia. It was little comfort that the third side was bordered by Russia.

The German plan was to deploy two army groups; Army Group North and Army Group South under General Feodor von Bock and General Gerd von Rundstedt respectively. These would drive directly into Poland and meet at Warsaw, encircling and cutting off the main Polish forces, which the Germans expected to be deployed in the western part of the country. Von Bock proposed a second, deeper pincer farther to the eastward, but that was not adopted as a part of the original plan.

Army Group North had about 630,000 men in two armies. It was supported by the 1st Air Fleet with 500 bombers, 180 Stukas or dive-bombers, and about 120 fighter aircraft. It had one armored corps in the 4th Army, west of the Polish Corridor, whose task

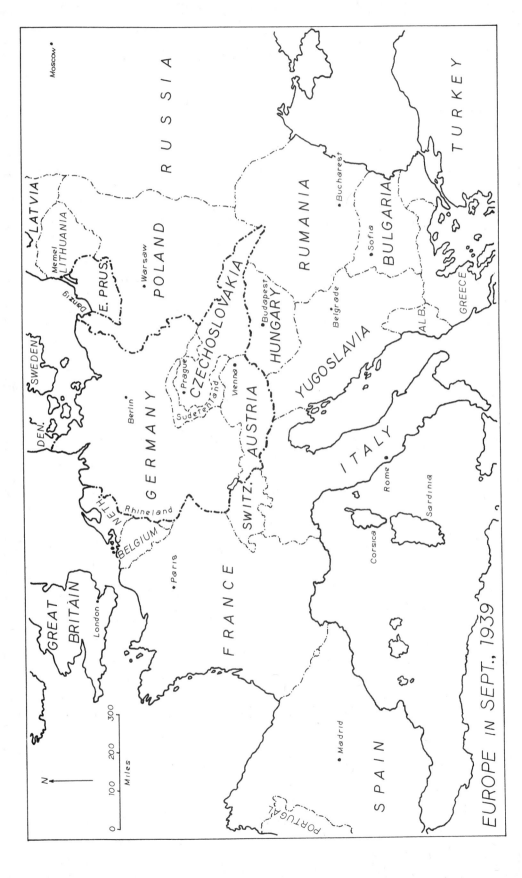

EUROPE IN SEPT., 1939

was to cut the Corridor, link up with the other army in East Prussia, and then drive due south on Warsaw.

Army Group South had three armies consisting of about 886,000 men. The 4th Air Fleet was in support, with 310 bombers, 160 Stukas, and again about 120 fighters. Its central 10th Army, with one Panzer or armored corps, was to drive northeast to Warsaw, while 8th Army protected its left flank from the assumed mass of Polish troops, and 14th Army protected its right flank while taking Cracow, one of the great historic sites of Poland and the kind of city the Poles might be expected to defend to the last.

Most of the navy was held in the west, on the other side of the Danish Peninsula, to guard against possible British intervention, but some units were allocated for the bombardment of the Polish port and naval base of Gydnia and Hel, at the end of the Corridor. The Luftwaffe held in reserve 250 Junkers Ju52 transports, which could be used in an emergency to drop paratroops.

Hitler's generals were extremely worried about what the Western Powers would do. The British Army was incapable of doing a great deal, but the Royal Air Force was by now formidable, while the French were perceived as a definite threat. Nevertheless, Hitler remained convinced the French would not take the initiative. He put on a major propaganda campaign to convince the world that Germany's western fortifications were impregnable; at the same time, he could spare only understrength infantry divisions and a few light air-force units to man the "West Wall." The whole concept of the campaign was to break through the Polish frontier crust as rapidly as possible and gobble up Poland before her allies could do anything about it. Then, having achieved a fait accompli, it would be time to decide where to go next.

In retrospect, it looks as if the old adage, "Whom the gods would destroy they first drive mad," might be applied to the Polish government in 1939. That is only the accuracy of hindsight. At the time neither the Poles nor anyone else expected the Germans to fight the kind of war they did. It is possible that the Polish Army might have held the eastern part of the country, defending the line of the Bug River or conceivably even the San. That would have meant abandoning Warsaw, Poland's industrial areas, and all the parts of the homeland that were most dear to the people. The Poles were tough, they had no illusions that the war would not come, and they were determined to make the hated Germans pay for every inch of Polish territory. The Polish high command, therefore, decided to hold on the frontiers in a linear defense, fall back as necessary under German pressure, and fight until the Western Allies came to their rescue.

To do this, the Commander-in-Chief, Marshal Edward Smigly-Rydz, had an army that at full strength would have mustered nearly 1,800,000 men. In the event, the Poles got about 1,000,000 called up, and of these about 800,000 actually seem to have gotten to their units and been taken on strength before Poland was overrun. These troops were disposed in six armies along the frontiers and one smaller "Operational Group" up near the juncture of East Prussia and Lithuania, plus a central reserve organized fifty miles or so south of Warsaw. The best of these armies, in terms of the modernity of its equipment, was the Poznan Army, at the western apex of Poland, in the area where the Germans did not intend to attack. The Poles had about 935 aircraft, almost all of them inferior to the equivalent German types, and no more than a few light tanks against the Germans' four armored divisions. They had impressive numbers of horsed cavalry, which they believed, probably correctly, to be the best in the world. Partly because of this they had not done much in the way of preparing field fortifications. The official Polish doctrine was that they would fight a mobile war, and that enemy penetrations would be quickly counterattacked and sealed off and destroyed, a doctrine that would have been adequate had their enemy possessed, as the Poles did, a World War I type of army.

The Germans had been violating Polish air space all summer, flying photographic reconnaissance missions which the Polish fighters were too slow to intercept. Perhaps because the Poles were jaded by the unending atmosphere of crisis, the attack when it came caught them by surprise. Instead of using the standard border clashes of a more leisurely era, the Germans hit with everything they had. At dawn on September 1 the Luftwaffe struck at Polish airfields, the German battleship *Schleswig-Holstein* moved into Gydnia at point-blank range to bombard Polish naval installations, and artillery and tank engines roared all along the frontier.

Contrary to popular opinion, the Luftwaffe did not wipe out the Polish Air Force in its first strike. The Poles had dispersed their planes to operational fields a few days before the attack. The Germans did, though, inflict serious losses, and that, coupled with the overwhelming numerical and design superiority of the Luftwaffe, was enough to destroy the Polish Air Force within the next three or four days. Polish fighters took a relatively heavy toll of the German planes—in some cases ramming them in desperation—but they were soon worn down, and the remaining fighters were pulled back for the defense of Warsaw. Their ground attack and tactical support aircraft, even more vulnerable than their fighters, were decimated in early attacks against the heavily armed German columns breaking across the frontier. The Luftwaffe was soon virtually free of opposition and turned its attention on the one hand to dive-bombing and strafing in support of the armored advance, and on the other to bombing communications and transport links, sowing confusion and despair in the rear of the Polish forces. Under this pressure, Polish mobilization broke down on the first day of the invasion, and was never completed.

The initial phase of the German attack consisted of the breaking of the frontier positions. This was achieved for practical purposes on the first day. The Polish idea of cut-off units establishing strongpoints until relieved by counterattacks was completely negated by the tank-aircraft combination. The counterattacks never got launched, and the "strongpoints" were quickly mopped up or dispersed by mobile artillery, by follow-up infantry units, or by dive-bombing attacks. The Poles fought stubbornly, and even, on occasion, tried their horses, swords, and lances against the German tanks. Nonetheless, by the evening of the first day, some of the German armor had made fifteen miles, and was practically into open country. By the 3rd, when Britain and France got around to declaring war, the Corridor was cut and the air force was all but wiped out. The last units holding on the frontier fell back on the 5th.

The linear defense being completely broken, the Germans entered the second phase of their operation, the pincer movement cutting off and destroying the remaining Polish forces. The Polish headquarters units were under constant air attacks, and the Poles were rapidly losing what little control they had over their battle. The roads were filled with panic-stricken refugees, and the motorized Germans could advance faster than the Poles could retreat. The Poznan Army was falling back eastward, seeking to reach Warsaw and defend it before the Germans could get there, but by the 7th, the German 10th Army, from the south, was only thirty-five miles short of the city. That day the Polish government left its capital and moved to Lublin.

The Germans won the race. They surrounded Warsaw on the 9th before the Poznan forces could get there. On the 10th, the Poznan Army, together with remnants of the other western Polish armies, about 100,000 strong, attempted to break out to the south. For four days the issue hung in the balance, while the Poles struggled desperately. The Germans pounded them with artillery and Stukas, and were at one point forced to fly in reserves, the pressure was so heavy. Yet the German grip tightened inexorably, and the crisis was past by the 14th; the survivors of the Polish attacks, about 52,000 strong, finally surrendered on the 17th.

The Poles by then were completely broken up, and their still-existent main units were all surrounded. The German Army high command had already adopted von Bock's earlier suggestion of a second deeper envelopment to gather in Polish forces escaping to the east. This pincer was complete by the 19th. From then on, it was a matter of cleaning up pockets of resistance. Remaining major units surrendered or dispersed in the third week of September. Warsaw held out, under constant air and artillery bombardment, until the 27th. By then, food was giving out, the water mains were broken, fires were raging out of control, and the city had collapsed. Aerial defense consisted mainly of loudspeakers sounding warnings and playing Poland's national music, Chopin's "Polonaises." Hospitals were out of supplies and swamped with both civilian and military casualties, unattached soldiers were shepherded through the city and out to fend for themselves, as the city did not need and could not feed them; organized life and with it resistance ground down, and finally there was nothing left to do but capitulate.

A few strongpoints lasted longer. Up on the Baltic, at the little naval base on the Hel Peninsula, the garrison of a few hundred soldiers, sailors, and civilian workers stood off attacks by tanks, artillery, dive-bombers, and German battleships until the first of October. Finally, after thirty-one days—about thirty more than required by the dictates of military honor—having nothing left to fight with, the Poles surrendered. The last organized resistance was at Kock, southeast of Warsaw, and here about 17,000 remnants put up the white flag on October 6.

No one knows what the campaign cost Poland; the breakdown was so rapid and so complete that accurate figures were never obtained. The Germans said they took 694,000 prisoners, and they estimated that about 100,000 escaped across neutral frontiers into Hungary, Lithuania, or Rumania. The Polish combat losses are unknown, as is the exact number taken by the Russians. The Germans themselves lost about 14,000 killed and about 30,000 wounded.

The whole German plan had been to overrun Poland quickly, and they had done so with a speed that astonished the rest of the world. Even so, it had not gone as rapidly as they had hoped. It was an essential part of Hitler's idea that Poland should be swallowed up in one gulp, before the West had time to react. As early as the 3rd, therefore, Hitler was asking that the Russians should fulfill, or take advantage of, their part of the deal and move in from the east. Essentially, the Russians were caught flatfooted by this and did nothing; the Germans repeated their request on the 10th, but it was another week before the Russians lurched into motion. On the 17th, they got two army groups moving, the White Russian Front in the north, and the Ukrainian Front in the south. There was little resistance as they crossed the frontiers, the Poles being fully occupied in the west, and by the 17th already collapsing. The Russians did gather up more than 200,000 prisoners among Polish troops and potential troops fleeing eastward. The Red armies then closed up to the German stop line; both sides were very careful to avoid any clash between units as a result of mistaken identity; it was not, after all, a very comfortable alliance.

In fact, the original nonaggression pact had called for a buffer zone between the Germans and the Russians, but this was now renegotiated, each took a sphere of Poland, and the Polish state once again disappeared from the map. Hitler then announced that the central European situation was satisfactory, that it could be a basis for a lasting peace, and he called for negotiations with the Western Powers.

The big question of the 1939 campaign is not what happened to Poland, or to Germany or Russia, but what happened to France and Great Britain. At a time when the Germans were almost completely committed in Poland, why did Britain and France not strike quickly and hard? This was what the Poles expected as help from their allies; this was, in effect, what Poland died for.

The saddest aspect of the whole matter is that the Western Allies could have done so. There is virtually no doubt that had they attacked vigorously, they could have broken through the thin screen of Germans to and across the Rhine. They could, and should, have easily defeated Germany, and the Second World War would never have gotten off the ground.

The French were fully mobilized while the Germans were still enmeshed in Poland. Facing the German frontier they had eighty-five divisions. Some of them were not fully worked up, but the lowest estimate by military experts gives the French seventy-two divisions. Against them the Germans had eight weak regular divisions, and about twenty-five reserve formations, some of them existing on paper, some made up largely of recruits who were not even half-trained. The Germans had 300 guns, the French had 1,600. The French had 3,200 tanks; the Germans had none—they were all in Poland. The French and British together had 1,700 aircraft; the Germans had almost none.

The French did undertake an offensive operation. They sent out patrols that penetrated about fourteen miles into German territory; they met no opposition. They then withdrew on order and never advanced again.

The Royal Air Force before the war had deliberately assumed a policy of building up a strategic bomber force. Now, with nearly 800 serviceable bombers against a virtually defenseless western Germany, it announced that its policy was not to use those bombers, but to conserve and build them up further. It would never again achieve a force ratio of 800 to nothing.

The facts seem to be that no one in the West really wanted to fight. German intelligence rated French morale as high, and the French Army as the most formidable possible foe; this was before its spirit was sapped by months of "phoney war." Yet the high command clung to its visions of French and Allied inferiority to German capability. Allied intelligence consistently overrated German strength, and underrated its own. The politicians were only too happy to listen to the generals, and the generals were afraid to risk a fight. Paralyzed by their fears and their memories, hamstrung by their doctrinal preconceptions, they wanted an absolutely guaranteed sure thing. Unwilling to accept the closest they would ever come to it, they let the opportunity pass. It was really a vicious circle; the military experts advised their governments that they were in a parlous position. The civilian leaders were therefore hesitant to dictate action. The military command drew the inference therefrom that the politicians were uncommitted to war, and might well be contemplating a deal with Hitler. That made the soldiers all the more reluctant to risk the issue of battle. So Poland went down, unaided. The French sat in the Maginot Line and let their army rot. The Royal Air Force dropped leaflets over Germany. The Allies' decision, or lack of it, would cost millions of lives and alter the shape of the world for the foreseeable future.

7. Northern Adventures

ADOLF HITLER WAS STILL on his winning streak, and immediately after the successful conclusion of the Polish campaign, he turned his attention westward. He wanted an offensive against France before the winter, but it was already late September, and his generals insisted that the sorting out and redeployment of the victorious army would take more time than was available. Grumbling, der Fuehrer let reality have its way.

Hitler was reluctant to do nothing; the Western Allies were reluctant to do anything. The French were more than content to wait passively, and not stir up trouble for themselves. Counsels were divided in Britain; Winston Churchill had been taken back into the government as First Lord of the Admiralty, and Churchill as always was a notable fire-eater. He pressed for offensive action. The Chamberlain government as a whole, however, was quite happy to defer to the French vision of how the war should be fought. Britain's position was somewhat embarrassing anyway. She had sent the British Expeditionary Force (B. E. F.) to France, but it consisted in its entirety of less than half a dozen divisions. It was therefore impossible to press the French too vigorously to fight, when it would be the French who had to do all the fighting. The French view, perhaps never overtly stated but constantly implied, was that if Britain wanted to fight, she should send over an army the size of France's and then she could fight as much as she pleased. Chamberlain found it easier to resist Churchill's internal than France's external pressure, so the government remained quiescent, and adopted as their slogan for the war the totally uninspiring "Business as usual." It was hardly calculated to arouse martial ardor, but it was what a public who could still remember World War I was thought to want.

An uneasy calm settled over western Europe as the fall rains and fogs rolled in from the Atlantic. The troops huddled along

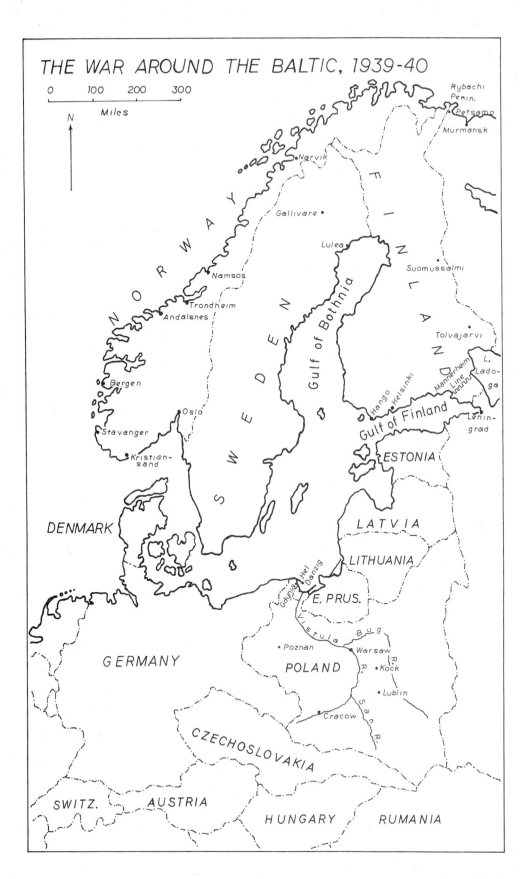

THE WAR AROUND THE BALTIC, 1939-40

0   100   200   300

Miles

N

NORWAY

SWEDEN

FINLAND

DENMARK

GERMANY

POLAND

CZECHOSLOVAKIA

SWITZ.   AUSTRIA

HUNGARY   RUMANIA

ESTONIA

LATVIA

LITHUANIA

E. PRUS.

Rybachi Penin.

Petsamo

Murmansk

Narvik

Gallivare

Lulea

Suomussalmi

Namsos

Trondheim

Andalsnes

Tolvajarvi

L. Ladoga

Bergen

Hango

Helsinki

Mannerheim Line

Oslo

Gulf of Bothnia

Gulf of Finland

Leningrad

Stavanger

Kristiansand

Gdynia

Hel

Danzig

Vistula

Bug R.

Poznan

Warsaw

Kock

Lublin

Cracow

San R.

the frontiers, the French in the Maginot Line relatively comfortable, those to the north of it, and the B. E. F. on the Belgian border, making the best of a boring, wasting time. They dug, drilled, they attended lectures on "Why we are fighting," and they wondered why they were not fighting. American correspondents, quick to flock to the war zone, soon christened the whole affair "the phoney war," a label that stuck to it. Surely there was going to be a deal; Chamberlain had characterized Czechoslovakia as "a faraway country of which we know little," and now, in the German propaganda phrase, no one was going "to die for Danzig." There was nothing to do but wait.

This was not universally true. The Russians were not waiting. As they rolled into Poland, they had firsthand evidence of the effectiveness of Germany's military machine. They decided that they needed even more cushion than the hundred miles of Polish territory they had gained. Along the southern shore of the Baltic, from Prussia eastward almost to Leningrad, was a string of three Baltic republics: Lithuania, Latvia, and Estonia. Residue of the great medieval Lithuanian empire, these areas had come under Russian domination as far back as the eighteenth century, and had formed the Baltic Provinces of the Tsarist realm. Like Poland, they had broken away in the general collapse of the Russian Revolution, and had been acknowledged as free states, in the post-World War I treaties. Somewhat precariously independent, they now formed a natural corridor from German East Prussia along the Baltic littoral to Leningrad, Russia's great industrial complex at the head of the Gulf of Finland.

As soon as the occupation of Poland was completed, the Russians put pressure on the three states. All three were pro-German by choice, but were not now in any position to exercise that choice. They each signed mutual-defense treaties with Russia, which had the effect of making them Russian satellites, and the Reds immediately moved troops in. Hitler was not pleased, but for the moment there was little he could do about it.

The Russians believed they were equally vulnerable in the north where Finland, another successor-state from the revolution, was seen by the Russians as a potential danger. The Finns had originally won their independence with the help of German troops and equipment, and they were pro-German, at least to the extent of being anti-Russian. The Russians therefore made the same kind of demands on the Finns they had made on the southern Baltic states. The Russians wanted fifty miles of the Karelian Isthmus, the strip of land that ran between the head of the Gulf of Finland and Lake Ladoga. They wanted islands in the gulf, and a long-term lease on the Finnish base at Hango, which dominated the mouth of the gulf. Finland also stretched north to a small shore along the Arctic, the Rybachi Peninsula. This threatened the Russian port of Murmansk, and therefore the Russians demanded cession of it too.

Finland could have lived with this; in fact, she has since the end of World War II. But Russia was the traditional enemy, and memories of Russian misrule formed the recent history of the country. The Finnish Commander-in-Chief, Marshal Mannerheim, had led the country in its revolt against Russia in 1918-19. On November 26, the Finns rejected Stalin's demands and mobilized for war, ready to play David to Russia's Goliath.

They knew they could not win a full-scale war, but they hoped the Western Allies might come to their aid, or barring that, that they could make the price so heavy the Russians would sicken and give up. On the 30th, the Russians responded to the Finnish rejection by air attacks on the capital of Helsinki, and hostilities opened all along the frontier.

The ensuing Russo-Finnish War or Winter War distracted everyone's attention northward, and filled practically the entire world with admiration for the Finns. They were a hardy people, as they had to be just to survive in their country, and though they were relatively few in numbers, they had adapted their defense well to the demands of the situation.

The Finnish regular army consisted of about 300,000 men. Nearly all of these were stationed on the Karelian Isthmus, in a fortified belt made up of pillboxes and Great War–style trenches known as the Mannerheim Line. It was not up to western European standards, but it was formidable enough. The 700-mile-long frontier from north of Lake Ladoga all the way to the Arctic was held mainly by reserve forces known as the Civic Guard, about 100,000 men strong. Additionally, the Finns had a women's auxiliary, also about 100,000 strong, to take over administrative duties. They had a small air force, flying mostly license-built or foreign-made British and Dutch aircraft, and a minuscule navy. They lacked any amount of heavy armor or equipment, but were well equipped for light, mobile, small-unit actions.

Against this force the Russians deployed some thirty infantry divisions and six tank brigades, roughly a million men, a thousand tanks, and about eight hundred aircraft. Nearly half their infantry and all but one of the armored formations were put in on the Karelian Isthmus, against the Mannerheim Line. Practically two separate wars were fought.

On the isthmus, the Finns were dug in and as prepared as they could be. Most of their artillery was used there, and they snuggled down in their pillboxes and trenches, disguised by the winter snows, dressed in white coveralls, ready for the Russians to come. The Russians, disdaining any kind of tactical finesse, drove forward in heavy masses. With scanty artillery preparation, and using their tanks to support crowds of foot soldiers, they rushed headfirst into the slaughter. Huge formations, cumbersome, unwieldy, inflexible, drove against the Finnish positions. They coupled their frontal attacks with heavy bombing of the Finnish cities, but the result was more to strengthen the Finns' resolve than to weaken their resources. They also tried amphibious attacks along the Gulf of Finland, but these too were beaten off.

By early December, the Russians on the isthmus were exhausted, and the Finns even tried a short-lived offensive, which cost them more casualties than they could well afford. The turn of the year saw both sides in the area fought out and waging a war of positions.

North of Lake Ladoga, all the way up along the frontier, the story had different details. The Russians launched five separate drives in corps strength. In the far north they made some progress, putting in an amphibious assault against the Arctic port of Petsamo and taking it. In central Finland, however, they suffered defeat after defeat. Here they readily broke across the frontier, but as their heavy columns advanced along the few roads, the Finnish Civic Guards coalesced against them like white corpuscles around a foreign body in the bloodstream. Just north of Lake Ladoga a Russian division and a tank brigade were stranded in the middle of nowhere and forced to surrender in February. Another division barely held on until it could pull itself out of the fighting; two more divisions were virtually wiped out at Tolvajarvi. Attacks were turned back in the north-central area, and at Suomussalmi the Finns added a small-action classic to military studies.

The frontier was crossed by a Russian division fresh from the open spaces of the Ukraine. It had heavy equipment which made it roadbound; as there was only one road this meant a thin column of vehicles, with soldiers floundering along in four feet of snow, and temperatures forty below zero. The first Russian division was followed by a second; together they made a column twenty miles long and one tank wide.

The Finns came in against them on skis, a squad or a platoon at a time, carrying rifles and light machine-guns. Their targets were less the heavy weapons and tanks that held the Russians to the road, than the machines that enabled them to survive: field kitchens, supply trucks—anything that could give shelter. Russian aircraft could not operate in the blizzards: reconnaissance patrols went out and usually did not come back. The Russian tanks tried to break out over the ice of frozen lakes; the Finns blasted holes in the lakes and drowned the tanks, forcing the survivors back to the choked road. The Finns got a few guns up and ranged on the road, systematically blockading it; Russian artillery fired blind in reply, hitting nothing. On Christmas Day, the first Russian division tried to break clear and was annihilated. The Finns turned their attention to the second division, broke through the column at several points, and then wiped out the pockets one by one. By the time it was over, the Finns had taken 1,300 prisoners and the full equipment of two divisions. They themselves had suffered 900 dead and about twice as many wounded. Nearly 28,000 Russians were killed or frozen.

Yet the Russians were no more prepared than the Finns to give up, and the Russians could afford their heavy losses better than the Finns their light ones. In February, they gave up their assaults in the north, where the country could not support their masses, and instead they concentrated on the Karelian Isthmus. They also did some housecleaning. To some extent their humiliation had been the price of the Stalinist purges, when political reliability and mediocrity had been more important than military expertise. There now came a ruthless weeding out of officers, and a re-emphasis on efficient staff work. They crowded twenty-four divisions into the isthmus, supported them with masses of tanks and artillery, and brought in large numbers of aircraft. On February 1, they launched heavy attacks with dense artillery preparation. For nearly two weeks they ground on, ignoring losses which reached fantastic proportions, and finally, on the 13th, the Finnish line cracked. Fighting desperate rear-guard actions, the Finns were pushed back to their end of the isthmus, and on March 1, exhausted and having no hope of rescue from the West, they opened negotiations. The war ended on March 12, and the Russians took pretty much what they had originally demanded.

* * *

The Winter War was extraordinarily fruitful of by-products, reassessments, and misconceptions. The greatest of these last was the widespread opinion that the Russians could not fight. After the war ended, the Russians busily replaced generals and reworked their military doctrines. Ironically, while they did so the rest of the world drew its own conclusion from the evidence presented, that the Russian forces were big but clumsy and that they would be no match for a modern army employing blitzkrieg-style strategies.

While the war was being fought, the question of the northern countries and their neutrality had become acute. The Allies had seriously considered active help to Finland; given the atmosphere after the Russo-German Nonaggression Pact, it seemed they might as well fight both totalitarian states as either one of them. They did send aircraft and artillery to Finland, and several thousand foreign volunteers, mostly Scandinavian, also went to her assistance, though few of them saw any fighting before the collapse.

It was the secondary motives that intrigued the Allies, though. The major obstacle to providing aid to Finland was the determined neutrality of Norway and Sweden. Baltic geography was such that the Allies could get help to the Finns only if they were granted transit rights through these two countries. Such rights were resolutely refused, both governments being justifiably afraid of giving Germany or Russia any excuse to intervene in the north. From the Anglo-French point of view, transit rights were highly desirable, because they would probably lead to more than that. If the British and French sent troops to Finland, they would do so across central or northern Norway and Sweden. The prize here was the control of Swedish iron ore being sent to Germany.

Swedish ore came out of the Gallivare iron fields, which were north of the Gulf of Bothnia. In summer, the ore was sent by rail to the Swedish port of Lulea at the head of the gulf, and then taken by ship south through the Baltic. In winter, however, the Gulf of Bothnia froze over. Then ore went by rail across the frontier to the Norwegian port of Narvik. It then went south by ship through Norwegian coastal waters, known as the Norwegian Leads, to Germany and the rest of the world.

The Allies, in the process of considering troops for Finland, centered also on Swedish iron. They were thinking in terms of economic warfare and blockade of Germany. If in transit to Finland they occupied the Gallivare fields, they would shut off a major supply of German ore. The British were also conscious of the desirability of making their naval blockade as tight as possible and they knew that the Germans had used the officially neutral Norwegian Leads heavily during the last war. The Royal Navy was therefore eager to mine the Leads, or to occupy Narvik, or indeed to do anything, under Churchill's eager prodding, that would make the war a little livelier.

As early as mid-February, the problem of the Norwegian Leads had become front-page news. The German supply ship *Altmark,* which had served as tender to the raider *Graf Spee,* was making her way back home to Germany. She was carrying nearly 300 imprisoned British merchant-navy men hidden below decks and was sailing down through the Leads. A cursory Norwegian search had failed to find the prisoners, so the British, after protestations of good intent, had sent in a destroyer division, violated Norwegian neutrality, boarded the *Altmark,* and rescued the sailors. The Norwegians protested, but were embarrassed by the fact that they had missed the prisoners. The British pointed out that the Germans were the original sinners, and they were just reacting to it. Hitler was furious at what he regarded as violation of his right to violate other peoples' rights. By mid-February, then, the Germans as well as the Allies were thinking of occupying Scandinavian territory, and everyone's plans matured soon after.

In March, the British and French had gotten close enough to action to be loading troops in northern Scottish ports, ready to go. They had then had the ground cut from under them by the Finnish collapse. Once the Finns asked for an armistice, there was no more pretense of going to their aid, and no excuse for moving into northern Norway and Sweden. They downgraded their operation to the mining of Narvik harbor and the Norwegian Leads. As they were doing this, the Germans struck.

The German plan and operation were both masterpieces of improvisation. On February 21, Hitler called in a relatively obscure general, Nikolaus von Falkenhorst, and told him he was to command the operation; von Falkenhorst spent the afternoon with a travel-guide book and came back with the nucleus of a plan and a list of his operational requirements. The navy, the key element in the affair, was called in only later, but the German machine slipped readily into high gear. Within a week, Hitler decided to occupy Denmark on the way by, as an afterthought.

The German flotilla put to sea late on April 7. By coincidence, that day the British were starting out on their mining of the Leads.

Churchill, moving more and more to the front as the pusher on the war in the British cabinet, had wanted to act earlier, but had been delayed by consultation with the French. The German forces were spotted by British reconnaissance planes, but the information was misinterpreted. The Admiralty knew something was going on in the north German ports, but it was preoccupied with the idea that the German fleet was preparing a breakout into the Atlantic. This preconception was reinforced by the fact that the sightings were of fleet units rather than transport vessels, as most of the German invasion troops were carried aboard warships. As the British Home Fleet sailed, therefore, it headed for an interception point that would block the breakout which never came, while the unmolested Germans followed the Norwegian coast north.

The Norwegian government was warned of what was afoot, but the army was capable only of local defense at best. It consisted of about 15,000 men, plus small reserve forces. The government hoped to the end that Norwegian neutrality could be preserved, and it was also to a certain extent victim of divided counsels. There were substantial numbers of German sympathizers in Norway, though the extent to which they sabotaged Norway's defenses has probably been overstated; in reality, there were few defenses anyway.

The Germans struck simultaneously in several places. Early on the morning of the 9th, heavy naval forces entered Oslo fiord, the long reach approaching the capital. They hoped that by speed and bluff they might even get ashore unopposed, but the coastal forts were waiting for them, and in the fiord they took severe losses, including the sinking of the heavy cruiser *Blucher*. The check allowed the Norwegian royal family to escape northward, but von Falkenhorst responded swiftly. He had originally intended to bring in troops by air as reinforcements for the seaborne landing; now he reversed that, and even while his ships were being held up, he landed troops at Oslo's airport, Fornebu. This small airborne force, only 3,000 men, managed to secure the city and keep it quiet until the coastal forts were subdued, whereupon the original assault force landed at the docks.

The Germans poured ashore right up the coast. They landed at Kristiansand, 2,500 men came in by aircraft at Stavanger, 2,000 by ship at Bergen, nearly the same number at Trondheim. Up in the north, ten destroyers supported by battlecruisers landed 2,000 men at Narvik. While all this went on, the Germans also moved into and occupied Denmark, against only sporadic resistance.

The Norwegians fought but they were caught by surprise, and their response was more a spastic reaction than a calculated campaign. In every case, the Germans were soon in possession of the ports and airfields, and the Norwegians were falling back in disarray into the countryside. The Germans rapidly brought in follow-up waves of reinforcements and heavy weapons and began in their turn fanning out to break up the Norwegians before they could fully organize.

There were chaotic and inconclusive naval clashes. Ships stumbled on each other through the fog and mists of the Norwegian Sea. The British destroyer *Glowworm* emerged from a squall to find herself facing four German destroyers and the pocket battleship *Hipper,* on their way to the landing at Trondheim. She responded to these daunting odds by ramming the *Hipper,* being sunk herself in the process. The Royal Navy might have been caught on the hop, but were still prepared to assert it was their ocean. The same day, a British submarine sank a German light cruiser in the strait between Denmark and Sweden, and the next day, dive-bombers of the Fleet Air Arm sank another one in Bergen Harbor.

Farther north, five British destroyers dashed up Narvik fiord and surprised the ten Germans who had landed troops there. They sank two and damaged three, for two losses of their own. On the way back out they ran into the supply ship carrying all the German ammunition for the landing force, and sank it too. Three days later, the British came back and finished the job, this time with the battleship *Warspite,* and the German Army units in Narvik found themselves all alone.

In the south the campaign hung in the balance. Within forty-eight hours of the landings the scattered Norwegians were trying to pull themselves together and hoping for help from the Allies. Air power decided the matter. German air control of southern Norway prevented the Royal Navy's operating in adjacent water, so the Germans were quickly able to consolidate there. In central and northern Norway, however, the British could work. Within a week they had put forces ashore at Andalsnes and Namsos, either side of Trondheim, about 30,000 all told. They also landed another 15,000 at Narvik and began pushing the Germans back toward the Swedish frontier.

The Andalsnes force advanced south and linked up with the Norwegians in the valleys leading to Oslo. German air superiority told, however, and they found themselves flanked, strafed, and slowly forced back to the north. Eventually, they were back at Andalsnes, and evacuated on the 1st and 2nd of May. The Namsos unit had little-better luck; the Germans leapfrogged their air units northward, the Trondheim forces turned the Allies back, and they were back on ship on the 2nd and 3rd of May. The British tried to supply air cover from carrier-based planes, but the planes were inferior to land-based types, and the carriers themselves were put under attack. The aerial units that operated from shore, usually from frozen lakes, were soon overwhelmed by the Luftwaffe.

Only in the north was some kind of equilibrium established. The Narvik area was out of range of German air cover, and the British and French forces landed here were numerically superior to the Germans left stranded by their naval defeat. The Allies handily held the town, but did not quite get up enough momentum to drive the Germans over the border into Sweden and internment. Before the issue was decided, however, the campaign of France had opened, and the Allied forces, by then built up to 24,000, were pulled out in early June as the magnitude of the French disaster overwhelmed all other considerations. By then, the last Norwegian units were breaking up, King Haakon VII and his ministers had escaped to Britain and set up a government in exile, and Norway, like Austria, Czechoslovakia, Poland, and Denmark, was gone.

The results of all this were problematic but significant, both in the long and the short term. The Norwegian campaign made the Allies look pretty inept. Britain had been confident that the Royal Navy ruled wherever the water would float a keel; no one up to that point had any real experience of the relative value of air power versus sea power, or the ways in which they might have to be combined. It was therefore an inordinate shock to the British view of themselves and of the way the war ought to be fought, that German air power might reach across the open sea and snatch a country practically from under their noses. Again, since it was difficult to judge the effect of air superiority on land fighting also, their military response had looked as ill-handled as their naval one. Probably the most important side effect of all this was the fall of the Chamberlain government. In early April, he had announced complacently in the House of Commons that Hitler "had missed the bus." Then came Norway. Ironically, it was partly through Churchill's riding off in all directions at once that the campaign went quite as badly as it did, yet popular fury hit on Chamberlain the appeaser, rather than Churchill the fighter. Chamberlain resigned on the 10th and Churchill came to power as a result of a disaster that he himself had done as much as any one man to engineer.

On the other side of the fence, Norway made the Germans look as good as it did the Allies look bad. There had been close cooperation between land, sea, and air units, and the machine had functioned smoothly; setbacks and shortcomings were promptly rectified, and the Germans showed themselves to be expert opportunists. They derived very real benefits; the Swedish iron ore supply was now secured for the rest of the war. They also had a safe funnel to get raiders out into the Atlantic, and later on they would have both air and naval bases from which to attack Allied convoys to north Russia. The British blockade was further loosened, and the problems of controlling the sea magnified for them.

But there were drawbacks to this as well. For practical purposes the German Navy had been crippled, and its efficiency and its numbers were diminished for months to come. Later in the year, one of the items that would militate against the invasion of Britain would be the weakness of the navy, stemming in good part from its wounds in Norway. There was also the fact that the more territory Hitler conquered, the more he would have to garrison. He was always tied up in fantasies about Nordic Scandinavia and its military significance, and eventually he would put more than a quarter of a million men in Norway and Denmark, and keep them there for the rest of the war. The effort might have been better placed elsewhere—but that can be said of everything in war, and indeed of war itself.

The Norwegian Army command finally surrendered on June 9. By then the unhappy story of the campaign was back-page news.

8. The Fall of France

THE CAMPAIGN THAT OPENED on May 10, 1940, was one of the world's great military masterpieces. As spring ripened into a beautiful early summer, the likelihood of war in earnest became apparent. The invasion of Denmark and Norway jolted the Allies out of their lethargy, and while it went on to its rapid and unhappy conclusion the Allied high commands tried to wrestle with the irreconcilabilities of their situation.

Hitler had made a peace offer back in October of 1939; this was probably not a serious one, and whether it was or not, the Allies refused to take it as such. Not too much had happened on the Western Front after that. The British had gradually increased their strength in France, and the British Expeditionary Force, under the command of Lord Gort, was up to a strength of nearly 400,000 men by spring of 1940. Against this, however, had to be set a noticeable decline in French morale. The army that had been fully confident of itself in September was less so by spring. There was disaffection, the troops had been quick to pick up the "phoney war" phrase, and inactivity in billets had led them to question the point of the whole exercise.

Neither of the Allies saw any real need for a reassessment of their view of the war. Though the British had increased their army commitment, they still believed that the economic pressure of the Royal Navy's blockade would finally win the war. They coupled with this the possibility of bombing by the Royal Air Force, but when they thought of that, they had no idea of the difficulties involved, nor did they really give too much thought to the fact that strategic bombing had not only to deal with the enemy, but also with friends. The French, worried about the power of the Luftwaffe, were adamantly opposed to the initiation of a bombing campaign. With the war eight months old, the R. A. F. had so far done precious little bombing at all.

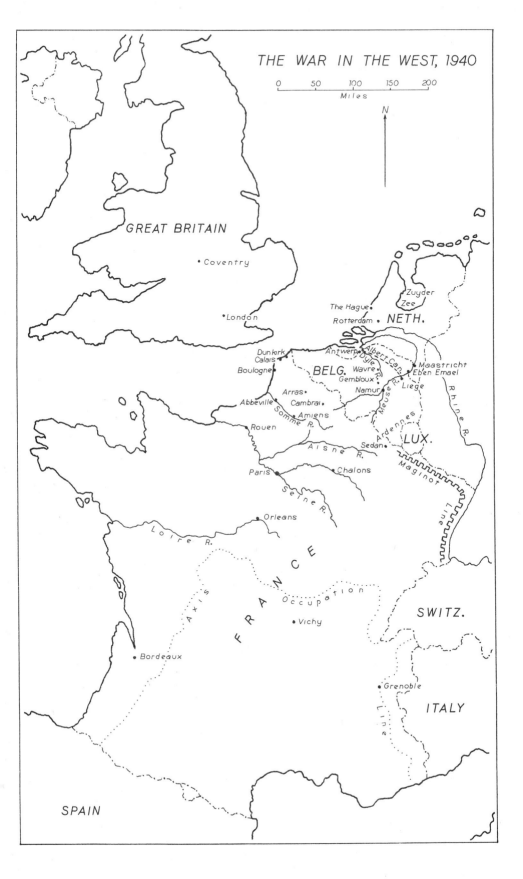

THE WAR IN THE WEST, 1940

0   50   100   150   200
Miles

N

GREAT BRITAIN

• Coventry

•London

The Hague
Rotterdam
Zuyder Zee

NETH.

Dunkirk
Calais
Boulogne
Antwerp
Albert Can.
Dyle R.
Wavre
Gembloux
Namur
Maastricht
Eben Emael
Liege

BELG.

Arras•
Abbeville •Cambrai
Amiens
Rouen
Somme R.
Meuse R.
Rhine R.
Ardennes
LUX.
Aisne R.
Sedan
Maginot Line

Paris
Chalons
Seine R.

•Orleans

Loire R.

SWITZ.

Axis

F R A N C E

Occupation

•Vichy

•Bordeaux

Line

•Grenoble

ITALY

SPAIN

The French were busy with internal problems. There was for one thing a government reshuffle. Premier Daladier resigned, and was replaced by Paul Reynaud. A smallish, slightly oriental-looking man, Reynaud was thought to be more of a fighter than Daladier; unhappily, his political position was weaker, and he achieved the premiership only by taking into his cabinet men who were not fighters at all. In balance the Reynaud government was hardly in a position to prosecute the war any more vigorously than its predecessor had been.

There were equivalent difficulties in the army command. General Maurice Gamelin was the Commander-in-Chief of the French Army, with his headquarters just outside Paris. As leader of all French troops everywhere, he was responsible not only for metropolitan France, including troops facing Italy and Spain as well as Germany, but also for the troops throughout the empire. To deal with the main battle front from Switzerland to the sea, therefore, the French appointed General Alphonse Georges as Commander-in-Chief Northeast. Under him were the various army groups and armies of the front. This command structure was practically designed to create confusion, and did. Gamelin did not want to interfere in Georges' direction of his battle but constantly did so; Georges wanted to run his own battle, but was never permitted to do it. Messages were shuttled back and forth and got lost, and in the end, neither Georges nor Gamelin was up to the task allotted to them.

Gamelin and his associates had refused to learn anything from the Polish campaign; they had decided before it started that the Poles were militarily negligible, and therefore the rapid defeat of Poland was no more than they expected. Since the campaign went as they supposed it would, there was obviously no lesson to be drawn from it. Through the 1939-40 winter Gamelin saw no need to restructure his defense system. The French did proceed with the leisurely equipping of armored formations, but no urgency underlay their endeavors. A more real problem for them was the attitude of the Belgians and the Dutch.

Both these countries had relatively respectable armies. There were twenty-two divisions in the Belgian, and nine in the Dutch. Between them they had a few hundred aircraft. The chief difficulty was their resolute insistence on their nonalignment. In spite of the experience of 1914, both states steadfastly clung to neutrality and therefore refused to have anything to do with the Anglo-French. It was impossible to coordinate any plans in such a situation.

Plans had to be made nonetheless; the Allies knew the Dutch intended to fight delaying actions as long as they could, and then to withdraw into an area between the Zuider Zee and the Rhine, known somewhat optimistically as "Fortress Holland." They knew also that the Belgians planned to hold the rough triangle Antwerp-Maastricht-Namur-Antwerp. Knowing this, the French based their operational plan on four assumptions.

These assumptions were, first, that the Maginot Line was indeed impregnable; second, that the Ardennes Forest north of it was impassable; third, that the Germans were therefore left with no option but a wheel through the Low Countries, a replay of the Schlieffen Plan of 1914; and fourth, that to meet and defeat this, the French would advance into Belgium and Holland and come to their aid as soon as the war started. The Anglo-French were sure, correctly, that the minute the first German stepped over the frontier, the Dutch and Belgians would hastily abandon their neutrality and start yelling for help.

The disposition of Allied forces reflected these assumptions and plans. On the seacoast was the French 7th Army under General Giraud; the most mobile and presumably best of all the armies, it would dash across Belgium and link up with the retreating Dutch to help hold Fortress Holland. It had the farthest distance to go, hence the assignment to it of the bulk of French motorized equipment. Next to it came the B. E. F., destined to advance into Belgium and link up with the Belgians, then the French 1st Army, also to help the Belgians. Finally came the 9th and the 2nd armies, under Generals Corap and Huntziger; the 9th was the pivot of the Allied wheel, and the 2nd was to hold in front of the Ardennes. With not-too-active roles to play, these were the weakest of the French armies. All five of these forces were under General Billotte, as Commander of Army Group 1. Two more army groups, consisting of four armies altogether, held the Maginot Line.

One remaining problem was how far into Belgium the Allied armies should advance. After a great deal of discussion, they finally agreed to go as far as what was called the "Dyle Line," roughly from Antwerp to Namur, or in effect the rear face of the Belgian fortified triangle. This not only covered Brussels, but it also covered a gap between Wavre on the Dyle River and Namur on the Meuse; known as the "Gembloux Gap," after a little town right in the middle of it, this was regarded as the classic invasion route through the whole of the Low Countries. Within twenty-five miles of it were Wavre, Namur, Liège, Charleroi, and Waterloo, names that had run down through European military history for three centuries and more. As the trees budded and burst into bloom, the French could say they had resolved their difficulties; they knew what the Germans would do, and they were as ready as they could be to meet them.

Materially, though they were unaware of it, the Allies were more than ready for the Germans. Figures vary so widely—wildly even—that one can choose any set to make any argument desired. In 1940, the French high command was speaking of 7,000 German tanks, deliberately overestimating them to cover themselves in the event of a disaster. What this did for French morale can readily be imagined. Figures now available give a comparison something like this:

	German	Allied	
Men	2,000,000	4,000,000	
Divisions	136	135	[94 French, 10 British, 22 Belgian, 9 Dutch]
Tanks	2,439	2,689	
Aircraft	3,200	2,400	[This includes all French (about 1,200), British in France (about 600), and Belgian and Dutch]

This gave the Germans a superiority only in aircraft, and even that depended upon what aircraft were counted, and on the inclusion of all types, as well as the exclusion of the Royal Air Force equipment retained in Britain.

What really mattered in all this, however, was less what either side had, than what either side thought the other had. Ultimately, the key factors were two: the French high command believed itself vastly outnumbered by the Germans, and it lacked a Hitler to force it to go ahead and fight anyway.

For the paradox was that if the French believed themselves outnumbered by the Germans, the Germans knew that they were outnumbered by the French. It was only on Hitler's oft-repeated demands that the German General Staff could be made to take the initiative at all. After his peace offer in October, he had ordered the General Staff to prepare for an offensive; they did not feel up to it, and between the lateness of the season and their dragging their feet, the offensive was gradually put off through the winter and into the spring. Finally, they produced Plan Gelb, or Plan Yellow, calling for a drive through the Netherlands and Belgium to secure the Channel ports, a sort of short-range Schlieffen Plan. This far they were in line with French strategic thinking.

Through the winter, however, the plan evolved. As early as November, when there was an invasion scare in the West that ended only with the advent of bad weather, Hitler and some of his subordinates began to have second thoughts. The original plan called for a drive north of Liège; Hitler now changed it to straddle Liège, that is, he moved the axis of the attack farther south. Finally, he was convinced by von Rundstedt's chief of staff, General Erich von Manstein, that the plan ought to be reversed. Instead of making the main effort in the north, the Germans would go through the Ardennes; instead of Schlieffen, there would be *"Sichelschnitt,"* a "sickle cut" that would slice through the French line at its weak point and envelop the northern armies as they rushed to the defense of the Belgians and Dutch. Manstein was an infantryman and was uncertain about the Ardennes; he approached General Heinz Guderian, the recognized German tank authority, who said it could be done. Hitler jumped at it immediately, and the plan was turned around. The assumptions on which the French had planned their campaign were now totally invalidated.

The tempo of events could not be completely disguised; it is impossible to move hundreds of thousands of men, their equipment, and supplies into a place for battle without anyone noticing, however hard one tries to hide it. As May opened and the long days came, the reconnaissance flights increased, the sound of birds was increasingly drowned by truck and tank engines; spring and war—the one so fruitful and the other so destructive—lay heavy on Europe.

In the early dawn of May 10 the Germans struck. There were the usual Luftwaffe attacks at Allied airfields and communications centers, and by full day the Germans were rolling forward all along the Dutch and Belgian frontiers. The whole plan depended upon making the Allies think it was 1914 all over again. Therefore, the initial weight of the attack was taken by General von Bock's Army Group B advancing into Holland. Strong infantry and armor attacks were carried out, along with heavy aerial bombardment, and paratroop and airborne landings on key airfields at The Hague and Rotterdam, and bridges across the major rivers. The Dutch hastened to their advanced positions, some of which they managed to hold for two or three days, others of which they were levered off almost immediately.

The whole campaign of Holland took a mere four days. The French 7th Army, rushing across Belgium to the rescue, arrived on the 12th, just in time to bump into oncoming German armor in full cry; the French, caught up in a wave of Dutch flotsam, were brushed aside and the next day were in retreat back into Belgium. Fortress Holland never even got organized; the Dutch government left for England on the 13th, to join the other exiles, and the army command surrendered on the 14th. In a last-minute mixup, an intensive bombing raid of Rotterdam missed the recall, and the "terror bombing" of Rotterdam became another example of Hunnish cruelty.

Almost if not quite the same thing happened in Belgium. The forward face of the Belgian defense position ran from Antwerp to Liège along the Albert Canal, and its southern anchor was the great fortress of Eben Emael, about seven miles out of Liège. The fortress was billed as impregnable, and the Belgians were very proud of it. It was a complex of tunnels, steel cupolas and casemates made of heavy concrete; self-contained and with a garrison of about 800 men, the fortress was the key to Belgium. The Germans landed an assault detail on it by glider, blew open the casemates and gun turrets with shaped hollow-charges, and were masters of the fort in twenty-eight hours, just in time to greet the armor forcing its way across the Albert Canal. The canal bridges were seized by similar if slightly less spectacular feats, and the whole Albert Canal line was gone before the Belgians knew what hit them. The Panzers roared on, past Liège, toward the Dyle and and the Gembloux Gap.

The British and French reached the Dyle on the 12th. They had left their more or less prepared positions along the French frontier, hoping and expecting to find the same thing on the Dyle. They found nothing. The Germans were on them before they had time to site their batteries. The Royal Air Force contingent in France, the Advanced Air Striking Force, made desperate attempts to bomb the bridges over which the Germans were pouring. The lumbering Fairey Battle bombers were decimated; the attacks won several posthumous medals for the R. A. F., but did not even slow the Germans down. The pressure was so great that all reports were sure this had to be the main attack; the Germans pushed over the Dyle by the 14th, but the frantic resistance of the Belgians, French, and British at last began to take effect, and it looked for a moment as if the northern front, minus Holland, might stabilize.

Between Namur and the northern end of the Maginot Line,

however, things were ominous. Corap's 9th and Huntziger's 2nd French armies had taken their positions on the western side of the Ardennes. As the 9th and 2nd waited on their quiet sector, three German armies, including seven armored and two motorized divisions, were bearing down on them. The Germans had poured through the Grand Duchy of Luxembourg and been swallowed up in the forest. But it was not impassable after all. It was garrisoned by a Belgian unit, the Chasseurs Ardennes, basically the government forestry workers of the area, put into uniform and issued rifles. They had no heavy weapons, and more important, no demolition material. The Germans were virtually unopposed. It took them two days of careful driving, and on the night of the 12th, they were on the Meuse, the main French defense position. With frantic reports of their arrival in force reaching him, Gamelin began shifting reserves north to meet them.

He was far too late. The Germans were operating at the speed of a truck or tank, the French at that of a marching man. The next two days were crucial. On the 13th, the Germans surged across the Meuse. Some of the French formations, made up of overage and underarmed reserves, fled precipitately before the tanks and Stukas; others fought to the last man, but nowhere were they a match for the constant German superiority of material and numbers at any vital spot. Corap ordered a retreat on the night of the 13th, but it was an order given to an army already out of existence. By next morning there was a fifty-mile hole in the French line, and within two days the German armor was on the Aisne, rolling into open country.

The whole situation was incredibly fluid. Here was this enormous gap in the French line, with Germans pouring through it. The German armor raced ahead, its flanks in the air. Stukas dive-bombed and strafed the retreating French, refugees jammed the roads and slowed down the troops. Behind the Panzers there was virtually nothing, just long dusty columns of dog-tired German infantry, slogging along and hoping to catch up. The Germans were wide open for a drive into their flanks.

But there was nothing to do this with. The mass of French armor was in Belgium and Holland and busy with its own battle. The French tried; they threw an armored division, newly organized under General de Gaulle, at the southern German flank. This attack later became one of the pillars of de Gaulle's reputation—he at least had fought—yet it achieved nothing more than the destruction of his division. The few gains the French tanks made could not be held against the Germans sweeping by, and they hardly noticed that there was anything special about this attack.

As the Germans went on toward Cambrai, toward the sea, the new British Prime Minister, Churchill, came over to see what on earth was going on. He visited Gamelin and looked at the maps. Surely, he said, if the head of the German column was far to the west, and the tail was far to the east, they must be thin somewhere. Why did the French not attack with their reserves? In his terrible French he asked Gamelin where the French reserves were. Gamelin replied with an infuriating Gallic shrug: there were no reserves. Churchill went home appalled.

The truth was, the Germans were indeed thin, and in many ways their high command was as scared as the French were. Von Rundstedt, in command of Army Group A, was so worried by his flanks that he tried to slow his Panzers down. The tank commanders, Guderian, Reinhardt, and Rommel, were aghast. When ordered to stop and wait for support, they asked permission to carry out local reconnaissances. This qualified permission granted, they drove on again full tilt. Occasionally, there was heavy fighting. On the northern shoulder of the drive, the French put up a good resistance, the French 1st Army giving them hard knocks around Arras a bit later. But the Germans were not going to bang their heads against failure. They just sideslipped their armor and kept on. The farther they went, the more the Allies lost cohesion. On the 21st, the Germans reached the sea at Abbeville; the northern Allied armies were cut off.

Gamelin was gone by then. Utterly outpaced by the speed of events, he had become completely defeatist; he could do nothing and therefore decided that nothing could be done. On the 19th, he was replaced by General Maxime Weygand, flown in from the French territory of Syria to take over. By the time Weygand figured out what was happening, he was too late to do anything but preside over the disaster.

Ordered to attack south and break through, the Anglo-Franco-Belgian forces were unable to pull themselves together, change fronts, and coordinate their efforts. Allied cooperation began to break down. The French still wanted to move south, but were incapable of doing it. Lord Gort, commanding the B. E. F., and mindful that his army was all Britain had, began thinking instead of evacuation. Out of these thoughts came the "miracle of Dunkirk," as well as a great deal of Anglo-French recrimination.

The Germans now held their southern shoulder along the line

of the Aisne and Somme rivers, and turned their attention north. The Allied forces began to contract into a perimeter around the small Channel ports, especially Dunkirk. Boulogne fell on the 23rd; Calais was reinforced from England and, isolated, held until the 27th. To the north, the Belgians, fought out, surrendered on the 28th. King Leopold believed he had done all he could, and he was probably right, but the Allies flung charges at him of leaving them in the lurch, and that was right too. The defensive perimeter shrunk and shrunk around Dunkirk, while the B. E. F. and the French 1st Army held off the Germans.

With no alternative now but evacuation, the British government hoped they might pull off 50,000 men. They organized everything that would float, and with the help of the French Navy as well, they started lifting men out of the port of Dunkirk, and even off the open beaches beyond the town. Destroyers, tugs, cross-Channel packets, paddle-wheel ferries, fishing boats, yachts, dinghies, swarmed in the Channel, prey to the Luftwaffe but determined to bring the soldiers home. Churchill and Reynaud agreed that the two armies should go off "arm in arm," but even the best intentions were lost in the general disaster. By that remark, Churchill meant one Englishman, one Frenchman; the French thought it meant proportional representation, and as there were a lot more Frenchmen than Englishmen in the perimeter, this would have meant more French than British were to be evacuated.

This kind of misunderstanding occurred all down the chain of command. The British were anxious to evacuate, the French still had some obscure vision of holding on as a sort of fortress; the British insisted that they would form the rear guard, but the run of the perimeter was such that they were squeezed out by the French, who insisted anyway that they ought to form the rear guard, and then tended to blame the British for letting them do so.

When the evacuation was finally over, on the night of June 3-4, the Allies had managed, incredibly, to lift off about 335,000 men. The British had gotten off about 215,000 out of perhaps 250,000 trapped in the north. The French had taken off only 125,000 out of about 380,000. It was both a triumph of the human spirit and a military disaster.

No one expected to get off anything like that, and it is probable that they would not have done so, had they not been helped by Hitler. For two crucial days, from the 24th to the 26th of May, days which allowed the Allies to organize both their defensive perimeter and their evacuation, he had issued a stop order for his armor. This order has puzzled students of history for many years, and gave rise to suggestions that Hitler really wanted a deal with the British, that he liked Britain, and so on and so forth. The truth seems to be a great deal more mundane. For one thing, von Rundstedt was by that time already looking south, and wanted to conserve the armor for the forthcoming drive against the remaining French armies. For another, the area around Dunkirk was low-lying, and crisscrossed by canals and ditches, and therefore not thought suitable for armor. Hitler also thought, incorrectly, that the Luftwaffe was capable of isolating the perimeter and thereby destroying the bottled-up forces in it. Finally, there does seem some ground for believing that the Germans were indeed overawed by the magnitude of their own astounding success so far. That, however, is a long way from the imputations that have been put on the whole matter. At bottom, it was a sound tactical decision plus a misassessment of the capabilities of the Luftwaffe that caused the stop order. They would make that mistake again.

For practical purposes Britain was now out of it. The campaign of France would last another three weeks. During that time Churchill and his government would make strenuous efforts to keep the French in the war, but they would make no material contribution to it. The few British forces south of the Somme would soon be evacuated. There was indeed only one thing the British had left that they could have contributed: the fighter arm of the Royal Air Force. To have sent this over to France would have left the British Isles absolutely defenseless, and in spite of French pleas for it, the British steadfastly refused to commit it. The French therefore, though only a few of them were churlish enough to say it, increasingly took the attitude that Britain was willing to fight to the last Frenchman. They could not believe that Britain either could or would continue the war alone, and even while Churchill tried to keep them up to the mark, Britain's weakness and inability to help told against his own arguments. There was little point in recriminations, and in pointing out that it was essentially the incredible deficiencies of the French command and war plan that had brought about that weakness. Current disasters came crowding in too fast to bother recapitulating past ones.

The French Army was now on its own. The nine Dutch divisions were gone, as were the twenty-two Belgian and nine of the ten British. The French had lost twenty-four of their sixty-seven infantry divisions, six of their twelve motorized or armored divisions. They had lost extensive amounts of equipment, and even the mechanized formations that remained were seriously depleted in strength and material. Perhaps half their army, the weaker half, remained to face the Germans along the Maginot Line, the Aisne and the Somme rivers. The Germans already had bridgeheads across the Somme at Abbeville and Amiens, and French attempts to squeeze them out failed. Defeat hung like a miasma over the Third Republic, and the higher one went, the worse it got. Weygand made futile attempts to pull his armies together and he issued orders of the day designed to inspire the troops to their utmost. But even in the most stirring government and military pronouncements of those weeks, despair lurked just below the surface. When generals begin talking of "satisfying the dictates of honor," the implied conclusion to the sentence is always "before surrendering."

While the French high command tried to sort out and organize the "Weygand Line" along the Somme and Aisne, the Germans were carrying out an impressive redeployment of their troops to face southward. They were ready to go by June 5, within a day or so after the completion of the Dunkirk withdrawal. With 120 divisions, they would attack all along the line. Von Rundstedt's Army Group A would break over the Aisne between Paris and the end of the Maginot Line, von Bock's Army Group B would storm across the Somme west of Paris as far as the Seine, then decide where to go from there. Meanwhile, General Ritter von Leeb's Army Group C would attack the southern end of the Maginot Line, break through, and link up with the Germans advancing south behind the line.

The attack opened on the 5th, and though the French fought desperately, things went pretty well as planned. The Stukas and tanks still proved a winning combination, the German bombers continually harassed the French rear areas, disrupting communications, and the French were simply too thin to inflict more than local checks on the Germans. Von Bock reached the Seine within three days. One of his tank commanders, Erwin Rommel, drove as far as Rouen on the lower Seine, then angled back up to the seacoast to gather up remnants of the French and British who had been holding along the coast. These were the last British fighting in France. To the east of Paris the French did a little better, but were slowly forced back to the Marne, and then, on the 12th, Guderian's tanks broke through their line at Chalons and took off south. It was the Ardennes all over again and, for practical purposes, with Guderian's breakthrough the campaign was won. When the news came in to headquarters, Weygand went to Reynaud and asked the government to seek an armistice.

There followed several days of grasping at straws. Reynaud refused immediately to consider giving up. Political and diplomatic questions of incredible complexity had to be answered. In a bid for time, Reynaud recalled France's hero, Marshal Pétain, who was then ambassador to Spain. Surely, he thought, the magic of Pétain's name would put fresh heart into the army and the people of France.

Tragically, Pétain proved to be a broken reed. He was a very old man, and his ideas had changed over the years. He now was obsessed with the idea that France had sinned and must be purged of guilt; he added his voice to those counseling surrender. Reynaud's position was further weakened.

The problem of relations with Britain was a major one. Back in March, France and Britain had rather offhandedly signed an agreement that neither would seek a peace or armistice without the full consent of the other. Little thought had been given to it at the time but now, in the face of disaster, it emerged as a major stumbling block. Asked if the British would release the French from it, Churchill's government backed and filled. To say they would not release France from the agreement was hardly fair, when France was bearing the brunt of the battle; indeed the French now insisted that the agreement had been predicated on the idea that each country would make an equal commitment to the war; this not being the case, some thought the agreement invalid anyway. But to acquiesce in France's seeking an armistice would only strengthen the hands of the defeatists.

Assorted alternatives were proposed. The French government might flee to North Africa, and with the strength of the empire behind it, carry on from there. An even more dramatic suggestion was one that came forward from some of the liaison people, especially Jean Monnet and de Gaulle, who was in close touch with the British representative, General Spears, and was adopted by Churchill and forwarded to France; it was for a total union of the two countries, shared citizenship, shared responsibility and effort. Perhaps it was utopian, but it was a gesture in the grand manner. The French turned it down flat.

As the war rolled on, Paris, flanked to east and west, was declared an open city. The government fled south followed by those who could get away. Reynaud launched pathetic appeals to

President Roosevelt in the United States to intervene, but the Americans would do nothing—could do nothing had they been willing.

The French, in their agony, had a sense of the vultures gathering; Britain would release France from her promises, but only if she were given custody of the French fleet. Roosevelt also suggested he would welcome the French fleet, and the French government's gold reserves as well. It was not only well-meaning friends who watched France's agony. Mussolini in Italy, thwarted so far of a share in the glory, could restrain himself no longer. He leaped in on the 10th and declared war on both Britain and France, though it was the 20th before his generals could launch an attack. The scanty French units on the Italian frontier beat it back with contemptuous ease.

The Germans roared on. Reynaud lost what little credibility he had left, and Pétain replaced him on the 17th. Over the radio he announced grandiloquently, "I give the gift of myself to France," then he added, "The fighting must stop. . . ."

By then, the remnants of the mighty French Army were back on the Loire. Orleans was gone, the Germans had reached the Swiss frontier behind the Maginot Line and the armies trapped there were too late to break out. There were isolated, ferocious little fire fights, where occasional units died rather than surrender. But no one wanted to be the last man killed in a war that was already lost. Any possibility of defense was hampered by the government's declaring that every town of more than 20,000 was to be regarded as an open city. Often even if the troops wanted to fight, local officials and civilians pressured them not to do so. The flood of refugees continued to the south.

There was some attempt to get overseas. A few planes fled to North Africa, some naval units did the same, some took shelter in British ports. De Gaulle at the last minute boarded a plane for England.

The rest was largely denouement, as far as the French and the Germans were concerned; Pétain's remark that the fighting must cease was taken as an injunction by the army. With armistice talks opened, the Germans rolled on unimpeded; Hitler would not end the advance until the Italians agreed to an armistice too, so though a cease-fire was signed on the 22nd, operations continued until the 25th. The Germans in the southeast were then at Grenoble and the Italians, still stalled on the frontier, begged them to cut in behind the French. But the German General Staff was not disposed to be overly helpful to the Italian Comando Supremo and they did little.

Hitler was determined to rub it in. The armistice talks were held at Rethondes, in the railway carriage where the Germans had surrendered to Marshal Foch in 1918. The Germans occupied northern France and a strip along the Atlantic coast down to the Spanish frontier. They retained the French prisoners of war, more than a million of them, and used them in effect as hostages for the good behavior of the new French government, set up at the small health resort of Vichy. They wanted the French fleet demobilized in French ports, but under German control. The French agreed to essentially everything; there was little else they could do but accept the humiliation of defeat. After their delegation signed the surrender terms, Hitler danced his little victory jig outside the railway carriage and ordered that it be hauled off to Germany. He left the statue of Foch, but the plaque commemorating Germany's surrender twenty-two years ago was blown up.

On the morning of the 25th, the sun rose over a silent France. The cease-fire had come into effect during the hours of darkness. The refugees could now go home or continue their flight unharassed by the dive-bombers. Long silent columns of prisoners shuffled east. The French generals and politicians began composing their excuses, the Germans paraded through Paris, visited the tourist sites, and began counting their booty. It had indeed been one of the great campaigns of all time, better than 1870, probably unequaled since Napoleon's veterans had swarmed over Prussia in 1806; Jena and Auerstadt were at last avenged, and there would be no more victories over Germany while the thousand-year Reich endured.

The casualties reflected the inequality of the campaign. The Germans had suffered about 27,000 killed, 18,000 missing, and just over 100,000 wounded. The Dutch and Belgian armies were utterly destroyed; the British lost about 68,000 men and all their heavy equipment: tanks, trucks, guns—everything. The French lost track of their figures in the collapse at the end, but the best estimates gave them about 125,000 killed and missing, about 200,000 wounded. The Germans claimed that they had taken one and a half million prisoners, which they probably had. Except for defenseless England, the war appeared all but over.

There were two footnotes, both fruitful.

General de Gaulle, the unsuccessful armored division commander, had gone to England. On June 18, the day that Churchill rose in the House of Commons to inspire Englishmen to their finest hour, de Gaulle broadcast over the BBC to France. He invited French soldiers and sailors everywhere to get in touch with him; the few who responded would become the nucleus of Free France.

The second footnote was Churchill's. Everyone but the British thought the British were done for. They would not fight alone, and they had no material to do it with even if they were willing. The American ambassador to Britain, Joseph P. Kennedy, thought they would cave in at any moment. Churchill, however, was determined to hang on. The key element now and for the foreseeable future was naval power; Britain's control of the seas was tenuous at best, and if the French fleet fell into the hands of the Germans, it, the German Navy, and the Italian Navy together would tip the balance. In a gesture that would restore that narrow margin, that would show the world, and especially the United States, that Britain was not going to give in, Churchill decided he must either control or destroy the French fleet.

On July 3, before daybreak, the British acted. French ships in British ports were seized by armed parties. The French squadron in Alexandria harbor found itself staring down the gun muzzles of its comrades of a couple of days ago and reached an accommodation. Most painful of all was what happened in the western Mediterranean. A British squadron appeared off the port of Mersel-Kebir, near Oran, and issued an ultimatum. It now appears that had either side known exactly what the other intended to do, agreement could have been reached. Instead, as so often happens, there were mistaken signals, misunderstandings, and a certain disingenuousness on both sides. Late in the afternoon the British opened fire; they sank the battleship *Bretagne* and the new battlecruiser *Dunkerque* and several destroyers. They killed 1,300 French sailors and wounded another 350. Then they sailed away, sick at heart, leaving the ruined port and outraged French behind them.

The whole episode has been argued ever since. It was brutal, to many it appeared merely spiteful, and it may well have been unnecessary. But whatever else it did, it showed one thing: Britain would fight. The war was not over yet.

9. The Battle of Britain

ADOLF HITLER STOOD TRIUMPHANT on the continent of Europe; he was master from the Neimen to the Pyrénées, from the North Cape to Sicily. No one for a century and a half had done what he had just done. His chief enemy may always have been Slavdom, or bolshevism, and the campaign in the West no more than a diversion of his true direction; in spite of all the words written about him, and quoting him, no one knows for sure. If he was just another military opportunist, then he had worked wonders; if his true aim was the Heartland of the World Island, then he had made a grievous mistake and like Caesar, grievously would he answer for it. As the leader who defeated the world's greatest military power in six weeks, his mark on history was already made. What next?

There remained England, aloof across the "greatest anti-tank ditch in the world." That twenty miles of water had once been a highway for invasion: Romans, Angles, Saxons, Jutes, Danes, Vikings, Normans, and Dutch William had all used it freely; for a millennium England was one of the most invaded countries in history. But then the English had put their house in order and their faith in a powerful navy, and the highway of invasion became an impassable barrier to it. This was not the Ardennes. Philip II, Louis XIV, and Napoleon had all gazed across that narrow body of water, failed to cross it, and turned elsewhere in disgust. The French, when they were not trying to cross it, did their best to disregard it; it was only *La Manche*, "the sleeve." But to Englishmen it became more than the Channel, it became the "*English* Channel." Now once again it stood between them and conquest.

In truth, it was about all that did stand between them and Hitler. While Churchill in the Commons was rallying his country with words that might well have been lifted from Shakespeare—"Come the four corners of the world in arms and we shall shock them"— Englishmen were desperately looking for weapons to fight with.

They dug holes in the fields to plant stakes against gliders; they organized a Home Guard, "Dad's Army," the newspapers called it; the hunt clubs of the southeastern counties turned out with their shotguns and fowling pieces, to be photographed wearing self-conscious looks of grim determination. The army rescued from Dunkirk was busy re-equipping and reorganizing; every day's new production from the factories was precious—yet at the height of the battle, Churchill would send the last seventy tanks off to Egypt; he later said, "I have not become the King's First Minister to preside over the liquidation of the British Empire."

Tanks, in the final reckoning, made little difference. If it ever came to using seventy tanks against the Germans the game would already have been lost. What counted now was whether or not the Royal Navy could hold the Channel: "It is upon the navy, under the good providence of God, that the wealth, safety, and strength of the kingdom do chiefly depend. . . ." For two hundred and fifty years the navy had never let down its guard. In time of danger it had always coalesced in the Channel and it had always held. Now to the question, Could the navy hold the Channel? had to be added, Could the Royal Air Force hold the air over the Channel?

The problems faced by both sides were enormous, and they had never been faced before. Never in history had one nation tried to defeat another from the air. The whole Battle of Britain was so new, and in the end such a near-run thing, that it is probably the most tantalizing of all the single episodes of World War II.

Hitler ordered preliminary planning for the invasion of Britain, Operation Sea Lion, while the Battle of France was still in progress. This presented the Germans with problems they had not previously considered; there was no tradition of amphibious warfare in German history. The Wehrmacht was a land animal; it could do a river crossing, but the Channel was not quite a river. The navy was not much help; it had no tradition of amphibious warfare either. The German Navy grew up out of a branch of the Coast Artillery, fathered by the vaulting ambition of Admiral von Tirpitz. Except for Norway, it had never landed on a hostile shore, and the British were not likely to be gulled the way the Norwegians had been. Could you use canal barges to cross the Channel? did you have to have a seaport or could you go over open beaches? how much backup shipping would you need for logistics? No one was sure, but being German, the Germans began working, and the plan began to take shape. The Dutch and French Channel ports began to fill with barges and tugs; the troops began to practice clambering in and out of them. The army needed time to reorganize from its sweeping victory over France; the navy was still in bad shape from the beating it took in the Norwegian campaign. But slowly, things began to fall into shape.

The urgency was less theirs than the Luftwaffe's, anyway. For the Germans to invade, the navy must dominate the Channel. But before it could do that the Luftwaffe must dominate the air over the Channel. By now, after Norway, both the British and the Germans recognized it would be naval suicide to take their big ships into the narrow waters under enemy air control. So it was up to the Luftwaffe; it must gain control of the airspace over northwest France and the Low Countries, the Channel, and southeastern England. In yet another of their legendary feats of organization, the Germans were getting set by the end of June. The units of the ever-victorious Luftwaffe moved into the Channel airfields of France, Belgium, and Holland. Though the newest of the Germans armed services, they considered themselves the elite; they were also particularly the "Nazi" service, built by Hitler, commanded by his old friend and close supporter, Reichsmarschall Hermann Goering. They believed in what they were doing. Unlike the "decadent" British, they marched out to their planes in the morning, singing. At least for a while.

They would be hampered in the coming battle by the inadequacy of their equipment. In the Messerschmitt Bf109e they had one of the world's great fighter aircraft; it was marginally better than the most plentiful British fighter, the Hurricane. Unfortunately, it was marginally inferior to the newer Spitfire. The Germans had a twin-engine long-range fighter, the ME110; it would prove disastrous. Their bombers, the Heinkel and the Dornier, were already obsolescent and would lack range, carrying capacity, and defensive armament. In the mid-thirties, the Germans had made their choice; they had gone for tactical aircraft and medium bombers. Now, with a strategic objective in view, they were about to overreach themselves.

This was not known at the time. Neither the British nor the Germans knew what was going to happen. No one even knew what it would take to achieve the kind of conditions desired. If the Germans overestimated their strength, the British underestimated their residual resources. They were hopelessly weak on the ground, and the army would stand little chance against the Germans

if it came to that. But the air force was still intact. Most of the
Advanced Air Striking Force had gone down the drain in France,
and there had been a steady bleeding of squadrons from Britain
into the fighting over Dunkirk and northern France. But they
reached a point where the Air Staff had put its foot down: if any
more squadrons were sent to the aid of France, they would not be
responsible for the safety of Britain. It was embarrassing for
Churchill to tell Reynaud, but it had the effect of preserving the
fifty-nine squadrons of the Metropolitan Air Force for home defense. There would be crucial problems of providing trained pilots,
but there was one advantage here: fighting largely over their own
territory, the British pilots would often live to fight again. German
pilots would go into the Channel or into P. O. W. cages. So crucial
would the question of pilot availability become that at one point
the British would order their planes to shoot down German air-sea
rescue seaplanes carrying the Red Cross, an order that was little
publicized and bitterly resented by the R. A. F. itself, whose pilots
knew they might well find themselves in the same situation as the
Germans someday.

The British did have one advantage over the Germans: they
had a radar net to give them early warning of the German approach. It was a crude system but it worked. Radio direction-find-
ing, as it was originally called, had been developed by both the
British and the Germans just before the war. It was, ironically, a
by-product of the search for a "death-ray" in the science-fiction
days of the early thirties. The Germans knew the British had such
a system; after all, they had a similar one themselves. Why they
paid it so little attention remains one of the mysteries, like so many
other things, of World War II.

In the last analysis, it was none of these material or techno-
logical matters that saved Britain in the summer of 1940. It was
intelligence misassessments and command failures—human errors.

The Battle of Britain went through a series of different phases,
marked by the Luftwaffe switching targets as they went along. In
the first of these, or the first two of them, depending on how one
counted, the Germans attacked the east coast shipping lanes and
then the port and docking facilities of southeastern England. The
whole period, lasting from early July to the second week of August,
was called by the Germans the *Kanalkampf*, the "Channel Battle."
This was only a preliminary phase, before the Germans really hit
their stride, and to a certain extent it was a misdirection of effort,

concentrating on what the eighteenth-century French Navy had called "the ulterior motive"; the primary motive was the destruction of the Royal Air Force. Nonetheless, Channel strikes were a two-edged sword: either the R. A. F. would defend the shipping, and be sucked into a battle of attrition, or it would not defend them, in which case the shipping would be sunk, leading to paralysis of the east coast cities and eventual strangulation of the battle area anyway.

British Fighter Command, led by Air Chief Marshal Sir Hugh Dowding, did not plan to protect the coastal shipping, so they soon found themselves caught in the bind of the initial German strategy. They committed minimal support to the convoys, which took heavy losses. The pressure on the R. A. F. to provide more cover mounted, and there was a steady attrition of aircraft and pilots. The R. A. F. was not tremendously effective in this phase. Pilots had to learn new tactics, the radar and communications nets were still clumsy, and whole system needed a good shakedown period. As the Germans too were just getting organized, both sides had their troubles. Still, the initiative lay with the Luftwaffe; it was the more-experienced service in combat, and the Germans were satisfied with the way the battle was developing.

More than anything else, the British were conscious of the necessity to husband their resources. They waited until the Germans were at the limit of their range, over the coast or at least the English side of the Channel, then they intercepted with small groups of fighters—a dozen was a large-scale interception—and they kept a tight control from the ground over their pilots. The early German tactic was to send over bombers with a high-level fighter escort. The British responded by sending their Spitfires after the German fighters to keep them busy, and then sending the slower Hurricanes after the bombers to break up their formations.

For all the retrospective appearance of order and logical sequence, both sides were groping in the dark. This had never been done before, and neither the Luftwaffe nor the R. A. F. was fully in control of its battle. In Britain there were arguments between senior commanders about the best way to counter the enemy, there were mistakes with the communications system, there were misassessments all along the line. On the other side of the Channel the Germans were striking out equally blindly. They hit at convoys, then they hit ports, then they hit scattered factories; they were waiting for the big day, but they were not entirely sure what to do while waiting, or if the things they were doing would bring that big day nearer. Over the summer of the battle, they played out the same kind of learn-as-you-go game the Allied bomber offense would play for the next four years.

One mistake both sides made: they invariably overestimated the extent of the damage they were causing the enemy. The British were sure they knocked down about twice as many German planes as they actually did, and in spite of a severe system of checking battle claims, they constantly said they were shooting down far more Germans than they were. The Germans made the same error, but since the casualties fell over enemy-held territory, they had even less check on their pilots' claims, and they seriously inflated their damage estimates. By the third week in July, they thought the R. A. F. was already within measurable distance of being wiped out. This would be a fatal mistake at the later stages of the campaign, and if any one mistake cost the Germans the battle, it was probably this one.

As July wore on, the problems of the R. A. F. became increasingly acute. The techniques of interception were running more smoothly, but the men and machines to effect the interceptions were disappearing. Maybe the Germans were right, and the R. A. F. would give out.

The fighter-production problem was solved by the appointment of an energetic Canadian businessman, Lord Beaverbrook, as Minister of Aircraft Production. His appointment had been one of Churchill's first moves as Prime Minister, and he rode roughshod over all the happy dilatory routines of peace. Factory managers and senior air force officers alike came to hate him, but without him, or someone equally acerbic, it is hard to see how the British would have lasted through that summer. He provided a steadily increasing flow of aircraft, so that in spite of losses of well over 100 percent of strength, the R. A. F. still ended the battle stronger than it went into it.

What Beaverbrook could not find were the pilots to man the planes he produced. Only about 3,000 R. A. F. pilots took part in the entire Battle of Britain, but the wastage was such that they became progressively less skilled and experienced as the battle wore on. They started at a disadvantage; even the regulars among them had little combat time, compared to Germans who had often fought in Spain, and then over Poland and France. As fighting and accidents took their toll, newer and newer pilots were filtered into the fight. The first few days were crucial, and if they lived long enough to acquire some skills, their chances got progressively better. Then they peaked off, and as fatigue and fear told against them, their chances weakened again. Though about 80 percent of the pilots were British, there was a good number of dominion fliers among them, a smattering of Americans, and quite a few Czechs and Poles, experienced pilots whose major problem was coping with the English language but who were fanatically keen to kill Germans; the high-scoring R. A. F. pilot in the battle was actually a Czech, Sergeant Pilot Josef Frantisek.

It was August before the Germans were fully ready for their main assault. Goering and the Germans designated it *Adlerangriff*, "the Eagle Attack," and August 13 was set for *Adlertag*, "Eagle Day." On the day before, as a useful preliminary, the Luftwaffe would send precision units in to knock out the main radar stations, and some writers date the attack from the 12th. The R. A. F. and its support system was to be the main target in this phase of the battle, and the Germans were going to go all out to achieve air superiority. On the 12th, they damaged but did not wholly destroy the radar chain on the south coast.

Next day, the day of the great assault, almost everything went wrong. The weather was chancy, and the assault was canceled. Only about half the units involved got the cancellation order, so half an attack was put in instead of the full-scale blow. The sky cleared in the afternoon, and the Luftwaffe came out in force, hitting radar stations, airfields, and aircraft factories. They flew almost fifteen hundred sorties, and the British responded with about seven hundred.

Two days later, the Germans decided on another all-out effort, with attacks not only from across the Channel but also from across the North Sea in Denmark and Norway. Again there was muddle and mix-up, with the weather playing tricks, and the Germans losing coordination. The R. A. F. lost about fifty planes, and the Germans perhaps slightly more. The Germans thought they had done poorly, however, and gloomily christened the 15th "black Thursday." More important, they decided that their attacks on the radar stations were not paying off—just as they were beginning to—and they discontinued them, another in their chain of fatal mistakes.

Unable to assess the results of their work, the Germans began shifting targets, thus giving any stricken element in the British defense time to recuperate. The British were also modifying their tactics; they began to intercept the Germans farther out, in an attempt to break up their formations before they reached the airfields; the Germans responded by flying closer fighter escort. By the last week in August, the battle was approaching a crescendo. The Germans believed they had the R. A. F. on the ropes, and they were nearly right. The fighter pilots were exhausted; new pilots were coming into the battle with only the most rudimentary training. Some of the air stations nearest to the Germans were virtually inoperable. The Germans were taking heavy losses as well, but Goering now demanded from his Luftwaffe commanders, Kesselring and Sperrle, an all-out effort. For the last week in August and the first week in September they gave it to him.

These two weeks were like the climax of a prize fight, when two boxers, lost in the fight and oblivious to blows received, stand up and slug away at each other toe to toe. The Germans concentrated on the airfields in Kent and around London. Both sides took heavy casualties and both overestimated the damage they were doing.

To get at the London perimeter airfields, the Germans often flew up the Thames. On the night of August 25, one German bomber got lost, and dropped its bomb load on the center of London, the City. There had already been attacks on the dock areas and on some of the suburbs, where aircraft facilities of one kind or another were located. Up to this point, however, the Germans had generally tried, within the loose limits of their equipment, to strike at obviously military targets. After the Rotterdam raid during the campaign of Holland, British Bomber Command had begun raids on the Ruhr Valley. Now, after this stray hit in the heart of London, they ordered an attack on Berlin. The German leaders branded this an atrocity and swore vengeance. Out of these two arguable accidents, the bombing of Rotterdam and the hit against central London by a lost German aircrew, came all the attacks on civilian targets during the next several years. Perhaps, in a world that had already seen Guernica and the Japanese bombing of Chinese cities, such escalation was inevitable; that did not make it less a blot on twentieth-century civilization.

By the first of September, the Germans were winning; the R. A. F. had no more fresh squadrons to provide rotations, on several days in this period they lost more planes than their factories produced, the factories themselves were under attack, and if the Luftwaffe could keep up the pressure, they were home free. Then they made another mistake: they decided to believe their own figures. They gave up the direct strikes against the Royal Air Force.

* * *

On the afternoon of September 7, nearly a thousand German bombers struck at London. Because of British misassessment of the objective, they were virtually unopposed. Covering a block of sky twenty miles wide by forty miles long, and almost two miles thick, they droned over the city sowing destruction. Goering himself came west in his special train, and he and his commanders stood not too far from Napoleon's statue above Boulogne, to watch the armada pass overhead. The "London Blitz" had begun.

In a contradictory way, it was just what the British needed. London was like a vast sponge, and it absorbed damage as a sponge does water. Casualties were heavy, but the British rose to the occasion. Many children had already been evacuated from the city and resettled in the country or overseas in Canada and elsewhere. For the Londoners, it became a point of honor to carry on. They slept in the subways, they fought fires and manned auxiliary posts, they at last made sense of Chamberlain's prosaic slogan "Business as usual." The whole Blitz should have been an object lesson for those theorists of air power who said that civilian populations would never be able to withstand aerial bombardment.

The German attack on London achieved three of Britain's objectives, and none of Germany's. It allowed the Royal Air Force to get its second wind and survive. The British came back so strongly, and so surprisingly, that the Germans went from daylight bombing to night bombing, a tacit admission that they could no longer match the R. A. F. in the air over England during daylight. Secondly, it provided justification for the British to use their strongest—their only—offensive weapon more freely. Bomber Command of the Royal Air Force continued its strikes against Berlin. At this stage they were not as massive as the German attacks by any means, but that would not always be the case.

The third result was a psychological one. However much war is fought with material, it is not fought with that alone. One of Churchill's great dreams, and his only real hope of ultimate victory, was that the United States would eventually realize that this war had more to it than a replay of World War I, that it was in the final analysis an assertion of human values against the negation of them, and that Americans would join in the war. He had an uphill struggle because of the residual attitudes from World War I, because of American isolationism, and because of the attitudes of leading Americans such as Ambassador Kennedy. But few things touched American opinion more than the photos of St. Paul's Cathedral outlined against the flames of burning London, or of school-children in trenches watching while the battle raged over-head. Slowly the tide of opinion began to turn.

Of these three things, however, only the first was of immediate benefit. Britain saved herself by her own efforts, not by future goodwill. It was a close-run battle, and at times it looked as if Britain were losing it. On September 12 the government put out an invasion alert, but the scare passed. It was the first week of October before the Germans were forced back to night bombing, and the Blitz went on through November and into the bad-weather months.

One of the most famous events of the Blitz was the bombing, in November, of the city of Coventry. Heavy damage was done, the great medieval cathedral destroyed, and many people killed or injured. By that time the British had broken the German codes, and some authorities have written that the government actually had advance knowledge of the impending attack, but decided to take no extraordinary measures, on the belief that the security of their code-breaking system was more vital to the long-term war effort than the preservation of one city. Other writers have maintained with equal vehemence that the raid was not known of in advance. The British reading of German signals did become increasingly important as the war progressed but still entailed agonizing decisions.

By then the "Battle of Britain" was over. The British people and the point of their sword, the Royal Air Force, had stood up to the worst the Germans could throw against them. There was no admission that the battle had ended, just a lessening of intensity. The Blitz went on. But as the days shortened, it became obvious that there would be no invasion. The barge fleets were dispersed, the soldiers drafted off to other tasks. Put whatever face they would on it, the Germans had not managed to bring Britain down. As early as mid-October, Hitler was turning his attention elsewhere, to the Balkans and ultimately, to Russia.

By later standards, it was all a pretty small affair. At its peak strength the R. A. F. had 570 fighters on the line; throughout the battle they lost 790. The Germans seem to have lost nearly 1,400 airplanes of one kind or another. Yet the results were hardly small; had Britain succumbed, it is difficult to see how the war against Hitler would ever have been won. Churchill's tribute to the Royal Air Force, "Never in the field of human conflict was so much owed by so many to so few" was well deserved, and it was indeed Britain's finest hour.

10. The United States and the War

BY THE FALL OF 1940, it was apparent that Adolf Hitler could not defeat Great Britain. Operation Sea Lion was postponed, and the German machine turned its attention to the East. It was equally apparent that at least for the foreseeable future Great Britain could not beat Hitler. Britain did not quite stand alone; she had the resources of the Commonwealth and Empire behind her, but these were not significant enough to make any substantial difference. As the Anglo-Axis war shifted to the Mediterranean, a kind of equilibrium had developed. The same sort of balance was being achieved in the Far East, where the Japanese had all but defeated China, but lacked the resources to carry their fight to a definitive conclusion.

Two great powers remained uncommitted, the entry of either of which might overturn this delicate balance; the first was Russia and the second was the United States. There were permutations in this; the United States was highly unlikely to join in on the side of the Axis; her ultimate entry into the war could only be on the side of the Allies. But Russia might go either way. She was already allied with Nazi Germany, and the alliance, if it was a bit uneasy, had worked fairly satisfactorily. Both partners had derived territorial and economic advantages from it. A Hitler-Stalin agreement to divide Europe and the Near East was no more unthinkable than some of the arrangements Europe had already seen. On the other hand Russia and Germany might fall out, and this is of course what did happen. Yet when Hitler did invade Russia, in June of 1941, he very nearly overran her as he had done France and all the other continental states, so that even Russia's entry into the war did not destroy the equilibrium created in late 1940. There was the further complication of Russo-Japanese relations, which

115

were at a low state in 1940 and 1941, and a Russo-Japanese war was not entirely out of the question.

Russo-German relations were crucial to the subsequent course of the war. The American diplomat George F. Kennan has pointed out that in 1941 the dictators were more powerful than the democracies, and if they had all managed to hang together—Germany, Italy, Japan, and the Soviet Union, plus all their satellites —they would almost certainly have won the war. As it was, with Russian power remaining an imponderable even after she entered the war, the question came back to the United States. Hitler did not know a great deal about the Americans, and did his best to ignore them. Churchill was immensely conscious of the United States, and consistently wooed her good opinion. Long before Pearl Harbor, American attitudes and policies were a vital factor in the war.

As the war hovered over Europe, the United States had been determinedly neutral. The passage of the Neutrality Acts showed the depth of American distrust of the European scene: that had been in 1937. In 1938 at Lima, the Americans had led the other Western Hemisphere states in reaffirming their opposition to foreign intervention. Affairs overseas could not be totally ignored, however, and after Munich the United States became increasingly conscious of its military weakness.

In January of 1939, President Roosevelt went to Congress to get money for defense measures. The American military leaders were especially worried about the security of the Panama Canal, and the government made extensive plans to fortify the Virgin Islands and Puerto Rico in the Caribbean, and the Pacific approaches to the Canal as well. Congress voted $552,000,000 for defense measures. As the year wore on, the President became more and more overtly sympathetic to the democracies. In April, he wrote a joint letter to Hitler and Mussolini asking them to refrain from aggression against specific states and suggesting reduction of armaments. He was either cold-shouldered or treated to contemptuous harangues.

Unfortunately, the Neutrality Acts were couched in such a way that they did not distinguish between aggressors and victims; all belligerents were put in the same class, and this simplistic lumping together of all foreign states tied the administration's hands when it came to encouraging the democracies. Nonetheless, the United States government permitted the French and British, particularly the former, to place large orders for aircraft with American manufacturers. To a very real extent the initial expansion that has enabled the American aerospace industry to dominate the world ever since 1941 was financed by French government contracts. Ironically, only a small portion of the orders was completed by the time of the fall of France. Some Curtiss fighters reached France, where they worked very well, and a few bombers got there; most of the orders were subsequently taken over by British purchasing commissions. The American government itself began placing orders for new aircraft. Yet in mid-summer, in spite of presidential pressure, Congress refused to modify the Neutrality Acts, and this weakened whatever effect Roosevelt's pleas and strictures to the European powers might have had as they went to war. On September 5, 1939, the United States declared its neutrality in Europe's new war.

From the outbreak of World War II, there began in the United States an increasingly heated debate on what role the country ought to play. Generally speaking, Americans were at least mildly sympathetic to France and Great Britain, but definitely not enough to get involved in the actual fighting. There were really three extremes: those few people who thought the United States ought to go to war on the side of the democracies; those even fewer people who thought the U. S. ought to support Germany—there was a minuscule American Nazi Party—and a much larger group who thought the United States ought to avoid any war under any circumstances. In newspapers and magazines there was a tremendous debate over the catchwords of the time: neutrality, isolation, intervention, America first, and all shades and colorations in between. There were quite violent divisions of opinion. William Randolph Hearst and the Hearst newspapers were isolationist and influential; Charles Lindbergh, one of the great heroes of the thirties, had been very impressed by the Luftwaffe and his treatment in Germany and was at least mildly pro-German. Most people were passively pro-British and pro-French and they tended to assume, with an ill-placed complacency, that Britain and France would win—without any help from them.

The fall of Poland came as a shock. Few people in the United States were very concerned about Poland, but the speed and ruthlessness of the Blitzkrieg proved alarming. Roosevelt responded by calling Congress into special session and asking it to amend the Neutrality Acts so that arms and ammunition could be sold to Britain and France—officially to all "belligerents," but as Britain and France controlled the seas, unofficially only to them. The session became a bitter six-week-long debate on neutrality, but in the end the Neutrality Acts were modified to the extent that belligerents could buy war materials if they paid cash for them and carried them on their own ships. "Cash and carry" became a halfway house to "lend-lease," but no more than that; Congress was determined not to acquire a financial stake in an Allied victory that might subsequently have to be redeemed.

Through the winter of 1939-40, the European scene was relatively quiet. Correspondents groused about the "phoney war," and there was a surge of interest in and sympathy for Finland. All Americans remembered, and were frequently reminded, that Finland alone had paid off her war debts to the United States. It was not until the spring of 1940 that the war came home with a jolt. The stunning German victories in Denmark, Norway, Belgium, Holland, and above all, France, raised the specter that the Allies might not win after all.

On June 22, as the French government was surrendering to the Germans, Congress passed a National Defense Tax Bill; they raised the ceiling on the national debt to what was then an unprecedented $49 billion and introduced taxes to produce almost $1 billion a year. A month later Congress voted $37 billion to produce a "two-ocean navy," guns and tanks for the army, and planes for the army air force and the navy. It was more money than the entire American cost of World War I. Meanwhile, Roosevelt was nominated for an unheard of third term as President.

Critics charged that Roosevelt wanted to be President forever, and rather more realistically, that he was dragging the country into war. Yet the hard facts were on the side of the growing number of interventionists. Americans watched fearfully as the Luftwaffe took on the Royal Air Force, and the support for Britain grew apace in the United States. Organizations sprang up to help the British, and the British government itself carefully played on American popular opinion. Both those who wanted to get involved in the war and those who wanted to keep out of it now agreed that the best way to achieve their ends was to bolster Great Britain. Thus, when Roosevelt traded Britain fifty overage destroyers for ninety-nine-year leases on base sites in the Western Hemisphere—an act that was technically illegal—there was not as great opposition as might have been expected.

It became increasingly obvious that just helping Britain might not be enough. In September of 1940, after lengthy and acrimonious debate, Congress passed the Selective Training and Service Act, the first peacetime draft in the history of the United States. "Selective Service" was just what the name implied; it was not a universal conscription such as was known in France or Germany. The act called for the registration of all men between the ages of twenty-one and thirty-six, and the training, for one year, of 1,200,000 soldiers plus another 800,000 reserves. In October, 16,000,000 men registered, and at the end of the month the first draftees were inducted. For a while the army was short of everything but bodies, but slowly the gears began to mesh. The Americans were slow to arm, but once they hit their stride, there would not be another country in the world capable of touching them, and American industrial and military might became one of the key elements in the entire war.

Roosevelt was re-elected in November. In January, he presented his annual State of the Union message to Congress, and it was at this point that he enunciated the famous "four freedoms"—freedom of speech, freedom of worship, freedom from fear, and freedom from want—that were ultimately to become the guiding principles for which the still-neutral United States and its future allies would fight the war. Like most utopian ideals, they were neither fully honored nor attained, yet that made them no less worth fighting for, and Roosevelt, like Churchill, was concerned that the war be perceived not as another sordid game of power politics, but as a struggle between good and evil. Only later on, when the victorious Allies got to the concentration camps, would they fully realize just how evil that evil had been.

During the last winter of peace in America, the government set up most of the machinery to administer the war. A huge number of agencies and offices began to transform the United States into what Roosevelt had asked for, the "arsenal of democracy." Aid to Britain became more overt, and was denounced by the Germans as "moral aggression." It was not in Germany's interest to bring about a war with the United States, however, and the Germans eventually put up with considerable provocation and ultimately, overtly belligerent acts without a declaration of war.

In March of 1941, the United States took another step forward, when Congress passed the Lend-Lease Act. Britain could not indefinitely afford to "cash and carry"; the new act empowered the President to lease or provide goods and services to any nation whose defense he thought vital to the defense of the United States.

This was almost but not quite a declaration of war. Through the spring the pace accelerated. Axis ships in American ports were seized at the end of March. A week later, the United States government announced it was taking over Greenland as a caretaker for Denmark, whose territory it officially was. The next day, the government allowed American shipping into the Red Sea, making it easier for American goods to reach the British fighting in Egypt. In May, fifty oil tankers were transferred to Britain, and ships belonging to Vichy France were seized. In May 21, a German U-boat torpedoed the freighter *Robin Moor,* and a week later the President proclaimed a state of unlimited national emergency. Axis credits were frozen, and consulates were closed in June. In July, American troops replaced the British garrison in Iceland.

There was a great deal of domestic opposition. The Lend-Lease Act especially was bitterly attacked, and isolationists saw it as a blank check by which Roosevelt could take the country into war. The strength of the opposition was clearly revealed in the debate over the renewal of the draft. The Selective Service Act of 1940 had been passed for one year. In August of 1941, it came up for reconsideration; the administration badly wanted it passed. In that month, the Germans were advancing toward Leningrad and into the Ukraine, the Japanese were occupying French Indochina, Roosevelt and Churchill met off Newfoundland to sign the Atlantic Charter—and the Selective Service Act passed the House of Representatives by a margin of one vote.

At Placentia Bay in Newfoundland, President Roosevelt and Prime Minister Churchill met and agreed on their war aims. Both had former connections with their respective navies, both arrived by ship, the President aboard the U. S. S. *Augusta,* a graceful, spick-and-span heavy cruiser, the Prime Minister aboard the battle-scarred *Prince of Wales.* The two leaders hit it off immediately and, in the course of several meetings, produced a basic agreement that Germany was their primary enemy. They also produced the Atlantic Charter, a statement of war aims that eventually evolved into the charter of the United Nations.

The Charter had its intellectual origins in both the old Fourteen Points of Woodrow Wilson, and the New Deal of President Roosevelt; rather more of it was American than British, but it was the Americans who had yet to be brought into the war and who had to be made to see that it must be fought. The two leaders announced that their countries sought no aggrandizement and no territory contrary to the wishes of peoples involved, that they respected the rights of states to choose their own form of government, and that they would restore sovereign status to those countries deprived of it. They favored equality of economic opportunity, access to raw materials, friendly cooperation. They incorporated Roosevelt's Four Freedoms, and ended with an explicit statement that only when the "Nazi tyranny" was destroyed could these things be achieved. The phrase about Nazi tyranny was Churchill's, and he wondered if Roosevelt would accept it; the President decided that Americans were ready for it, and were coming to recognize that if they wanted the world they said they wanted, they would sooner or later have to fight for it.

It turned out to be sooner. The United States Navy was already at war, though it had not yet been declared. The logic of events was dictating that the United States could no longer stand aloof. If the Americans were going to provide all aid short of war to Great Britain, it made no sense for them to fill up ships with materials, and then see those ships sunk in the Atlantic because the British were critically short of escort vessels. Even before the Newfoundland meeting, the navy was escorting convoys through the Western Atlantic as far as Iceland, where they were picked up by the Royal Navy. This placed the Germans in a considerable dilemma; officially they wished to avoid infringing American neutrality, but on the high seas that became more and more difficult. American destroyers were picking up German U-boats and shadowing them until they could call in British boats for the kill. Some sort of collision was inevitable.

On September 4, the U. S. S. *Greer* received a signal from a British patrol plane that there was a submarine ahead. *Greer* picked up the contact and held it for three hours: she made no attacks, but the British plane dropped depth charges on the sub. Finally, the U-boat fired a torpedo at *Greer*; it missed, and *Greer* went in to attack with depth charges. They missed too, but now both sides had exchanged shots. The respective governments expressed their indignation, and Roosevelt announced that the Germans were little more than pirates, and from now on American ships would shoot on sight. It is easier to continue fighting than to start it, and public opinion in the United States was on the whole supportive of the tough line, whatever the legal niceties of the matter. On October 16, U. S. S. *Kearney* was hit by a torpedo in the middle of a wolf-pack attack on the convoy she was escorting, but she made it to Iceland. Then on October 31, the *Reuben James*, an old four-stack destroyer, was hit and sunk 600 miles west of Iceland.

The Congressional response was an alteration of the Neutrality Acts. By clear, though certainly not overwhelming, majorities, both houses of Congress amended the acts so that American merchant ships might be armed, and declared that they might now sail into war zones. Congress also extended a $1 billion Lend-Lease credit to the Soviet Union.

The German government still chose not to respond to what was in fact American belligerence. Both parties had now committed overt acts of war against each other. In a court of law, the United States would have been declared the aggressor against Nazi Germany, and the U. S. Navy in the Atlantic was on a war footing; in fact, it was doing more in 1941 than it would be able to do in 1942, after it became officially involved, because then almost all its efforts were of necessity thrown into the desperate fight to stop the Japanese.

The United States and Germany were at war, and yet they were not at war. Sailors from the Atlantic convoys came back to a country that still pretended it was at peace. The last six months of 1941—at least until December—were a sort of twilight zone, and it was in the interest of neither party to alter the status quo. Roosevelt was doing all he could, and the domestic opposition had already branded him a warmonger. War industry had brought the United States finally and fully out of the Depression; few people really wanted to go any farther than that. It was extremely unlikely that the American public could be carried into the war on behalf of a couple of sunken destroyers; too many Americans would charge that the destroyers should not have been where they were anyway.

If the United States were to go to war, some massive overt shock was required. But Hitler was deeply embroiled in Russia, with his invincible armies marching on Moscow. In the first week of December of 1941, the Wehrmacht was closing in for the kill in Russia. Americans were concerned bystanders, but most of them still thought it was not their war.

11. The Battle of the Atlantic

In 1917, GERMANY HAD very nearly brought Great Britain to defeat and starvation by the use of submarines. She never came quite that close in World War II. There were periods when the Germans were actually winning, but in the longest and most crucial battle of the war, to keep the sea lanes to the United Kingdom open, the Royal Navy mastered the challenge. The Battle of the Atlantic was a super-scale Battle of Britain, spread out over five years.

There were several different aspects to it. The longest and most dangerous was between the escort vessels and the German submarines, and it started with the declaration of war and did not end definitively until the last German U-boat surrendered in May of 1945. This campaign passed through several phases, dictated both by geographical shifts of emphasis, and by the introduction of new tactics and techniques. When people speak of "the Battle of the Atlantic," it is the submarine campaign they are usually thinking of.

Besides that, the Germans also had a respectable surface fleet. They did not hope to challenge the Royal Navy for overall control of the sea; their own fleet was not that strong. Instead, they used their battleships and pocket-battleships as raiders, sending them out on sorties designed to catch and destroy the occasional convoy. This was expensive for the British, for it meant that many of their large fleet units had to be employed as convoy escorts, in case a German battleship should suddenly loom over the horizon. But it was also expensive for the Germans, because the British eventually caught or ran to earth almost all of their major units. Some naval authorities argue that the whole surface effort on the part of the Germans was a vast and costly diversion, and that if the money, men, and material that were put into battleships had gone into submarines instead, Germany would have won the Battle of the Atlantic—and possibly the war.

This argument, which is central enough to the course of the war to explore for a moment, goes essentially back to the American naval theorist Alfred T. Mahan. Writing at the end of the nineteenth century, Mahan analyzed how Britain had gained her supremacy at sea and held it. His conclusion was that the dominant element in sea power was a large battle fleet able to destroy an enemy fleet, or blockade it in its harbors, so that one kept the seas open for one's own use. Mere commerce raiding, he said, had never been decisive, and had always been a second-class alternative for a second-class power.

Just before he wrote, there was a French school of naval thought known as the *Jeune école*; its writers maintained that commerce raiding could indeed be decisive, especially against a state such as Great Britain that depended increasingly upon imports for its livelihood. Most writers and naval leaders, however, agreed with Mahan, and at the opening of the twentieth century all the navies of the world were busily building battleships. It was this race that produced the German High Seas Fleet which challenged the Royal Navy, and lost, in World War I.

The irony of Mahan's writings was that at the very time when they were uncritically accepted, technology was producing weapons that challenged their validity. Steam and oil made close blockade increasingly difficult and the development of the submarine provided a commerce raider that was so effective that perhaps commerce raiding could win wars after all. The submarine in its early days, however, was not seen as a raider—Europe was too civilized for that—but rather as a weapon against enemy warships. Only as World War I progressed in nastiness did the submarine achieve its true role as a killer of merchant ships. When it did, the Germans very nearly won the war with it. Had they had more subs and fewer battleships, they probably would have won.

In 1939, both sides went to war with the experience of World War I fresh in their minds. The junior officers of the first war were the senior officers of the second. The Germans therefore immediately began submarine warfare, and the British immediately instituted their countermeasures, foremost among them the convoy system. Both sides enjoyed advantages, and suffered disadvantages, that they had not had in the last war.

First among these was geography. The advantage in this lay definitely with the Germans. At the start of the war, things were much as they had been before, with one exception: the independence of Ireland. In 1914-18, the British had operated large escort forces out of their base at Queenstown on the southern coast of Ireland. When the Irish Free State gained its independence the British lost the base. This pushed their escort forces back at least a hundred miles to the east, which meant two hundred miles coming and going; that in turn made the mid-Atlantic operational gap wider, and many British sailors would die in the waters off Iceland because of Irish neutrality.

After the 1940 campaigns, geography took another turn against the Royal Navy. The Germans occupied Norway and were able to operate out through the Norwegian Sea into the northern waters. When Russia came into the war the British convoys to North Russia were harassed all the way by attacks from Norwegian bases, and the convoys to Murmansk and Archangel had to run the gauntlet of U-boats, air attacks, surface ships, and even small motor torpedo boats. A sailor abandoning ship or a pilot shot down from the sky was dead in less than a minute in the waters off northern Norway, and the casualty toll on the Russian runs ran ten times higher than on the North Atlantic run.

The Germans also occupied the entire Atlantic coast of France, and were able to base their U-boats at Cherbourg, Brest, and Lorient as well as the smaller ports on the Bay of Biscay. From Brest and Lorient they were as far west as the British themselves, so geography was definitely on their side, compared with what it had been in the last war.

The British enjoyed some advantages, too. In World War I it took them three years to bring in a convoy system, because they thought the complexity of loading, marshaling, sailing, and unloading steamships would make it impossible. They found when they finally tried it that they had been wrong, and the convoy system, passive defense though it was, became the major anti-U-boat instrument. Now, in 1939, they resorted to it immediately. The Admiralty had the plans all worked out, and the whole mechanism began with the very declaration of war.

An underlying assumption of the convoy idea is that it is as difficult to find a block of fifty ships in the immensity of the ocean as it is to find one ship. Therefore, if you concentrate the ships in such a block, you have immediately reduced by fifty times the odds of their being spotted by an enemy. Further, if they are concentrated, it becomes possible to provide an armed naval escort for them. The enemy has to come to the convoy to destroy it, and that brings him to the escort as well, and it can destroy him. So you have fewer—if slightly larger—needles in the haystack, and you have some protection against the man looking for them.

The British problem was that they had few escorts, and the German problem was that they had few submarines. In fact, the Germans had only about thirty-nine U-boats at the outbreak of war, and that included several short-range training boats for the Baltic. Out of roughly thirty, a third would be on overhaul and a third in transit to operating areas at any given time. That left them only about ten boats actually on station to sink ships.

But the Royal Navy was almost as short of escort vessels. Destroyers were too expensive, and they were critically short of them anyway. They hoped at first to escort convoys with armed tugs and fishing trawlers, but these simply could not stand up to the North Atlantic. The answer eventually was found in the slower-speed escort vessel known as the corvette—the Americans called it a frigate—and these uncomfortable little ships finally bore the brunt of the Battle of the Atlantic. There were not too many of them to begin with, but the lull from 1939 to the end of the Battle of France gave the British just enough time to bring numbers of them into service. Both sides were slow to get started, but on balance, the British profited more by the breathing space.

The first ten months of the war, until the fall of France, was a period in which the contestants groped their way toward some conception of what was actually going to happen. Prior to war, the Germans had signed agreements restricting the use of submarines against merchant shipping, but these soon went by the board. The British expected that they would, and even before war began they were making plans to arm their merchant vessels. After 1945, both sides threw charges against the other of the "he-did-it-first" variety, but these are largely retrospective rationalizations. The U-boat was just too good a weapons system, and the merchant ship too crucial a target, for either side to be unduly concerned with the niceties of behavior. It is difficult to think of an instance in history when a weapon that was available and effective—gas was not—has not been used by the state possessing it.

On the day war was declared, the German U-30 torpedoed and sank the passenger liner *Athenia* with no warning and with large loss of life. The British made capital out of this, and the Germans did their best to deny the matter; in fact the U-boat commander either acted against his orders or misread them, but the damage had been done. After that beginning the campaign slowed down, and until June of 1940, the Allies were ahead on points, sinking more U-boats than the Germans commissioned, for their own loss of 222 ships, about 100,000 tons a month. The Germans calculated that they would have to sink about three-quarters of a million tons a month to defeat Britain, so 100,000 a month, whatever agony it meant for those involved, was not an unacceptable loss. More serious in this period were the German air strikes against convoys along the vulnerable east coast of Britain, for which the Royal Air Force had made no provision.

Equally important right from the start was the influence of new techniques and new technology. The British found, for example, that their Coastal Command air patrols were an effective anti-submarine device, and this element would increase in importance until the U-boat was mastered. The Germans introduced a new wrinkle by sowing magnetic mines in the Channel, and the British were for a while at a loss to counter them. The magnetic mine sat on the sea floor, and when a ship passed over it, it was detonated by the magnetic field generated by the ship. The whole British minesweeping service was set up to deal with moored contact mines, which float just below the surface of the water, and are moored to the bottom by a long cable. To defeat these the mine-sweeper cuts the cable, the mine floats to the surface, and the sweeper destroys it with small arms fire. With no vulnerable cable to be cut, the magnetic mine was for a while unbeatable. Fortunately, in November a mine was dropped on a tidal flat, the British retrieved and examined it, and were able to develop countermeasures. One of these was a device known as degaussing, in which an electric cable was run around a ship's hull. A current activated through this cable counteracted the magnetic field of the ship itself, so that there would be no disturbance to detonate the mine.

Throughout the war, there was a constant battle by the scientists to invent new weapons, and to counter them, so that the war had two incongruous aspects: on the one hand, the completely objective and scientific search for improvement, on the other, the physical, dangerous business of putting those weapons to use. The war produced its own schizophrenia.

In October, the Germans scored another striking material, and even greater propaganda, success when U-47 worked its way inside the northern British naval base at Scapa Flow in the Orkneys, and torpedoed the battleship *Royal Oak*; she took more than 800 men to the bottom with her, and the whole matter was a severe blow to British pride.

The U-boat campaign began to increase in intensity after the fall of France. Norwegian and French bases were now available, and the Germans were putting more effort into submarine construction. The British had lost heavily in their destroyer and escort forces in the Norwegian campaign and at Dunkirk; the new corvettes were not ready until late in the summer and early in the fall, and the services of the French Navy were also lost. Late 1940 saw the American destroyers-for-bases deal, but in spite of extensive news coverage, the fifty old American ships needed a great deal of work, and had no more than a marginal effect on British needs.

Losses mounted steadily. From June of 1940 till the end of the year, the British lost 638 ships, almost a threefold increase over the previous period. In the first six months of 1941, they lost more than seven hundred. They tried various expedients; Coastal Command was strengthened, and attacking the U-boats got equal priority with reconnaissance. The arming of merchant ships continued, and the use of the Q-ship was increased. This was a heavily armed vessel disguised as a merchant ship; the idea was to fool the submarine into thinking that it had an easy target, so that it would surface to finish it off with gunfire. Then the decoy ship would let down false partitions and stagings and sink the U-boat with its hidden guns. It was a pretty hazardous business, and in a sense it was self-defeating, for if the Q-ships succeeded often enough, the Germans would soon learn not to surface, but to rely on torpedoes instead.

The British discovered that aircraft were among the most effective means of countering the submarines, but not until the production of the small escort carrier, with a flight deck built on a merchant ship hull, did they have enough ships to provide most convoys with air escort outside the range of land-based planes. As an interim measure they introduced the catapult fighter. They put steam catapults on some merchant ships, and mounted a Hurricane on them. When a German reconnaissance plane was sighted, or a submarine on the surface, the Hurricane would be shot off from the catapult and do its bit. The obvious limitation on this was that the Hurricane was not a seaplane. Once in the air, if it could not make it to land, it had to ditch, hopefully alongside an escort which would then pick up the pilot. It was a pretty desperate business, but 1941 and 1942 called for pretty desperate measures.

The Germans responded by producing bigger and better U-boats that could range farther into the Atlantic, to the areas beyond the effective reach of the short-range escorts or the land-based planes. The British then had to develop means of refueling their escorts at sea, so they could go all the way across to Halifax in Nova Scotia, or St. John's in Newfoundland. That eventually got rid of the mid-ocean gap, but it increased the strain and the wear and tear on men and ships. The German shift to mid-Atlantic brought increasing conflict with the United States, but that did not unduly hinder the submarine operations, though there was some falling off of sinkings in the second six months of 1941.

Hitler's U-boat commanders introduced new tactics, too. They had originally operated independently, and like successful trout fishermen, the leading aces had their own private fishing grounds. Now they brought in group tactics; the first U-boat to spot a convoy would surface and radio a report to U-boat headquarters, which would then signal other U-boats in the area. Or German long-range reconnaissance planes, the famous Focke-Wulf Condors, would radio back reports. The subs would home in on the convoy, form a "wolf-pack," and systematically attack it and whittle it down. The British intercepted the radio signals, and in their turn warned their escorts what to expect. Each night the submarines would make their attacks; in the morning they would meet behind the convoy, figure out what to do next, and sail on the surface to get ahead of their victim. The U-boats were generally faster on the surface than were the convoys, zigzagging and tied to the speed of the slowest merchantman. Night would come and the subs would close in again, sometimes with spectacular results. A tanker would burn for hours, unless it were loaded with gas, in which case it would go in one huge flash. A ship loaded with iron ore would sink in less than a minute. The escorts would churn about frantically dropping depth charges and trying to keep the subs away from their victims, and in the morning, the convoy would close up its empty spaces and plod doggedly along.

Sailors developed a grim appreciation of their chances, measured in how you slept: if you carried iron ore, you slept on deck, for if hit by a torpedo, there were only seconds to get clear. If you carried general cargo, you could sleep below decks, but had to leave your door open, and sleep with your clothes on so you would have time to get out. If you were on a tanker carrying aviation gas, you could undress, close your cabin door, and have a good night's sleep, because if you were hit, it wasn't going to make any difference at all; you'd never get out anyway.

Eventually, to deal with the wolf-packs, the British introduced the hunter-killer group. This was an escort group that was unattached, a sort of fire-brigade free to come to the rescue of convoys under attack; once it found a wolf-pack, it could harry the U-boats just as they had harried the convoy. But this came only later, when the Allies had sufficient material to afford such luxuries.

In early 1942, with the entry of the United States into the war, the U-boat campaign hit its stride. For the Germans the first six months went down in legend as "the happy time" or "the American hunting season." The Americans were by no means fully organized for war, and U-boat operations shifted to the eastern seaboard. Large replenishment submarines known as "milch cows" brought fuel, torpedoes, and supplies over to submarines which remained on station off New York, Boston, Charleston, and Gulf Coast ports. The American cities were in many cases not even blacked out, and the Germans had a field day sinking ships silhouetted against the lights as they moved along the coast. It got so bad for a while that there was a "reverse Lend-Lease" with British and Canadian corvettes turned over to the Americans and Royal Navy ships escorting American merchantmen up and down the Atlantic coast. In two weeks the Germans sank twenty-five ships—200,000 tons—off the coast of Florida. The Florida towns refused to turn their lights off at night because it would damage their tourist trade. In February, 432,000 tons went down, 80 percent of it in American coastal waters. By spring the Germans were winning the war.

The crisis continued through the summer, but both the British and Americans rallied to it. Massive shipbuilding programs in the United States began to catch up with the losses; increased numbers of air patrols kept watch over the convoy lanes. At sea there was a deadly equilibrium, with the escorts and the U-boats locked in a death grapple. But between the new escorting tactics and the accelerating production, the situation began to stabilize. November of 1942 was the last month in which shipping losses outpaced construction. By the end of the year, though it was hard to be certain, the Allies had turned the corner.

Through 1943 the Allies tried to retain the advantage, and the Germans strove desperately to recapture it. Both sides were now fully aware of the importance of the Atlantic, both knew that whoever won that battle would eventually win the war. When they met at Casablanca in January of 1943, the Allied leaders decided the U-boat was their absolutely first priority. They diverted their strategic bombing campaign to U-boat bases and building yards, they increased their production of ships, escorts, escort carriers, and anti-submarine patrol aircraft, and through 1943 they brought these new weapons and their new tactics into use.

The Germans too increased their efforts. They built bigger and better submarines, armed them with more anti-aircraft weapons, laid more mines and developed better ones. The search for new weapons continued. The Allies produced the hedgehog, a multiple projectile that would fire ahead of the escort while it still had sonar contact with the sub; it was several times more efficient than the old World War I–style depth charge. The Germans riposted with the acoustic torpedo, which would home in on the noise of the ship's propeller, follow the wake of the ship, and hit in the stern. The Allies answered that with a towed box that imitated a propeller's noise and caused the torpedo to detonate prematurely. The Germans, just too late, introduced the snorkel breathing tube, similar to that used by skindivers today, so that a sub could get air and recharge its batteries without surfacing. At the end of the war, one German submarine went from Norway to Argentina on its snorkel; the crew turned green, but they made it.

Through 1943 and after, things went downhill for the Germans. The Allies gradually gained the upper hand; finally, in 1944, as the ring closed in on Germany, the U-boats' Atlantic bases were lost one by one; all the old aces disappeared—bombed, depth-charged, rammed, or sunk by gunfire. New replacements drafted out of the surface navy went to sea and never came back. U-boat sailors who survived one patrol became veterans, those who survived two were old men at twenty. The happy days were gone, and gone forever. The seas calmed, the wreckage disappeared, the sinkings stopped.

The statistics of the Battle of the Atlantic defy the imagination. More than 2,600 ships were sunk, totaling over 15,000,000 tons. The British alone lost about 30,000 sailors of the Royal Navy, and 30,000 of the merchant service. The Germans built 1,162 U-boats during the course of the war; 785 of them were sunk, 156 surrendered at the end of the war, and the rest were either scuttled or otherwise destroyed. Almost 41,000 men served in the U-boats; 5,000 were taken prisoner, and 28,000 were killed. In balance the campaign was more costly for the Allies than for the Germans, but they could afford the losses better—they had no choice in the matter.

The merchant ships, corvettes, and submarines were always there. They hit the headlines only when there was some spectacular disaster, such as befell the famous Convoy PQ17, a north Russian convoy, in midsummer of 1942, when it lost twenty-two out of thirty-three ships. But for the most part the battle of the convoys went on almost unheralded. It was when the big ships clashed that excitement peaked.

The major surface units of the German fleet, all of them new, were qualitatively among the best in the world. Ship for ship they were superior to the equivalent units of the Royal Navy, most of which were older and designed to meet a wider variety of needs. The Germans, for example, did not have the imperial responsibilities that required British ships to sail all over the world; with fewer habitability problems, they were able to provide better damage control facilities, and such factors counted heavily in battle. But there were not enough German ships to make an open challenge, and therefore they reverted to the classic role of the inferior power, the *guerre de course*, the attempt to destroy the enemy's maritime trade. Their super battleships became powerful but expensive commerce raiders.

Some of the Kriegsmarine's ships were at sea when war was declared. One of them, the *Deutschland*, managed to sink only two merchant ships before coming home through the Denmark Strait; afraid of the propaganda effect if a ship with such a name were sunk, Hitler rechristened her *Luetzow*, after a cruiser given to Russia. Far more spectacular was what happened to the other pocket-battleship at sea, the *Graf Spee*.

Under Captain Hans Langsdorf, *Graf Spee* was at large in the mid-Atlantic in early September. For two months she ranged the south Atlantic and into the Indian Ocean, sinking 50,000 tons of shipping. She then returned to try the rich hunting off the South American coast, and it was there, early on the morning of December 13, that she was run to earth by a British squadron of one heavy and two light cruisers, *Exeter, Ajax,* and *Achilles*. Someone on *Graf Spee* made a costly recognition mistake, and assessed the enemy as a light cruiser and two destroyers rather than what they really were. The Germans bore on to attack. The British split into two divisions, forcing *Graf Spee* to divide her fire; *Exeter* was very badly hurt, but so was the German, and though Langsdorf could probably have finished off his opponents, he broke away instead and took refuge in Montevideo. While the Germans hastily made all the repairs they were allowed in a neutral port the British mustered the watchdogs around the lair. On the evening of the 17th, huge crowds watched as the battered German raider steamed out to sea for her last fight. Then, to everyone's surprise, instead of going down in a blaze of glory, the Germans set off charges and scuttled the ship in the Plate Estuary. Three hours later, the minuscule British squadron that *Graf Spee* dared not face sailed triumphantly into the harbor. Poor Langsdorf shot himself to refute any charge of cowardice, but the world drew its own conclusions about how long it takes to build a naval tradition and how Britannia still ruled the waves.

There were already examples of that. In November, the Germans had shaken loose two more raiders, the beautiful battle cruisers *Scharnhorst* and *Gneisenau*, at the time the finest ships in commission in the German Navy. On the 23rd, they sighted an armed merchant cruiser on the Northern Patrol; H. M. S. *Rawalpindi* signaled "Enemy battle cruisers in sight" and took her six-inch guns into battle against the Germans' eleven-inch guns. They finished her off in sixteen minutes, but then they scurried back home, successfully evading the pursuing British main fleet units.

The spring and summer of 1940 were busy with the Norwegian affair, the fall of France, and the unhappy episodes of British ships attacking the French fleet. Not until October of 1940 did the big ships clash again. The pocket-battleship *Scheer* got out then, and on November 5 she ambushed an eastbound convoy of thirty-seven merchantmen, escorted only by another armed merchant cruiser, H. M. S. *Jervis Bay.* Captain Fogarty Fegen of *Jervis Bay* steamed straight for the giant, and though the old merchantman never had a chance, her destruction took long enough for the convoy to scatter. *Scheer* caught only five of them. The German cruiser *Hipper* broke loose in early December; on Christmas morning she attacked a troop convoy, but the heavy escort drove her off, and she eventually went to Brest.

In January of 1941, the *Scharnhorst, Gneisenau,* and *Hipper* all went to sea together; they were at large for sixty days and sank twenty-two ships before they returned to French ports. That was just a warm-up for the main event, however. In May, the mightiest ship in the world, the brand-new *Bismarck*, sailed from Gotenhavn in company with the cruiser *Prinz Eugen.*

The ensuing chase was the high point of the naval war in the Atlantic. The Germans went far north of Iceland, then came south through the Denmark Strait, close to the ice ringing Greenland. Five days out, they were sighted by H. M. S. *Suffolk*, a cruiser on the Northern Patrol. *Suffolk* shadowed them while heavy British units closed in to contact. The first to meet them were the *Hood* and the *Prince of Wales,* one long the pride of the Royal Navy, the other brand-new and still carrying dockyard workers who were caught aboard the ship as she hastily put to sea.

The giants opened fire at each other in the long Arctic dawn on the 24th, Empire Day, at a range of about twelve and a half miles. The ships were positioned in such a way that only the forward British guns could fire, while all the Germans' bore on target. They concentrated on *Hood*, and at 0600 *Bismarck*'s fourth salvo hit her four-inch-gun magazine, aft of the mainmast. The explosion flashed into the main after-magazine for the fifteen-inch guns. There was a huge pillar of fire that soared a thousand feet into the air, a horrendous explosion, and *Hood* broke in half; her bow and stern reared up out of the water, and within ninety seconds she was gone. She took 1,418 men with her; three members of the crew survived. The Germans raced on south, and the badly hurt *Prince of Wales* turned away, after hitting one of *Bismarck*'s fuel tanks.

The Admiralty now concentrated every effort on closing a ring around the Germans; their net eventually included five battleships, two aircraft carriers, nine cruisers, and eighteen destroyers. For some of these, such as the old battleship *Ramilles*, detached from duty as a convoy escort, meeting the Germans would have been little short of suicide, but there was no way they would allow *Bismarck* to get away.

Yet the sea was wide, and Admiral Gunther Lutjens, flying his flag in *Bismarck*, might well survive his foray. To the south of him there remained huge gaps. German U-boats were concentrating below Greenland to provide a cordon for him, and if he turned east and managed to shake off pursuit, he might get under the air umbrella from the French coast. At dark on the 24th, he detached *Prinz Eugen*, and she eventually got home safely. The British cruisers were still successfully shadowing *Bismarck*, though, and at midnight she was attacked by Swordfish torpedo planes; they scored one hit, but it was right on her main armor belt and did no damage. Soon after that, Lutjens turned southeast, and the British lost contact.

For the next thirty-six hours the Germans had the sea to themselves. The British net was gradually tightening, but they were not totally sure the quarry was inside it. They assumed Lutjens was making for the French coast, but they could not be certain. Then at mid-morning of the 26th, a Catalina flying boat sighted *Bismarck*, only 690 miles from Brest. By now the ships in the British ring were getting low on fuel, but if they moved properly, they would still catch her.

Soon after the Catalina sighting, aircraft from the carrier *Ark Royal*, operating hitherto in the Mediterranean, picked up the German, and the cruiser *Sheffield* got her on radar and took up the role of shadower. *Ark Royal* sent off fourteen Swordfish to make a torpedo strike; in the heavy weather and poor visibility they attacked *Sheffield* instead; fortunately, all the torpedoes missed, but the language on *Sheffield*'s bridge qualified this as one of the hottest actions of the war.

A second strike fared better. There was another hit on the armor belt, and more important, a hit aft that jammed *Bismarck*'s rudder. During the night the British moved in for the kill. A destroyer attack achieved little, but at daylight two battleships, *Rodney* and *King George V*, closed in from the north. In two hours the great *Bismarck* was a silent, flaming hulk. The British finished her off with torpedoes and rescued 110 survivors of her crew of more than 2,000.

From that high point—or low point, depending on where one stood—the German surface campaign gradually deteriorated. They were forced increasingly into a defensive posture. The British torpedoed *Luetzow* as she steamed into northern waters, and bombing raids damaged *Gneisenau*, *Scharnhorst*, and *Prinz Eugen* in their French shelters. They hunted down supply ships and converted merchantmen acting as raiders, and slowly the surface threat receded.

The Germans still kept a few tricks up their sleeve. One place from which they could operate surface vessels was Norway, where their ships could make short-range dashes out against the North Russian convoys. As 1942 came in, that presented a problem. Opportunity lay in the north, but most of the major ships remaining were in French Biscay ports. In February, the Germans carried off a daring coup, when *Scharnhorst*, *Gneisenau*, and *Prinz Eugen* made a dash up through the Channel to German ports under heavy air escort. Both the Royal Navy and the R. A. F. were caught napping; they mustered everything they had available and launched torpedo aircraft, bombers, motor torpedo boats, and a destroyer attack. *Gneisenau* hit a mine, and *Scharnhorst* hit two, but the ships made it home, to the considerable embarrassment of the British.

Still the attrition went on. *Gneisenau* was bombed in port and made useless. *Scharnhorst* made one more significant appearance; she came out against a North Russian convoy over Christmas of 1943. On December 26 the British caught her up in the Barents Sea, and in the icy waters off the North Cape, they pounded her to death. Only thirty-six of a crew of nearly 2,000 survived.

That left only one threat, the new *Tirpitz*, sister ship to the *Bismarck*. Her career was far less spectacular than that of her older twin. She spent most of her life operating out of Norway, constantly hounded by the Royal Navy and the R. A. F. They bombed her several times, and in September of 1942 they got at her with midget submarines and planted mines under her hull that immobilized her for six months. From 1943 on, the British launched increasingly heavy bombing attacks, eventually hitting her with 10,000-pound "blockbuster" bombs. At last, reduced to the ignominy of a floating battery in Tromso harbor, she was hit hard and capsized.

That was late in 1944. Germany's proud fleet was gone. Bombed, mined, depth-charged, torpedoed, sunk by gunfire, U-boats and battleships alike disappeared. Victory for the Royal Navy was a costly, near-run, tedious affair. There was no sudden ray of light at the end, just a gradual clearing of the atmosphere. Slowly the enemy's presence was less obvious, and it all ended in May of 1945 when the last survivors of the U-boats came sullenly to the surface and hoisted black flags of surrender. Once again the Royal Navy had mastered all the challenges a brave, daring, and vicious enemy could throw against it.

12. War in the Mediterranean

AFTER THE BATTLE OF BRITAIN, and indeed before it was ended, Hitler turned his attention to the east, and began planning to finish off Russia. The focus of the war shifted not eastward, however, but southward. For the next nine months, and as far as Britain was concerned for the next three years, the main theater of the war was the Mediterranean.

Few questions about the conduct of the war have been argued at greater length than that of the so-called Mediterranean strategy followed by Great Britain. On both sides of the Atlantic, writers have claimed that it was either basically sound or wastefully divergent. Some have said that it arose out of Churchill's failure at the Dardanelles in 1915 and his subsequent determination to prove that he had been right in World War I by winning World War II from the south, and Churchill himself coined the infelicitous phrase "the soft underbelly of Fortress Europe." There has been endless argument about the British preference for a peripheral strategy as opposed to the American desire to go straight to the heart. In fact, the diversion into the Mediterranean grew out of the logic of events. Whatever responsive chords fighting in the middle sea may have struck in Winston Churchill, if any one man may be said to have caused the war to center there, that man was not Churchill, it was Mussolini. Almost everything followed from Il Duce's inability to sit quietly and mind his own business.

At the start of the war Germany had neither territories in nor access to the Mediterranean. War did not come to that sea, therefore, until Italy declared war on France and Britain in June of 1940. Then, ringed by states that were either belligerents, potential belligerents, allies or colonies of belligerents, the Mediterranean heated up very quickly. From west to east on the northern side of the sea there were Spain, France, Italy, Yugoslavia, Albania, Greece, and Turkey. On the southern side there was French North

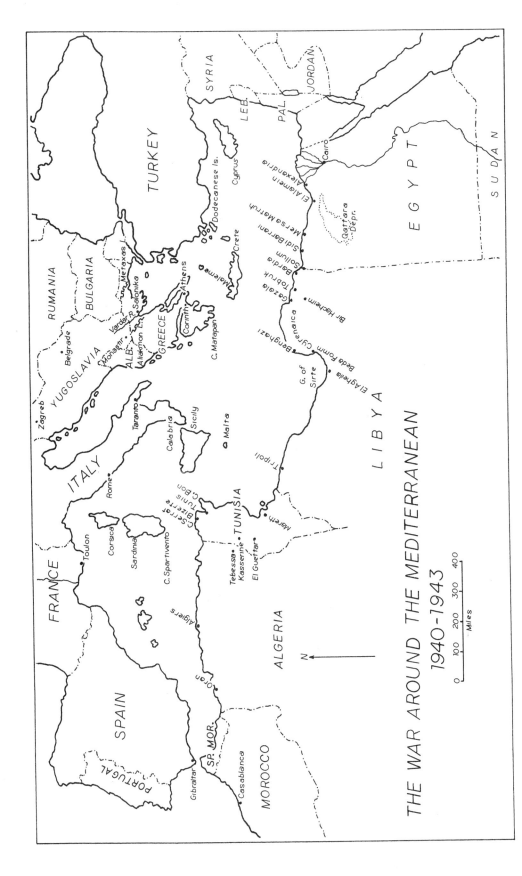

THE WAR AROUND THE MEDITERRANEAN
1940-1943

0   100   200   300   400
Miles

Africa, divided into the colonies of Morocco, Algeria, and Tunisia, then Italian Libya, and then British-held Egypt. This parceled-out arrangement continued right down the Red Sea coast to the horn of Africa, where there were Egypt and the Anglo-Egyptian Sudan, then Italian Eritrea and Ethiopia, then French and British Somaliland, and finally Italian Somaliland. Once Italy was in the war it was inevitable that fighting would flare over all the colonial territories.

Mussolini entered the war less because he coveted British territory than because he coveted French. From the time of Italian unification in the 1870's there had been the hope of a trans-Mediterranean Italian empire that would stretch from the peninsula through Sicily and across the Sicilian Narrows to the north African hump of Tunisia. Italian ambitions had been forestalled by the French, who declared a protectorate over Tunisia in 1881. The territory was often referred to in France as "our largest Italian colony," and it was this colonial frustration that made Italy join the Triple Alliance in 1882. One of Mussolini's chief motives for declaring war on France was the hope that Italy would take over the French North African empire as her share of the victory.

Unhappily, the Italian reach exceeded Mussolini's grasp. The Germans overran France so fast, and the Italians contributed so little, that Mussolini was able to make few claims in the armistice negotiations. He made none on French overseas territories, and French North Africa remained under the control of the Vichy government, with the exception of a few unimportant equatorial colonies that rallied to the dissident General de Gaulle. Frustrated in his westward-looking ambitions, Mussolini turned his attention from the French to the British. As an uneasy calm settled on the western territories, the war burst over the eastern Mediterranean.

The whole Allied position in the Mediterranean had been predicated on close cooperation between British and French units. In World War I the two navies had divided the sea between them, the French taking responsibility for the western end and the British the eastern end. The same sort of agreement was now invalid, and the British and Commonwealth forces were left to hold the central position of empire all by themselves. The British seaborne line ran from Gibraltar to Malta to Alexandria, squarely across the Italian line from southern Italy and Sicily to Libya. Both British and Italians had respectable fleets in the inland sea, and through 1940 and 1941 they fought a series of battles in which the British quickly achieved moral mastery, and more slowly gained physical mastery, of the seas.

The British on land were even thinner than on the water. The commander of all British land forces in the Middle East was General Sir Archibald Wavell. Under him was a motley collection of units from all over the empire, totaling about 63,000 in Egypt and Palestine, and another 19,000 in scattered garrisons throughout East Africa. They included Australians, South Africans, New Zealanders, Indians, Africans, and British. Though they were potentially magnificent fighting material, they were largely underequipped and lacking in cohesion. As usual, it was a case of running the empire on a shoestring, and Wavell's instructions were fundamentally: hang on with what you have, and hope nothing happens.

The Italians, however, had an itch to accomplish something. There were about 200,000 troops in Libya, commanded by Field Marshal Graziani, and there were nearly 300,000 in Ethiopia, about a third of them Italian, the rest native troops. This gave them odds of roughly fifteen to one in East Africa, and they overran British Somaliland in August with relatively little difficulty. They got really busy in the fall. In September, they advanced about sixty miles from Libya into Egypt and stopped just past Sidi Barrani. In October, other Italian forces, operating out of Albania, began the invasion of Greece. While the British prepared a military riposte, the Royal Navy struck at the Italian Navy in its base at Taranto. Launching a surprise torpedo-plane attack with the ubiquitous Swordfish, of which they lost two, the British crippled half the Italian Navy for the next six months.

That was on November 11. A month later the British jumped off on an offensive in the Western Desert, as the Cyrenaican hump of Libya and Egypt was called. This was slated as a local offensive to recapture Sidi Barrani. The town was retaken in two days, along with 38,000 Italians. The British then decided to continue. Within a week, the Italians were back on the frontier. Still the British kept on; in early January, they took Bardia, then Tobruk. Wavell's desert general, Richard O'Connor, next sent his armor into the unknown desert to cut the Italians' retreat. Finally, in February, surrounded at Beda Fomm, the dazed Italians surrendered. In eight weeks they had lost 130,000 men, nearly a thousand guns, almost 500 tanks, and immense amounts of trucks, stores, and ammunition. British losses were fewer than 2,000 men, and Libya lay defenseless before them. Wavell sent out troops as far as El Agheila, and asked permission to go all the way to Tripoli; he believed he could wrap up the whole North African campaign in a couple of weeks. He was probably right.

Unhappily, he did not get the chance to prove it. Instead of being allowed to press on, he was told to set up a defensive position and a holding force at Benghazi while most of his troops went off to help bail out the Greeks. He left an armored brigade and an infantry division in Cyrenaica, which he assessed as sufficient to hold the Italians. It would not, in the event, hold the Germans. The Greek diversion would cost Great Britain, and eventually the United States, many months of fighting and many hard knocks.

Though it does not look it on the map, the eastern end of the Mediterranean Sea is a strategic unity, and events in one country influence those in another. The unity is created by the sea, and whoever dominates the waters of the Mediterranean is in a fair way to being master of the adjoining lands. To master the waters meant to master the air over them too, but that problem came later.

In early 1941, it was the Royal Navy who ruled the eastern Mediterranean. In actions off Calabria, at Cape Spartivento, and in the Fleet Air Arm attack at Taranto, they had sent the Italians running. They had constantly fought convoys through to Malta in the face of air and surface attacks by the enemy, and the Mediterranean Fleet enjoyed a comfortable feeling of superiority over the Italian Navy. It was not that the Italians were no good; their training state was high, and their ships were in many cases better than the British. Their problem was the unwillingness of their high command to risk its vessels; ships tend to be expensive prestige items, and navies trying to establish a naval tradition are often reluctant to risk the material, not realizing that the tradition depends less upon the possession of the ships than upon the way they are used—and even the way they are lost. The Italian Navy saved its ships, and lost its soul.

The definitive proof of this came in March of 1941 when a British force, after an all-day chase, sank three Italian cruisers and two destroyers off Cape Matapan in southern Greece. The Royal Navy lost one airplane. The victory came when it was badly needed, for things elsewhere in the theater were not going well at all.

In the fall of 1940, the attention of the Axis leaders focused in the Balkans. As Hitler's roving eye lit there, so did that of the local dictators. The desirable prize was Rumania, with its wheat and its oil fields, and in September, as the Italians were crossing the Egyptian frontier, Hungary, Russia, and Bulgaria all demanded and took parcels of Rumanian real estate. The next month the Germans arrived and took over the remainder; officially Rumania joined the Axis powers, but in fact she became a German dependency.

None of this pleased Mussolini. Thwarted in the west, he now saw himself upstaged in the east as well. He therefore decided to expand from his Albanian holdings, and he demanded concessions, including air bases, from the Greeks. The Greeks and the Italians had hated each other with Mediterranean intensity for centuries, and the Greek government summarily refused Mussolini's bid. Late in October, the Italian forces attacked out of Albania, and drove across the frontier into Greece in four columns.

The Greeks fought; moreover, they won. And on top of that, they invited the British to send in R. A. F. units to help them win. Hitler had hoped to gain by diplomacy a secure southern flank for operations against Russia; now, in early November, he had a half-baked little war down there, and as a result of it, he had British bombers on Greek soil, within range of his newly acquired oil fields of Rumania. He was not pleased.

Through the winter of 1940-41, the Greeks slowly pushed the Italians back through the mountains of the Greco-Albanian frontier. The Germans watched with increasing interest, and finally took a hand. In March, they got Bulgaria to join them in the Axis; they put pressure on Yugoslavia to come in too, and they also became more active in the North African theater. They sent Luftwaffe units to Sicily, and they dispatched General Irwin Rommel and the first units of the German Africa Corps to Tripoli.

In the Balkans, the Yugoslav government did not wish to become involved. Its military forces were weak and ill equipped. Under German pressure it caved in, however, and on March 25 agreed to join the Axis and permit transit rights to German troops. The next day there was a military coup d'état, the Prince Regent, Paul, was forced into exile, and the new Yugoslav government decided to sit pat. Hitler blew up, and ordered the Wehrmacht to make immediate plans for the overrunning of Yugoslavia.

The British sent a military mission, and the Greeks proposed that they and Yugoslavia form a common front that would have protected all of Greece but abandoned about two-thirds of Yugoslavia; that had little appeal. The Yugoslavs also applied to Russia for help, but the Russians with problems of their own were unwilling to become embroiled. There remained little for the Yugoslavs to do but sit and wait, and that was what they did.

The German staff planners turned in their usual virtuoso performance. They were in the midst of preparing their Russian operation. Now a rapid shuffle of units and tasks took place, and within ten days, they were set up and ready.

On April 6, the attack opened with the usual Luftwaffe strikes. Bombing Belgrade, the Germans killed about 17,000 civilians and completely disrupted the communications of the Yugoslav Army. German units broke across the frontier on the same day, and within another day or so were in the open. The Yugoslav units that were fully mobilized and equipped fought fiercely but they were few and far between. In many areas, units made up of ethnic minorities, mostly Croats, deserted or mutinied and a rival Croat government set up in Zagreb welcomed the Germans as liberators. The Germans occupied Belgrade on the 12th, and an armistice was signed on the 17th.

Again it looked very impressive. The Germans had about 500 casualties; they captured 330,000 Yugoslavs. They roared on toward Greece without even stopping to clear up their back areas. But many Yugoslavs slipped into the hills and mountains. The national tradition was not for conventional fighting as practiced in western Europe; it was for guerrilla warfare and killing in the dark of the moon.

While the Germans were preparing their move on Yugoslavia, and supplying troops to their new ally Bulgaria, the British were moving ground troops into Greece. Up to this point the Greek government, with an army of half a million men doing well against the Italians, had been reluctant to have British Army units, for fear of unduly antagonizing Hitler. But now they had little choice. The northern Greek frontier was long and thinly fortified. It ran along Albania, where things were proceeding satisfactorily; Yugoslavia, with whom the Greeks were on friendly terms; and Bulgaria, a country which the Greeks hated above all others. The Greeks had fortified the Bulgarian frontier with a belt called the Metaxas Line, and they were not disposed to give this up without a fight. But they were wide open to an attack coming down the Vardar River Valley from Yugoslavia toward Salonika.

The British recognized this, and their commander, General Sir Henry Maitland Wilson, took his troops north and put together a position known as the Aliakmon Line. This covered the Vardar Valley to his front, but left his flank wide open still to an attack from Yugoslavia through the Monastir Gap. There was little Wilson could do about this, except tell himself that the Germans would be slowed by the Yugoslavs, and when necessary, he would have time to fall back and cover the gap.

That was precisely what did not happen. The Germans operating out of Bulgaria hit the Greeks at the same time they hit the Yugoslavs, and within three days, by April 9, the Metaxas Line was swamped, Salonika was taken, and the German armor was pouring through the Monastir Gap. The British were pushed off the Aliakmon Line before they ever got dug in; it was the Dyle in Belgium all over again.

Wilson then withdrew to Mount Olympus, but got pushed off that as well. The Germans had air supremacy, and their armor moved through territory supposed to be unsuitable for tank operations. The British had few anti-aircraft guns, and their tank commanders were reduced to parking the tanks on as steep hills as they could manage, hoping in that way to elevate their guns enough to get a shot at German aircraft; the method served more as a vent for frustration than any practical purpose.

As the British columns were harried southward, the Greeks on the Albanian front got cut off. Reluctant to give up the few tangible gains they had so far made, they hung on too long and suddenly found their retreat cut. The western Greek armies surrendered on April 23.

By then the British were back across the Plain of Thessaly and almost to Athens. The Greek commander, General Papagos, told them they had beter get out or be forced to surrender, and Wilson's weary army, its air component outnumbered ten to one, hurried down into Peloponnesus; the Germans dropped paratroops at the isthmus of Corinth, but they cut off only some stragglers.

As usual, it became the navy's task to rescue the overextended army. Under heavy air attack, the destroyers and cruisers raced into the little southern Greek ports, loaded up, and raced out again. By the end of the month there were no British troops left at large in Greece. The campaign cost them about 12,000 men and substantial amounts of equipment, almost all the casualties coming during the evacuation when ships were sunk and machine-gunned unremittingly by the Luftwaffe.

As a footnote, the British then decided that even if they could not hold Greece, they could hold the island of Crete. Hitler was not too interested in it, but Hermann Goering convinced him that if Crete were taken, Luftwaffe units could break the Royal Navy's hold on the eastern Mediterranean. Hitler agreed, and the Germans decided to take Crete from the air, the first major independent airborne operation in history. The British left a scratch garrison of about 28,000 men, supported by 14,000 Greeks, under General Bernard Freyberg, the famous commander of the New Zealand Division. Unhappily, the troops were the usual mixed remnants of the earlier disaster on the mainland, and they lacked proper equipment and material.

The Germans opened their attacks on May 20 with paratroops and gliders on the main airfields. The British were ready for them, however, and for thirty-six hours it looked as if they might hold on. Vicious fighting swept back and forth across the key positions, and the Germans were in serious trouble. On the second afternoon they resorted to desperate measures and landed troops by transport on the Maleme airfield in the middle of fighting. It was costly, in both men and aircraft, but it turned the tide, and by nightfall the Germans had an airfield. The Royal Navy broke up attempts to bring troops over from the mainland on captured Greek shipping, but the Germans steadily reinforced by air, and on the 28th, Freyberg decided to evacuate. His haggard soldiers made their way through the mountains to ports on the south coast of the island, and again the navy came in under heavy air attack to pull them off. About 12,000 soldiers were left behind, but 18,000 were rescued. Against the heavy losses Admiral Cunningham reminded his staff that it took three years to build a new ship, three hundred to build a new tradition. It cost the navy heavy damage to two battleships, a carrier, six cruisers, and seven destroyers, and three more cruisers and six destroyers were sunk. Greece was lost, and both the British Army and the Royal Navy so weakened that their hold on the entire Middle East became tenuous indeed.

The decision that Greece had to be helped, and Crete held, was a political one, and the British paid a heavy price for it. Its wisdom has been hotly argued. In the end, Greece was not materially helped, and there are those who claim she would have been better off—or at least no worse off—without the British intervention. In the long run, the Greek campaign showed little more than that the British were willing to come to the aid of an ally; in that it may have demonstrated only the difference between Chamberlain and Churchill. In the end, not only was Greece lost, so was the chance of wrapping up the North African campaign relatively quickly.

In support of the intervention, some have argued that the campaign set back the German timetable for Russia. It is maintained that the Germans had planned to invade Russia by May 15, that because of Greece they had to postpone it until June 21, and that that five weeks at the end of the season allowed Russia to make it through to winter. This would be a satisfying justification for the tragedy of Greece if it were correct; unfortunately, it is not. The May 15 date for the German invasion of Russia was not the planned beginning of the campaign, but rather the operational readiness date. The Germans wanted to be ready by then, and to invade any time after that. To the extent that they were diverted at all from their timetable by the Balkan affair, it was the takeover of Yugoslavia rather than beating the Greeks that cost them time. Further, the real crux of the matter was not what happened in the Balkans, but what happened to the weather in central Europe. Spring was very late in 1941, and the ground was not sufficiently hard for the passage of armor until the third week in June. If anything caused a delay in the German invasion—and thereby saved Russia—it was not Greek or British or even Yugoslav courage, it was Polish mud.

As their campaign in the Balkans reached its sad conclusion, the British were also busy tidying up other areas of the Middle East. Indian, South African, and local troops had finally pulled themselves together sufficiently to take the offensive against the numerically superior but isolated Italian forces in East Africa. It took them about three months of occasionally heavy fighting, and a great deal of chasing around the desolate mountainous country, to run the Italians to earth. Many of the Italian native forces deserted, and by late May East Africa was secure. The Italians lost or surrendered nearly 300,000 troops; British casualties were about 1,200 in battle and 75,000 to local diseases, chiefly dysentery and malaria. Perhaps the prevalence of disease explains why Mussolini's troops were not that eager to fight for Mussolini's empire.

There was also the Levant. In April, a pro-German politician named Rashid Ali staged a coup d'état in Iraq. With their oil supply threatened, the British scraped up a few troops, moved in and took over. They then learned that the Germans were being supported by Vichy-French Syria, so in June they invaded that too. They sent along Free French units that had been contributed to the Middle East command by General de Gaulle, in the hope that Frenchmen would not fire on each other. The hope proved tragically wrong, and there were several bitter little fights before the Vichy troops finally capitulated.

None of these small successes was much to lay against the

losses of men, equipment, and prestige in Greece. Even worse, that loss soon had to be coupled with a disaster in the Western Desert.

Erwin Rommel has become something of a cult figure among World War II buffs. Whether he deserves to be is a matter of some disagreement, but the status of hero was accorded him by the British fairly early in the war. Much of this arose from the conditions of the war in the African desert. In peculiar ways it was a "pure" war, with both sides facing exactly the same problems of supply and local conditions, and with no civilians around to clutter up the battlefield. The armies went back and forth, back and forth, repetitiously over the same country, until it became familiar, and for all its harshness, almost friendly. It was a private war, fought, though that now seems either absurd or hopelessly romantic, without rancor, and both sides behaved with occasional touches of chivalry that at a later stage of the war would seem unthinkable. When they are not actively killing each other, soldiers have to live like other people, and it was not uncommon for patrols to share each others' waterholes and even gas or rations once in a while.

The desert war was in many senses a naval war, and that accounts in good measure for its repetitive quality. Equally hostile to both sides, the terrain provided nothing. Everything to sustain life and war had to be brought in from the outside world and then had to be carried forward to the fighting front. The crucial aspect of the campaign was logistics. How far forward could you place your main supply points, and how much of your matériel would you have to devote to supply and sustenance? The main Axis supply port was Tripoli, but they could possibly leapfrog forward to the ports of Benghazi or even Tobruk. To go any farther would bring them under the British air control reaching out from Alexandria, so as they approached the Egyptian frontier their supply line necessarily got longer and in itself consumed more material. The main British port was Alexandria, but they could conceivably jump forward to Tobruk or even Benghazi. To go any farther than that put them under the Axis air umbrella, so as they got out past Benghazi to the Gulf of Sirte and El Agheila, their logistics problem too became insurmountable. The reasonable area for the fighting thus fell in Cyrenaica, roughly between El Agheila at the bottom of the Gulf of Sirte and Sidi Barrani, just past the Egyptian frontier. Depending upon whose supplies were coming in more frequently, the war swung back and forth across Cyrenaica like a pendulum.

When Wavell had been ordered to break off his operations in the Western Desert and go to the aid of Greece, he left only a small force out in Cyrenaica. In March of 1941, Luftwaffe units operating out of Sicily neutralized the port of Benghazi. Meanwhile, Hitler had offered Mussolini two divisions for Africa, commanded by Rommel, who had won laurels in France. Rommel arrived in March with orders to stand strictly on the defensive, and not make trouble for his superiors. Late in the month he launched a heavy raid against the advanced British post at El Agheila; the British fell back. Always one to exploit success, Rommel pushed on. The British fell back again. Early in April he captured Benghazi, and kept on going. Most of the British armored brigade was wiped out, and General O'Connor was captured. By the second week in April, Rommel was all the way to the frontier, regaining everything the Italians had lost the winter before. The British in Egypt, with most of their combat troops in Greece, were thoroughly scared by this turn of events; ironically, so was the German high command, which was distressed to find its field commander so cavalierly disobeying his orders.

The British had managed to build up a perimeter around the Libyan port of Tobruk, and Rommel attacked that on April 10, but was repulsed; gradually strengthened, Tobruk withstood an eight months' siege and became a perpetual thorn in the Axis' side. Meanwhile, Wavell was pressed by Churchill to regain the lost ground. In June, the British launched an ill-prepared counteroffensive that broke down with heavy losses. The Germans brought their big anti-tank guns right up alongside their tanks and knocked out the British armor piecemeal. Wavell, forced into the attack by Churchill before he was ready, was relieved of command and sent off to India, replaced by General Sir Claude Auchinleck.

"The Auk," as he was fondly known to those who served under him, was now given the supplies and reinforcements that Wavell had lacked. Rommel, on the other hand, was starved as the Germans put everything they had into the attempt to finish off Russia before the winter. Late in November the British attacked. They managed to surprise the Germans and Italians, but Rommel got his reserves up quickly and there was hard fighting for two weeks, with small armored columns blundering into each other, before the Germans broke. The chase then went streaming away to the west. Early in December, the long siege of Tobruk was lifted, and by the end of the year, the Axis were all the way back at El Agheila again.

It was practically the only bright spot in the whole world that New Year's Eve. The Germans were deep in Russia, and the Japanese running rampant in Southeast Asia. Rommel immediately began preparing his reply; soon the disasters would be universal.

13. The Invasion of Russia

ADOLF HITLER'S DECISION to invade Soviet Russia brought the first of the two great neutrals into the war. In terms of its long-range consequences, still being worked out, Hitler's choice may well have been the single most important political decision of the twentieth century. From a generation after the fact, it seems incredible that he could have believed Germany was strong enough to defeat Russia as well as all her other enemies: Britain, the Commonwealth, and an increasingly hostile United States. Not only did he think he could do it, he very nearly succeeded.

Neither partner to the Russo-German Nonaggression Pact was wholly satisfied with it. The Russians were not quite as subservient as the Germans thought they should be, and the Germans were far more successful in the West than the Russians wanted them to be. Russian pressure on Finland and Rumania threatened German sources of raw materials. As early as the end of July in 1940, Hitler said that he really wanted to settle affairs with Russia. However, the Battle of Britain was just getting underway then, and Hitler realized the desirability of avoiding a winter campaign. He decided to wait until the spring. In August, the German high command began military planning, but just on a contingency basis. The Russian Foreign Minister, Vyascheslav Molotov, visited Hitler in Berlin in November of 1940. That was the famous occasion when Hitler told him Britain was finished, and Molotov replied, "Then whose bombers are those overhead, and why are we in this bomb shelter?" Hitler tried unsuccessfully to convince Russia that she should turn her attention eastward. The Russians and the Japanese had already engaged in heavy fighting in Mongolia, but rather than allow this to blow up into a full-scale war, both sides by 1940 were negotiating and damping down the flames. The Japanese felt betrayed by Germany when it signed the Nonaggression Pact, and the Russians did not want to be further involved in eastern Asia when things

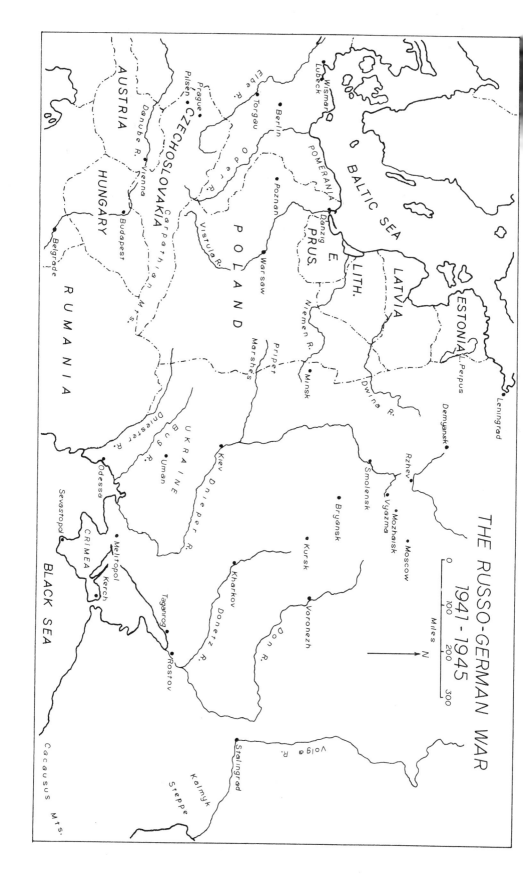

looked so chancy in Europe. Hitler's urgings therefore fell on deaf ears. Russia continued to entertain both Baltic and Balkan ambitions.

In December, Hitler issued Fuehrer Directive No. 21, in which he set out the basic lines of Operation Barbarossa, which was the code name for the destruction of Russia. Frederick Barbarossa had been the great medieval Emperor who had led the German contingent to the East on the Third Crusade. Apparently, Hitler forgot that he died there.

As it evolved through the winter, Barbarossa called for a two-stage operation. In the first, the main elements of the Russian forces would be encircled and destroyed as close up to the frontier as might be managed. The second phase was to be a rapid pursuit of whatever remnants were left, and the establishment of a line that ran roughly from Archangel in the north to the Caspian Sea in the south. The Russians were to be definitively finished off by the end of this stage. For the longer-range future, the area from the German stop line as far east as the Ural Mountains was to be dominated by the Luftwaffe. Any surviving Russians could live a precarious, hand-to-mouth existence east of the Urals, where they would be incapable of mounting any threat to the Greater Reich.

Three army groups were assigned to achieve this. Army Group North under General Ritter von Leeb was to attack toward Leningrad, Army Group Center under General von Bock was to head for Smolensk, and Army Group South under General von Rundstedt was to drive for Kiev. In discussion of the plan, Hitler's generals said they would prefer that the central drive be directed right on Moscow, some 200 miles farther on than Smolensk, but Hitler decided to go for the nearer objective, and keep his options open so that units might be diverted to the north or south as necessary. In this discussion lay the seeds of much future argument and recrimination. The plans were finalized, and troops and commanders allotted in January of 1941, everything to be ready by May 15.

Two things were especially remarkable about the concept. One was the magnitude of it; here were the Germans proposing to take on the largest state in the world, and telling themselves they would knock it out in eight to twelve weeks at the most. The Luftwaffe was a bit uncertain, bothered by the problems of distances, and the Foreign Office was opposed, not from any military qualms, but because von Ribbentrop was the architect of the Russo-German rapprochement. The army remained quite confident, however, that the Russians would give them little trouble.

The other surprising thing was that the Germans were operating in a military intelligence vacuum; they had little idea of how big the Russian Army was, or what its equipment was like, or how good it was. The Russians had showed poorly against Finland, and Hitler insisted on regarding them as *Untermenschen*, subhumans. For all their reputation for thoroughness, the Germans were remarkably casual about what they were likely to encounter in the Red Army.

Russia was indeed walking soft after the fall of France. Her military experts too had regarded the French Army as the greatest in the world, and the apparent ease with which Germany had overrun it had had a sobering effect on the Russian Army and government. Stalin did not back the Yugoslavs when they appealed for his support, and the Soviets generally took a restrained attitude on the whole Balkan question. They were busily tidying up in other areas, though, and did achieve, in April, a treaty of neutrality with Japan, a major clearing of their flanks that was of great help. The general failure of the Axis powers to concert their diplomatic and military moves was one of their chief shortcomings throughout the war. Stalin himself clung to the hope of peace; he dismissed the German concentration in Poland as merely spring maneuvers and troop rotation. Both the British and the United States governments warned Russia that an invasion was imminent, but Stalin regarded this as a western trick designed to embroil Russia with Germany. He resolutely refused to send out an alert to his armed forces. Not until the early morning hours of June 22 did a war warning go out to the Red Army; most units never got it.

Though both sides disposed of massive forces, neither one was in overwhelming strength. The Germans had about 188 divisions, including a weak fourteen of the Rumanian Army, and a good twenty of the Finnish Army, which called this the Continuation War. Nineteen of the German were armored, but the increase in Panzer divisions was achieved by taking the available tanks and thinning them out through more formations. It looked better on paper, but probably weakened the fighting capacity of the armor. At this time, German industry was operating at well below peak strength; in fact it was at almost peacetime levels of production. Germany had still not faced up to the likelihood of a long war. All of these divisions totaled just over 3,500,000 men, about a million of them non-Germans. There were 3,350 tanks, 7,200 guns, 600,000 vehicles, 625,000 horses—three times as many as Napoleon took to Russia with him—and about 2,500 aircraft of one type or another.

The Russian figures are largely estimates, as Russia has continually been shy of releasing material. They seem to have had about 200 divisions, of which 158 were in the west and facing the German attack; the rest were still in the Far East on guard against the Japanese; later on, the arrival of these battle-tried units was a major factor in stemming the German tide. They had forty-six motorized or armored brigades; at this time Russian armor was not organized on a divisional basis, and these brigades worked out at about twenty-two or -three divisions. All told there were probably 2,300,000 soldiers in European Russia. Of their roughly 6,000 aircraft, most types were obsolete or inferior to their German counterparts. On the other hand, they may have had as many as 10,000 tanks, the best of which came as a very rude surprise to the Panzers.

On the night of June 21-22, 1941, the entire German Army crouched in its jump-off positions, like a cat ready to spring. The Russians remained determinedly unconcerned, and German soldiers in position along the Neimen watched the last Russian trains chugging over the bridges, pathetically fulfilling Stalin's bargain with Hitler, bringing supplies of strategic materials to Germany. The Russians were concentrated in depth along the frontier, ripe for the deep envelopment tactics the Germans were going to employ, and completely unaware of the danger in which they lay. Later on, their retreat—for those who survived to make it—was billed as Stalin's plan to draw the invader deep into Russia and destroy him, but their initial dispositions belied this; they were caught absolutely flat-footed. Democratic governments are not the only ones taken by surprise.

At 0300 on the morning of the 22nd, the front opened up with a flash and a roar. Guns lighted the sky from the Baltic to the Black Sea; it was as if the sun were rising in the west. Tanks lurched across the frontier, and the Luftwaffe droned overhead, on its way to Russian airfields where the planes were lined up in neat rows, ready to be bombed and strafed in the first light of dawn. The Russian units on the frontier were swamped, tumbled out of their huts and holes before they even knew they were at war. As the sun climbed the eastern sky, the battle that was to be over in eight weeks, the battle that was to be the culmination of Adolf Hitler's life and the justification of his philosophy, the battle that ended in the ruins of Berlin some two hundred weeks later, began at last.

Wherever they could, the Russians fought. Fierce and tenacious fighters, expecting little mercy and giving none, units rallied and tried to pull themselves together. But they had not extensively fortified Poland or the Baltic states; the speed of the Germans was so great that there was little to rally around. In many places, the chain of command simply collapsed, and the Russian high command appeared completely stunned by the attack and its viciousness. While some formations held hard and either fought their way clear or faded into the forests to continue their battle, others milled helplessly about, bombed and strafed, then shelled by passing tanks, until they fell before the advancing infantry. Within the first few days it looked as if the Germans were well ahead of their own predictions, and the war would soon be won.

Army Group North, advancing toward Leningrad, had no trouble clearing the Baltic states; they reached the Dvina by the end of the month, and by the first week of July they were on native Russian soil. Only as they neared Leningrad itself did they begin to slow down, with their tanks and their supply system both overextended. Army Group Center made fantastic progress, surrounding and taking a quarter of a million prisoners west of Minsk. They rolled on toward Smolensk, where they took another quarter of a million. Time and again the Panzers slashed through weak Russian lines and encircled thousands of still-fighting soldiers, who then, cut off and with supplies dwindling, surrendered or were wiped out. Army Group South was slowed by rains and strong Russian resistance, but nonetheless made steady progress toward Kiev. The Russians were hampered by their lack of prepared positions, by their antiquated command structure and poor communications, and by their party apparatus, which put political commissars at all levels and made them co-commanders, so that military decisions were constantly being upstaged by political posturing. Within two weeks, the German high command believed that the first phase of its operation was complete, that the Russian Army was all but wiped out, and that the Wehrmacht was ready to enter the pursuit and mopping-up phase.

In late July and early August, the Germans threw the game away. The flaws in the plan, and indeed in the entire German system, began to show. On both the military and the political level, things started to go wrong.

Dictatorships not being subject to the sort of press and public criticism that other states are, Adolf Hitler had by now come to believe in his own infallibility; so far, every time his generals had said one thing and he had said another, he had been right. They had been wrong about the Rhineland, he had been right; they had been wrong about Czechoslovakia, he had been right; and so it had gone. It did not occur to him that these previous encounters had been matters of political intuition, and that now he was meddling in affairs of military professionalism. The generals wanted to drive on straight to Moscow; they assessed that Moscow was the heart of Russia and of communism, and that Stalin would be forced, want to or not, to commit everything he had to the defense of the city. Once he did so, they could destroy the remnants of the Red Army, and the war would be won.

Hitler waffled. He decided that the armor ought to be pulled out of Army Group Center, which could continue its advance solely with its infantry formations. This armor would be allocated to Army Group North, to help it get to Leningrad, and to Army Group South, to bolster its increasingly successful advance toward the Crimea and the industrial area of the Donets Basin. There was about a week of protest and argument by the generals, which only served to reinforce Hitler's conviction that he was right, and then the transfers began. The result was that the Russians gained badly needed breathing space—this became their equivalent of the "miracle of Dunkirk"—and the German armor, though it had some time to catch its breath, lost it again by running back and forth parallel to the front. The decision and the reorganization attendant upon it cost the Germans more time than the side-trip into the Balkans before the campaign began.

The other difficulty was that military considerations became subordinated to some of the more hare-brained Nazi ideological preconceptions. Communism was not popular in large parts of Russia; the vast, rich Ukraine, for example, had tried to break away from Russia after the Revolution and into the twenties. As an ally it would have provided an enormous amount of territory, resources, and population for Germany. When the first German Army units entered the Ukraine, they were greeted as liberators by the local inhabitants. Not since the Anschluss had German troops been treated to girls throwing flowers and men breaking out the wine bottles for them. Nazi ideology, however, dictated that Ukrainians were Slavs, and Slavs were subhuman, fit only to serve as slaves for the Master Race until they died off. Within weeks in the rear areas, the Jew-hunters and the political squads were at work, rounding up, exterminating, robbing, raping, and killing. Soon there were no more pretty girls by the side of the road throwing flowers; there were only bitter men throwing Molotov cocktails. The Master Race found that even it could not afford gratuitously to alienate several millions of people.

What Hitler casually threw away, Stalin picked up. In the early weeks of the war, the regime appealed to all Russians to help save communism, and to wage war to the utmost against the bourgeois Fascists who came to destroy the one true state. The response to this was limited, and as the crisis mounted, as the enemy neared the gates of Moscow and Leningrad, there was a change of emphasis. The political commissars disappeared from the army units, and communism was less stressed in the propaganda broadcasts. It was now the sacred soil that was under the boot of the oppressor; Holy Mother Russia was in danger, and peasants who were at best lukewarm to world communism had no doubts about the worth of Holy Mother Russia. Later, communism would come out of the shadows triumphant again, but in the dark hours of 1941 and 1942, Russians fought for the Motherland, and as they always had, they fought with a stolid tenacity that ultimately took its toll of German machines and men. Germany not only bled to death in Russia, she also made enemies of millions who might have bled for her.

While Hitler and his generals squabbled, the drive went on. All through a hot August the tanks and infantry plowed across the great plains. Army Group South now began to break clear and around Uman it surrounded twenty Russian divisions and wiped them out. By the end of August, it was closing up to the Dnieper River; Odessa was surrounded and cut off. A huge mass of Russians was surrounded at Kiev, and late in September more than half a million surrendered. Now, on the entire southern half of the front, it seemed as if the Germans faced little but the remnants of Russian units. In the north, Ritter von Leeb had closed in on Leningrad; coming up through the Baltic states the Germans were again hailed as liberators from the hated Bolsheviks. The Finns in the farther north returned to their old frontiers, and then stopped. And up at the very top of the map, General von Falkenhorst, hero of the Norwegian campaign, had made some progress toward Murmansk when increasingly bad country, terrible weather, and Hitler's decision that taking Murmansk was unnecessary brought him to a halt.

The machine was showing wear by now. The troops were dog-tired, and the vehicles were in need of overhaul. There were beginning to be partisan attacks on the supply lines. The Russians looked to be almost finished, yet it took most of the German attention for most of September to wipe out the Kiev pocket and to straighten out a line that ran roughly from Leningrad to the Crimea.

While this was going on, Hitler changed his mind once again. He decided his generals might have been right after all—not that he phrased it that way—and that the Germans should indeed go for Moscow. So he pulled the Panzers out of Army Group North and sent them south once more. Leningrad was to be blockaded and starved to death, rather than taken. And in the south, though he would let von Rundstedt continue to Rostov on the Don, he again withdrew armored units and sent them back to Army Group Center. Once more his tired tankers ran up and down behind the lines, wearing out treads and engines. Nonetheless, by the first of October—with a touch of fall in the air—they were ready to go again.

All these diversions and to-ings and fro-ings had given the Red armies in the center about six weeks' respite, and they had built up firm defenses on the direct route from Smolensk to Moscow. The Germans hit these with everything they had on the first of October, and within a week, the firm defenses were shattered beyond repair. More than 650,000 men were entrapped around Bryansk and Vyazma, and left to the infantry to clear up while the Panzers rolled on. With one eye on the calendar, the army commanders urged their tired soldiers forward.

On October 7, it began to rain. It rained for three weeks. Trucks, guns, and tanks went belly-deep and were hauled forward by brute strength. The troops shivered and tried without success to find dry spots somewhere in the sea of Russian mud. But though the advance was slowed, it was not stopped. Up in the north, von Leeb extended his lines and pushed east toward the areas from which Leningrad drew its supplies across Lake Ladoga. Von Rundstedt reached Taganrog, the last town before Rostov, and his troops broke into the Crimea. The Russians threw in what ought according to German intelligence to be the end of their reserves in front of Moscow, but Mozhaisk fell on October 20, and it was the last town before the capital. The German General Staff began planning the big, ultimate battle of encirclement and annihilation that would take Moscow, and wipe out Bolshevism and the Red Army once and for all. As an omen of success, the rain stopped at the end of the month.

Both sides were at their last gasp. Both knew that they had only a few more weeks to go. Winter would come soon; overnight the ground would freeze, and everything else along with it, and the snow would whistle across the steppes. If the Germans could not wrap up the campaign before that, they could not do it this year, maybe not at all. If the Russians could only last until General Winter came to the rescue, they might well live to fight again. Everything hinged on the next few weeks, perhaps even the next few days, for no one knew when winter would arrive.

By any reasonable numerical measure the Germans had won already. They were in possession of two-thirds of Russia's coal reserves, and three-quarters of her iron ore. Thirty-five million Russians were in occupied territory. Thousands of Russian tanks, guns, and aircraft had been destroyed or captured, and the Red Army had been all but wiped out. In fact, if there were really two and a half million Russian soldiers in European Russia in June, it had been wiped out almost twice already. It had even now been the greatest campaign in history; Napoleon's efforts were amateurish compared with this.

The Germans had paid a price for it. Their tanks were down to one-third strength, and their divisions at little more than half-strength. There were few supplies and no reserves. As the rains dwindled and the ground hardened in early November, the Wehrmacht gathered itself for the last spring; the way home led through Moscow.

Army Group Center jumped off on November 15. It made gains north and south of Moscow. But in front of Moscow the Russians replied with a desperate counteroffensive that held the central German forces on the defensive for two weeks. Day after day the Reds came down the road from Moscow to Mozhaisk, taking monstrous casualties, but pinning the Germans where they were. The Russians were now throwing better planes into the battle, and the Luftwaffe no longer quite had the sky to itself. Then there was another ill omen: a Russian armored brigade showed up riding British tanks; when Hitler invaded Russia, the great anti-Communist, Churchill, rose in the House of Commons to announce in his gravelly voice, "If Hitler were to invade Hell, I should find occasion to make a favorable reference to the Devil." Here now was the first fruit of that favorable reference. The new Russian T-34 tank was in action, better by far than anything the Germans possessed. Even more surprising, the Russians seemed to be finding new troops, this time battle-hardened divisions fresh from facing the Japanese in Siberia. The dead piled up along the Moscow road. Still the Wehrmacht ground forward, but at increasingly heavy cost.

The first real Russian success was in the south, where von Rundstedt's advanced units got cut off by a counterattack at Rostov. When von Rundstedt asked permission to pull out, Hitler sacked him; there was to be no retreat.

That was incidental; around Moscow the great decision was being taken. The Germans were still making progress on the first of December. They still hoped to close a great pincer around the city, the heart of both communism and the entire Russian military and communications network. To the north, they were even with the city; to the south, they were well past it, and turning northward. The trap was beginning to close. It looked as if victory were within their grasp.

The hand froze before it could clutch. Winter arrived early, the earliest and the hardest winter in half a century. The Germans had expected to win by now; they had summer uniforms, summer equipment, and lightweight oil in their guns and engines. Overnight the temperature dropped and kept on dropping; it finally clunked to the bottom at forty degrees below zero, with the wind blowing straight from the North Pole. A last spastic effort carried the German 3rd and 4th Panzer Groups to within twenty-five miles of Moscow. That was as close as they ever got; no free German would march through Red Square in this war, and precious few of those German prisoners who did would ever come home to tell about it. The German drive collapsed on the 5th; the Russians, incredibly, opened a counteroffensive on the 6th. The next day, the Japanese bombed Pearl Harbor.

14. Japan and the Road to Pearl Harbor

THE JAPANESE AIR STRIKE at the United States Pacific Fleet in its base at Pearl Harbor on the morning of Sunday, December 7, 1941, transformed the wars in Europe and Asia into one gigantic, global struggle. Ever since 1939, the United States had moved closer and closer to war, without getting fully involved in it. Except for ships on the North Atlantic convoy runs, Americans were still determinedly aloof; finally, it was not escalation of the U-boat war, but the quite uncoordinated activities of Japan in the Far East that catapulted America into the ranks of the belligerents. The ultimate irony of the whole situation is that Japan went to war not because she thought she could defeat the massive industrial power of America, but because she was already frustrated by her inability to defeat China.

Ever since the China Incident in 1937, the Japanese armies had moved from triumph to triumph on the Asian mainland. They overran large areas of northern China; they forced the Chinese government twice to move its capital. In 1938, they adopted a policy of military occupation of the coastal areas, and therefore of economic strangulation. Early in the year they took Tsingtao. The Chinese rallied, but after some checks in the spring the Japanese advance resumed. The old nineteenth-century treaty ports went one by one, Amoy, Suchow, and on down the coast. On the Manchurian border ebullient Japanese troops clashed with the Russians. In September, the nucleus of a puppet government was established, and in October, after months of ruthless and indiscriminate bombing, they took the city of Canton, upriver from British Hong Kong, and the greatest port of entry remaining to the Chinese; Hankow fell a few days later and the Nationalist government of

161

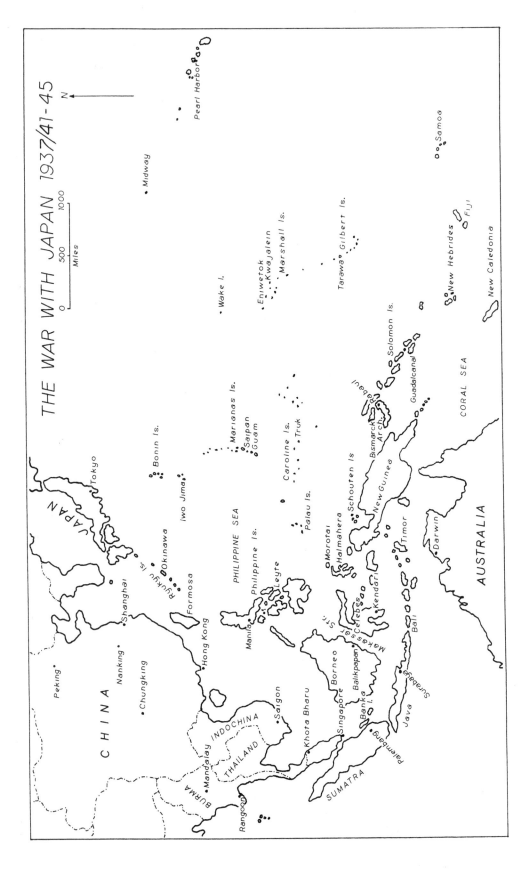

Generalissimo Chiang Kai-shek fled upstream to Chungking. The Western Powers protested ineffectually, but by early 1939, most of China's access to the outside world was gone. Only a few tenuous links were left; through Russia, up from the south through Burma, and up the Red River from French Indochina. As the imperial powers became more and more preoccupied with matters nearer home the Japanese turned to economic and political pressure designed to drive them completely out of China.

For all their victories, the Japanese could not, in Clausewitzian terms, win the war. The Chinese people had consolidated behind Chiang's government, and all parties, even to some extent the Communists, cooperated against the enemy. The ultimate aim of war is to break the opponent's will, so that he no longer offers opposition; the Chinese refused to be broken. The string of victories seemed endless, but the reservoir of Chinese seemed inexhaustible. Like others before her, Japan was wearing herself out killing Chinese.

The Japanese were also bothered by European affairs. As they were willing to take advantage of the early 1939 crises to enhance their own Asian position, so they felt threatened by the Russo-German Nonaggression Pact. This seemed to be encouraging Russia to turn east, and in fact was regarded in Japan as a considerable betrayal by Hitler. The army lost some of its political prestige through this, as it had been strongly pro-German. Through the last months of 1939, there was some diminution of the direct pressure on China as a result of events elsewhere.

The campaigns of 1940 and the fall of France changed all that. The all-too-apparent weakness of the democracies and their imperial holdings in the Far East encouraged the Japanese to increase their pressure once again. Though active fighting in China was burning down from mutual exhaustion, the economic stranglehold was tightened. The Imperial Navy too became increasingly interested. Hitherto, the Japanese Navy had had little to do with the China Incident; China had no navy of her own to speak of, and the sailors had been more or less bystanders to the soldiers' war. Now Japan's naval leaders cast increasingly covetous eyes southward. A move into Southeast Asia and the islands of the East Indies might achieve much. Occupation of Thailand, Burma, Malaya, French Indochina, and the Dutch East Indies would give Japan enormous opportunities for exploitation. There were tungsten, rubber, tin, rice, oil, quantities of things Japan needed and did not have; there was the chance to cut off all western access to

China. There was also the chance for the navy to make its contribution to Japan's bid for hegemony.

Even better, there was not too much in the way. French Indochina was garrisoned by a weak and isolated force getting orders, but not much else, from the Vichy government. The British were fully committed in Europe; they were running Malaya and Burma on a shoestring. The Dutch government after May of 1940 was in exile, operating out of rented space in London. Russia had no interests in the south, indeed would be delighted to see the Japanese turn in that direction. The only power still able to do anything about a Japanese advance into the "Southern Resources Area" was the United States. The Japanese planners assessed that if the Americans would not fight for Paris, they would not fight for Saigon.

For the next two years, therefore, from early 1940 to late 1941, the Japanese gradually expanded their influence and their control in the direction of Southeast Asia. Slowly the tension between them and the United States mounted.

In June of 1940, Japan demanded that the Vichy government grant it concessions in Indochina. Vichy agreed, being able to do little else, and Japanese warships immediately appeared in Indochinese ports. Troops entered the northern part of the country in September. Meanwhile, the British, under the same kind of pressure, agreed to close the Burma Road, the last line by which supplies could be pushed through to the Chinese Nationalists. In August, the British pulled their garrisons out of the international settlements in Shanghai and northern China. At home in Japan, a new cabinet under Premier Prince Konoye began to reorganize the government along militarist and totalitarian lines. Konoye's Minister of War was a man named Hideki Tojo. A soldier, former military attaché in Germany, he had been chief of the secret police in the Kwantung Army in Manchuria, then its chief of staff. He was known as a leading militarist, and his promotion into the cabinet meant a measurable escalation of militarist attitudes.

In September, Japan reaffirmed her relations with Germany and Italy; in spite of the Russian affair the community of interest among the dictators was too strong to be ignored, and they now signed a tripartite pact which pledged them to full support should any one of the three become involved with a country not yet at war. The Germans thought that clause applied to Russia; the Japanese thought it applied to the United States. By the end of the year Japan had allied wih Thailand, and in 1941 she concluded a neutrality pact with Russia, and then in July fully occupied the remainder of Indochina, leaving the Vichy French to lead a sort of half-life under Japanese domination. By then, too, Japan had decided to go to war with the United States.

As Japan became more overtly expansionist, the United States became more overtly disapproving. Each Japanese territorial initiative was matched by an American diplomatic or economic response. Gradually, the two countries moved onto a collision course. It was the Japanese rather than the Americans who faced, and accepted, the logical conclusion of this course of events.

With the Hitlerian domination of Europe, the United States moved more and more into the forefront as the protector of imperial interests in the western Pacific and east Asia. American protests went back right to the start of the China Incident, and had become so routine that they were completely discounted in Tokyo. The Americans had condemned the initial Japanese aggression against China, with no result. The sinking of the gunboat *Panay* in 1937 was explained away by Japan. In late 1938, Secretary of State Cordell Hull told Japan that the United States continued to regard the nine-power treaty of 1922, byproduct of the Washington Naval Conference, as the basis for all action with regard to China. The Japanese politely pigeonholed the American note.

Early in 1940, the 1911 trade treaty between the United States and Japan ran out. The American government refused to renew it and said it would trade with Japan only on a day-to-day basis; that bothered the Japanese; they were heavily dependent on American industrial imports. But the collapse of western Europe encouraged them to press on; the opportunities were too good to miss, and the Americans seemed disposed only to talk.

The American attitude was indeed equivocal; the man in an argument who wants to talk but not fight is at a disadvantage against the man who is willing to talk, but even more willing to fight. The Americans favored China, rightly but usually for the wrong reasons; because of missionary involvement of long standing, and because Madame Chiang Kai-shek was American-educated. The Americans saw Chiang as the defender of democracy in China, which he may have been, but not as the most successful of the warlords, which he also may have been. The American public, correctly if a bit simplistically, saw China as the good guys and Japan as the bad guys. The Japanese understood neither that

nor why American politicians had to take any account of it anyway. They met American moral protestations with suggestions that
the two powers cut up the east Asian pie between them. Figuratively as well as literally, the two sides spoke different languages.

In February of 1941, the Japanese sent Admiral Kichisaburo
Nomura to the United States to negotiate on existing disagreements,
but Nomura made little progress. Every time he and the American
State Department seemed about to reach a meeting of minds, the
Japanese forces in Asia took another leap forward, and the ne-
gotiations had to start all over again.

They began to near the flash point in July. When the Japanese
completed the occupation of French Indochina, the British and
American governments responded by freezing Japanese assets;
Roosevelt had to do it by presidential decree, but it was done
nevertheless. The Americans also began to look seriously to their
Far Eastern defenses, such as they were. General Douglas Mac-
Arthur, at the time head of the United States military mission to
the Philippines, which were being groomed for independence, was
named Commander-in-Chief Far East, and assumed command of
both the Philippine armed forces and the weak American garrisons
there. In August, President Roosevelt warned Nomura that Japanese aggression must cease. Japan was still sufficiently dependent
upon imports that this was in effect presenting her with an either-or
proposition. Either she could give up her ambitions completely,
including getting out of China, or she could go to war with the
United States in order to obtain the materials that would enable
her to fulfill those ambitions. The Americans somewhat naively
hoped the Japanese would choose the former; instead they chose
the latter.

In October, General Tojo replaced Prince Konoye as premier;
this was an indication that Japan was firmly committed to her forward policy. The next month both sides took what were effectively
final positions, with little common ground between them. The
Japanese proposed that the United States unfreeze their assets,
reopen trade, and that the two countries cooperate in the East
Indies, i.e., divide them. The United States countered with the suggestion that Japan get out of China and Indochina, and recognize
the Nationalist Chinese government, after which the United States
and Japan would sign a trade agreement. For practical purposes,
negotiations had collapsed by late November.

The Japanese had of course recognized that even before it
happened, and they had been planning war since at least mid-

summer. Once the Americans had frozen Japanese assets, the military planners had gone to work. Army and navy leaders sat down together and worked out their war plans. The most noted of their military men was an admiral, Isoroku Yamamoto, internationally known and widely respected in naval circles. Yamamoto spoke fluent English, having spent several tours of duty in the United States. He was an expert on oil and on naval aviation. He was also remarkably ambivalent in his attitudes toward the Americans, swinging between contempt for their casual approach to affairs—their navy was "a social organization of golfers and bridge players"—to undisguised admiration for their industrial power and their organizing ability. He was practically the only high-ranking Japanese officer to say that for Japan to fight the United States was folly. Having said that, he then went ahead and planned the war.

In 1894, an ostensibly weak Japan had gone to war with China. Launching a preemptive strike, she had seized what she wanted, and then negotiated peace. In 1904, she had done the same with Russia. Now she was going to do it with the United States. Yamamoto guaranteed his government six months of victory; after that it would be an open ball game. But the Japanese military planners said they had all the oil they needed to start their war. Six months would enable them to overrun the Southern Resources Area and the islands of the western Pacific. They could establish a defensive perimeter based on the East Indies and the mandated islands of the mid-Pacific. After that the Americans could do as they pleased. Let them bang their heads against the perimeter until they learned to accept the situation. Americans were not fighters, and eventually they would make a negotiated peace; Japan would have what she wanted. In all of the western Pacific, indeed from Panama all the way to Suez, there was really only one obstacle to Japanese aggrandizement: the United States Pacific Fleet.

Just how strong that was, or how strong the Allies were, was a matter of conjecture. On both the Japanese and the Allied side, force levels were fluctuating rapidly, and both sides had extensive commitments already.

The armed forces of the United States consisted of about a million and a half men, over a million of whom were but partially trained and poorly armed. The United States Army Air Force had 1,200 combat aircraft, including 150 four-engined bombers. The United States Navy possessed 347 warships, including seventeen battleships and seven aircraft carriers. A substantial amount of this American strength was committed to the Atlantic or to the defense of continental United States, however. It was more realistic to count what the Allies, the United States, Britain, Australia, the Netherlands East Indies government, had in the Pacific. There were about 350,000 troops, all of them poorly equipped and scattered here and there in penny-packet garrisons. There were about ninety warships, and less than a thousand aircraft, many of them obsolete. These forces were spread from the Indian frontier all the way to the American West Coast. The only major homogeneous unit was the Pacific Fleet. After the spring maneuvers of 1940, the fleet was based out of Pearl Harbor rather than its usual West Coast ports, as a means of putting pressure on Japan to behave. Late in 1941, the British too agreed to increase the pressure, and sent the battleship *Prince of Wales* and the battlecruiser *Repulse* out to Singapore. They wanted to send an aircraft carrier as well but could not spare one.

The Japanese had about 2,400,000 trained troops and a partly trained reserve of nearly three million more. They possessed 7,500 aircraft, including 2,675 first-line planes, most of them much better than the Allies'. They were producing another 425 each month and were training nearly 3,000 pilots a year. Their navy was first-class, and unlike the army, was not deeply involved in China. It had about 230 combat vessels. They had a relatively weak merchant marine of about six million tons. But above all, they enjoyed the inestimable advantages of interior strategic position, homogeneity of units, unity of command, and singlemindedness of war aims. They knew what they wanted and they knew what they had to do to get it. They began planning the destruction of the U. S. Pacific Fleet.

Phase one of the Japanese war plan called for them to operate in two areas simultaneously. What they wanted to obtain was control of the Southern Resources Area. They proposed therefore to move south from the home islands and Formosa, and attack the Philippines and Hong Kong; moving from China and Indochina they would hit British Malaya at the same time, and advance on Singapore. So far they were in line with American strategic thinking. Through the prewar years the U. S. Navy, sure that someday it would have to fight Japan, had produced a series of war plans. All of these were seriously compromised by the war in Europe and the high-level decision that Germany was the enemy with first priority. Faced with that, United States planners were forced to adopt a defensive stance in the western Pacific. When war began, the Americans, British, and to a lesser extent the Dutch, would hold on as long as they could against the southern Japanese advance. If necessary they would fall back on the so-called Malay Barrier— Malaya and the East Indies—which they would hold. While this operation was in effect, the Pacific Fleet would come to the rescue, the Japanese would be defeated, and the Allies would move north again, quite possibly relieving the Philippines before they even fell. It all depended upon how fast the Pacific Fleet mobilized and got out to the islands, and how soon they would be able to beat the Japanese in an open fight.

The Japanese first phase offensive contained another area of operations, however. As early as January of 1941, Admiral Yamamoto had suggested that if Japan were to go to war with the United States, she might as well do it in a big way, and he therefore proposed that she launch her war by a strike at the Pacific Fleet in its home base at Pearl Harbor. The Japanese military leaders were thoroughly scared by this and regarded it as far too risky even to contemplate. Yamamoto contemplated it anyway and began training his aircrews and his officers for the attack. Not until October did he get the green light, and by then his forces were fully ready.

In November, the heart of the striking force, six aircraft carriers under Admiral Chuichi Nagumo, gathered in the fog-bound Kuriles Islands north of Japan. Choosing a northern approach route that would keep them clear of foreign ships and American patrol planes, they sailed late in November. The Japanese government took its final decision on December 2, and that evening sent out its message: "Climb Mount Niitaka." By then the carrier striking force was well on the way to Pearl Harbor.

All went well. They crossed the International Date Line about halfway between Midway, the farthest outpost of the Hawaiian chain, and the Aleutians, and turned southeast on the 5th. At dark on the 6th, course was changed again, due south. Dawn on the 7th put them some two hundred miles north of the island of Oahu; as far as they could tell, they were completely undetected. A radio station in Honolulu promised a clear and warm day, perfect island weather.

The Americans knew something was going to happen. They had broken several of the Japanese codes; they knew that Admiral Nomura in Washington had been instructed to burn his code books and present a note to the United States government precisely at 1:00 P.M. on the 7th. They even knew what the message said, but its significance, as well as that of the time—it would be 0730 in

Hawaii—was not especially noted. The British had spotted troop transports and fleet units in the Gulf of Siam, and all signs pointed to an attack on Malaya.

The American armed forces had indeed sent out an alert which was billed as a "war warning," but they thought again that it applied more to the Far East than anywhere else. There was some consideration of a possible attack on the Panama Canal. Hawaii, however, was well prepared, and the chief danger anticipated there was sabotage. The military and air force garrisons responded to this threat by lining up all their planes and equipment in neat rows so they could be more easily guarded.

Most of the fleet was in port for the weekend. The navy was involved in a heavy training schedule, and Saturday night was time for some relaxation. The three aircraft carriers of the Pacific Fleet were at sea, one on the West Coast, two delivering aircraft to mid-Pacific garrisons. One battleship, *Colorado*, was in the States having an overhaul. The remaining eight were at Pearl, seven lined up along Battleship Row, just off the naval airfield on Ford Island.

The fates conspired against the United States that morning. The Japanese first attack wave was picked up on a vintage radar set, but there was a flight of new bombers due in from the West Coast. Even though these planes were coming from the wrong direction, no one reacted.

Not until the first wave struck, and the first bomb dropped, at 0755, did the Americans realize they were in a war. There were about 190 planes: fighters, dive-bombers, high-level bombers, and torpedo planes. The pilots of the latter had been especially trained and equipped to make their attacks in the shallow waters of Pearl Harbor. While the fighters attacked the air stations around the island, the rest went for the fleet. Within minutes, Battleship Row was a shambles: *Oklahoma* capsized, *West Virginia* was hit by torpedoes; counterflooding allowed her to settle on the bottom, her guns still firing. *California* too lodged on the mud. *Nevada* alone, at the inboard end of the row, got underway, but was badly hit and beached before she could clear the harbor. *Arizona* took several torpedo and bomb hits, including one in her forward magazine; surrounded by burning oil she sank with more than a thousand of her crew trapped inside.

The first Japanese attack cost them only nine planes. The second wave came in after a lapse of about twenty minutes, and was hit by everything the Americans could throw at them; it was not much, but it brought down another twenty planes, and several more had to be written off after they got back to their carriers.

In an hour the United States forces lost about 150 planes, and another hundred damaged. Every battleship at Pearl was damaged, though only two, *Oklahoma* and *Arizona*, were total losses. Several smaller vessels were sunk or damaged. There were 4,575 casualties. Perhaps more important than what the Japanese hit was what they missed. The carriers were at sea, and they would prove the queen of naval warfare. The repair facilities were not seriously damaged, and Pearl remained a usable base; most of the fuel storage was intact.

Still, Yamamoto's six months of victory had gotten off to a tremendous start. Pearl Harbor was one of the greatest surprise attacks of all time, a fair rival to Hitler's invasion of Russia. The Japanese could unroll the map of conquest, with very little to challenge them from San Francisco all the way to Suez. In the first two hours of hostilities they had swept the board almost clean. But in London, Winston Churchill's first thought was "We have won the war!" and he later wrote that that night he went to bed and slept "the sleep of the saved and the thankful." All reservations cast aside by the galvanic shock of Pearl Harbor, the United States was in at last.

PART III: "THE HOUR WHEN EARTH'S FOUNDATIONS FLED. . . ."

15. Allied Conferences and Plans

THE COALITION THAT FOUGHT the Second World War was probably the most successful in history. Even taking into account the dissensions and difficulties of working together, on which undue stress has been placed by the memoir-writers, the coalition achieved its ends, and did so with an economy of effort that defies ready comparison. It is, however, in the nature of coalitions to be uneasy. Nations go to war for different reasons, against different enemies, they have different national backgrounds and attitudes, and all of these become particularly apparent at two times: when coalitions near defeat, and when they near victory.

The primary aim of a state, by definition, is its own self-preservation. Though a parent may sacrifice himself for his child, or a friend for his comrades, the nature of the political entity does not lead it to this kind of self-abnegation. As Palmerston once said in a moment of unwonted candor, "Britain has no eternal friends or eternal enemies, Britain has only eternal interests." As a coalition nears defeat, the interests of the individual members assume paramount importance. The breakdown is invariably accompanied by recrimination and charges that the other partners failed to fulfill their obligations. Thus in 1940, when the strain of the war became too great for the Belgian government to sustain it, Belgium signed an armistice. Her allies accused her of gross betrayal. Less than a month later, the French were negotiating their armistice in their turn, they and the British each feeling let down by the other. The chief aim of the French government was that the French state should survive, not that France should sacrifice herself for Great Britain. Looking back, one can say the French politicians made the wrong choice, but that is the luxury of hindsight by those who were not faced with the agonizing necessity of decision.

Ironically, victorious coalitions tend to break up in the same kind of distrust and divergence as do defeated ones. Military victory is the sine qua non of survival, but it is not an end in itself; it is but the means to some larger political end, defined and perceived by the state and its leaders. Each state will have different ultimate aims, arising out of a variety of factors—historical, geographical, and ideological. As the military crisis is faced and surmounted, the differing political ends become more apparent, and the coalition, the more successful it waxes militarily, becomes shakier politically. As the potential postwar situation is partially predetermined by who takes what where, and what it costs him to take it, the political problems become increasingly acute, and few wartime coalitions long survive the war. In 1814, the about-to-be-victorious Allies signed a twenty-year alliance against France. A year later, half of them were threatening to go to war with the other half, and both sides were courting French support. In 1914-18, the Western Allies promised Russia things that they had spent a century denying her, just to keep her in the war. Yet by 1918 they were mounting massive military interventions in Russia, while Britain and the United States were refusing to ally with France. World War II, both in spite of and because of the aims for which it was fought, went the same way.

The major determinants of the course of action pursued by any given state depend upon the historical circumstances of the state, its situation at successive points in the conflict, the strength and predilections of its leaders, and their war aims, either announced or assumed. As a means of understanding why World War II went the way it did, and why so many of the postwar decisions were taken almost by default, it is worthwhile examining the three major allies on these points.

Nations are molded by their geography and by their history. Time, and its expression through historical development, is a fourth dimension for the individual and the group. In Great Britain, the most important event of recent history was World War I, and her strategy and her attitudes in World War II were extensively conditioned by the experience of the First World War. This was true at all levels of command and leadership. During the third battle of Cassino, as the New Zealanders were fighting through the ruins of the town, General Alexander asked if one more push would win; the corps commander, General Freyberg, replied with one evocative word: "Passchendaele." There was no British soldier alive who, faced with recollections of the horror of Flanders in World War I, would continue a run-down assault, and Alexander accordingly called off his battle.

This experience was a national, not an individual one, and it is possible to trace it throughout the British handling of the Second World War. Compared to the continental powers, Britain had always been weak in manpower, but strong in geography. She had traditionally fought her wars at sea, and used the profits therefrom to subsidize continental allies against her enemies. William of Orange had started the fashion by taking over England not because he loved the British constitution, but because he wanted British gold to fight his lifelong enemy, Louis XIV. The pattern he set had been followed for two and a half centuries. It was British money that raised coalition after coalition against Napoleon, and eventually brought him down. The British always made their military contribution too—Marlborough in the Low Countries, Wellington in the Peninsula—but they usually kept it secondary; they lacked the manpower to do more than that.

In World War I, this policy had gone awry. Germany proved so strong that she nearly defeated both Russia and France, and the British found themselves dragged increasingly into a large-scale land commitment in Flanders and northern France. It ended up nearly ruining her, and in World War II a major concern of her leaders was that they did not have the manpower that the United States or Russia had. Much had been made of the British preference for a peripheral strategy, nibbling around the edges as it were, but once France went out and Mussolini came in, Great Britain, as we have already seen, had little choice.

By the middle years of the war, Britain was relatively weak in men and resources, given the massive strength of Russia, and the even more massive potential of the United States. She made up for this by mobilizing far more fully than the United States did, and by being much more sophisticated militarily than the Russian war machine ever became. Through 1942 and 1943, Britain dominated the wartime coalition through her seniority, her experience, and her expertise. Unfortunately for her, her relative strength declined as the war went on. In 1944 and 1945, as Russia survived and turned the corner to victory, and as the full power of the United States was mobilized, Britain and British interests became less important to the conduct of the war. The ultimate effect of this was to go far toward robbing Britain of the fruits of victory that she paid such a high price to win.

Both Britain's past and present were magnificently summed up in Winston Churchill. It is little disservice to Roosevelt, and certainly none to Stalin, to say that Churchill was probably the one indispensable leader among the Allied Powers. The product of a classical education and an already long career in public life and affairs, he was pre-eminently the right man at the right time. His leadership and oratory rallied Britain when there was precious little else for her to rally behind, and through the early years of the war he dominated the Allies as no one else could have done. Stalin remained a Russian rather than a world figure, and Roosevelt the leader of a neutral or at best still very junior partner. As the war went on, however, Churchill found himself outpaced by the growing strength of his allies. If he did not perceive the "Red menace" as fully and as early as he later said he did, he nevertheless found himself increasingly frustrated, through 1944 and into 1945, by the Russian and the American insistence on their own policies. Ultimately, just as the war was ending, his leadership was repudiated by his own war-weary people; even the British could not sustain indefinitely the heroic heights to which he aspired.

His war aims and those of his country were fairly straightforward: to put down Germany, to restore a balance of power in which the British were conveniently on the top of the heap, and to preserve the British Empire and Commonwealth, in which Churchill was a fervent believer. Doing that would also preserve the moral and ethical systems which Churchill saw negated in Nazi Germany and Hitlerism and which he devoutly believed were embodied in Britain and her empire. He was, perhaps, the product of an old world of politics and diplomacy, but he represented the best of that old world.

The United States too was conditioned by its immediate past history, and by its experience in the Great War. That experience, however, was far different from Britain's. The Americans had arrived late and faced a German Army that was on its last legs. Though experience of combat in World War I was one of the keys to command in World War II, American soldiers had fought in numbers only when the war had opened up again in 1918. None of them had the soul-destroying, bone-wearying years in the trenches of the British or the French. Europeans tend to stereotype Americans as big, brash, ebullient, outspoken, and energetic. As with most stereotypes, there is some truth in it, and many Americans saw themselves the same way. In 1918, American divisions were twice the size of British or French ones, and General Pershing fondly remarked of his 1st Division that it was "the best damned division in any army in the world!" He was quite possibly right, but if so, it was because no American unit suffered the more than 3,000-percent casualties that some British regiments had in the course of the war. To many Americans then, even to professional military men with experience of European warfare, the way to fight the war was to get to Europe and beat up the Germans, and then as quickly as possible get on and finish off the Japanese who, after all, were the ones to attack the United States. With a quite different historical experience of World War I from that of the British, Americans developed a quite different view of how World War II ought to be fought.

That divergence of view was compounded by their diametrically opposite situations as the years went on. British strength peaked in the middle years of the war, while the Americans were just beginning to get organized. The long grace period from 1939 to the end of 1941 gave the United States time to gear up its industry, and the demands first of Cash and Carry and then of Lend-Lease provided a shot in the arm to American business, but it takes a long time to design a successful tank or airplane, or build a battleship, and the new materials of war were just beginning to come on the line by the time of Pearl Harbor. The United States armed forces were weak in 1942, and given their worldwide demands, were operating on a shoestring even in 1943.

In the long run, the American economy had much more disposable fat than did the British or Russian or German, however, and as American production finally hit its stride, the United States became a veritable cornucopia of the resources for war. American fighting men had a wealth of equipment and impedimenta that astounded the British, as the British themselves astounded some of the east European refugees, such as the Polish troops who fought in the 8th Army.

So great indeed was the strength of the United States that the country never was completely mobilized for war. Industry was neither as fully controlled nor directed as in Britain, labor was not regulated to the extent it was in other countries, and individual freedoms were much less restricted in America than elsewhere. It is quite probable that had the war lasted another year or so government control would have gone further, but in the event it proved unnecessary. At full production, the American economy could produce and equip huge armed forces, its own as well as those of much of the rest of the world, and still generate some surplus for home consumption.

Nor did American military power ever reach full strength. Ironically, in one of the richest and most populous countries of the world, the actual burden of combat was borne by a relatively small percentage, not just of the population, but even of the armed forces. In 1941, the U. S. Army estimated that global war would require it to produce a total of 213 combat divisions. The army never came near it. The demands of navy, air force, support services, and domestic war industry prevented the ground forces from mobilizing more than ninety-one divisions in the course of the war. Germany mobilized 300, Russia about 400, and even Japan produced more than the United States did. On the United States' side, the hard business of doing the real fighting in the war was done by a surprisingly small number of men.

With all this, the Americans still, toward the end of the war, surpassed the waning strength of Great Britain, and usurped her dominance of the western alliance. As late as mid-1944, there were more British troops than American fighting in Europe, but by the end of that year, it was the Americans, and American views of what the end of the war should bring, that were taking over.

There has been a great deal of argument over American leadership and war aims, and one of the earliest commentators on them, the Australian writer Chester Wilmot, set the stage by charging that American naivete and shortsightedness gave away the victory. Wilmot in *The Struggle for Europe* accused the Americans of being babes in the wilderness, and of allowing Stalin and the Russians to carry off all the prizes of the war. The argument does not seem wholly tenable a generation later; much of what Wilmot said the Americans gave away now looks like things that the Russians had already taken anyway, and because of the dictates of strategic geography could hardly have been prevented from taking.

Even setting all that aside, two things told against American handling of the political aims of the later part of the war. One was the fact that Franklin Roosevelt was pre-eminently a domestic politician; in spite of his favoring the Allies before the United States became a belligerent, in spite of his growing interventionism, he still thought largely in American terms, and appeared somewhat simplistic in his view of world affairs. He believed imperialism was undesirable and therefore was not disposed to spend any effort on recreating the British Empire. He may have been right, but he also believed the Russians at bottom were not much different from the Americans, and that they could be dealt with. His background was such that he had little in common with Joseph Stalin.

The second fact was that as the United States assumed increasing leadership, Roosevelt was a dying man. He had for many years waged an exhausting and courageous battle against polio, but by 1944 his illness and the incredibly heavy burden of office were perceptibly wearing him out. In few other states of the world would a political leader in his condition have continued to function as actively as Roosevelt did, and he compounded the difficulty by confiding very little in his potential successor after 1944, Vice-President Harry S Truman.

One of Roosevelt's problems was that of producing credible, acceptable war aims. The United States was not in acute danger of invasion—though after Pearl Harbor it thought it was. The enemy was distant, and until Pearl Harbor most Americans had a hard time believing that the Japanese, or even the Germans, were a real threat to them. After December 7, most Americans wanted to jump in with both feet and beat up the Japanese, and then go on to the Germans. As noted earlier, the government had already decided that Germany should be defeated first, and then Japan. Though this was not a major problem, it was certainly a minor complication to American strategy. For overall war aims, however, Americans, dealing with a distant war, were forced to generalize what they wanted to achieve. It was not enough to defeat Germany and Japan militarily, they must be destroyed so they could never again unleash the kind of evil they and their war represented. The Four Freedoms and the Atlantic Charter became universalized goals. Given the imperfections of humanity, they may even be called mythologized goals, and to the extent that they were incapable of achievement, by military means or any other, Americans were to be disappointed in their war aims. Not because they did not win— they unarguably won—but because their aims were not wholly realizable.

Especially for an ally of Stalinist Russia.

Unlike the Americans, insulated with a large ocean to either side of them, the Russians are a people often invaded. One of the dominant themes of Russian history is fear: the fear of the outsider, the invader, the conqueror—or the would-be conqueror, for though many have tried, few have succeeded. The Tartars did from the east, and the Vikings from the north, but in modern times a whole series of westerners has failed to overwhelm Russia. Charles the Great of Sweden, Napoleon, Wilhelmine Germany, assorted Poles, all have come to grief in the vastness of the Russian plain. All they left in Russia were their bones, their military reputations, and a deep residue of distrust for the West among the Russian people and leaders.

When to this historical relationship is added the ideological problems of communism, and its outcast status among the nations of the world, the basis of Russian fear becomes readily obvious. No matter that every challenge from the West had ultimately resulted in a westward extension of Russian territory and influence; such extensions were achieved only at the cost of untold suffering and misery, and over the centuries the Russians developed a love-hate relation with western Europe, wanting the material and political advantages enjoyed by the West, fearing western power and aggressiveness.

As a country of immense potential, much of it still latent in the 1940's, Russia's role in the war fluctuated wildly. She did her best to avoid it as long as she could. When finally invaded, she came within a few miles or a few days of total disaster. Until the end of 1942, it looked as though she might still succumb. While the danger was pressing, the Russians were comfortable allies, grateful for the help the Western Powers could or would accord them. From 1943 on, as Russia's situation improved, her demands increased. She claimed, truthfully enough, that she was bearing the brunt of the fighting. Without a great navy, she discounted British efforts at sea; without a strategic air force, she paid little account to the western Allied air offensive. The Russians chose to count as meaningful only what they had most of, soldiers on the ground fighting the Germans. More difficult allies as they were more successful, the Russians fought the war on their own terms; they paid an immense price for their victory, but in the end they got most of what they wanted.

At least part of that was the result of the fact that Joseph Stalin was unhampered by the limitations that beset Churchill or Roosevelt. There was no domestic opposition in Russia; it had all been liquidated in the purges before the war. Stalin was not only a ruthless, crafty leader—they all were, in their ways—he was also able to set his own goals and follow them or abandon them as the needs of the moment dictated. He knew what he wanted, and as the war progressed, Russia was in a position to achieve his aims.

Those were, in their simplest sense, to gain as great a buffer zone as possible between Russia and her potential enemies. He wanted to ruin both Germany and Japan as possible rivals; happily the United States was going to ruin Japan, and Russia, if she played her cards right, would reap the benefits while doing little of the work. She could concentrate her efforts on Germany, and on creating a Russian-controlled ring of satellites, Communist-run, in central Europe. An age-old problem of any state is to find a defensible frontier. Russia is relatively defensible from the Neimen, better from the Oder, and in fantastic shape if her frontier is on the Elbe. This view, too, is oversimplistic, but that is part of its attraction. Stalin's war aims were not generalized or universalized; he was fighting for the security and power of Russia; "freedom from fear" did not mean quite the same thing to him as it did to Roosevelt.

These three states essentially decided the shape of the postwar world. The only other claimants for great-power status were China and France, and both were allowed into the councils of the Allies purely on sufferance. Chiang Kai-shek lacked the world view or world status of Churchill, Roosevelt, and Stalin; for most of the latter part of the war China was a poor relation kept alive by Allied help and goodwill. To say that is to underestimate her contribution to the war effort in tying up the bulk of the Japanese Army, but by the accidents of geography and strategy that is the way the war developed.

The other great-power aspirant, France, was kept afloat less by Charles de Gaulle than by Churchill's backing of him. De Gaulle was the prickliest of allies, Roosevelt thoroughly disliked and distrusted him and did his best to cut him off, and even his champion, Churchill, once grumbled that the heaviest cross he had to bear was the Cross of Lorraine. The French had a contribution to make, both as an occupied people and as a military force working from North Africa, but their whole position was an immensely complicated one, and only after a series of Byzantine convolutions did they reappear as an almost-great power.

Throughout the war the Allied leaders met at a series of conferences and meetings, sometimes all three of them, sometimes only two, occasionally with their foreign ministers and representatives of the top leadership. In the early stages of American participation in the war, these meetings were mostly concerned with organization and strategic planning; as the war proceeded, the leaders turned their attention increasingly to postwar matters.

In late December of 1941, just two weeks after Pearl Harbor, a British-American meeting convened in Washington. This was known as the Arcadia Conference. The Anglo-Americans reaffirmed the decision taken at Placentia Bay to defeat Germany first. They decided on air bombardment of Germany through 1942, and the clearing of the North African coast if at all possible. They set up the Combined Chiefs of Staff, consisting of the British Imperial General Staff, headed by General Sir Alan Brooke, and the American organization of the Joint Chiefs of Staff, headed by General George C. Marshall. They also agreed to invade continental Europe in 1943, though even at this first conference, the British preference for peripheral operations came into conflict with the American desire to invade Fortress Europe at the first possible moment.

This American desire for what the British considered a premature invasion led to a second conference in April. General Marshall and President Roosevelt's personal advisor, Harry Hopkins, went to London; there the Allies agreed to a large buildup of American forces in Britain as a preliminary to the invasion, at that point to be code-named Operation Bolero-Roundup. Even while agreeing to the operation, however, the British stressed their desire to go elsewhere, and this Bolero Conference eventually led to the later decision to invade French North Africa in the fall of 1942.

The next major Allied meeting came at Casablanca in January of 1943. By that time North Africa was all but liberated, but several new problems had arisen. Chief among them was what to do about the French, and much of the behind-the-scenes maneuvering at Casablanca was a jockeying for position between Churchill's protégé, de Gaulle, and Roosevelt's candidate, General Giraud. The latter, last seen leading his army into Holland in May of 1940, had been imprisoned by the Germans, had escaped, emerged as a potential alternative to Vichy France, and then been picked up by the Americans. Roosevelt's dislike of de Gaulle stemmed largely from the Frenchman's imperiousness. Giraud, who had the attraction of not being well known to Roosevelt, proved in the event even more imperious, and even further divorced from the reality of war and politics as they were in 1943. After a short reappearance in the limelight, he was discreetly shunted into the background and eventually upstaged by de Gaulle, and dropped by the Americans.

Roosevelt and Churchill also agreed to name an American to the Supreme Command in the Mediterranean theater, and the nod went to General Dwight D. Eisenhower, a fast-rising regular soldier who had no battle experience, but who proved to be a wonder-worker at resolving problems among what George Bernard Shaw called "two countries separated by the bond of a common language." They further decided on the invasion of Sicily, as a continuation of operations in the Mediterranean. Finally, in a subsequently hotly debated political move, Roosevelt broached the idea of "unconditional surrender"—the enemy powers were not to be allowed to surrender on terms, but must, to end the war, throw themselves completely on the mercy of the Allies. There had been discussion of this among the Americans, and Roosevelt had mentioned it to Churchill, though the two had not agreed upon it formally. Roosevelt therefore sprung it on a press conference, and the somewhat surprised Churchill quickly backed it.

The idea has aroused considerable argument, because some writers maintain it lengthened the war. Cutting the ground from under domestic opposition to Hitler, Mussolini, and their regimes, it is possible that unconditional surrender encouraged the Axis to fight on to the bitter end. In part, the announcement was a response to particular pressures of the moment. Churchill and Roosevelt had been accused of making back-room deals with some of the Vichy French leaders, and in the immediate political sense, their enunciation of unconditional surrender policies was designed to show the western peoples that their leaders were super-clean. In a larger sense, however, the idea was inherent in the Rooseveltian and Churchillian view of the war. If it was indeed a struggle between good and evil, then evil must be completely expunged, and good could not taint itself by treating with evil. It could not even deal with those fellow-travelers of evil who had themselves become partially infected by association. From that viewpoint unconditional surrender was but the logically inescapable conclusion to the Allies' idealized war aims. Clausewitz said war is an extension of politics. The Allied leaders took war beyond politics and made it a crusade.

From the heights of Casablanca the planners returned to the more mundane levels of strategic discussion. In May of 1943, there was a Trident Conference in Washington. The British and Americans agreed to go from Sicily to Italy, a British desire, and set a firm date for the cross-Channel invasion, May 1, 1944, an American desire. As the price for Italy, the British agreed that the forces buildup would henceforth be concentrated not in the Mediterranean but in England. This put the British in a dilemma; with one hand they gained a decision to continue in the Mediterranean; with the other they gave away the resources that would have given point to that decision. The whole Mediterranean adventure was henceforth to be dogged by this unresolved conflict.

In August, the Allies met at Quebec City in the Quadrant Conference. They reaffirmed their intention to invade across the Channel, in spite of a Churchillian rear-guard action in support of the Mediterranean. At the insistence of the Americans, the British also conceded an upgrading of the Pacific offensives against Japan and a greater allocation of resources to that area.

Roosevelt and Churchill finally met with Stalin for the first time at Tehran in November. There was a wide-ranging discussion of military matters, in which Stalin laid great emphasis on what Russia was accomplishing, and asked repeatedly about the invasion of France. Roosevelt responded by stressing how much the Americans were committing both to the Pacific and to the cross-Channel scheme. Churchill was the widest-ranging of the three, and while stressing that Britain too looked forward to the invasion, he continued to explore Mediterranean and Balkan possibilities. Not only had he the most imaginative view of the three, he was also the most strategically opportunistic. Their ultimate agreement was on the invasion of France and a Russian offensive timed to support it by distracting the Germans.

They also began, hesitantly, to look toward the postwar world. It was agreed there should be some form of supra-national organization, but its outline was still dim. Roosevelt proposed that it should contain a subgroup of "Four Policemen": Britain, the United States, Russia, and China. Stalin thought China would not make the grade and that the idea would not be too welcome to the rest of the world anyway. He was more definite about what Russia wanted—a major sphere of influence in central Europe, and some way to keep Germany down in the future. This boded ill for the future of the former central European states, but Churchill seemed at this time no more than mildly concerned over that, and Roosevelt was not concerned at all. Everything was too far in the future to worry yet, certainly too far off to upset the solidarity of the alliance.

Ironically, by the time the Big Three met again, at Yalta in February of 1945, and finally at Potsdam in the ruins of Germany in July of that year, it was too late to worry about the future.

The Western Powers, represented at Yalta by Churchill and a dying Roosevelt and at Potsdam by their replacements, Clement Attlee and Harry Truman, saw Europe already rearranged in Stalinist terms. All the talk in the world was not going to move Russian troops out of Poland by then. Throughout the whole war, it was always either too early or too late for political deals and decisions. It was as if the ghost of Bismarck had risen from the past to echo, "The great decisions of our times will not be decided by speeches . . . they will be decided by Blood and Iron." It was still the time of blood and iron.

16. Occupied Europe

WHILE THE AVENGING FATES gathered, the Germans continued to build the Thousand-Year Reich. At its greatest extent the German empire extended from the North Cape of Norway to the Peloponnesus, and from the Pyrénées to the Caucasus Mountains. This included Germany's allies and satellites, but for practical purposes they might as well have been conquered territories, for their treatment was only marginally better than that accorded the victims of outright military aggression. German relationships with all the states and territories under their domination varied, both from one state to another, and from time to time as the war progressed. Yet through all the changes on the theme, there were perceptible patterns, and there was some attempt to impose a coherent scheme of empire on the German conquests.

In principle, Germany and Italy divided prostrate Europe between them. In practice, Italy got Albania, the Dalmatian coast of Yugoslavia, and a few unimpressive bits of Balkan real estate. The bottom line of Hitler's philosophy was that might makes right, and that as conquerors the Axis Powers could do as they pleased with their victims. They even went further than thinking that they might do as they chose; they believed, or professed to believe, that what had enabled them to conquer Europe was the superiority of their ideology; democracy had bred weakness and therefore did not deserve to survive; totalitarianism bred strength and it therefore not only deserved to triumph, it also enjoined upon its practitioners the necessity of conversion, or of full implementation of its tenets. If the conquerors were free of the toils of representative government and the burden of criticism, they were no less imprisoned by the demands of their own beliefs—or what was even worse, they were all imprisoned by the demands of Hitler's beliefs.

The normal assumption is that the loss of freedom in a dictatorship is compensated for by the gain in efficiency; that is in fact usually the justification for the restriction of freedom. An examination of the Hitlerian empire, however, reveals that it was not nearly as efficient as is usually thought by admirers of Teutonic thoroughness. It was unwieldy, with the necessity for constant control militating against the factors that would make for a ready response to crisis. It was also full of junior empires, all seeking to enlarge themselves at the expense of competitors, all in the long run working against each other. Not only were there the personal problems and rivalries inherent in any human organization, but at bottom some of the guiding principles of the system blatantly contradicted other guiding principles. Ultimately, the whole creation was a huge inverted pyramid, resting on a tiny point named Adolf Hitler.

The omnipotent Fuehrer divided his world into segments, territorially and topically. Topically, all of his underlings competed with each other to enlarge their own spheres of influence. Joachim von Ribbentrop, for example, was Minister of Foreign Affairs. A man completely bereft of talent, his one purpose was the serving of his master; as ambassador to Great Britain before the war, in one ludicrous instance, he had greeted a startled King George VI with an outstretched arm and a loud cry of "Heil Hitler!" Fortunately for Germany, under Hitler there was little for the Foreign Ministry to do. Von Ribbentrop's greatest days ran from 1935, when he negotiated the Anglo-German Naval Treaty, to 1939, when he was instrumental in gaining the Russo-German Nonaggression Pact. He was never anything more than the mouthpiece of Hitler, however, and in a war situation the Foreign Office gradually lost whatever usefulness it ever had. None of that prevented von Ribbentrop from building up his office, from fewer than 2,500 to more than 10,000 personnel, and from parroting the party line and pushing the claims of his own little bailiwick whenever possible.

Far more important was Hermann Goering, not so much in his capacity of head of the Luftwaffe as in his role of economic director of the Reich. Goering amassed titles and responsibilities the way he collected medals and uniforms. A fascinating mixture of characteristics, a war hero from the First World War, Goering was the second-highest man in Germany. A man of considerable intelligence, he faded badly through the war, partly perhaps because of drug addiction, which seems to have been acquired by taking pain-killers, partly because he was one of the few in Hitler's immediate entourage to recognize where they were all going. As the war progressed, he adopted an *"Après moi le deluge"* attitude, and more or less retired to enjoy the good life as long as it lasted. Yet he had still gained a great deal of power under Hitler, and he remained a formidable member of what would later be called the Nazi Leadership Corps right to the end. He was a total failure as an economic director, however; he knew little of economics and cared less. It was left to others, eventually, to put the German economy on a war footing.

Another competitor was Alfred Rosenberg, who was regarded as the Party Theorist, in capital letters. Anti-Christian, anti-Slav, violently anti-Semitic, he was slated in the days of peace to lead the educational renaissance of Germany in the paths of righteousness. After war began he was eventually given the title Reich Minister for the Occupied Eastern Territories. His administration never really got anywhere, as he and his followers were constantly outpaced by Goering's people, by the army, by the SS, and by everyone else who was in on the pickings east of the Vistula. Yet it was Rosenberg who approved the plan to bring pre-teenagers west from Slavdom with the double aim of making them work for Germany and reducing the reproductive potential of Russia. Rosenberg was really a pseudo-intellectual nonentity, lost among the bully-boys of nazism, but he owed his position to the fact that his volumes of turgid writings gave a veneer of class to Hitler's philosophy.

The propagandist of the movement, as opposed to its philosopher, was Josef Goebbels. In terms of running the empire, he appeared as the exponent of German *Kultur*, so that his minions were trying to convince the occupied peoples of German superiority while other Germans were robbing and enslaving them. Goebbels therefore had something of an uphill struggle; but as Hitler's most faithful follower, doglike in his devotion, he enjoyed a privileged base from which to operate.

Diametrically opposed to Goebbels' task was that of Heinrich Himmler, head of the dreaded SS or Schutzstaffel, the military formation of the party that replaced the massacred SA and eventually became a rival to the army itself. As Reichsfuehrer SS, Minister of the Interior, and master of a host of other offices, Himmler was more feared perhaps than Hitler himself. His was the control over the concentration camps, his the responsibility for carrying out Nazi views on "racial purity." A precise, almost effeminate man, Himmler exuded the kind of fearful, devious power that had once emanated from Cardinal Richelieu; the SS as a body were modeled in part on the Jesuits with their stress on loyalty and obedience.

They were an almost archetypal example of virtue perverted, of the world turned upside down.

Finally, competing with all the myriad other organizations and claims to authority, there were the military forces. The army, navy, and the Luftwaffe all had their problems and their needs, and they were forced to fight with the assortment of civilian groups for priorities, for materials, for men, and for power.

If this were not sufficient to confuse the schematic diagram of the empire, there was a territorial or geographical pecking order as well. Preferential—or more appropriately, non-preferential—treatment went to different areas, generally as they were more or less "Germanic" or "Aryan." Nazi ideas of "race" were hopelessly confused, but concentrated essentially on the "purity" of Germans and Germanic peoples. Such notions, though scientifically bizarre, were of long historical standing. As far back as the Middle Ages the superiority of tall blond Germanic types was extolled, and during the unification movement of the nineteenth century, German historians praised their distant ancestor, Arminius—Hermann—for defeating the legions and refusing to be corrupted by the decadence of Rome. A series of writers expatiated on the superiority of the Germanic type, and when the idea found its way into the heart of nazism, it was reflected in the treatment given to different states.

First of all, of course, came the German Reich. This included not only the Germany of the Peace of Versailles, but also the Germany of all the territories rescued from the foreigner: Austria; the Sudetenland taken from Czechoslovakia; Poznan Province, Upper Silesia, and the Corridor taken from Poland; the former free city of Danzig; the Grand Duchy of Luxembourg; and Alsace-Lorraine taken from France; also, after 1943 and the collapse of Mussolini's Italy, the ex-Italian Tyrol, this in spite of the fact that a rescued Mussolini had set up the Salo Republic and was still ostensibly fighting side by side with his partner.

Next favored were Norway, the Netherlands, and Denmark. Though they all remained occupied by the Wehrmacht, they were still regarded as "Aryan" states and were allowed a degree of self-government, or at least self-administration, under regimes that were willing to collaborate with Germany. The most notable of these was in Norway, where a Norwegian Nazi named Vidkun Quisling gave his support to Germany and his name to be a synonym for one who betrays his own country. How much independence any of these regimes enjoyed depended basically upon how subservient they were to German demands, and the military situation at any given time. The Germans did make some attempt to deal "correctly" with them. They also recruited soldiers from these countries—indeed by the end of the war they were recruiting soldiers everywhere—and exploited them in any way they could.

Rather below them in preference were the non-Germanic satellite countries officially regarded as allies. These included Bulgaria, Rumania, Hungary, and the rump of Czechoslovakia, now known as Slovakia. There was also a lesser ring of satellites, the Protectorate of Bohemia, and the so-called Government General of Poland. Where the allied states secured some small measure of independence and autonomy, the latter two were directly subordinated to German control.

Finally, the vital military areas, non-Vichy France until late 1942 and all of France after that, Belgium, Greece, and much of the conquered Russian territory, remained basically under the control of the military forces, though subject to incursions by all the other competing authorities. The navy controlled ports, the SS hunted Jews, the labor organizers rounded up forced labor, and on and on.

Through all the conflicts engendered by these competing authorities and diverse relationships, there ran several common threads of exploitation. The German planners, to the extent that they had a consistent philosophy, believed in the self-sufficiency of Europe, and in the creation of an independent closed system, in which Europe's resources would enable it to live by itself. Though this was never entirely achieved, they did do fairly well at it, and in terms simply of resources and materials, they managed to sustain their war effort much longer than might originally have been expected.

A corollary idea was that in any considerations of priority, Germany was to be supreme, and all the other areas were to serve merely as hewers of wood and drawers of water for the Master Race. Non-German Europe was to be exploited as a colonial area for Germany. How much France or Holland or any other state might be left depended upon how much surplus it could produce over German needs. As the war turned increasingly sour, the demands of the German economy became more voracious, and by late in the war, even the supposedly favored territories such as Holland and Denmark were being ruthlessly looted and exploited to meet German quotas.

The financial underpinning of all this was provided by a series of agreements between Germany and the conquered states, in which the currency value and exchange rates were arbitrarily fixed in favor of the German mark. The mark was pegged artificially high, and competing currencies were fixed artificially low; the result of this was that Germans could buy foreign goods at ludicrously cheap prices, while German goods were far too expensive for non-Germans to afford. This created a one-way flow of manufactured items and luxury goods into Germany, with no corresponding outflow. The Germans also, in the time-honored tradition of conquerors, assessed the occupied countries for the maintenance costs of the armed forces. Thus, Belgium not only was occupied by German troops, the Belgian government had to pay for the privilege.

Setting aside the jugglings of high finance, the Germans resorted to a form of legitimized robbery under the name of requisitioning. In all combat areas, the German forces simply commandeered what they needed. In eastern Europe, with a relatively low-level economy, and a Slavic population, they left a desert behind them in many areas. In western Europe, they were at great pains to be more "correct" in their approach, which meant for practical purposes that they robbed more politely. As the war went on, the veneer of correctness became progressively thinner. Eventually, they were skimming off most of the products of non-German Europe. They took over the Hungarian grain production, Danish dairy products, Dutch garden crops, Norwegian timber. They requisitioned iron ore from Lorraine, oil from Rumania, coal from Poland, copper from Yugoslavia. They took virtually all the French bauxite and all imports from the French Empire while Vichy was still afloat: iron, phosphates, oil—everything they could get.

They also took over businesses and factories. French firms built German aircraft and tanks under license; Czech firms built German guns. The business infrastructure of Europe was overlaid with a web of German control, with all normal considerations subordinated to German needs. The Nazis were careful to maintain friendly relations with German capitalists and manufacturers, so they became the agents of the regime in handling business deals that put them at an advantage over foreign firms, and enabled private German businessmen to reap incredible profits from the general situation. The result was a temporarily integrated though imbalanced European economy.

Another factor making for integration was the need for labor.

As more Germans went into the armed forces, and as the country eventually awoke to the needs of a long war, the need for factory and farm labor gradually increased. Germany began to draw on foreign labor pools. First, in spite of international agreements to the contrary, they started putting prisoners of war to work. There were something like a million French soldiers in Germany as prisoners after 1940. The Germans drafted many of them into their factories. This was not nearly enough, as the war continued, so they began to conscript foreign labor outright. In Vichy France, there was a labor draft; at first it was presented to the French as a patriotic gesture: if France would send so many volunteer workers, the Germans would release an equivalent number of prisoners of war. Needless to say, volunteering was not too popular, and the Vichy authorities were soon forced to resort to outright conscription. One result of this was to send large numbers of young men into the hill country, where they became recruits for the Resistance movement.

Eventually, there were as many as ten million foreign workers in Germany, manning the factories, working on the farms, doing the jobs that would ordinarily have been filled by young Germans. The young Germans were at war. It was a vicious circle; in the name of Nazi ideology—racial purity, living space, and all that— millions of Germans were fighting and dying in Russia, North Africa, and the mid-Atlantic. To make up for their being away, millions of Russians, Czechs, and French were at home in Germany, keeping the economy going so that more millions of Germans could go off and fight—so that more millions of foreigners could be brought into Germany, and so forth. In the long run the Germans were trading their own blood and that of their allies and subjects for other peoples' goods and services, and finally they would run out of blood.

The compulsory labor system helped generate the Resistance movements, and it provided the greatest displacement of peoples since the barbarian migrations. Yet it was merely a footnote to the larger policies for which Hitler's Germany will always be remembered. The Nazis are inseparable from their policy of systematic terror in eastern Europe, and the worst expression of it, the attempt to wipe out the Slavs and the Jews.

One of the ostensible reasons for which Germany launched the war was her need for *Lebensraum*, "living space." It was a Hitlerian idea that Poland and western Russia should be cleared of inhabitants and colonized by Germans. Bizarre though it sounds, it was again an idea with deep roots in German history. The German migration to the east had gone on since the Middle Ages, and indeed, most of twentieth-century Germany was land originally colonized by German settlers moving east from the Rhine or the Elbe. The Hanseatic League, the Teutonic Knights, the German share of the partitions of Poland, the large access of territory claimed from Russia in 1918 at the treaty of Brest-Litovsk, all were expressions of the same urge to eastern expansion. The difference between Hitler and his predecessors was that they had come in as overlords and reduced the inhabitants to dependent status; he planned to kill them.

The Poles bore the brunt of this. They were conquered two years before the invasion of Russia. The southern Slavic states were in some sort of allied status, so it was primarily in Poland, and then later in Russia, that German policies received their most thorough development.

The Germans started by drawing up lists of Poles. Germans who had come to live in Poland through the drawing of boundaries at peace treaties were now welcomed back into the fold. Part-German Poles were accorded some degree of security. Pure Poles became "protected persons," and Jews and Gypsies were classified as "reserved"; neither term meant what it sounded like. "Protected" meant, in effect, that Poles were not protected at all; they could not own real estate, they could not go beyond primary education, they could not form any associations, they could not go to libraries, museums, or theaters, they were paid at the lowest wage scale, they received fewer rations than Germans, their movement was restricted, they had to have special permission to use a bicycle, and they could be sentenced to death for anti-German gestures.

The intelligentsia and upper class, the business leaders, the educators, the priests, were all systematically eliminated. Cut out of their jobs and positions, they were sent to prison camps or work camps or killed out of hand. The Poles were to be reduced as a people to the level of trained beasts. Anything of value that was distinctly Polish was looted or destroyed; art works were carried off, churches desecrated, museums closed, newspapers proscribed. There were successive reclassifications of Poles, constantly skimming off any surviving leaders or potential leaders, with the ultimate aim of producing a race of helots. In the end, Poland, over whom the Western Allies went to war, suffered the greatest proportional losses of lives and property of any country in World War II.

This was not only the Nazis' doing. In 1943, German troops near Smolensk came across mass graves in the Katyn Forest. In the time between the Russian occupation of eastern Poland and the German invasion of Russia, thousands of soldiers, officers, and leading Polish civilians had been imprisoned by the Russians. About 15,000 of them had disappeared completely; survivors and Poles who were in the west made frantic inquiries and efforts to find them, but no trace appeared until the Germans discovered the graves. Delighted to be able to accuse someone else of massacre, the German government gave the Katyn finding wide publicity. Eventually, more than 4,000 bodies were exhumed, of which nearly 3,000 were identified by name, the rest by their rank. All were officers or officer cadets, or—in the case of the civilians— teachers, professors, doctors, and engineers. All had last been seen alive in Russian prison camps; all had been shot in the back of the head; some had their hands tied behind them, their overcoats pulled over their heads, mouths stuffed with sawdust; some had wounds from the unique four-sided Russian bayonet blade.

Russians and Germans both, then Germans, then Russians, combined to destroy the Poles as a people. To be a Pole was almost —but not quite—the most unfortunate thing a person could be in World War II.

Russians under German control fared equally badly. The Germans had several millions of Russian prisoners of war. It happened that Russia had never signed the Geneva Convention on the treatment of prisoners, and the Germans used this as an excuse to rid themselves of the Russians. Prisoners were drafted into work camps or put in concentration camps. They were systematically maltreated, denied proper rations or medical facilities and, as much as possible, worked to death. Nor was this treatment confined to "legitimate" military opposition; civilians under German occupation were handled the same way. In the spaces of Russia and the Ukraine, the war achieved a depth of savagery unmatched elsewhere. In the midst of the winters, retreating Germans would burn and destroy housing and drive the peasants into the cold to die. Very soon the Russians were burning their own housing, so it would not shelter the enemy; the "scorched earth" policy reduced vast stretches of European Russia to a desert. Civilians lived a precarious hand-to-mouth existence between or behind the lines. Those who could hid in the countryside. In the great Russian forests, partisans gathered, ambushing trains, killing sentries, being killed themselves, with no mercy expected or shown by either side. Only slowly did the Soviet government take an interest in and start supplying the partisans, but once it did, their attacks increased in numbers and, if possible, in ferocity.

The Germans responded by taking hostages, executing them and, in many cases, wiping out whole villages. Himmler announced that one of the aims of the Russian campaign was to reduce the population of "Slavdom" by thirty million, and the anti-partisan operations were partly used as an excuse to do so.

There were of course ironic and tragic side-effects to all this. As the Germans needed more men, thousands of non-Communist or anti-Communist Russians were recruited into the German Army. Just as Russians who had tried to wipe out Poles later raised Polish bodies of troops, whom they eventually released to the West, so Germans who had tried to wipe out Russians raised Russian bodies of troops. A captured Russian general, Andrei Vlassov, was used as a rallying-point for Russian prisoners. Relatively few joined him, mostly to escape death in one form or another, and the force never became effective; the Germans could not overcome their ideological preconceptions and frittered away whatever chance there might have been of sowing political confusion in Russia. Not that there was much chance once their policies created opposition, anyway. In all, probably three of the five million prisoners taken by the Germans died, as well as fifteen to twenty million Russian soldiers and civilians. Nothing could overcome the hatred generated by that fact.

The survivors of the German camps did not fare much better once they were released. Official Communist doctrine was that it was a sin to surrender to the enemy. At the end of the war returning prisoners were treated very badly; many of them went from German prison camps to Russian labor camps, in some cases not to be released until the death of Stalin in 1953. Needless to say, German prisoners of war in Russia were treated the same way.

If Poles and Russians were to be reduced to subhuman levels, the Jews were to be exterminated. This policy developed during the war. Before 1939, the Germans were content to rob, beat, and deport German Jews; their ideas evolved with success. In the early stages of the war, they moved toward the creation of a super-ghetto in the Government General of Poland, herding Polish Jews into it and then gradually bringing in Jews from other conquered areas as well. When they took over France, they toyed momentarily with the idea of creating a great Jewish ghetto in the French colonial territory of Madagascar. The idea lacked practicality, however, so as they moved into Russia, and brought several million more Jews under their control, they hit on a logically more satisfying approach, a "final solution" to their problem. To Hitler and his followers the Jews represented all that was decadent and despicable. They would, therefore, produce an aesthetically and philosophically satisfying answer to what to do with them: they would kill them all.

The problem of how to do it was handed by Goering to Reinhard Heydrich of the SS. By late 1941 and early 1942, things were moving. The Germans had already introduced mobile vans into the Government General. Jews were placed in these, ostensibly for delousing, and gassed, after which the truck simply drove off with the bodies. It was a relatively small-scale operation, however, and the Germans soon moved to the idea of extermination camps, based on their own already existent concentration camps. They built four of these in Poland—Belsen, Maydanek, Sobibor, and Treblinka—and converted a labor camp in Silesia named Auschwitz. The Jews were systematically rounded up, loaded aboard trains or truck convoys, and taken on their one-way journey to the camps. Auschwitz achieved for its rulers a proud record of peak performance: 12,000 victims a day, sorted, gassed, cremated, disposed of. There were "scientific" experiments as well: how long could a man stay in freezing water before it killed him; how much faster could you operate without anesthetics; would a woman sacrifice herself to prevent her child being bludgeoned to death. By 1943, Himmler was urging his minions to greater efforts to fulfill their duty to the Fatherland.

Not only Jews went to the camps. Thousands upon thousands of Slavs died, the Gypsies were virtually wiped out in Europe, the retarded, the insane, the senile, all went down the via dolorosa to the camps. Rumors of what was happening reached western Europe in 1942, but most people in the West regarded them as nothing more than war propaganda. It was too horrible to be true, there were no words to describe it, and eventually a new one had to be coined: genocide, the murder of whole peoples.

No one knows how many people actually died in the camps, on their way to them, or as a result of having been in them. The official figure for the Jews is usually put at six million, in the camps themselves. Those are the best documented, as a result of the thoroughness with which the Germans kept their records, records which Himmler boasted, "have written a glorious page in our history." But there is little doubt that nearly that many more died outside the camps, and the end product was very near what the Germans wanted, the wiping out of European Jewry. Before the war there were four million Jews in Poland; today there are seven thousand.

The fact that some Jews and Slavs survived at all is mainly the result of the contradictions of German policy. If the Jews were gassed, the Poles shot, the Russians starved to death, who would be left to do the work? The answer was no one, and eventually the policies had to be modified; from a quick death for everyone, the Germans moved to a policy of imposing a slow death by malnutrition while making prisoners work as long and as hard as possible. Had it not been for the demands of industry, the death toll would have gone even higher.

How much the German people, as a people, knew of all this remains problematical. The domestic opposition to the Nazis was weak, usually short-lived, and in the main ineffectual. If in the occupied countries German policies sparked the flames of resistance even while attempting to liquidate it, at home little was done. Only those who have never had to fear the knock on the door in the middle of the night can afford the luxury of criticism, and as the Nazi tentacles fastened ever more firmly on civilization, occupied Europe became what Churchill, as he so often did, summed it up: "a monstrous tyranny, never surpassed in the dark, lamentable catalogue of human crime."

17. The Japanese Offensives in the Pacific

As THE JAPANESE carrier pilots returned triumphantly to their ships on the morning of December 7, exciting vistas of conquest opened before them. Behind them on the mud of Pearl, in the midst of the fires, the wreckage, and the oil, lay the one instrument capable of impeding their advance. With one sudden blow they had altered the balance of power in the Pacific for the foreseeable future. They were now to embark on a string of victories that would carry them to the doorsteps of Australia and India. By the only means worthy of a race of warriors, the Japanese were going to claim their place in the sun.

Coinciding with the Pearl Harbor strike, the Japanese launched simultaneous offensives on all fronts. The first stage of their plan was the taking of the Southern Resources Area. Stage two was to be the establishment of a wide-ranging defensive perimeter. The Japanese high command calculated that it would take the United States at least eighteen months to recover sufficiently to reply. By then the defensive perimeter would be secure. They moved forward confidently to the conquest of the southern regions.

Their initial offensive was composed of two main thrusts, plus several subsidiary ones. The main thrusts were a southwestern one into Southeast Asia, which would advance down the Malayan Peninsula and branch both left and right into Burma and into the Dutch East Indies; and a southeastern one from Formosa down through the Philippines to meet the western thrust in the islands of the Indies. The subsidiary drives would take Guam in the Marianas, Wake Island north of the Marshalls, and would extend Japanese control down into the Gilbert Islands, south of the Marshalls. If successful, these drives would achieve three results: they would destroy Allied power in the western Pacific, they would complete the isolation of China, and they would lay Southeast Asia and the islands open to Japanese exploitation.

They did succeed, even beyond their projections. In the smaller operations, the Japanese moved into the Gilberts with no opposition. The unfortified island of Guam fell on December 10. Wake proved a tougher nut to crack, and its minuscule garrison beat off a landing attempt on the 11th before succumbing to a stronger one on the 23rd. The defense of Wake was looked on as a tiny epic by the American public in that dark December, but it had no effect on the overall course of the war, and the last message, "The issue is in doubt. . . .", seemed to sum up all too accurately the state of the world as Christmas neared.

In the western drive the main target was Malaya, but there were a couple of side operations also to be wrapped up. The Japanese wanted to take Hong Kong, the last British-held territory on the China coast. As a base it was completely untenable, but the British insisted for prestige reasons that it be held as long as possible. In November they had beefed up its garrison of four battalions by the addition of two Canadian militia battalions. This was regarded by the British as a show of force. They had few guns, fewer naval units, and six old planes to defend the island, but some among the garrison were convinced the island was impregnable, and the Japanese no more than third-rate troops.

The house of cards came tumbling down on December 8, the same day as the attack on Pearl Harbor on the other side of the International Date Line. The first Japanese air strike wiped out the British aircraft, and in a day they broke through the mainland British defense position, which had been scheduled to hold out for three weeks. The British were pushed off the mainland and back onto the island of Hong Kong by the 11th. After a week of heavy bombardment the Japanese stormed across on the 18th, split the defenders into two parts, isolated them, and drove them to the ends of the island. By Christmas Eve, the British defense was collapsing, and on the 25th, the British commander, General C. M. Maltby, surrendered. The British suffered 12,000 casualties, the Japanese 2,800.

The imperial bastions crumbled like sand castles before the advancing tide. Simultaneously with their attack against the outpost of Hong Kong, the Japanese initiated their major western drive, against Malaya and Singapore. Troops moved direct from Indochina into Thailand and started down the Kra Isthmus toward Malaya. Meanwhile, troop convoys crossed the Gulf of Siam and landed forces just above the Thai-Malay border, and just below it at Khota Bharu.

Singapore is a low-lying island off the southern end of the Malay Peninsula. It had been a great trading city back in the Middle Ages, and had then been destroyed by its rivals. In 1819, an enterprising Englishman named Stamford Raffles had leased it from its nominal ruler, the Sultan of Johore, and had established a duty-free port city there. Through the nineteenth century it had flourished and grown, become a naval base as well as a trading port, and gradually became the center of seaborne empire east of Suez. The British undertook extensive fortifications of the island in the 1920's, but they were never completed, falling prey both to heavy costs and to confusion about the problems of land bases versus air power. The British decided that Singapore would be held as a main base for the navy. If war broke out in the Far East, the army would hold Singapore until the Royal Navy sent out a fleet that would destroy any invaders of Malaya. They failed to fortify the shoreward side of the islands, however, and then in the thirties they decided that air power was the key to control. But when war came they could not afford the aircraft to defend Malaya.

In December of 1941, the area commander, Air Chief Marshal Sir Robert Brooke-Popham, had under command about 80,000 combat troops, generally poorly trained and deficient in artillery and armor; about 150 aircraft—precisely half of what was considered necessary for defense—and a naval force whose mainstays were the newly arrived *Prince of Wales* and *Repulse*. In other words, his ground forces lacked material, his air forces were short of planes, and his naval forces had no air cover. All the British really had for comfort when the Japanese landed on the Malay Peninsula was the belief that the enemy could not advance through the jungles. Of that happy ignorance they were swiftly to be disabused.

The Japanese forces under General Tomoyuki Yamashita were well trained and battle tested in China. There were four divisions of them, plus adequate support from air and naval units. Unlike the British, they had a tough, integrated, well-coordinated force. By launching air strikes early on the 8th, the Japanese quickly gained air supremacy. They followed it by winning naval supremacy as well.

The outbreak of war found *Repulse* and *Prince of Wales* at Singapore; the fleet commander, Admiral Sir Tom Philips, was in Manila conferring, or commiserating, with his American opposite number. Philips flew back to Singapore immediately, and when news came in of Japanese convoys up the coast, he sailed into the China Sea to intercept them. He asked for air cover from shore-based units, but cooperation broke down between the rapidly changing situation and the inadequacies of the British command and communication structure. Instead of British planes, Philips got Japanese. Scouts picked up his two huge ships at sea, naked to their enemies, and before noon on the 10th the two great ships were attacked by a series of bomber and torpedo aircraft. Both ships went down that afternoon, giants killed by insects. They were the last standard-bearers of Allied naval might in the Pacific, and the first capital ships ever sunk in battle by aircraft alone. When a Japanese patrol plane dropped a wreath over their graves, it acknowledged not only a brave enemy, but the end of the dreadnought era as well.

Air power and naval power gone, the defense of Malaya now rested on the shoulders of the land commander, General A. E. Perceval. He had two divisions scattered about the Malayan Peninsula, and one in reserve holding the approaches to Singapore. Within days the Japanese were all over his forward troops, moving through the supposedly impassable jungle, sending tanks down the tracks and roads to ambush the British, cutting in behind them and setting up roadblocks. Harried, confused, cut off, the British fought a series of rear-guard actions that turned into a shambling retreat. By the first week of January they were pushed out of the Malay States and into Johore, only fifty miles from Singapore. The British hoped to hold there, but once again the Japanese flanked them and levered them out of their positions. By the end of the month, Perceval was off the mainland, his troops pulled back to the island of Singapore itself.

The Strait of Johore, which separates Singapore from the mainland, is shallow and narrow. The British had built some defenses along the island, but had not extensively fortified the area. The great naval guns in their fixed positions were across the island, pointing resolutely out at the empty sea. After a week of intensive bombardment and air attack, Yamashita put three divisions across the strait, and by the morning of February 9 his troops were firmly ashore. The British, Indians, and Australians of the garrison did their best to hold a line through the center of the island, but this went too; the linear defenses and static ideas of 1916 simply could not withstand the Japanese tactics of penetration and infiltration. They lost the reservoirs in the center of the island and by the 15th were back in a tight perimeter around the city of Singapore, while a pall of smoke from burning oil hung over everything, a funeral beacon for empire.

That afternoon British envoys came out of their lines under a flag of truce. Later a humiliated Perceval signed a document of "unconditional surrender," and at dark the shooting stopped and an uneasy quiet fell over Singapore. The Japanese troops moved into the city the next morning, and the British moved out to three and a half years of captivity. In total casualties, the Japanese had suffered 9,800; the British losses were 138,000. It was the single greatest disaster ever suffered by British arms, and it left the Indian Ocean and the East Indies wide open to conquest.

While the western Japanese forces roared down the Malayan Peninsula toward Singapore and the eastern forces fastened a stranglehold on the Philippines, the Japanese split off a third force that went for the heart of their objective, the East Indies. Navy, army, and air force units crashed into the so-called Malay Barrier and ran riot. The Allies had little with which to resist; they improvised an organization called ABDACOM, for American-British-Dutch-Australian Command, and gave its direction into the hands of General Sir Archibald Wavell, sent out from the desert where he had recently fallen from grace with Churchill.

ABDA was longer on initials than it was on fighting strength. The British and the few available Australian troops were trapped in Malaya, and the Japanese by their drive through Thailand had cut off the hope of reinforcement through India. The Americans were very thin in the Philippines, and Pearl Harbor had forestalled any hope of American relief. The Dutch troops in the East Indies were primarily native levies, armed only for internal security, and not overly friendly to their colonial masters at that. ABDA was left with a few obsolete aircraft, British and the Netherlands East Indies Air Force, and a series of scratch naval units under the command of the ranking Dutch sailor, Admiral K. W. F. M. Doorman; the ships lacked even common codebooks; in fact, they lacked a common language. The Malay Barrier was a myth.

The Japanese hit this myth in four separate but coordinated groups, a carrier striking force to the eastward, then an eastern, central, and western force. All operated the same way. Air bases were isolated by naval air strikes, then landings were put in; local control was quickly consolidated, and the navy and air units moved on to the next target. The separation of forces was unorthodox, but against a weak and ill-organized Allied effort, it was highly successful. The ABDA units were reduced to running back and forth like firemen with a blaze out of control, and the Japanese swept them off the board a few at a time.

Disasters came fast and furious. In mid-December the Japanese landed on British North Borneo, the state of Sarawak, ruled by the descendants of "Rajah" Brooke; the territory was occupied by Christmas. By the second week in January the enemy was in northern Borneo and landing in northern Celebes too. From there they jumped to Kendari in southern Celebes, and Balikpapan, halfway down Makassar Strait on the eastern side of Borneo. Here an American striking force ambushed them. Admiral Glassford started out with two cruisers and four destroyers; one cruiser grounded and had to turn back, the second developed engine trouble; the destroyers, all World War I relics, got in among the Japanese transports on the night of the 23rd-24th, shot them up, and sank five, before fleeing back down the strait.

ABDA could operate only at night. With the dawn came the ubiquitous Japanese search planes, and anything that floated was in trouble during daylight. On February 4, Doorman took four cruisers out of Surabaya, his main base, to make another strike against Balikpapan. Planes caught them and hit two Americans, *Houston* once and *Marblehead* twice; the raid finished the latter. After temporary repairs she limped painfully back to the States. Next, Doorman swung west to try to stop the Japanese from reaching Palembang, the great oil refinery on Sumatra. He got as far as Banka Island where Japanese planes bombed his fleet so heavily he had to call his attack off. Another key island was gone, and the Japanese were now closing in from east and west on the central ABDA position of Java.

Their next target was Bali, just east of Java. Doorman decided to hit their transports and sent his forces in in poorly coordinated waves, first mainly Dutch, then mainly Americans, and finally an attack by torpedo boats. There was a great deal of firing, several ships on both sides were hit, but little was accomplished, and soon Bali was gone too. Java was now all but cut off. Some reinforcements were coming in through Darwin in northern Australia and the eastern island of Timor. The Japanese took time out from Java, occupied Timor, and on the 19th their carrier force hit Darwin, catching the city completely by surprise, and destroying virtually all of the port and its military installations.

The Java forces were now substantially reduced. Wavell left

for Australia, and naval command devolved on Dutch Admiral Conrad Helfrich. There was a last futile attempt to get air support to the island, and the result was that the American aircraft transport *Langley* was sunk, loaded with planes, a hundred miles south of Java. Her survivors were transferred to the oiler *Pecos*; a few days later the Japanese got her too. In two assault convoys totaling well over a hundred ships, the Japanese closed in on Java. Helfrich decided on a last death-or-glory battle, gathered up all the ABDA forces he could find, and went forth to meet them.

Sallying out from Surabaya, Helfrich had nine destroyers and five cruisers, the exhausted remnants of Allied power in the western Pacific. All his ships went into the fight with previous battle damage; on the American cruiser *Houston* the after main battery turret had been inoperative since her bomb hit early in February. The crew of all the ships were on the point of collapse; ammunition and fuel were low. As dark came on the 27th, they ran into the Japanese covering force, four cruisers—heavier than the Allied five—and fourteen destroyers.

The Battle of the Java Sea was an incredibly confused tangle; the ABDA forces were reduced to following the leader in the dark, ships blundered into each other, gun flashes stabbed briefly out of the blackness. Helfrich made repeated efforts to get in at the Japanese transports, while the Japanese admiral, Nishimura, with his superior tactical control herded him away from them. Badly hit early on, the British cruiser *Exeter* limped back to Surabaya, followed by the four American destroyers who had spent all their torpedoes defending her and had just enough oil left to get back to port. The other destroyers were hit by gunfire and torpedoes, and one ran on a mine close to shore. Finally, just before midnight, Helfrich made a final desperate dash for the transports with his four remaining cruisers.

Suddenly, the Japanese heavy cruisers appeared on parallel courses and opened up with full broadsides. Both Dutch cruisers, *Java* and *de Ruyter*, took torpedo hits. As *de Ruyter* sank under him, Helfrich signaled wounded *Houston* and the Australian *Perth* to run for it. They could not run; they could barely hobble off into the darkness.

The denouement was just as bad. *Exeter* left Surabaya the evening of the 28th. The Malay Barrier had become a trap, and all the surviving Allies wanted to do now was break through to the south, to get away to fight again. But on the 29th, *Exeter* and her two destroyers were caught by four heavy cruisers and a destroyer screen. In 1782, an earlier *Exeter* had been surrounded by six French ships; asked what to do, her captain had said, "Fight her till she sinks." Now she fought till she sank. One of the destroyers went with her; the other was caught by the merciless carrier aircraft and sank an hour later.

That left only *Houston* and *Perth*. Trying to get through Sunda Strait they ran into what they had been searching for for days, a Japanese transport force. They waded in with all guns blazing and sank or drove ashore four loaded transports. The scene abruptly changed when the Japanese covering force arrived, three big cruisers and ten destroyers. *Perth* took several torpedo hits and sank, *Houston* fought on alone till she went dead in the water; then, her gunnery controls gone, her sailors loading the shells and training the guns by hand, she lay there while the Japanese pounded her into a shambles, and then she sank beneath her still-fighting crew.

Java was gone by the first week of March. ABDA was gone; the United States Asiatic Fleet was gone. The triumphant Japanese were through the Malay Barrier and ranging into the Indian Ocean.

For the British it was unmitigated disaster. The fall of Singapore was a military defeat of the first rank, and a humiliating one at that. Nothing could be worse, but things almost as bad were still to come. In cutting off Malaya and the East Indies from India, the Japanese moved west through Thailand and north into Burma. Burma had been British territory since 1885, a prosperous, relatively quiescent backwater of empire. It was also an isolated territory, only tenuously connected by land with India; it was rich in rice and oil, and the Japanese decided it would make an ideal buttress for the western bulwark of their new empire.

They moved out of Thailand in December, striking against the weak British forces in southern Burma. The panhandle of Tenasserim was quickly occupied. Rangoon came under heavy air attack. The British tried to hold as far south and east as they could, but they overreached themselves. The Japanese were better in the jungle than they, the enemy had air control, as always, and the British found themselves constantly flanked and driven back. Rangoon fell on the 7th of March, and the litany of retreat began all over again. With help from the Chinese, the British tried to hold at Prome, a hundred miles north of Rangoon; they could not do it, and by the end of April the Japanese were in Mandalay and Lashio. China was cut off for fair, the Burma Road was gone, and the tired, wasted columns of British, Indians, and Chinese were trekking back along the narrow paths to the mountains and the Indian frontier. It looked as if they would do well to hang on there. A Japanese naval force raided into the Bay of Bengal, mounted air strikes at Colombo and hit the naval base at Trincomalee on Ceylon. They caught an aircraft carrier and two cruisers and sank them, as well as 100,000 tons of merchant shipping on the east coast of India. By late April, the only Allied forces left in the Northern Hemisphere between Ceylon and the Hawaiian Islands were the Americans in the Philippines. And they were soon to go.

The Philippine Islands, one of the largest and most beautiful archipelagoes in the world, had been ruled by the United States since Admiral Dewey had steamed into Manila Bay in 1898 for the commencement exercises of the new United States Navy. Among the more benevolent of the area's unending stream of foreign rulers, the Americans had promised the Filipinos they would receive their independence in 1946, and through the thirties had made moves toward preparing them for self-government. The threat of war increasingly hung over Philippine development, however. As 1941 moved along, General Douglas MacArthur was reinstated in active duty and entitled Commander United States Army Forces Far East. As with ABDACOM, the title was more grandiose than the forces under him. Though there were officially about 130,000 troops in the Philippines, only a fifth of them, one infantry division, and armor, engineer, and support troops were American, and these were the only ones ostensibly fully trained or up to normal establishment. The Filipinos themselves consisted of a large number of training cadres, still in a state of organization, and a few small units fully worked up, such as the Philippine Scouts.

Washington had for practical purposes written off the Philippines anyway, when it made its Germany-first decision. MacArthur, however, was not one to accept decisions made by someone else. He was convinced that he could hold the islands, and even more that, with the new B-17 bombers being stationed there by the Army Air Force, he might well carry out offensive missions. He saw the Philippines not as a hostage to fortune, perched way out on a very thin limb, but as an advanced base that would be the springboard for assaults against Japan.

In spite of this vision, he was reluctant to act when the news of Pearl Harbor came in. His air force people urged an immediate attack on Japanese bases on Formosa, well within range of the B-17. MacArthur hesitated; he had to consider relations with the

Philippine government, and he did not want to lose their support by committing the first overt act of war. He did not know that the Japanese had already hit targets here and there in the islands. Later in the morning the big bombers took off, milled around helplessly in the air for a while, and returned to Clark Field. The fighter pilots flying cover over the bare airfields came in for lunch.

Just after noon the Japanese hit them, wave after wave, high-level bombers, dive-bombers, fighters coming low to strafe the neatly parked planes. It was not so much that the Americans were caught napping as that they were psychologically unprepared for what was happening. Up till now they had lived in a fool's paradise of a world at peace; the reality of war hit them hard. When they could, they fought back with their outclassed fighter planes and their antique anti-aircraft weapons. But when the exuberant Japanese got back to Formosa, they had lost only seven fighters, and no bombers. They had shot down twenty-five fighters and destroyed seventy bombers and fighters on the ground. MacArthur no longer had to worry about an "overt act." All he had to worry about after "little Pearl Harbor" was that he had nothing to hit back with.

The first Japanese landings followed soon after their initial strike. Small detachments landed in the northern part of Luzon. MacArthur's defense plan called for holding the central part of the island, and then withdrawing into the Bataan Peninsula, where he proposed to hold on until help came. Messages from Washington assured him that help would soon be on the way, though they did not say what it would be or where it would come from. Following his plan, MacArthur refused to be gulled by the first landings. He believed the main landing would come in Lingayen Gulf, and while his smaller units withdrew slowly before the northern advance, he husbanded his main forces for the big battle.

The Japanese came all right. On the morning of the 22nd, 43,000 of them stormed ashore in Lingayen Gulf. Unfortunately, the Americans expected them to land in the south, at the head of the gulf. Instead they landed halfway up it, and met very little serious resistance. They immediately started moving down the central plain that led from Lingayen toward Manila. MacArthur's commander in the area, General Jonathan Wainwright, had a series of withdrawal positions from which he hoped to inflict successive checks on the Japanese, but none of these held long. Further Japanese troop convoys were sighted converging on Luzon, and MacArthur ordered the Americans and Filipinos to fall back into Bataan in as orderly a fashion as they could manage.

By the day before Christmas the Japanese were landing in Lamon Bay, on the east coast of Luzon, and the American forces were hustling back toward Bataan. Manila was declared an open city, and while the Northern Luzon Force desperately held back the attackers, the southern defenders hurried across their line of communications and into the peninsula. Given the difficulties under which everyone was laboring, it was a very successful movement; its end result was to put the defenders of the islands into a bag, but there was no alternative anyway. By New Year's the Americans and Filipinos were holding their main battle line on Bataan.

Both sides were now faced with a siege. The Japanese general Homma was actually inferior in numbers to the Americans and Filipinos, but his troops were better trained by far and they also were better supported. They commanded the sea and the air and they could get reinforcements of whatever might be necessary. In Washington, General Marshall still hoped to rescue MacArthur, but the U. S. Navy had already said that was impossible. A convoy en route to the islands with reinforcements and supplies had had to be diverted to Australia; Marshall wanted it fought through to Manila, but the navy was sacrificing all it had in a futile attempt to hold the Malay Barrier, and that was a good thousand miles south of the Philippines. There was no help for it; MacArthur would have to sink or swim with what he had. Yet the general knew the Japanese too were stretched thin; seemingly impervious to the navy's problems and to disaster all around him, he kept insisting he could win if reinforced.

On the Japanese side, they were actually reducing their forces. With no idea of how many men were opposing them, the Japanese pulled out one of Homma's divisions for the leap into the East Indies. They were still ready to go, however, and on the 15th of January they opened heavy attacks against the Allied line in the middle of the peninsula. The Americans were pushed back, counterattacked, and after a week's bitter fighting in the jungle-choked country, held their position. It did them little good; with the troops exhausted and few supplies coming up, they had to fall back and take up another line farther down the peninsula.

They stopped on a line running from Bagac to Orion, and here MacArthur intended to fight it out to the end. In vain the Japanese butted against it for two weeks in late January and early February, then they settled down to regroup and pull themselves together. The Americans and Filipinos did the same, but there was now heavy wastage caused by exhaustion and malnutrition. Their rations were cut to thirty ounces of food a day in early January and to fifteen in April. Supplies were not getting through. MacArthur himself was ordered out late in February and left on March 12, he and his family and staff going south on PT-boats, then flying to Australia. Many of the troops, though they accepted the logic of it all, felt bitterly betrayed, and MacArthur's famous "I shall return" had a hollow ring to those who were not allowed to leave.

Homma, losing face over the delays, was ready again by April 3. After an intense bombardment he crashed through the center of the Bagac-Orion Line, and found almost nothing ahead of him. The reeling Americans and Filipinos were done; they never again put together a coherent position on Bataan, and on the night of the 8th the Luzon Force surrendered. Homma had gambled on a complete surrender of the entire archipelago, and was furious when he failed to get it. The survivors of the peninsula were sent off to prison camps in what became known as the "Bataan Death March."

In part, the infamous death march occurred because the Japanese had no idea that 76,000 Americans and Filipinos plus another 26,000 civilians were crowded onto the end of Bataan; they expected about 25,000; what provisions they had made to escort prisoners north the hundred-odd miles to camps were soon swamped by numbers. But that was only part of the cause; the other was the attitude of the Japanese. A Japanese warrior expected to die for his Emperor; surrender, to him, was so shameful that it was virtually inconceivable, and there was no such thing as an honorable capitulation. A man who surrendered was utterly without honor, unworthy of respect or humane treatment. Enemies should not surrender, they should have the grace to die. When they did not, the Japanese often killed them. The route of the march soon became lined with bayoneted, shot, and beheaded men. Those who fell out, suffering from exhaustion, dysentery, malnutrition, wounds, were clubbed or bayoneted. Estimates are that 3,000 to 10,000 of the men who started the Death March died on the way. Japanese soldiers expected little mercy from an enemy; after Bataan they would get little.

There remained a number of scattered forces in the rest of the Philippines, especially on the southern island of Mindanao, and these were still fighting against other Japanese forces. Homma, however, was preoccupied with the island of Corregidor, a rock square in the middle of the mouth of Manila Bay. He bombarded and bombed it for a month, by which time the weakened defenders were reduced to a state of complete collapse, hardly aware that they were by three months and a good thousand miles the last defenders of the great colonial empires. On the night of the 5th-6th of May, a Japanese assault battalion crossed from Bataan and got ashore. The opposition was weak and sporadic, the defenders were utterly worn down. On the afternoon of the 6th, MacArthur's successor, General Wainwright, opened surrender negotiations. This time Homma was not to be cheated of his prize; he insisted Wainwright surrender all the troops in the Philippines. Under the threat of reprisals Wainwright finally did so, and after agonizing arguments and shifts, the Americans and Filipinos everywhere in the islands laid down their arms.

Many of the Filipinos took off their uniforms and went home; many of the Americans went into the jungles as guerrillas, but the majority, led by Wainwright, went into prison camps, where they remained for the rest of the war. Homma went home in disgrace, for having taken so long to win his campaign. Still, the victory, though belated, was complete. The Japanese were masters all the way to Australia and the islands of the southern Pacific. Now they had what they wanted; now in leisure they could prepare their defensive perimeter. It was the slack high tide of empire.

Yamamoto had guaranteed six months of victory; his masters believed they were going to get eighteen months' grace. He was right and they were wrong.

In the United States, after the first initial shock, there was an explosion of fury. The Americans might have been extremely dubious about participation in the war, but all that doubt was swept away by Pearl Harbor; if ever a nation leapt to arms, it was the United States in December of 1941. That was little help to the hollow garrisons of the western Pacific, but it seems to be the fate of regular soldiers and sailors to buy time for their carefree civilian masters. While American soldiers in the Philippines and sailors in the Java Sea bought that time, the mightiest—and the luckiest— nation in the world flung itself into the war effort with frantic energy.

The apparently unending stream of Japanese victories only inflamed the American public; the tide must turn. But until it did, there was an increasing public clamor for offensive action. The clamor coincided with the desires of the military leadership; engraved on every soldier's heart was a cardinal principle of war: it is the offensive which brings victory. Defense only staves off defeat.

The most important thing for the moment was to secure the

supply route to Australia. As the Japanese lapped eastward past the Indies and New Guinea and threatened to spill down into the Solomons and the Coral Sea, strategic attention had to go to this area. To the American public, however, strategic maneuvering east of Australia was not very exciting. They wanted dramatic action. The military Chiefs of Staff for once agreed with them and decided that a surprise move would throw the enemy off stride. It could be no more than a pinprick, but it might develop into something. They agreed to bomb Tokyo.

On the morning of April 18, sixteen twin-engined B-25 bombers groaned off the heaving deck of the carrier *Hornet*. Sighted by a Japanese picket ship, they had to go 150 miles farther than planned. The extra distance meant they would be unable to return to the carrier and would have to fly to the Asian mainland. Led by Colonel James Doolittle, thirteen of the planes roared over Tokyo; the others hit Nagoya, Osaka, and Kobe. They carried only four bombs apiece; they did almost no damage. Swooping over their targets, they were cheered by civilians who thought they were Japanese planes. Within seconds they were gone, on to China or Russia, where the planes crashed, out of fuel. The few fliers captured by the Japanese were tried as war criminals and some were executed.

The raid, harmless as it was, got banner headlines in the Allied world, but its greatest effect was on the Japanese leaders. They had blithely assumed that the home islands were inviolate. Where had those planes come from? They were army bombers; they were too big to fly off carriers. It was barely possible they had come from the Aleutians, or from Midway, though both seemed pretty far. President Roosevelt would say only that they were from "Shangri-la"; wherever they came from, it was obvious that the vaunted "defensive perimeter" was either too thin, or not far enough out, to be secure. The Japanese began planning a further extension in the northern Pacific.

Three weeks later they ran into trouble off Australia. Here too they had decided to extend a bit farther than originally planned. Everything had gone so well that the Japanese were now wildly overconfident. They had pushed out along the northern coast of New Guinea and taken the Bismarck Islands with the great harbor of Rabaul on the eastern end of New Britain. Rabaul was to be their major base in the area and the southeastern anchor of the defense line before it swung northward. To secure the approaches to Rabaul, they began to push down into the Solomons. They also decided on an end run around New Guinea, to take Port Moresby on the southern side of the island. New Guinea has some of the worst terrain in the world, its central spine formed by a range called the Owen Stanley Mountains. The Japanese had tried to cross this, and been held up by a handful of desperate Australians. The two spearpoints of empire, both racked by malaria and dysentery, had fought each other to a standstill on the track to Kokoda, so the Japanese sought to go by sea and cut the Australians' base out from under them.

Instead they got ambushed. An American carrier task force was operating in the Coral Sea; the Americans had long broken the Japanese operating codes, and knew something was going on in the area. The resulting battle of the Coral Sea, fought from May 4 to 8, was the first naval action in history in which the surface ships never sighted each other. The aircraft carrier took its place as the dominant element in naval warfare. Both sides flew off a series of air strikes, and traded punches somewhat like prize fighters in the dark. The Japanese, who had three aircraft carriers, lost a small one, *Shoho*; the Americans, with two, lost a big one, *Lexington*. Their second carrier, *Yorktown*, took heavy damage and limped off to Pearl, out of action for the immediate future. When the smoke finally cleared, it was the Americans who were worse hurt, but they won the day: the Japanese turned back, and the threat to Port Moresby and northern Australia was gone, as it turned out, forever. The only positive fruit of the action for Japan was a new holding down in the Solomons, a seaplane base at Tulagi, and the start of an airfield on a larger, all but unknown island called Guadalcanal.

The Japanese believed they had a clearcut material victory; they thought they sank both American carriers. They knew the remaining two were last seen in the north Pacific—these were Doolittle's "bases," though they did not know that—and therefore the central Pacific was wide open. Still supremely confident, the Japanese now launched the extension of their perimeter; they aimed operations at the Aleutians, and at Midway, the western end of the Hawaiian chain.

They planned to use virtually the entire Imperial Fleet in this, and they scattered ships all over the map. As a battle, Midway was fairly simple in broad outline, extremely complex in detail. As a human drama it conformed to most of the dictates of great literature in plot, scene, and characters, and a great deal has been written about it.

Using their by now standard eccentric strategy, the Japanese planned a diversion that eventually took the unmanned Aleutian islands of Attu and Kiska. The effort diverted more of their forces than it did of the Americans, so although the gain in territory was a positive benefit of the campaign, it was quite possibly achieved at the cost of the larger battle.

Their main fleet was directed on Midway, a tiny sandspit a thousand miles from Hawaii—famous as the home of the gooney bird—of some small value as an advanced outpost for either side. To take this the Japanese used a fleet of six aircraft carriers, eleven battleships, thirteen cruisers, and forty-five destroyers, plus submarines, minesweepers, transports, and assorted other craft. The whole armada was under the direction of Admiral Yamamoto himself, though in practice the fleet was divided up into packets, at one time as many as ten, spread all over the central Pacific. The heart of it was Admiral Nagumo's Mobile Force, with four carriers, *Akagi, Kaga, Hiryu,* and *Soryu.*

In Hawaii, Admiral Chester W. Nimitz mustered his forces to meet the onslaught. They were thin enough. He had the aircraft based on Midway itself, but afloat there were only three carriers, eight cruisers, and fourteen destroyers. *Hornet* and *Enterprise* were battle-ready; the third carrier was *Yorktown,* just back from the Coral Sea. Estimates were that she required three months in the dockyard to make her ready for sea. She staggered into Pearl on May 27. Three days later she put to sea again, patched rather than fixed, but ready to fight. Nimitz ordered his commanders afloat, Admirals Fletcher and Spruance, to be governed by the principle of the calculated risk, do as much damage as possible, suffer as little as possible. On June 4, the American carrier force, northeast of Midway, surprised the Japanese carrier force northwest of the island.

The battle was a series of air strikes, the Japanese hitting Midway, then being hit by a succession of American attack waves, from both Midway and the carriers, then striking back at the carriers. The climax came at mid-morning. The Japanese had been under attack by planes from Midway and by torpedo planes from the carriers. Virtually every one of the latter—slow, lumbering, obsolete —had been shot down with no damage to the enemy. But they served the purpose of drawing the Japanese fighter aircraft down low, and when the American dive-bombers appeared on the scene the sky was clear. Streaking down they dropped their bombs right in the midst of the Japanese flight decks, covered with planes busy refueling and rearming. Within a matter of minutes three of the big carriers, *Akagi*, *Kaga*, and *Soryu*, were blazing infernos. The fourth was slightly out of position, and was untouched. She in turn launched a strike that put two torpedoes in *Yorktown*. Late in the afternoon the Americans came back and caught *Hiryu* and wrecked her too. The submarine *Nautilus* fired three torpedoes at the already sinking *Kaga*, with one dud hit, and the Americans almost saved *Yorktown*, but a Japanese sub got her in turn. The Japanese fleet pulled back, the Americans followed and caught a cruiser, *Mikuma*, before they gave it up and turned away, wary of an ambush.

In a war involving millions of men and thousands of ships and aircraft, the loss of four carriers on one side, and one on another, may not seem of immeasurable consequence. But it was. For the first time the Americans had emerged the clearcut victors in a battle with the Imperial Navy, and that victory was counted in the one indispensable currency: aircraft carriers. In one short day the balance in the Pacific was restored. Midway was the great crisis and the climax of the Pacific. The Americans were not going to give up, and the fundamental assumption of the Japanese war planners, that it would be a short war, was proved wrong. From now on it would be American expertise and productive capacity against Japanese staying power. The long road from Pearl Harbor to Tokyo Bay had reached its turning point, just six months after December 7. For the first time the strategic initiative lay with the Americans. Now they had to decide what to do with it.

18. The Battles for North Africa

ERWIN ROMMEL HAD BEEN SENT to North Africa to mount a successful holding operation. He had managed to turn what the Germans regarded as a sideshow into a major theater of the war. By the use of daring and tactical initiative he had carried the reluctant Italians along with him and made even them look like winners. Time and circumstance had aided him immeasurably, and he had hit the British when they were at their lowest ebb in the eastern Mediterranean. As soon as they were able to regroup and rebuild their ruined forces after the Greek disaster, they struck back, and in their turn overran the Western Desert. Then, over the end of 1941, both sides settled down; it was a matter of supply, and the one that could build up fastest in the Western Desert would gain the edge and the initiative.

Here Rommel was at a disadvantage. The Germans were throwing everything they had into first stopping the Russian winter offensive, and then reopening their own drive deeper into Russia. Relatively little of their material was sent south. Rommel was left to his own resources. The British, on the other hand, put their major effort into the Mediterranean. At enormous costs of shipping and supplies they tried to give Auchinleck enough of a shot in the arm that he could continue his offensive. Yet even though the British put more into Egypt than the Germans sent to Libya, within the theater itself they faced great difficulties. It was Rommel who was pushed back on his bases, and the British who now had the long tenuous supply line out from Alexandria all the way to El Agheila. As they built up their dumps along the coastal road, Rommel got a helpful convoy in early January of 1942. Two weeks later, still thin but seizing the moment, he jumped off on his second offensive.

The British were caught on the hop and were quickly pushed back out of the Cyrenaican hump; they lost large amounts of the supplies so painfully carried forward; rations, ammunition, trucks, and fuel now were gratefully used by the Germans and Italians. The retreat ended temporarily on a line just west of Tobruk, the Gazala-Bir Hacheim Line, and the rapid withdrawal went down in the troops' folklore as "the Gazala gallop."

Once again both sides paused to gather their breath. Now it was Rommel who was the more distant from his supplies, and he noted with concern that the British were still building up more rapidly than he. Rather than await the inevitable swing of the pendulum, he decided to attack again and he reopened his offensive on May 26.

The Gazala-Bir Hacheim position was about thirty-five miles long, running south from the coast into the desert. The British field commander, General Neil Ritchie, had extensively fortified it with minefields, wire, and a series of infantry strongpoints. The southern end of the line was held by the Free French brigade dug in around Bir Hacheim. Ritchie's idea was that he would use his armor to shore up his strongpoints, and keep the Axis forces from breaking through. He also kept a heavy concentration of armor behind his open southern flank to catch the Germans should they break around it. The British had a substantial superiority in tanks, about 700 to 560 of the enemy, and nearly half of those 560 were light Italian vehicles. Besides that, during the course of the battle the British got the first 200 American Grant tanks, which outgunned the Germans.

The battle that began on May 26 was a remarkable one. Rommel's infantry and some armor put in a straightforward attack against the main British line. While they did that, his mobile armored force moved south, around Bir Hacheim, and then fought its way into the rear of the British line. The British slugged it out every inch of the way, and with their main line four-fifths surrounded, still refused to budge. Rommel was then forced to bring his armor back into the main line—from the British side of it—and hold onto a strongpoint of his own, aptly named "the Cauldron," resisting the attacks of Ritchie's armor while he managed to re-supply. Meanwhile, he sent everything he could spare south against the now isolated Bir Hacheim. The cut-off French held for ten days against heavy attacks led by Rommel personally, then, out of supplies, the survivors broke out and faded into the desert. It was after Bir Hacheim that de Gaulle changed the name from "Free French" to "Fighting French," and their stand brought the French credit with the Allies they had not so far enjoyed.

With Bir Hacheim secured and with his armor regrouped,

while the British had frittered theirs away in piecemeal attacks on the Cauldron, Rommel was ready for the climax. On June 11 he broke through to the eastward. The British armor managed to hold him for two days while most of the infantry scooted out of their strongpoints, then the whole affair gathered momentum, and the pursuit dashed off to the eastward. Ritchie ended the battle losing more than 90 percent of his tanks. The Germans leaped forward and this time grabbed Tobruk before the British could organize it for a siege, gaining several thousand prisoners and immense amounts of stores. Hitler responded by promoting Rommel to field marshal, and it looked as if the end of the North African campaign were in sight.

As the British 8th Army streamed in disarray toward Alexandria, General Auchinleck moved in and took over the army command. His position was almost intolerable from several points of view. He was faced with disaster to his front, and to his rear, relations with Churchill were becoming increasingly acrimonious. Churchill constantly wanted to intervene in the course of the battle, he was the bane of his military advisors at home, and he was now falling out with Auchinleck as he had with Wavell; at one point he inspired an anguished Brooke to cry out, "I tell you you must either back your Commander-in-Chief or sack him!" and "to back him or sack him" became a constant problem. Just now Churchill would do neither the one nor the other.

In spite of this Auchinleck pulled the situation together. He slowed Rommel just across the frontier at Sollum, and more seriously with a stand at Mersa Matruh, and then stopped him definitively at El Alamein. The Germans had finally run out of steam, and the position stabilized at the end of June, with the British on a very strong line between El Alamein on the coast road and the Qattara Depression, a great impassable sinkhole thirty miles to the south. It was a far better anchor than Bir Hacheim, and they were safe for the moment. They were also a mere sixty miles from Alexandria.

Midsummer of 1942 brought alluring prospects for the Axis. For a few moments German troops gazed on the Caspian Sea, and at times it looked again as if Russia would collapse. Japanese carriers were raiding Ceylon, and Rommel was on the doorstep of the East. The situation has conjured retrospective visions of the three great Axis Powers meeting each other somewhere in the depths of south-central Asia. Such visions are of course but an illusion. The

Japanese forays into the Indian Ocean were no more than diversions, the Russians recovered in the late summer, and Rommel never got past El Alamein. On a straight calculation of so much energy, matériel, and manpower required per mile of conquest, the Axis simply did not have the goods. But that knowledge too is retrospective. At the moment, practically the whole world was locked in the throes of the greatest war ever seen, and the future boiled down to thousands of young men in cylinders in the sky, steel compartments in the sea, and holes in the ground.

For the British the supply buildup had to be done all over again. All the material so painfully shipped to Egypt, trucked and carted forward with such immense effort, was now being enjoyed by the Germans and the Italians. Once more the convoys made their way around the western hump of Africa, past the Cape of Good Hope—old Bartholomeu Diaz wanted to call it the Cape of Storms, but the fifteenth-century Portuguese had their public relations men too—up through the Red Sea, and into the teeming ports of Egypt. Malta was reinforced as well, the unsinkable aircraft carrier that became the single most-bombed target in the world, and every day the fighters and bombers sallied forth to harry Rommel's convoys. Both sides raced against time to tip the balance their way in Egypt.

Refusing either to back him or sack him, Churchill kept pestering Auchinleck for an offensive. "The Auk" demurred; he did not feel ready, and through July and August his troops sparred ineffectually with the enemy. Neither side yet had the advantage. In mid-August, Churchill lost patience and made up his mind; Auchinleck went, and a new team came out to try its luck in the desert graveyard of reputations. Churchill had never been unreservedly behind Wavell, and was even less so behind Auchinleck, but the new commanders were his stars, General Sir Harold Alexander as area commander, and Lt. General Bernard Montgomery as the 8th Army commander. They told Churchill exactly what Auchinleck had, that they were not ready to advance yet. This time he listened, and gave them the support they wanted. Montgomery promised that when he did move, he would win.

Rommel moved first again. At the end of August he launched the battle of Alam el Halfa, his attempt to break through the El Alamein position. The plan was a straight replay of the Gazala-Bir Hacheim battle, but this time the British were ready for him. Once again they had built up faster than he, though the two sides were nearly equal in armor. Montgomery did have one startling advantage not enjoyed by his predecessors: he had a copy of Rommel's operation order.

The Germans were still unaware that the British code-breakers were reading their signals. Up to this time the cryptographers in London had been able to provide useful snippets of information to the commanders in the field, but now a whole spate of signals between Rommel, Field Marshal Kesselring in Rome, and the German high command gave the British not only Rommel's complete order of battle and a count of his available supplies, but also a full outline of his tactical plan as well. With this in his pocket, Montgomery was able to astound his staff by stepping up to the map and saying that Rommel would do this and the British would do that, and the battle would be over. Montgomery never mentioned the code-breaking in his memoirs, but to be fair to him, at the time they were written it was still a state secret.

Anyway, all went exactly as planned—by the British. Rommel hit the southern end of the line hard on the last day of August. It floated back, and the Germans turned north. Instead of running into soft rear areas, they encountered armor and infantry dug in deep on the Alam el Halfa ridge. Here Montgomery's true talent showed up; he had assessed Rommel's trick of gulling the British armor into attacking him in the open, and then destroying it with his anti-tank guns. This time the British refused to be drawn, Rommel had to go forward, and it was his armor that took a beating. Under heavy air attacks, he was forced to pull back, and by the 7th the British were still holding their original line, with only a few dents in it. The battle was over. So were Rommel's offensives.

Churchill immediately took up the old refrain of an offensive, but Montgomery would not be rushed. He was not an improvisor and he wanted everything to be ready. Alexander backed him, and he had the prestige of Alam el Halfa behind him as well. Therefore, while the supplies piled up and the troops trained, the British got ready. This time there were to be no half measures.

For six weeks the matter hung fire, both sides preparing as best they could for what both knew was coming. The only constraint Churchill now put upon the timing was that the battle must come before the first week of November, because the Allies were planning at that time to invade French North Africa; when they did, they wanted the French to be in no doubt as to who was winning the war.

The battle that opened on the night of October 23-24 was the greatest so far fought in North Africa. The British and Commonwealth troops, about 200,000 strong, outnumbered the Germans and Italians in men and tanks by two to one; they enjoyed complete air superiority. They started with an intensive, World War I-style bombardment by more than 800 guns, and then, in the darkness, the British crashed into the Axis positions. The attack opened with the Australians moving along the coastal road. To their left the Highland Division, bagpipes wailing in the night, drove toward the desert ridges. To their left again were New Zealanders, then South Africans, Indians, and a Greek brigade, more British, and the French down on the end of the line. The Germans and Italians held hard; they had dug in extensively, they had laid minefields and strung wire and sited their anti-tank guns. For three days the British bludgeoned their way forward, only to be held to no real gain. On the fourth day Rommel sent his armor out in a vicious counterattack, but the British tanks and aircraft stopped it cold.

Montgomery had hoped to break his armor through, set up blocking positions, and then mop up the enemy infantry. The Germans were holding too hard for that, and the battle resolved itself into a straight slugging match. Finally, on the night of November 2, the New Zealanders broke into the clear, shored up a corridor through the main line of resistance, and British armor rolled on into the open. Late on the 2nd, Rommel acknowledged his battle was lost. He began to pull out, then made the mistake of asking Hitler if it was all right. The order came back next day to hold fast, no retreat. It was a mistake and Rommel knew it; reluctantly he canceled his withdrawal order, and the result was that the whole position fell to pieces, units facing in every direction, some moving, some trying to hold on. Aided by this confusion, the British punched another hole in the line on the 4th, caught an Italian armored division in flank as it moved up from the south, and wiped it out after it had put up a gallant stand. The rest of the Italians, cut off to the south, were left to their fate and the Germans, disregarding Hitler's orders, began to fade away. On the 5th, Hitler said they could go after all.

Montgomery paused to pull his winded troops together. The battle cost him 13,000 casualties and more than half his tank force but he was quickly reinforcing and bringing in new material. The Axis lost twice that many men and half that many tanks and could afford neither.

Now the hunt was up. On the 7th, the British just barely missed cutting off the retreat; on the 11th, they crossed the Libyan frontier. For 1,400 miles, all the way to Tunisia, the 8th Army and the Desert Air Force harried the Axis and snapped at their heels. The Germans never really put a position together. The Royal Navy kept leapfrogging supplies forward from port to port. The fliers moved their airfields as fast as the armor went, and at one point even flew in and set up a temporary airfield ahead of the retreating Germans. Time and again the British armor lanced into the desert, racing to get ahead of the Germans and cut them off. They never quite succeeded, for the fleeing enemy could travel faster along the coast road than the British could through the rough scrub and shale of the desert. Repeatedly, though, they cut the tail of the column, and the Axis retreat was marked by a long suppurating trail of broken-down vehicles, abandoned when their fuel ran out, guns left behind, aircraft parked on overrun fields. Australians drank the wine stored by gourmet commanders, and Indians marched thousands of prisoners back eastward. It was one of the greatest and most exhilarating pursuits in history, and the old familiar desert names appeared in the communiques one after another: Tobruk on November 13, Benghazi on the 20th, El Agheila in mid-December, Sirte on Christmas Day—not for two years had the British been close to Sirte—and the climax, Tripoli, on January 23, 1943. By the end of the month the British were into Tunisia, and closing up on the end of the long desert campaign. El Alamein was one of the great turning points of the war, fairly won and exploited to the full. The only sour note in the whole symphony was that they had failed to bag Rommel himself. In February he and the tattered remnants of the mighty Deutsches Afrika Korps sought refuge behind the Mareth Line, an old French fortification in southern Tunisia, and turned at bay. The Desert Fox was cornered at last, but he was still going to fight.

The Allied invasion of French North Africa, the other half of the pincer that was to wreck Axis hopes in the Mediterranean, was the product of a great deal of discussion and even argument among the Allied leaders. As soon as the Americans entered the war they sent planning staffs to Britain, and projected a great troop buildup for an invasion of France at the first possible moment. At the Arcadia Conference, the British broached the idea of wrapping up North Africa, and the Americans reluctantly agreed. As their forces buildup began to gather momentum, they tried to shelve the idea at the Bolero Conference in London. The British clung to it, pointing out that they must come to grips someplace as soon as possible, that to be able to use the Mediterranean would ease their shipping problems. The argument went on for months, and at one point the American Joint Chiefs of Staff became so unhappy they urged a reordering of American priorities and a major emphasis on the Pacific instead of Germany—an attitude dear to many American hearts anyway, and one always lurking beneath the surface.

Assorted evidence of German strength in France refused to deter them. For example, to test some of their preconceptions about invasion plans, the British mounted a major raid on the French port of Dieppe in August of 1942. Up to this point the Allies believed they might have to land at a port, as supply over open beaches for an invasion force was considered impossible. The Dieppe raid was carried out by a force of nearly 7,000 men, 5,000 of them Canadians who had been in Britain since 1940. The whole raid was a shambles. The Canadians barely got off the beach in front of the town, and in nine hours of heavy fighting they suffered well over 3,000 casualties in killed, wounded, prisoners, and missing. It was a costly way to prove the Allies could not invade Europe in the immediate future, and the Canadians, who had been asking for action for two years, still have bitter memories of the way they got it.

The decision to go to North Africa was eventually kicked upstairs to Roosevelt, and he came down unequivocally on the British side. Politically, he believed it was imperative that American ground forces come into combat with the Germans at the earliest possible moment, and obviously North Africa was the only reasonable place to do it in 1942. That the invasion of French North Africa may have delayed the invasion of France for a year remains arguable; both the Russians and the American public demanded more action by the Western Allies and demanded it immediately, and that determined this issue. The British got their way: North Africa it was. Operation Torch was set for early November of 1942.

With General Eisenhower appointed as commander of the invasion forces, the British and Americans then fell to arguing over where they should land. Roles were reversed now, and the British, whose caution led to North Africa instead of France, now wanted to move as far east as possible. They wanted a landing near the border between Tunisia and Algeria that would enable them to move rapidly east into Tunisia, and grab it before the Germans and Italians could rush troops in to hold the territory. The Americans, who had wanted to go boldly into France, now wanted to go cautiously into Africa. They were afraid Spain would come in, or that Axis air power would catch them at sea in the Mediterranean. They therefore wanted to land on the Atlantic coast of French Morocco, and move from there. The British thought this was pretty wasteful, and would just involve the Allies in another campaign such as they were already waging in Egypt.

Eventually they compromised. A Western Task Force, entirely American in composition, would sail from the United States and land off Casablanca on the Atlantic coast of Morocco. A Center Task Force, also American, sailing from Britain, would land inside the Mediterranean at Oran. An Eastern Task Force, British and American, would land at Algiers. The first two would prevent a German move through Spain and across the straits into Spanish Morocco; the third would dash east and secure Tunisia before the Germans could get there. The British agreed that all three operations should look as American as possible, in the hope that the French would not resist them.

That was the big question: would the French fight? The French said they would. The Vichy French government had been a faithful collaborator in the Hitlerian New Order, and one reason they had forestalled German occupation of the rest of France, as well as their North African empire, was that they had managed to convince the Germans they were capable of defending their territory against the Allies and willing to do so. When the British had seized Syria in 1941, the French had fought; when the British took over Madagascar in May of 1942, as a means of guarding their approaches to India, the French had fought again. They had lost both times, but their weak forces had still done the best they could. So there was little doubt they would fight the British; it was an open question whether or not they would fight the Americans. No one knew the answer to that, not the Germans, not the British or Americans, indeed not even the French.

French soldiers at the time faced an extraordinary moral dilemma. They were servants of the state, sworn to defend it; the accidents of war had made the legitimate French government a tool of the conqueror, yet it was still the official French government. It took a special kind of person to throw aside the norms of a lifetime, to make the lonely decision that there was a higher loyalty, a higher duty, than that he had always acknowledged, and in the name of some abstract moral principle to work against his own government. Thousands did make that decision, but the vast majority continued to work within the comfortable parameters of routine and convention.

Nor was it a purely academic decision. The German occupiers did not say anyone was free to choose as conscience dictated. Half of France remained unoccupied, a hostage to good behavior. It would stay that way only as long as the French Empire behaved itself and resisted the blandishments of de Gaulle or the Allies. If a French pilot in North Africa defected and flew his plane to Gibraltar, his family in France was going to suffer for it.

The French government was little help. Pétain was contemptuous of the Germans but wrapped up in his own delusions and determined to get along. Imperceptibly, he moved more and more fully into Hitler's orbit. He was helped along this path by Pierre Laval, the malign influence who was France's most eminent collaborator with the Germans. A third figure in the power equation was Admiral Jean Darlan, the head of the French Navy. Darlan had done much to build up the prewar navy, and considered it his private fief. In his last "free" order to the fleet before the capitulation in 1940, he had ordered it to scuttle itself rather than fall into the hands of the Germans, if they ever subsequently attempted a takeover. But he was publicly anti-British, and no one knew how he, or the fleet still loyal to him, would react in the event of an Allied invasion of French North Africa.

In spite of all these convolutions, there were officers, especially at the middle and junior levels, who were desperate to bring France back into the fight. As the United States had never broken off diplomatic relations with Vichy, but maintained consular services in the French Empire, American officials and these middle-grade officers gravitated together. Out of these contacts came some degree of collusion and incomplete plans that the French would stage a near-coup, seizing power and allowing the Allies to get ashore unopposed.

These plans failed to reach fruition because the Allies could not, at the last moment, bring themselves to trust the French completely; they kept secret the date of their landings. The result of the whole imbroglio was a large degree of confusion, some very unhappy fighting, and a good deal of residual recrimination.

Things went best at Algiers. The Anglo-American Eastern Task Force, commanded by the American general Charles Ryder, arrived on the morning of November 8, just as pro-Allied officers had seized temporary control of the city. By chance, Admiral Darlan was in Algiers, visiting his son, and the Vichy forces under his overall direction regained command of Algiers at mid-morning. The damage was already done, however, and the British and Americans were securely ashore by then. They had landed on both sides of the city and were rapidly closing in on it. Fighting ended at nightfall, when the Vichy remnants surrendered. Darlan was taken by the Allies, and he then ordered all French units to cease fighting. When this order was received in metropolitan France an angry Pétain quickly disavowed it and ordered the French to continue the struggle. This sort of confusion continued for the next three days.

The Central Task Force under General Lloyd Fredendall landed at Oran. The plan here was the same as at Algiers, landings on both sides of the city and a pincer movement to isolate and capture it. The flank landings were both made successfully; an attempt to push two destroyers loaded with troops straight into the harbor was practically wiped out. The Americans also made parachute drops against the inland French airfields, but the paratroops missed their target by nearly twenty miles. Nonetheless, the Allies had naval and air superiority; the French made some fairly determined counterattacks on the 9th, and surrendered at midday on the 10th.

The heaviest fighting was on the ocean side, where General George S. Patton's Western Task Force, coming all the way across the Atlantic, went ashore near Casablanca. Again the landings flanked the city, and the assault waves, in one of the few instances of the war, waded ashore carrying American flags, in the hope that the French would not fire on them. The hope proved illusory, and the defenders, mostly French colonial troops, fought hard before they were pushed back and the landings secured. There were substantial French naval units in Casablanca, and trapped as they were, they fought. Five ships were sunk, and the incompleted battleship *Jean Bart* engaged in a losing gunnery due with the American *Massachusetts*. Allied planes raked the harbor and took on the obsolete Vichy Air Force—American pilots in American planes versus French pilots in American planes bought back in 1940. Finally, after hard fighting, the French surrendered on orders from Algiers early on November 11.

The landings were but a prelude to a whole series of problems: What would the Germans do to France, what would happen to the

French fleet, what sort of deal would the Allies make with the French in the empire, and what would the Germans do about that? The answers were not long in coming.

In Metropolitan France the German response was a quick take-over. Disregarding the protestations of loyalty by the Vichy government, the Germans immediately moved troops across the demarcation line, and swept south over hitherto unoccupied France. Vichy collapsed precipitately, its little remaining credit gone forever. The army, known as the Armistice Army, dissolved with no show of resistance. From now on, the facade was stripped away, and France, like all the other defeated territories, was laid open to the direct rule of the Germans. The Vichy hand had been played out.

The French fleet in its southern base at Toulon, however, remained true to its chief. It takes several hours to fire off boilers and raise enough steam for a ship to get underway. The French ships were helpless, unable to move. Rather than have the vessels fall into the hands of the Germans, the crews scuttled the ships. It was a sad, negative act of self-destruction, but it kept the fleet out of German hands.

Difficult as the decision to scuttle the fleet was, it was nothing compared to the complexities of the power situation in North Africa. The French Empire, though weak in modern equipment, contained large numbers of trained troops. There were several aspirants for the right to lead them, thereby bringing France back into the war and ranging her alongside the Allies. First there was de Gaulle, deliberately kept in the dark on the North African operation and shunted into the background by the Americans. De Gaulle was the one man who could claim to have been on the side of the angels from the very beginning, but he had no credit among the former Vichy officials. In his place the Americans flirted with General Henri Giraud, whom they initially liked better. But the man who had the support of the Vichyites was Admiral Darlan. It was a three-way standoff: de Gaulle was pure, but anathema to the Vichyites; Darlan was Vichy's hero, but the Allies distrusted him; Giraud immediately proved utterly inept, so neither side wanted him.

Eventually, the Allies decided Darlan was their man, and Eisenhower, coming over to North Africa, agreed to recognize him as "head of the French state" in return for committing French troops to the war against the Germans. There was an immediate protest from the American and British publics against dealing with a man who had so openly connived with Germany, and Darlan began to be a considerable embarrassment. That embarrassment was removed on Christmas Eve when the admiral was shot by a young assassin. The assassin was captured and precipitately shot in his turn by the French authorities. In an incredibly confused welter of plot and counterplot, the assassin seemed to think he was acting on behalf of the Count of Paris, current claimant to the throne of France, who had been serving in the French Foreign Legion, as royal pretenders were not allowed to serve in the regular forces of the republic. Whatever the details, it was the Gaullists who profited by Darlan's removal; de Gaulle quickly outmaneuvered Giraud and ended up the holder of the reins of French power.

All of that was but a sideshow. The primary problem was what the Germans would do. As usual, they reacted rapidly. The key to saving the situation in the Mediterranean was the control of Tunisia, which at its closest point is a mere hundred miles from Sicily. The French military commander in Tunisia, General Georges Barré, received a string of orders from both Pétain in France and Darlan in Algiers which not only flatly contradicted each other, but even contradicted themselves from one message to the next.

While the French dithered, the Germans acted, and on the 9th the first German units began arriving by air from Sicily. Barré's outclassed forces pulled back out of Tunis and retreated westward to meet the British, frantically trying to leapfrog troops forward from Algiers. But Tunis is farther from Algiers than it is from Rome, and the Allies hardly had a firm operating base in the confusion of Algiers anyway. The Germans handily won the race and by the third week in November had created a thin line running along the mountain spine of Tunisia from Cape Serrat in the north about halfway down the country to El Guettar. The Allies managed to move the British along the coast, so that as they came up against this German line, they had the British 1st Army in the north, then a wide sector held by weak French patrols in the mountains, and then Americans coming into the line at the southern end.

Through November and into early December, the British made a try for Tunis, but German air superiority and then the advent of the winter rains stopped them. The Germans then launched attacks against the thin French patrols in the central sector, who had to be shored up by the diversion of arriving American armor. January was spent in sorting out the Allied forces on the one side, and in the arrival of Rommel's remnants from Egypt on the other. By early February the Germans believed they had the situation in hand; their lines were secure, and they decided they could risk an attack. They chose the weak U. S. IInd Corps sector. The American public and leaders had wanted to get their troops in combat in the European theater; now they were going to get more than they had bargained for.

The Battle of Kasserine Pass was a limited engagement for the Germans; they wanted to buy time and shake up their enemies. There was not a great deal more than that that they could hope to achieve. For the Americans it was a confused nightmare, a baptism of fire that showed them they were newcomers in a tough league.

Early on the morning of February 14, the Germans opened an assault with two armored divisions, supported by fighters, dive-bombers, and mobile artillery. The Americans expected it, but not in such strength. The Germans cut off an infantry regiment and wiped it out; the Americans counterattacked with an armored regiment, and the Germans wiped it out too. The American Stuart tanks failed even to dent the heavier Germans, and the medium Shermans soon showed their shortcomings as well. In five days of steady driving, the Germans made nearly seventy miles, through Kasserine Pass toward the town of Tebessa. They lost their momentum, however; Rommel disagreed with the Tunisian commander, Jurgen von Arnim, and the Americans gradually regrouped. The Germans finally ran out of push on the 22nd, having achieved little more than a large-scale raid, and soon the lines were back where they had been before the battle. It cost them about a thousand casualties, and they inflicted well over 6,000 on the Americans. It was a small affair as battles went in World War II, but it marked two things: it was the end of American military innocence, and it was also the end of German offensive action in North Africa.

From then on it was a matter of squeezing. Montgomery linked up with the American tail of the Allied Tunisian line, and the Germans were henceforth in a pocket. Hitler thought he could hold it and he kept putting troops in, running the gauntlet of Allied air power across the Sicilian Narrows. Rommel went home sick, and left von Arnim to fight it out. Late in February, Montgomery got around the Mareth Line—his direct assault failed—and the Germans fell back; by mid-April all they held was the northeastern tip of the country. Hitler still thought he could hang on. The final Allied attack opened on April 22. The Germans and Italians held firm under heavy, steady pressure for ten days, but then they began to weaken. The Luftwaffe pulled out, leapfrogging its planes and whatever it could salvage, back to Sicily. French and Americans, now on the left of the line, pushed into Bizerte on May 7, and British troops entered Tunis. Too late, the Germans were trying to scuttle out. Convoys of the transport planes were badgered across the narrows by the R. A. F. and the Royal Navy, who hoped in vain the Italian fleet would come out to the rescue.

The final resistance collapsed on the 13th, when the Italian 1st Army, the last cohesive unit, laid down its arms. More than a quarter of a million prisoners went into the cages, the biggest Western Allied haul yet and an entirely appropriate match for the great Russian victory at Stalingrad. The southern shore of the Mediterranean was free at last, and the Hitlerian empire reduced to Fortress Europe.

19. Crisis in Russia

THERE IS AN OLD proverb that Russia has two unbeatable commanders: Generals January and February. In 1941 she had a third, General December. The early winter hit the Germans just as their final drive for Moscow ran out of steam; Hitler had frittered away his weeks in the late summer, and they were never regained. Napoleon once remarked, "Ask me for anything but time." Now the chance for easy victory was gone.

The Russians, dressed for the cold and employing primitive tactics and equipment, struck back on December 6. In the frozen steppes horse-drawn sleds, ski troops, and mounted cavalry were better than German tanks with their engine blocks frozen solid. The Russians employed large masses of men; as throughout the war, they ruthlessly sacrificed troops in the line while building up massive reserves for their own offensives. Now their drive gained power, rolling over the ill-prepared Germans, weak from their extended operations, and disgusted by their failure to win the war before the arrival of winter.

On December 8, Hitler approved an Army high command order placing the forces in Russia in a defensive position. For the next ten days the commanders were free to maneuver, shorten their lines, and improve their situation by falling back to defensible positions. Then Hitler got angry; large amounts of equipment were being abandoned to the cold and the enemy. He stepped in and fired his Chief of the General Staff, von Brauchitsch, and took over supreme command himself. He had had enough of the generals with their subtly superior ways and their foolish ideas that military requirements took precedence over the dictates of Nazi ideology. The withdrawals were to stop; there would be no more retreat; units would fight where they were, and there they would stay. Within a month all three army group commanders were fired and replaced by men who realized what a command from the Fuehrer

232

really meant. On Christmas Day, Hitler fired Guderian too, for allowing a retreat without permission from his master. When General Hoeppner made a snide remark about "civilians" in high places, Hitler dismissed him as well.

Firing generals was one thing, stopping the Russians was another. It was all right to issue standfast orders from Berlin or East Prussia, but the troops in the field, ill equipped and on half rations, kept on falling back. The Russians launched massive attacks in the Crimea, and the Germans there were hard put to contain them. They broke through the center of Army Group South's front and created a large salient in the German line. Up north they very nearly surrounded large numbers of Germans fighting around Demyansk; Hitler ordered them to hold on, and the Luftwaffe began supplying them by air, setting a precedent for what might happen later.

The worst news was in front of Moscow. The Reds broke the Germans both north and south of the city and drove them back nearly 200 miles. Rage as he might, there was nothing Hitler could do about it; eventually he had to agree that there might be "limited" retreats on the front. Ninth Army of Army Group Center ended up in a huge sack, but the Russians were not quite able to close the neck of it. The Germans organized all-around defense positions which they called "hedgehogs," and inflicted such heavy losses on the Soviets that even they began to feel they were running out of bodies. By late February they were played out, and the lines stabilized at last. Hitler claimed that it was his policy of no retreat —slightly modified—that prevented complete disaster and utter rout. He may have been right; on the other hand, his generals and critics claimed that his orders cost the Wehrmacht immense casualties, and that in the end the Germans were back on the more or less defensible line they had wanted to retreat to anyway. As March rains came on and the front dissolved in mud, the Russians could feel they had gained breathing space at last. Their greatest accomplishment may have been their forcing Hitler into supreme command where he was free to make mistakes.

Little could be done by either side through April and into May; the mud forced both Russian and German to wallow about cursing. All either could do was make plans for the coming campaign, which both recognized had become a life-and-death struggle. A process of stabilization which neither immediately recognized was now taking place. The Germans, with their economy still not fully geared to war, were becoming weaker. The Wehrmacht of 1942 was poorer than that of 1941; its tank formations had fewer vehicles, many of its infantry battalions were down almost to half-strength. This attrition continued as the war made increasing demands on Hitlerian Germany. Eventually, Albert Speer replaced Goering as economic dictator, but his genius was applied too late to reverse a trend apparent in 1942. Between Hitler's amateurish meddling in development and the great overextension of German responsibilities, their problems grew until they became insurmountable. In the simplest terms, they bit off more than they could chew.

The Russians too were relatively weak in 1942, but as the German graph slid downward, theirs went up. At the start of the spring campaign they were even short of rifles and small arms for their infantry, but they gained day by day. Part of this gain, though only a part, come from the West. In 1942 and 1943 the British, Americans, and Canadians turned out more than 10,000 tanks which were sent to Russia. Most of them were not up to Russian standards, ironically, and they were generally employed on quiet sectors, with the exception of some British infantry-support tanks heavy enough for Russian needs.

Rather better results were achieved with western aircraft. A total of just over 14,000 American aircraft was sent to Russia, nearly 10,000 of them fighter planes. The largest single type was the P-39 Airacobra, one of the less successful in the American inventory, which had already been rejected by the British as unsuitable for combat. The Russians liked them and used them extensively as ground support and attack aircraft. The British added another 4,000 planes, mostly Hurricanes and Spitfires. These figures impressed western observers more than they did Russians. The American aircraft industry produced about 300,000 planes during the war; Russian industry built 142,000. The Russians felt that 10 percent of their needs, and only 5 percent of American production, was not a great deal.

The greatest contribution of the Western Allies, however, was in trucks—more than 385,000 of them—clothing, rations, raw materials, signal equipment, and all kinds of items which enabled the Russian war industry to concentrate on producing its own guns and tanks. It was American trucks and half-tracks that really motorized the Red Army. Not until 1943 did these items reach Russia in large proportions, but they were a major addition to Russia's war effort. If the Russians did not appear as grateful as the British and Americans thought perhaps they should be, the

Soviet response was brutally simple: we are doing the fighting. It was November of 1942 before the first American troops were in action against the Germans in even divisional strength. At that time the Russians had more than four million men facing the German armies.

That was far more Russians than there were Germans about. The Axis had in midsummer of 1942 just over three million men in Russia; more than half a million of them were from the satellite countries: fifty-one divisions of Rumanians, Hungarians, Slovakians, and Italians. There was a Spanish division as well; though Franco remained determinedly neutral in Hitler's war, he did allow the dispatch of an all-volunteer division to join the fight against communism. Few of them came home to Spain again.

The Russians needed to be stronger because, though they were improving, they were still far less sophisticated than even a weakened German war machine. Their staff work was not as good, their troops were poorly trained, forced to learn as they went along—if they survived to do so—and the Reds still employed tactics that were wasteful of manpower. More than any other army, except possibly the Chinese, they were willing to trade lives for time and space. Yet as their communications techniques developed and as their planning staffs gained confidence, they became increasingly adept. Once again, as Russian matériel—human and otherwise—got better, and German matériel got worse, the two lines on the graph neared and finally crossed. The place where they ultimately met each other was at Stalingrad.

Hitler's plans for 1942 were grandiose indeed, when viewed on a map. He decided by a four-stage operation to clear the great bend of the Don River, close in on Stalingrad on the Volga, and then drive down into the Caucasus where he would seize the Russian oil fields and bring the Russian war machine squeaking to a halt. The weakness in these plans was that they made the oil fields the primary objective and reduced the Red Army, which had to be pushed out of the way to get to them, to a secondary position. Going for towns or space on the map was the basic error of commanders in the eighteenth century, the "era of indecisive decisions"; Hitler, the gifted amateur, contemptuous of professional advice and relying on his intuition, was now making that error once again.

The Russians beat the Germans to the punch and in May launched an attack on Kharkov from the salient they had gained during the winter. The Germans responded ferociously, breaking the attack and cleaning out the salient as well, and when the smoke cleared, the Russians had lost a quarter of a million men and more than 1,200 tanks. The Germans continued with their preparations for the Caucasus.

Stage one of the operation was a necessary clearing of both flanks. In the south the Germans at last completed the conquest of the Crimea. They drove the Russians into the sea at the Kerch Peninsula, inflicting 150,000 casualties on them, and they vigorously pushed their siege of Sevastopol. The Russians had dug extensive fortifications around this, their major Black Sea base. As long as they could they supplied it by sea. When the German artillery got too close for surface vessels, they brought in material by submarine. Inexorably, the German noose tightened, and late in June they broke through and reached the harbor on the northern side. The main part of the city and the Russian works were to the south, however, so on June 28 the Germans made an assault crossing of the harbor, catching the defenders to the south by surprise; the city was theirs by July 1 and another 100,000 Russians gone with it.

Clearing the northern flank of the Don bend meant taking the key Russian city of Voronezh. This was done by means of the now-standard enveloping attack. Early in July the Germans punched two holes in the Russian line, and a week later the city fell. The Russians were surprised, in spite of taking prisoner a German staff officer with the complete operation order in his briefcase.

The next stage was a deeper envelopment to the south, while the Hungarians held a blocking position north of Voronezh. The German 6th Army drove eastward and met the Voronezh force coming down the river. Resistance was weak, but the Russians managed to pull back without getting trapped. Sixth Army in its turn wheeled right and began to slide down the Don toward its easternmost point, the great bend forty miles from Stalingrad.

While 6th Army pushed on, Hitler opened the third phase of the drive. The southern part of Army Group South, now reorganized as Army Group A, drove past Rostov at the mouth of the Don. The Russians broke easily here, many troops deserting while others fled back in complete disarray. It looked for a moment as if all the southern Red armies would be caught in a gigantic trap between 6th Army and Army Group A, just as the original German plan for this stage had intended. Then Hitler did it again and diverted Army Group A toward its final objective. Instead of letting it continue eastward to link up with 6th Army at Stalingrad, he wheeled it right, and the leading elements took off for the Caucasus with almost nothing ahead of them. Instead of being trapped in the Don bend, hundreds of thousands of Russians escaped into the Kalmyk Steppe; by their own willfulness the Germans had created a funnel instead of a trap, and the Soviet forces lived to fight again.

On August 1, 6th Army, supported by 4th Panzer Army, was forty miles from Stalingrad, driving hard for the city. The long-range intelligence forecast was gloomy. The Germans believed they had destroyed well over a hundred Russian divisions, but they had identified elements of more than three hundred more. They figured that the Russians outnumbered them in soldiers by at least 50 percent. The Russian manpower pool was estimated as being three times greater than Germany's, and in spite of the amazing advances they had made on the map, the Germans thought the Russians had preserved the capability to launch another winter offensive.

By late August the Germans were in the western Caucasus Mountains. Here the Russians finally slowed them down and held on firmly to the passes in the hills. Eastward, the Germans flowed over the steppes, gradually halted not so much by the Russians as by distance and their inability to supply themselves. Their tanks gobbled gasoline faster than they could bring it up to the front. Hitler became more and more angry with his commanders, and there was another spate of dismissals: Halder lost his job as Chief of Staff, and Army Group A's Field Marshal List was fired for lack of aggressiveness. Hitler took over the army group himself, which made him the world's most distant field commander. It had little effect; by late November the German advance had ground to a stop, defeated by time and distance, two things that neither the Wehrmacht nor Hitler could control. The great Caucasus drive was over, and it had netted only thin air.

Meanwhile, Army Group B, the other half of the former Army Group South, had been sucked deeper and deeper into the morass whose center was Stalingrad. Under Field Marshal von Weichs it had seen its spearpoint, 6th Army, under General Friedrich Paulus, close up on the city in early September. Here the advance stopped; the Russians had retreated as far as they were going. Stalingrad stretches for miles along the great bend of the Volga, where that river and the Don approach each other. It is on the western, higher side of the river, with banks and bluffs falling off to the waterfront. It was then a major industrial center and, during the fighting, Russian workmen in their factories were building tanks which drove out the doors with guns firing at the enemy. By November 1 there were five Russian armies defending the city and the area immediately around it, and two German armies—6th and 4th Panzer—fighting their way into it.

The battle raged unceasingly. Every night the Russians ferried supplies over the river, and the troops worked their way into the rubble and hunkered down behind piles of bricks and mortar; every house, every cellar, every room, became a strongpoint. City fighting is a nightmare for troops and commanders alike; for the troops all the skills developed in open country are negated. The need for constant alertness saps vitality, and even perpetual caution is not proof against sudden surprise, the sniper, the mine, the booby-trap, the man who leaps around the corner and shoots first, the grenade that comes sailing in out of nowhere. Commanders lose control of their battles and watch their forces disappear into a choked mess that defies description. The Germans did not like it, and neither did the Russians; but this was where the Russian high command decided to make its stand. Stalingrad became the Verdun of World War II, its monuments today evoking the same kind of pilgrimages that Verdun's did after World War I.

As the focus of interest narrowed down on the city and the gigantic battle raging in its heart, the Germans were forced to neglect their long fronts lying either side of Stalingrad. Due south was the Kalmyk Steppe, wide-open territory with few defensive features to it, held only by the relatively thin screen of the Rumanian 4th Army. To the north lay the long line up the Don as far as Voronezh. This too was weakly held, by the 3rd Rumanian, 8th Italian, and 2nd Hungarian armies. All of these were low-priority units; all had German forces attached for stiffening. The Germans openly regarded their allies as second-class troops, which did a great deal to make them so, but even without that, their formations were numerically and materially weaker than the German, as well as poorer in morale.

By November 1 the Germans had split the defenders of Stalingrad into four groups. They had not completely isolated them but they had reached the point where communication between them had to be carried out on the other side of the river. On the 12th the Germans actually got to the Volga itself at one point in the southern outskirts of the city. Casualties were extremely heavy on both sides; the Russians who crossed the river were told not to come back, and the Germans kept pulling in more and more troops from their other fronts. Stalingrad had now become the worst kind of battle, one whose cost far exceeded its value. Hitler had lost his head over it and was absolutely determined to have it; just because of that, the Russians were equally determined to hold it, and the battle went on.

Meanwhile, German intelligence was picking up vague hints of Russians massing north of the city, opposite the front held by the Rumanians. Here the Reds still maintained a precarious toehold on the western bank of the Don, and they were suspected of moving troops into it. Belatedly, the Germans pulled one Panzer division out of Stalingrad and sent it north to bolster their allies. The troops were delighted to be reprieved from the fighting in the city.

The Russian plan, in its classic simplicity, possessed a terrible beauty. The Germans had piled themselves into a lump at Stalingrad, leaving their flanks screened only by thin supporting troops. Trading the lives of the defenders of Stalingrad for time, the Russians waited for two things: the arrival of frost that made the ground hard enough to move armor across country, and the Allied invasion of French North Africa, rightly seen as tying down German reserves in western Europe. Now, stealthily, they had massed two full armies, one of them armored, against the Rumanians south of the city. North of it, where Rumanian 3rd Army held its long line, were hidden five armies—seven, counting those slated to move on Stalingrad itself.

On November 19 the Red armies opened a massive artillery barrage all along the Don River. At mid-morning huge masses of infantry, staggering forward in human-wave attacks, came out of the Russian bridgehead. The Rumanians held them up for a few hours, putting up a stronger resistance than anyone had any right to expect, but they were soon swamped. By suppertime of the first day the Red armor was out in the clear, and the German and satellite remnants were breaking up, fleeing over the open plain and being rounded up by triumphant Russians.

The next day the Russian drive south of the city opened as well. Here there was not even a defensible front, just a long line of patrols. The Rumanians broke immediately, and again the Russians took off. The two arms of the pincer linked up a day later, fifty miles west of Stalingrad. Sixth Army was trapped.

By dithering, the Germans lost whatever opportunity they

might have had to break out. Weichs urged Paulus to move quickly; Paulus, waiting for Hitler's decision, lost his chance. Hitler took counsel, appointed General von Manstein as commander of Army Group Don, and told him to rescue 6th Army. Unfortunately, Army Group Don existed only on paper, a command shuffle of the original two army groups. While Manstein tried to get something together, Hitler talked to Goering, and the air force leader promised that Stalingrad could hold out. He personally would see that the supply requirements were met. The Luftwaffe would commit itself to getting in 500 tons a day, enough to keep 6th Army alive and fighting.

While Paulus sat and slowly froze, and his men defended the shrinking perimeter against heavy attacks, Manstein put together a striking force. It was December 12 before he could launch his attack but he made steady progress when he did; most of the Russian forces had turned inward against the Stalingrad pocket. After a week, Manstein was within thirty miles of the German lines, as close as he was going to get. He ordered Paulus to attempt a breakout and linkup. Paulus waited again for orders from Hitler. The Russians beat him to it and shored up their defenses between the two. By Christmas Eve, Manstein's relieving force was fighting for its own life and just barely able to cut its way back out of the salient it had made. The relief attempt was over.

Inside Stalingrad the Germans hung on grimly. The weather was brutal—snow, wind, cold, and more snow. The Luftwaffe pulled planes in from all over Europe, many of them antique types long since relegated to the training schools. Nothing they could do was enough. Five hundred tons a day, Goering had promised; the greatest daily delivery was 180; the average was sixty. Ammunition was handed out a cartridge at a time, there was no gasoline, rations dwindled. Hitler responded in characteristic fashion: he promoted Paulus to field marshal and ordered him to hang on to the death.

Even that would be a useful service, for the Russians were now running rampant over the southern front. The pursuit was up, and the Germans went reeling back from the Don, back across the Donets. By late January, Army Group A was cut off from the main forces, its communications having to go back through the Crimea. Army Group B had gone back 250 miles, and Manstein's Don Group was hard put to hold Rostov.

In Stalingrad seven Russian armies slowly strangled 6th Army. The perimeter got smaller and smaller; by late January it was a mere ten miles across. German soldiers sat down to write their last letters home, letters which on arrival in Berlin were seized by the authorities and analyzed to see how well the German soldier stood up under adversity. On the 23rd the Russians captured the last airstrip. Then they cut the remaining Germans into two pockets; the southern one was overrun on the 30th, and Paulus surrendered with it. On February 2 resistance ended; twenty-two divisions, reduced from more than a quarter of a million to a mere handful of 80,000 men, were left to march off into captivity. Hitler raged and fulminated: the "cowards" who surrendered should have had the decency to shoot themselves. The Verdun of World War II was over; the Russian steamroller so fondly envisaged in World War I had become a reality at last.

The great struggle for Stalingrad was only the most dramatic of the battles in Russia in 1942. All along the line, from northern Finland to the Black Sea and beyond, the two massive armies were locked in a fight whose magnitude defies ready comprehension. All through the campaigning season the Germans had pushed eastward, and the Russians had pushed back. Stalingrad had provided the great break, and in the early months of 1943 Russian tenacity finally paid off. In January they had attacked toward Leningrad and at the cost of more than a quarter of a million casualties they had opened a corridor through to the city. The long siege was ended at last; Leningrad had survived to take its place with Stalingrad among the epics of the Great Patriotic War. In November of 1942 the Reds had mounted an immense offensive against Rzhev, west of Moscow; it broke down with huge casualties, but they came back again in February, forcing the Germans out of a salient a hundred miles wide by a hundred miles deep. The space and distances covered were enormous; the Rzhev salient was nearly as big as the whole of German East Prussia. In the south the Germans viciously counterattacked the oncoming Soviets around Kharkov, and the momentum engendered by the Stalingrad offensive was finally lost. Manstein inflicted enormous losses on the Soviets once more, and by the time the rains came in March and the blessed or cursed mud arrived, the lines were back roughly where they had been a year ago, at the start of the great 1942 offensive. A whole year, and millions of casualties, and it was all for nothing.

The Russians now had a four to one superiority in men; they were receiving large amounts of Lend-Lease matériel from the

United States and Great Britain; and they were gaining increasing air superiority over the front, as more and more Luftwaffe units became absorbed in countering the Anglo-American air bombardment of Germany. Short of a miracle, there was no way the Germans were going to stem the tide of military power massing to the eastward. In 1918, after the failure of their spring offensives on the Western Front, Ludendorff had asked Hindenburg what to do; the old field marshal had burst out, "Do! What to do? Make peace, you idiot!" Adolf Hitler did not believe in making peace; he believed in miracles.

The Germans lacked troops and material for a straight defense of their long line in Russia. Skill and maneuver had to offset their weakness. Now, if ever, was a time for the art of generalship. Intelligence said the Russians would attack in the south. Manstein wanted a phased withdrawal, and then a slashing counteroffensive that would catch the Reds strung out and destroy them in open country. The high command decided instead on a spoiling attack, and in July of 1943 the Germans mounted a great drive around Kursk, where there was a bulge in the lines. The Germans delayed their offensive for a month while they re-equipped some of their armored formations with the new Panther and Tiger tanks; by the time they jumped off, the Russians were ready and waiting for them, with wide belts of mines and anti-tank guns by the hundred.

Kursk was the greatest tank battle in the war. The Germans used nearly 3,000 tanks, the Russians about the same number. In the southern part of the pincer, under General Hoth's 4th Panzer Army, nine of the best divisions in the Wehrmacht, massed along a short thirty miles of front. It was blitzkrieg on a massive scale. But it was still the same old thing, and the Russians, with their larger numbers, had now learned how to handle it. The new tanks were a disappointment; the Panthers burned too easily. The Tigers were stronger but their defensive armament was limited; they were the dreadnoughts of the tank era. When they outsurvived or outpaced the smaller tanks who acted virtually as escorts, the Russians were all over them. Proof against anti-tank guns, they were defenseless against Russian infantry who clambered over the still-moving monsters, squirted flamethrowers in their vents, and dropped grenades down their hatches. The Russian artillery never let up, and the Russian tanks proved as good as and better than the Germans. Operation Citadel, as the Germans called Kursk, marked the graveyard of the great Panzer armies. The German mobile forces never recovered their verve after that.

If Kursk did not use up the Germans' last reserves, it definitely weakened them for the battles to come. The Russians were now free to attack as they chose and they alternated blows from one end of the line to the other. A variety of appealing choices lay open to them. In the north they were on the point of driving back into the Baltic states and eventually to East Prussia; in the center they could move toward Poland and Germany itself; and in the south they could head for the Balkans and the fulfillment of the age-old Russian dream of closing up on the Dardanelles. They chose to do all three.

In the fall they hit Manstein's Army Group South. The Germans hoped to hold the line of the Dnieper River down to its bend, and then across country to Melitopol, which would secure their access to the Crimea. Instead, the Russians pushed them back to the river along its whole length, and the end result was the isolation of the German 17th Army in the Crimea. That was by the end of November. Farther north the Russians had taken Kiev, and were pushing south of the Pripet Marshes. The fall rains and effective German defensive tactics slowed them down, and at last the Wehrmacht got a chance to catch its breath.

It was no more than a slim chance, though. In January of 1944 the Russians shifted their attention northward and set off an offensive near Leningrad. This had been quiet since last spring, and the Germans were weak and unprepared. In February the Germans were back in Estonia, around Lake Peipus, where Alexander Nevsky had defeated the Teutonic Knights in 1242.

As if to show that they had a plethora of men and matériel and could do whatever they pleased whenever they pleased, the Russians then returned their attention to the south. In January the battles began again. The Dnieper Line was gone, and in March the Russians crossed the Bug, rolling toward the Rumanian frontier. In April they put massive forces into the Crimea. Hitler wanted it held; from the Crimea, Russian bombers could reach the Rumanian oil fields. But by May the last of the Germans there were gone, most saved by sea, as the Russian Black Sea Fleet hesitated to come to grips with the German evacuation. Early April also saw the Germans back from the Bug to the Dniester, and now the whole southern flank of Russia was cleared, and the Reds were poised for a drive into Rumania and the Balkan states. Farther north they were a mere twenty miles from the old Polish border. When Stalin met with Roosevelt and Churchill at Tehran in November of 1943, he had promised a great Russian offensive to coincide with the Allied landings in Normandy. That offensive would carry the Red armies from Odessa to Budapest, from Smolensk to Warsaw, and from Estonia to East Prussia. As the Russians regained their former frontiers, Hitlerian Germany had one year left to live.

20. Allied Strategic Problems: Upgrading the Pacific

IN THE LAST SIX MONTHS of 1942 the war approached an equilibrium. The Allies were no longer losing it and they now began to have sufficient men and material to consider various options of one kind or another. The Russians, though hard pressed, were obviously surviving; the Japanese advance had slowed and then ground to a stop, and victory was just down the road in North Africa. It was time to get out the maps and look ahead to the future.

For the Western Allies, the next big operation after the clearing of the southern Mediterranean shore had to be an invasion of the European mainland. Where would it be? The German conquests included nearly all of the Continent, so there was a number of possible choices. They could invade France, they could move north to Scandinavia, or they could continue in the Mediterranean. There were advantages and disadvantages wherever they went.

Invading Scandinavia was set aside as essentially fruitless. The recovery of Norway would achieve only a safer route to North Russia, and was probably not worth the effort. Better to let the Germans keep their quarter of a million troops on occupation duties up there, and leave them alone. The invasion of France was clearly the key matter; everyone knew it had to be done, and the only real question was how soon, and what ought to precede it. An invasion of northern France and a drive due east to the Rhine and into Germany was a knife thrust to the heart, one which the Germans could be expected to counter with everything they had. The best estimates were that the Allies were not yet ready, and that therefore operations ought to continue in the Mediterranean. That at least was the way the British thought about it; the Americans were less certain. General Marshall and the American Chiefs of

Staff already believed that they had been shunted into the North African operation. They saw themselves the victims of a vicious circle; unable to invade France immediately, they were forced to divert forces elsewhere; the more they diverted forces elsewhere, the more distant the proposed invasion date became. It was with an increasingly ill grace that they listened to the British sing their Mediterranean song. Yet they found themselves undercut by events. After Kasserine Pass and the serious shaking the Americans took in Tunisia, even their field commanders such as Eisenhower were prepared to accept the British view, that the Germans were too tough at the moment for a successful Allied invasion of France. The Mediterranean it had to be.

Within the theater itself there were several possibilities. The whole northern shore of the sea is made up of a series of peninsulas or islands, any one of which might serve as a stepping stone into Europe. First there was Spain. The Allies were not impressed by Franco's official neutrality and they would have invaded Spain had they seen any real profit in it. But as Henri IV said in the seventeenth century, Spain is a country where small armies are defeated and large armies starve. To invade Spain meant a long fight through the Iberian Peninsula, with the Pyrénées and another long fight through France after that.

Next came the islands of Sardinia and Corsica, the former Italian, the latter French and occupied by the Italians. These possessed very considerable appeal. A landing here would threaten further landings all along the Italian coast and the French Riviera. Large numbers of German troops would be tied down to counter such threats. Additionally, the islands would provide bases for the bomber offensive against southern German targets. To the French, though their influence was not great in Allied councils, Corsica offered the enticement that it was French territory, and could be used as the basis not only for military operations but also for a political offensive to reclaim control of the homeland. Some planners remained convinced that invading the islands would lead to southern France itself, and that a drive up the Rhone Valley and into southern Germany was a more profitable approach than across the Channel and through northern France. Although the idea did not gain sufficient support in late 1942, it came to the surface again later.

Moving east, the next natural target was Sicily. The large island sat like a bone in the throat of the Mediterranean. If Sicily were occupied, the Italian Air Force, or Regia Aeronautica, and the

Luftwaffe would lose important air bases from which they had perpetually attacked Malta and the Malta convoys. A clearing of the central Mediterranean would mean an immense saving in shipping, as it would permit the use of Mediterranean routes instead of the long passage around the southern tip of Africa. In early 1943 shipping remained a major problem for the Allies, and eventually it was Sicily on which they agreed as their next target.

The other possibility was the Balkan Peninsula, and it had some attractions, especially for Churchill. The Russians were opposed to this, however, and so were the Americans. Though there was some appeal to a drive through Greece or Yugoslavia to the Danube Basin and the Rumanian oil, neither Russia nor the United States wanted to see the Western Allies involved there. The Soviet Union had its own ambitions, while the Americans had no desire to play what they regarded as imperial games for Britain in the eastern Mediterranean.

Across the world, there were the same kind of choices to be made in the Pacific and in the war against Japan. The offshoot of the Midway operation—the occupation by Japanese troops of Attu and Kiska—opened up the Aleutians as a theater of war. The Aleutians is the shortest route from the United States to Japan. Unfortunately, it also possesses the world's worst weather, especially for aircraft operations. Though it would not really be a serious contender for priority, the Aleutians nonetheless remained American territory occupied by the enemy, and thereby engendered an emotional reaction that eventually placed several hundred thousand troops up in the north and led to some short but very brutal fighting.

More-realistic possibilities lay to the south and west, and through 1942 the Allies divided up the war against Japan in a way that, though it contained certain anomalies, worked pretty well on the whole. The Japanese invasion of Southeast Asia had cut the British off from Australia, which now became a major base for the American buildup. The British therefore accepted that they should have command over the Indian Ocean and operations originating from there, i.e., the campaign in Burma, and eventually, the return to Malaya. Everything east of that, including China and Australia, was to be under American control.

The Americans divided the Pacific into three commands, though only two of them really counted, the South Pacific Area being beyond the reach of the Japanese. The North Pacific was put under the basic direction of the U. S. Navy, and the area was commanded by Admiral Nimitz. His control was extended south for the Solomons campaign. The Southwest Pacific Area, including Australia, the East Indies, and a lump north of the Equator to include the Philippines, went to the U. S. Army and General MacArthur. China was also placed by the Allies under the strategic direction of the United States, though in practice that did not mean a great deal. The Chinese generalissimo, Chiang Kai-shek, did what he could and got support where he could. The Americans exercised their strategic direction largely through an advisor, General Joseph Stilwell, "Vinegar Joe" behind his back, a brilliant, unpopular eccentric who labored under immense difficulties, not least of which was his own personality.

A nearly isolated China was something of a sideshow as far as the Americans were concerned. More crucial to them were the central and the southwest Pacific areas, where American troops were in contact with the enemy. Yet all the fronts—Aleutians, central, and Southwest Pacific, China, Burma—cried out for troops to fight and matériel to fight with, and decisions on priorities were not solely conditioned by geography or even by strategy, but by politics and interservice rivalries and by personal likes and dislikes. Burma remained a poor relation for the British, and in American planning, MacArthur and Nimitz waged a constant struggle for top billing and allocation of resources. As a soldier, MacArthur ended up with practically his own private navy to support his drive up past New Guinea and into the Philippines. Nimitz on the other hand ended up with his private army, the Marine Corps, as the navy worked its way west through the islands of the central Pacific. The converging strategy eventually proved to be sound, but it was achieved only after a great deal of argument. The Americans haggled among themselves in the Pacific theater almost as much as they did with the British in the European theater.

The one item on which everyone, British and American alike, could agree was the necessity of improving the shipping position. It was this problem that led the Allied leaders at Casablanca in January of 1943 to give priority to defeating the U-boats. This was carried even to the point of disrupting the strategic bombing schedule and diverting it to attacks on U-boat bases and yards, much to the dismay of the bombing planners. It also led to the agreement to invade the island of Sicily. Some things were already happening to improve the situation. The scuttling of the French fleet at Toulon removed a large potential threat, and the return of the remainder of it to the war on the Allied side provided a small boost. Later in 1943 the defection of the Italians from the Axis side had the result of subtracting an important amount of shipping from the enemy, and adding it to the Allied ranks. By then the U-boat menace was being contained, so the whole naval situation improved throughout the year.

Things that were achieved as by-products of other developments in Europe had to be won by battle in the Pacific. Through late 1942 and into 1943 the Americans and the Japanese hammered at each other. The anvil of their operations was an island in the Solomons called Guadalcanal.

In the late spring of 1942, as the Japanese extended eastward to New Guinea and past it to Rabaul, they decided that by ranging a bit farther southeast they could threaten the American supply route to Australia. As part of their Coral Sea-Port Moresby venture they sent a small force down into the Solomons to set up a seaplane base at the little island of Tulagi. Across a twenty-mile-wide strait lay the much larger island of Guadalcanal, ninety miles long by nearly fifty wide, and here they began laboriously hacking an airfield out of the scrub and jungle.

After Midway the Americans enjoyed for the first time a marginal superiority over the Japanese. In spite of their official adherence to the Germany-first policy, they had shipped much larger numbers of troops to the Pacific than to Europe and had allocated the even greater proportion of shipping needed to sustain them over the longer Pacific distances. Most of this was the work of Admiral Ernest J. King, former ambassador to Vichy France, now Chief of Naval Operations, something of an Anglophobe, and an absolutely determined pusher of the U. S. Navy and its aims and ambitions. The American Secretary of War, Henry Stimson, once wrote that after a visit to the Navy Department he came away feeling that he had been in a place "where Neptune was God, Mahan was his prophet, and the U. S. Navy the one true church." He might have added that Admiral King was the current Pope.

In spite of King's power over events and resources, the American superiority, as noted, was only marginal. It was, however, going to grow immensely; the Americans were producing for war, the smaller Japanese industrial base still was not; but in midsummer of 1942 a limited operation with limited resources was all the Americans could manage. MacArthur wished to take over most of the navy and go straight for the main Japanese base at Rabaul.

The navy, not wanting to gamble in confined waters, countered with a proposal that they advance step by step up the Solomons, while MacArthur did the same up the northeastern side of New Guinea. Then they would converge on Rabaul. Not until July 1 was the navy's position adopted by the Joint Chiefs of Staff; they decided on a landing on Guadalcanal a month hence.

Overall direction of the area and the operation went to Admiral R. L. Ghormley in New Caledonia. The business end of the American expedition was the 1st Marine Division, commanded by General A. A. Vandergrift. Admiral R. K. Turner commanded the Amphibious Force. It in turn was protected by a screening force under a British admiral, V. A. C. Crutchley, and all of these were to be covered by a carrier task force under Admiral F. J. Fletcher which would operate southwest of the Solomons. The landing was to go in from the north between Savo Island and the flat Lunga Plain area of Guadalcanal where the airstrip was being constructed.

On the morning of August 7, after a predawn bombardment, the Marines clambered down the nets into their landing boats and made for the black-sand beaches. The Japanese forces did not contest the landing, and by nightfall there were 11,000 Marines ashore, spreading along the beaches and beginning to edge into the tropical jungle. Opposition was sporadic. Though the Americans did not know it, there were only about 2,000 Japanese on the island, most of them laborers. Only a few snipers and machine gunners contested the American advance, and they were soon overrun. For the moment all was well.

What might have happened was shown across the strait on Tulagi and a couple of neighboring islets. Here the small Japanese garrison was dug in and ready to fight. The intensive naval bombardment that preceded the landing achieved nothing, and it eventually took 3,000 Marines to overcome the 750 soldiers protecting the seaplane base.

The Japanese, who were concentrating their efforts and attention on Port Moresby, were initially slow to respond to the threat in the Solomons. But when they did, Guadalcanal and the battles for its approaches became the focal point of the Pacific war. The fight lasted for seven months, and included what one authority has called the most prolonged, intensive, and destructive naval campaign since the Anglo-Dutch Wars in the middle of the seventeenth century.

The key to the island was control of the water around it and the ability to land men and supplies to reinforce the ground troops.

On the afternoon of the 7th the first Japanese planes showed up, and the amphibious force was subjected to a series of weak attacks all through the next day. Fletcher's carrier planes accounted for most of the attackers, but with considerable losses himself, and feeling crowded in the waters off Guadalcanal, Fletcher decided to pull his carriers out late on the 8th; they were too valuable to risk at that stage, he thought. That decision left Turner with no air cover, so he announced he would withdraw his amphibious fleet as well, but he would stay one more day to unload further supplies for the Marines who were now settling into a defensive perimeter.

While Turner was making that decision, a Japanese surface squadron of seven cruisers and a destroyer came racing down "the Slot," the channel inside the Solomon island chain. Crashing into Crutchley's screen early in the morning of the 9th, it ran temporarily wild, then turned back, to get away before daylight. In half an hour's good work the Japanese sank three American cruisers, *Quincy*, *Vincennes*, and *Astoria*, and blew the bow off *Chicago* with a torpedo, and sank as well the Australian cruiser, *Canberra*. An American sub torpedoed a cruiser as they retreated northward, otherwise they would have gotten away scot-free. As it was, the Battle of Savo Island went down as the most humiliating defeat ever suffered in a fair fight by the United States Navy. Had the Japanese admiral Gunichi Mikawa known of Fletcher's withdrawal of the carrier planes, he could have hit the transports too and made it a massacre. Turner stayed around the next day, salvaging what he could, landing more supplies, then he sailed away at dark with most of the landing force's heavy equipment and supplies, and indeed, with 1,400 troops still aboard the transports. On the island, the Marines settled down to short rations, supplemented by captured Japanese rice.

The deadly naval pavane continued as both sides sought to reinforce. In the third week of August the Japanese sent in a small convoy. Fifteen hundred troops sailed from Rabaul, escorted by the entire combined fleet—battleships, carriers, and all. The Americans met them in what was called the Battle of the Eastern Solomons. When it was all over, the Japanese had lost a carrier and a seaplane tender and ninety planes, for American losses of fifteen planes and damage to one carrier.

On the island the Japanese put in a premature attack against the Marines' perimeter. Nearly a thousand men stormed up to the wire and machine guns at the Tenaru River and were wiped out. The Marines suffered just over a hundred casualties. The Americans now had planes on the airstrip, named Henderson Field, and they kept the Japanese ships away from Guadalcanal by day. Each night, therefore, the Japanese crammed troops and supplies aboard destroyers and raced them down the Slot, unloading and scooting back out under cover of darkness. The destroyer runs were nicknamed the Tokyo Express. By early September there were 6,000 Japanese troops on the island, and they were ready for a major attack. They launched it on September 12, trying to clear high ground south of Henderson Field. All night and the next day the Japanese tried to take Bloody Ridge, but the Marines, with heavy machine-guns, howitzers, and mortars, were too strong for them. After a last Banzai charge they gave it up, again with casualties of ten to one, 1,500 Japanese to 150 Americans.

Then it was the navy's turn again. At the end of August a submarine torpedoed the carrier *Saratoga*, putting her out of action for the next three months. That left only the *Wasp*, smallest of the fleet carriers, and she went to the bottom in mid-September after two torpedoes found her. In mid-October both sides moved troop convoys in, and the escorting forces met off Cape Esperance. The superior American force got its revenge for Savo Island, sinking three destroyers and a cruiser, and crippling two more cruisers. This time the Americans had radar, while the Japanese had none. They capped the Japanese "T" and opened with full broadsides, and would have gotten away virtually unscathed had not the cruiser *Boise*, preferring to do things the old way, switched on her searchlights to find a target. She took six hits immediately, and then her magazine exploded. Still, the honors for the night went to the Americans, who by now badly needed a morale-raising victory.

The Japanese riposted by sending two huge battleships down to bombard Henderson Field, which they did with impunity while more troops were landed. Up till now, Guadalcanal had been a sideshow slowly impinging on their attention while they still were preoccupied with New Guinea and Port Moresby. But if this was where the Americans wanted to fight, so be it. For two days they poured troops in, supported by the battleships, until they slightly outnumbered the Marines, about 23,000 to 20,000. They planned to seize Henderson Field, get land-based planes in, then move in their carriers and take on the U. S. Navy for a fight to the finish.

In the third week of October they launched their main effort to get the field. The Marines were well dug in and ready for them. The Japanese came on with fanatical bravery, but with poor tactics, and ill-timed and poorly coordinated human-wave attacks that left bodies by the hundreds strung along the American wire. With more than 2,000 killed and probably three times as many wounded they finally gave it up. American losses were fewer than 300, and they now began the expansion of their perimeter. From this point on the Marines were on the offensive.

At sea the struggle went on. Ghormley was relieved by Admiral William F. Halsey, and Fletcher by Admiral Thomas C. Kincaid. The Marines had been accused of not attacking, and had replied that they needed better support from the navy than they were getting. Halsey was determined to supply it. While the battle for Henderson Field raged ashore, he sent Kincaid after the Japanese main fleet. Striking each other with carrier aircraft, the Americans damaged two Japanese carriers, while the Japanese damaged the *Enterprise* and sank the *Hornet*. Losses were more or less evened by the fact that this battle of the Santa Cruz Islands cost the Japanese more than a hundred carrier planes and pilots, and their pool of trained pilots was now getting dangerously low.

Both sides were convinced that victory was within their grasp, and as long as neither would concede the matter, the fight went on. The Japanese pushed in more troops, until they outnumbered the Americans by several thousands; they also had naval superiority, with battleships and carriers outnumbering their enemies. But Halsey was determined to give the Marines the support they needed and he stripped troops out of areas all over his command. In spite of the impending North African invasion, the Americans sent ships and planes from all over; the problem reached the President, and Roosevelt himself intervened in the allocations and the scheduling of resources. Guadalcanal was to have the highest priority; this was where the fight was.

In mid-November the Japanese mounted yet another reinforcement convoy, scheduled this time to deliver 13,000 men. As in the previous month, they planned to cover it with a battleship bombardment of the American position. They sent two battleships, a cruiser, and fourteen destroyers into the waters north of Guadalcanal, now known, ominously, as Ironbottom Sound. The Americans, also scheduling reinforcements at the same time, could not match that strength, but Turner sent his escort commander, Admiral D. J. Callaghan, into the sound with five cruisers and eight destroyers and orders to break up the bombardment. It was a cast of desperation, but fortunately for the Americans, most of the Japanese magazines were loaded with high explosive for the shore bombardment, rather than the armor-piercing shells that would have wiped out the American squadron.

After dark on November 12 the Americans waited in ambush in Ironbottom Sound. In spite of their radar they were still surprised when the huge Japanese force entered the sound just past midnight. What followed was a melee in which neither side was able to exercise any real control. For about half an hour ships blazed away at each other, sometimes hitting the enemy, sometimes hitting their own comrades, sometimes firing at shadows. Ships loomed up suddenly out of the tropic darkness, fired into each other, and surged apart again. Shell splashes and torpedo wakes churned the confined waters between Savo and Guadalcanal. Losses were extremely heavy on both sides. On the American side, Admiral Callaghan was killed, the cruiser *Atlanta* was sunk, *Portland*, another cruiser, was a wreck with no power, and the battered *Juneau* was sunk by a submarine—700 of her crew went down with her; and four destroyers were lost as well. The Japanese lost two destroyers, and the battleship *Hiei* was hit more than fifty times, so that she was dead in the water when American planes found her and finished her off next morning.

In spite of the losses, the first phase of this Naval Battle of Guadalcanal was an American victory; Turner got his convoy through, while the Japanese turned back. Over the next two days there were ferocious air battles, the Americans trying to bomb the Japanese convoys as they dithered back and forth in the Slot, and the Japanese tenaciously trying to move in to bombard Henderson Field. This second phase accounted for seven Japanese transports and two cruisers, but the Japanese were still not ready to quit. On the night of the 13th-14th they sent their remaining battleship, *Kirishima*, four cruisers, and nine destroyers in for another covering bombardment.

The Americans countered with four destroyers and, this time, two battleships of their own, *Washington* and *South Dakota*. The latter took a hit that put her temporarily out of action, and for a while it was *Washington* and the destroyers against fourteen Japanese. With her radar-controlled gunnery she sank *Kirishima* and a destroyer; then *South Dakota* came back on the line, and the Japanese had had enough. They fled northward.

The mid-November battles effectively turned the tide in the waters of the Solomons. The Americans were now in superior strength, and the Japanese tacitly acknowledged the fact. The direct challenge was over. They were by no means ready to quit completely, however. At the end of the month when Japanese Admiral Tanaka was caught off Tassafaronga Point with a replenishment squadron, he attacked furiously and, badly outnumbered though he was, he hit three American heavy cruisers and sank a fourth, for the loss of only one of his destroyers.

With naval supremacy, the Americans increased their advantage on the island of Guadalcanal. Japanese reinforcements dwindled, and for supplies they were reduced to running their ships offshore and throwing over oil drums, hoping they would drift to land. The American troop buildup continued, and they gradually outnumbered the enemy. In December, the 1st Marine Division, what was left of it, was finally withdrawn, and the fever-wracked, young-old men came out of the line at last. The Japanese now threw up their own defensive lines east of Henderson Field, and defied all efforts to dislodge them. Wasteful of manpower in a charge, they were indefatigable diggers and burrowers, each foxhole a stronghold containing a man willing to die if he could take an American with him.

By January of 1943 the Americans had 50,000 men on the island. The Japanese were down to about 12,000 half-starved survivors. They had another 50,000 to the northward but could not run them down the Slot in the face of American naval power. Reluctantly, they decided to cut their losses and get out. In early February they ran a series of high-speed destroyers down to their perimeter and, under the Americans' noses, lifted their troops off the beaches. It was the most successful evacuation of its type since the British pulled out of the Dardanelles in 1915. But evacuations are not victories. Now both at Midway and at Guadalcanal the Americans had started out the weaker and ended up the winners. The Japanese had frittered away their strength and their advantages, committing themselves piecemeal, and losing opportunities while the enemy quickly improved. Yamamoto's remark about a navy of golfers and bridge-players was coming home to haunt him.

Elsewhere the story was the same. A thousand miles west of Guadalcanal, MacArthur was forging his way up the Papuan coast of New Guinea, past Buna, Gona, Salamaua, Lae. The Australians finally stemmed the Japanese advance through the Owen Stanley Mountains and sent them back from Kokoda, slowly at first, and then routing them triumphantly. The country was horrible: swampy, insect-ridden jungle and sharp mountain ridges where man was not the only, but the most deadly creature.

What began in 1942 continued through 1943. Germany still had priority, but the industrial power of the United States, coupled with that of its allies, was capable of fighting two wars at once. American military and naval commanders were not going to wait for Germany to be defeated before turning on the treacherous enemy who had attacked Pearl Harbor. Roosevelt's two-ocean navy could be used only peripherally against Germany, so more and more of the new ships were dispatched to the Pacific. In all the theaters of the Japanese war, the pressure was applied.

China could do little; the ground war there was at a stalemate. Millions of people in China died of famine in 1943, and Chiang Kai-shek could do almost nothing about it. The Japanese undertook local offensives called "rice offensives," designed to procure supplies for themselves and deny them to the already starving Chinese. Relations between General Stilwell and the generalissimo continued to degenerate, and Stilwell was upstaged by American Air Force General Claire Chennault, whose former Flying Tigers had now become part of the Army Air Force. With Chiang supporting him, and later on with backing from Roosevelt too, Chennault managed to upgrade American air operations over China. By the end of 1943 the United States planes dominated Chinese skies and were striking even at Formosa. Things did not go so well on the ground. The earmarking of supplies for the air forces meant that the Chinese armies did without. Chiang was also increasingly preoccupied with the Communist problem and diverted substantial numbers of divisions to a blockade of the Communist-held territories, further reducing his effectiveness against the Japanese.

The British in 1943 launched two Burmese offensives, though relatively little was achieved in either. The earlier of these was called the First Arakan campaign; General Wavell, anxious to restore his troops' confidence, attacked before he was really ready for it, in January. The Japanese held hard, then counterattacked brutally, employing their usual encircling and infiltration tactics. The result was that the British took heavy losses, and the troops lost rather than gained confidence; they were more convinced than ever that the Japanese were unbeatable in the brush.

The second attempt was rather different. One of Wavell's brigadiers was a visionary named Orde Wingate; he believed that the counter to Japanese penetration was for the British to penetrate even more deeply into the enemy lines. Organizing a special raiding force known as "Chindits," Wingate mounted a long-range penetration of the jungle, hoping to interdict Japanese supplies. One of the dicta of the strategic bombing enthusiasts was that the nearer the front the interruption was, the more immediate the result; the farther back, the more profound. Wingate believed the same thing, but the method he proposed to achieve the interruption was different. The Chindits infiltrated Japanese territory in several small columns, then united for operations. They stirred up a hornet's nest, and the Japanese quickly chased them back out, and nearly a third of the Chindit force, more than a thousand men, were casualties. The Chindit campaign too was therefore regarded as a failure, though it did serve as something of a morale booster. Later in the year there was some hope of British-Chinese cooperation in northern Burma, but it came to nothing, lost in the morass of internal Chinese problems.

Away up in the far north, the Americans retaliated against the Japanese-held islands of Attu and Kiska. Reaching out through the Aleutian chain, they built air bases nearer and nearer to the islands. Eventually, they isolated them by naval action as well, and in the small battle of the Komandorski Islands an American and a Japanese squadron fought the last of the old-style naval battles, ships against ships with no aircraft around to interfere. In May soldiers of the U. S. Army landed on Attu. The 2,500-man Japanese garrison fought to the bitter end, then launched a suicide charge that finished in a hand-to-hand struggle in the American line; only twenty-nine of the Emperor's soldiers survived the battle, and in proportion to the forces involved, Attu was bloodier than any battle in the Pacific except Iwo Jima. Later in the year the Japanese slipped away from Kiska, and the Aleutian chain was secure from then on.

In spite of the war raging in all these areas, the southwest and the central Pacific remained the crucial points of conflict. The Japanese high command was still not entirely unhappy with events. They had expected to shift to a defensive strategy once their perimeter was achieved, and all of their setbacks so far—the Coral Sea, Midway, Guadalcanal, even Papua in New Guinea—had occurred beyond the perimeter as they originally envisaged it. Most of the losses could be explained away, though the consequences were awkward; they were bothered by the diminution in the number of their trained carrier pilots and they initiated an intensive training program. They could still hope that a few hard defeats on the main line of the perimeter would make the Americans give up. But as 1943 rolled on, the skies began to darken for them.

The Americans did not give up, and the process of nibbling away at the empire went on with increasing energy. MacArthur and Halsey kept pounding at the approaches to Rabaul. It was the end of 1943 before the Japanese were cleared off the Huon Peninsula of New Guinea, and the Americans leaped to the west end of New Britain, the island on which Rabaul sits. At the same time they worked their way up the Solomons, and the litany of pain, defeat, and victory begun at Guadalcanal went on: Rendova, New Georgia, Kolombangara, Vella Lavella, Bougainville. Flyspecks on the globe became engraved forever on hearts in the United States, in Australia, and in Japan. The constant drainage of men and materials hurt the Japanese more than it did the Americans and the Australians; the Allied forces could afford it better.

In the central Pacific it was an ocean war; the carrier task forces ranged over the great spaces. In March of 1943 the Allied chiefs approved a second approach to the Philippines, due west from Hawaii, and turned the navy loose. Admiral Nimitz wanted to go for the Marshalls, but lacked sufficient troops for that. He decided instead on a landing in the Gilberts, farther east, and picked the island of Tarawa as his target.

Tarawa is an atoll, the top of a submerged mountain forming a circle of islets. The largest of these islets, Betio, was only a few feet above the water, containing a scant 300 acres of sand and coral and palm trees. The Japanese had put 4,700 troops ashore here and they had done their best to make the island a fortress. Betio was ringed by two coral reefs; the inner, unknown to the Americans, rising high enough that landing boats would not be able to get over it. The few breaks in the reef the Japanese mined and wired. On the island itself they brought in eight-inch guns from Singapore, built redoubts, dugouts, pillboxes, and bunkers. They mined and wired again, and set up interlocking zones of fire. Then they sat down to wait it out.

The Americans showed up on November 13. First there were heavy air strikes, followed by a lengthy pre-invasion bombardment from the navy. Neither of these did as much damage as the Americans hoped. Flat-trajectory naval guns had but a limited effectiveness against deeply dug positions, which required plunging fire to reduce them. Then, on the 21st, while the army overran the nearby island of Makin, the Marines went ashore.

Almost everything went wrong. The landing boats grounded

on the inner reef, where the Japanese had their guns ranged. Under heavy fire the troops clambered out of the boats and into waist- and chest-deep water and began to wade the several hundred yards to the beach. The Japanese machine guns opened up on them in the water. The amphibious tractors that clambered over the reef immediately became targets for mortars and artillery. Many were hit, some broke down, some made it to the beach, then could not get up over the palm log barricades. With Marines on the beach the navy stopped its shore bombardment for fear of hitting its own people. The Marines were pinned down to a few square yards of sand in front of the barricades; there was no way back across the bloodstained waters of the lagoon, and no way forward. All that long day they clung to their strip of sand; by nightfall, of the 5,000 who had started for the shore, 1,500 were dead or wounded.

Relief came with the dark, and some tanks and artillery got to the beach. By next morning the Marines had enough of a foot-hold that they could call in carrier support aircraft to make strikes on the Japanese positions. The divisional reserve came ashore that day, though it lost 350 officers and men just reaching dry land. Inch by inch the Marines fought their way forward, the Japanese fighting back for every step. By nightfall on the second day, the Americans had secured the western end of the island. That night the Japanese launched a suicide charge that left their dead piled up in front of the Marine positions, and the next day, the 23rd, the last pockets and pillboxes were cleared out. Tarawa was secured.

The cost, to both sides, had been horrible. Of the 4,700-odd garrison, a hundred Korean laborers were taken prisoner. Only seventeen combat soldiers were taken alive; all the rest fought to the death. In killing them the Marines suffered 985 dead and 2,193 wounded, roughly ten casualties per acre. The ratio mounts even higher if one accepts the estimate that half the Japanese casualties were suffered by the air and naval bombardment.

Tarawa taught the Americans many lessons about the tech-niques of amphibious landings. They needed better pre-invasion reconnaissance, better and different types of fire-support, better ship-to-shore communications. But it could all be done. After the Dardanelles in 1915-16 military men came to the conclusion that opposed landings were doomed to failure. By 1943 that decision was reversed, and American planners believed that an amphibious assault could get ashore, no matter what the obstacles. The price might seem prohibitively heavy, but improved tactics, weapons, and the new masses of material would remedy that. New ships, new planes, and thousands of trained men were pouring out of the United States. The western Pacific lay ahead: the Marshalls, the Carolines, the Marianas, the Philippines, and at the end—the home islands, Japan itself. At whatever price, the theme begun at Guadalcanal would reach its climax in Tokyo Bay.

21. The European Resistance Movements

THE GERMAN CONQUEST of Europe was intended to be permanent. The First Reich was the old Holy Roman Empire, and it had been laid to rest by Napoleon after the Battle of Austerlitz; the Second Reich was the Hohenzollern Empire; proclaimed in the Hall of Mirrors in Versailles in 1871, it collapsed with the Kaiser's abdication in 1918; the Third Reich was to last for a thousand years. At least so Hitler said, and so he meant. He was building for the ages.

Not everyone agreed with his concept of the Master Race and the inherent superiority of the Aryan peoples. In western Europe, though at first the Germans behaved themselves, the shock of conquest and defeat soon wore off, and as soon as it did, men and women began thinking of ways to thwart the conquerors. General von Senger und Etterlin wrote in his memoirs of being billeted in a chateau in Normandy after the French surrender, and visiting with the owners and exchanging pleasantries. In 1939 and 1940 there was still some sense of European community among the well-to-do and well educated of the Continent, and French and German had conquered each other so often that there were recognized modes of behavior for such situations. There were also strong currents of authoritarianism in right-wing French circles, and a substantial number of Frenchmen initially preferred the Germans as masters to their own French Socialists, or even worse, the Communists.

The sense of community wore off when Frenchmen realized that these Germans were not quite what they were thought to be. As Neville Chamberlain had earlier discovered, the Nazis were not gentlemen. Temporary occupation, requisitioning, a certain degree of traffic in art work and monuments, all these were still within the code. Labor conscription, holding prisoners of war as hostages, blatant robbery of personal as opposed to state property, persecution of Jews, these were outside the code. The Germans ceased to be tourists in *Feldgrau*, and became the enemy.

In eastern Europe the Germans made little pretense of being anything other than permanent conquerors, and their murderous policies served almost immediately to alienate those peoples who had initially seen them as marginally better masters than the Bolsheviks. The conquest of the eastern lands lacked even the veneer of civility shown to western Europe.

As a result of this, there grew up in every subject state of the German empire a resistance movement. There was even one in Germany itself, "Germans" versus "Nazis." The Resistance has attracted considerable attention, though it remains a difficult affair to study, for so much of its activity was clandestine, fragmented, and individual. Historians disagree widely on how valuable it was and opinions vary from those of orthodox military historians who discount the whole matter as the bungling of right-thinking amateurs, to theorists and advocates of "popular war" who contend that the Resistance won the war—or could have done so—practically alone.

The movements in each country had their own peculiarities. The Resistance in Belgium, relatively open and built up, was different from that in Greece or Yugoslavia. Resistance in Norway, where access to the outside world was at least possible, was different from that in Poland. There were even differences within countries. A member of the Resistance at the Renault works outside Paris worked within a different set of limits from his fellow in the rough country of the Vosges or south-central France. In spite of all these necessary variations, the French historian Henri Michel has found a series of constants in the development of opposition to Hitlerian Germany. The movements had several common characteristics and they all went through similar phases of development.

The rock-bottom common denominator to all of them was that they were patriotic movements aimed at the liberation of one's own territory from the invader. For whatever other reasons he might be an enemy, the basic one was that the German was there, on another's land, doing and taking by might what was someone else's by right. For patriotism as for religion, few things provide a more effective spur than persecution.

It was not just that the Germans were in occupation, however. Because of the essentially negative nature of the Nazi ideology, the Resistance movements also became a reaffirmation of the essential worth and dignity of man. Here was one of the major differences between the Hitlerian empire and the Napoleonic one. However much he may have warped the concept, Napoleon claimed to be the standard-bearer of European progress and the culmination of the Enlightenment, and until they went sour, the Napoleonic conquests were welcomed by bourgeois, liberals, and intelligentsia. The German conquests were sour right from the beginning, and made no pretense to universality of appeal. Their basic argument was brute force, and the attraction of that was limited. Those who opposed the Germans had widely divergent views on the worth of man, and the proper social or political system under which he should live, but there was a common ground for agreement, and for action, in their detestation of nazism. Thus the paradox of Communists, Catholics, Protestants, and liberal agnostics fighting side by side against the enemy.

Not everyone felt that way, though. One of the most painful aspects of the whole war was that the Germans did possess some appeal to certain classes and types of people in every country. They did attract supporters, either those who became collaborators from conviction or ambition, or those who were caught up in an organization that was by the policy of its own government committed to a degree of cooperation, such as the French police organizations under the Vichy regime. In all of the countries of Europe, or nearly all of them, the war became a civil war as well as a conventional one, and in many places the worst excesses were committed in the struggle between the members of the Resistance movements and the collaborators with the Germans. In France, for example, as young Frenchmen took to the countryside and became the Maquis, the Germans organized French paramilitary forces called the Milice, and Maquis and Milice waged war on each other with a breathless fury. In Yugoslavia there was open warfare between the Communist Resistance led by Joseph Broz, who took the name Tito, and a pro-monarchist leader, General Draja Mikhailovitch, leader of the "Chetniks." Eventually, the British backed Tito, as the more active and the more anti-German of the two; Tito went on to win, and Mikhailovitch was executed by him in 1946—as a Fascist.

The timing of the different phases through which each nation's Resistance movement passed depended upon a variety of matters: the circumstances of its defeat, the extent and brutality of its occupation, the condition of its government, whether it was in residence like Vichy or in exile like Holland, and similar factors. Nonetheless, all the movements had similar stages of development.

The first of these is the most difficult to document or treat historically, for it was intensely private and individualistic. This was the phase of rejection, of refusal to submit. The state was conquered; if the national government existed, it was either in exile or had made some sort of accommodation. The individual therefore was left to make his own decision, and it was a necessarily lonely, painful, and dangerous one. In Poland one could be shot for a gesture of ill will toward a German. Yet all over Europe, one at a time, people made such gestures. A Frenchman who habitually sold newspapers to Germans would one day watch a convoy of Jews being shipped off; the next morning when the Germans came for their papers, they found the vendor suddenly understood no German. When Germans entered a café, conversation stopped. Silently the patrons finished their drinks, paid, and got up and left. Such acts were small but they were still dangerous, and a small act because it was dangerous thus became an act of patriotism.

Thousands of Europeans who did no more than turn their backs when a German parade marched by could still feel they had committed an act of defiance. The Germans forbade listening to the overseas service of the British Broadcasting System; it therefore became a patriotic act to gather behind closed blinds and listen to the evening news. There were jokes about the enemy, and the Germans, like most conquerors, notoriously lacked humor. A classic was the tale in France that at nine-twenty a Jew killed a German, cut his heart out, and ate it; why was this story untrue? For three reasons: first, a German has no heart; second, Jews do not eat pork, and third, at nine-twenty everyone is listening to the BBC anyway.

The second phase was that of organization. Like-minded people began to seek each other out and slowly to coalesce into groups and units. This development was fraught with danger; mistakes were easily made. Many people who were willing to turn their backs on Germans were not willing to move to active participation of the kind that might land them in jail, or before a firing squad. There was also a great problem of differing aims. Groups developed to get men to England, and to take soldiers and sailors, and later downed fliers and place them on routes back home. But other groups wanted to educate and propagandize; still others wanted to gather intelligence, and a few hotheads wanted to kill Germans in the streets. These last were the most dangerous, for the Germans soon adopted a policy of reprisals: one dead German was worth fifty to a hundred executions, and eventually they were wiping out whole towns and villages, especially in eastern Europe, as punishment for killings or assassinations.

One of the most notable examples of this kind of situation occurred in Czechoslovakia. In May of 1942 Himmler's number two man, Reinhard Heydrich, the Protector of Bohemia, was assassinated by a group of Czechs who had been in exile in Britain. They had been infiltrated into the country, and had set up an ambush in Prague. When Heydrich's car passed by, they opened fire, and he was fatally wounded. The plotters were betrayed, run to earth in an old church, besieged, and killed. The assassination had been opposed by the British, but ordered by the Czech government of President Benes, in exile in London. The Resistance in Czechoslovakia itself had also been opposed to it for reasons that quickly became apparent. The Germans arrested nearly 500 people immediately, following this with the execution of more than 250. They then mounted a military operation against the village of Lidice, rounded up all the inhabitants—men, women, and children—and massacred them as a warning and a reprisal.

In Holland the assassination of a German officer resulted in the deportation of nearly 700 people to concentration camps. Eventually, the Resistance movements decided that this kind of direct action was probably too costly and that it ought to be avoided. There were exceptions to this decision, however. In Poland there was no cessation of the bloodshed; the Poles were so badly treated anyway their condition could hardly be worse, and throughout the war they fought furiously and indiscriminately against the conqueror. Particular assassinations and reprisals were part of an ongoing cacophony of terror there.

The Communists too tended to take a cold view of affairs. In many countries they were leaders of the organizational phase. They possessed the necessary background; they were used to acting clandestinely, to being persecuted, to having to live carefully. Resistance for them was little more than an extension of their normal activities. There were variations on this theme, too. The earliest French resisters found the Communists completely uninterested in them; the Reds marched to a drum beaten in Moscow, and as long as the Russo-German Nonaggression Pact was in force, they were well behaved. As soon as Germany invaded the

Soviet Union the Communists became violent anti-Nazis. They were also quite willing to shed blood, their own as well as others'. They believed that if killings caused reprisals, the reprisals in turn caused more killings, and they were content to see villages wiped out if that would ultimately bring more people into the fight against the Fascists. Ideologically, everyone who was not a Communist was an enemy, so it meant little to them if innocents died. "Innocent" was not a word in their vocabulary.

The differing ideological views of the resisters, the different types of work done by different groups, the rivalries within and between them, the fear of infiltration by enemy agents, all made organization difficult. Gradually, the small cells did coalesce; safe houses became parts of escape routes; occasional broadsheets became newspapers; isolated intelligence-gatherers became networks. Few were as successful as the Dutch, who set up shop across from German headquarters in Amsterdam and ran a line across from the German central switchboard so that they could listen to all German calls. But within a relatively short time, the individual resisters had become the Resistance. As they moved to yet a further stage, the outside world began to take an interest in them.

As soon as they were chased off the Continent, the British began thinking how they were going to get back. Harboring a large number of governments in exile, maintaining ties and contacts wherever possible with the occupied territories, the British soon realized that the more Germans who could be tied up in internal security operations, the fewer there would be available for the battlefield. They established a group known as SOE, Special Operations Executive, to control and coordinate the activities of the various Resistance groups. Initially, there was some hope that SOE would become a "fourth arm," equivalent to the army, navy, and air force, but it never got that far. Personality conflicts, the excessive demands for supplies and resources, the inability to control matters, all militated against this. Conventional service chiefs were extremely skeptical of Resistance-type operations, and indeed, the regular service officer tended to make a poor Resistance leader. Subversive warfare called for different skills, in fact for a different type of mind altogether, than that attracted to the regular army. In France, for example, few officers from the Armistice Army became successful Resistance leaders; the necessary mental leap was too great for them to make.

As the British began supplying the Resistance, they also sought to control and direct its activities. They were not overly successful in this; for one thing, they often wanted slightly different things than the Resistance people wanted. For another, it was difficult to direct and control from afar. They also had to contend with the desires and directives of the various governments in exile, so there was at least a three-cornered tug of war for control in most cases. In spite of all this, the Resistance reached the third stage, that of giving battle to the enemy.

For the Resistance, "battle" was different from what it was for the regular forces. It might include overt action, an ambush or a derailment of a train; it might be the fomenting of a strike, or some kind of industrial sabotage. Overt action varied from place to place, and time to time.

In Russia where large numbers of Russian troops were cut off in the early days of the invasion, guerrilla or partisan operations began early. Large numbers of German units were forced to operate behind what were officially the front lines, and attacks on supply and communication lines were frequent. The same sort of thing happened in Yugoslavia, and though the Germans officially occupied the country, they never subdued it. At one point there were twenty divisions of Germans and Italians—as many as were fighting on the Italian front—busy in Yugoslavia attacking the partisans.

In France things were slower getting off the ground. The Vichy regime and the Armistice Army took some of the sting out of occupation initially and led to a degree of confusion as to who was actually the enemy, and where effort ought to be directed. Resistance grew up in both the occupied and the Vichy zones, but the simple existence of an ostensibly legitimate government served to make overt resistance a matter of argument. When the Germans occupied all of France after the Allied invasion of French North Africa the issue became clearer. The Armistice Army dissolved, Vichy was removed as an intermediary, and the French stood face to face with the conqueror. By that time there was already a cadre of resisters living in hiding, not only the normal underground resisters, but also the genesis of a partisan army, spawned by the labor draft and the roundup of Jews. Young men had taken to the hill country, where they lived a hand-to-mouth existence, eventually being organized, and armed and supplied in large measure by the British. They emerged to fight and by early 1944 they actually controlled substantial segments of France, on the borders of which they fought pitched battles with the Germans and the German-controlled Milice. At the time of the Normandy invasion the French Resistance made substantial contributions to the Allied effort, tying up German communications and interfering with their reinforcements.

An outstanding example of what the Resistance could achieve, and some of the difficulties under which it labored, was the affair of the Norsk Hydro Plant in Norway. At the start of the war the plant was the world's only commercial producer of heavy water, a vital component for the creation of an atomic reaction. When the Germans took over Norway, they immediately made plans to increase the heavy-water output and took such an ill-concealed interest in Norsk Hydro that the matter soon came to the attention of the British. The question then was raised as to what should be done to cut off the supply to the Germans.

Eventually, the Allies mounted four separate attacks against the heavy-water plant, by three distinct methods. The result was a major vindication of unconventional methods.

The first attempt was a commando-type operation staged in November of 1941. Two bomber aircraft took off from Scotland towing two gliders. All four crashed in Norway without getting anywhere near their objective. The aircrew were killed in the crashes, and the soldiers who survived the landing were rounded up by the Germans and shot, in accordance with Hitler's order to execute commandos. Cost of the operation: two bombers, two gliders, and forty-seven lives, for no result except to alert the Germans of British interest.

The second attack was by SOE, which sent in a team of nine specially trained Norwegians. At the end of February in 1943 the Norwegians penetrated the Norsk Hydro plant and blew up 2,000 pounds of heavy water, temporarily wrecking both the storage and production facilities. They got away without a shot being fired at them and believed they had set the German program back two years.

They were correct in assuming they had scored a phenomenal success, wrong in their estimate of the German recovery time. By August the Germans were producing at a rate exceeding pre-attack levels. Now the Americans entered the affair, and the head of the American atomic bomb project asked General Marshall to take an interest in Norsk Hydro. The result of this interest was an attack by 115 Flying Fortresses of the U. S. 8th Air Force. On November 16, 1943, they dropped nearly 200 tons of bombs on the plant and the adjacent town of Rjukan. They killed twenty-two Norwegians, including one several miles from the target, wrecked Rjukan, and never even hit Norsk Hydro. The Norwegian government in exile delivered a stiff note of protest to both the British and the Americans, neither of which paid any attention.

The Germans responded by planning to transport all the existing heavy-water stocks south to Germany. On Sunday, February 20, the Norwegian SOE operatives sabotaged the shipment, and as the heavy water was being ferried across a lake, they sank it in 1,300 feet of water. Several Norwegians went down with the ferry, but the heavy water was lost for good.

The heavy-water strikes were somewhat atypical, in that the plant and its products were ideal targets for unconventional operations, while very difficult ones for the regular forces. Nonetheless, they gave some idea of what might be achieved, and have continually been cited by those who maintain that covert operations and industrial sabotage are far more cost-effective, as well as far cheaper in lives, than indiscriminate and imprecise area-bombing. How much more might have been achieved in this way, as the Resistance moved toward its fourth and final stage, was a matter of argument.

The ultimate aim of all that had gone before was a full-scale uprising, a national war of liberation that would drive the enemy from the homeland. Hopefully, the entire country would participate in this. If every single Frenchman or Belgian were out pulling down telephone wire, changing road signs, blowing up culverts, and—if possible—sniping at Germans, the whole untidy affair would make occupation physically impossible. It would be organized chaos, planned anarchy, and it would topple the German empire. In the midst of this mass action the shadow government of the Resistance would come out into the open at last, and as German power faded from the scene, the liberation, and the moral regeneration that went with it, would be accomplished.

That was the ideal, visionary situation, and it never happened. In some places, the Resistance came close to achieving this aim. Yugoslavia was probably the most nearly successful. Tito controlled large areas of Yugoslavia by 1944 and he and the Axis forces engaged in pitched battles. Late in 1944 Belgrade was occupied by Soviet and Titoist forces, but Tito was strong enough to pursue an independent line and to keep the Soviets from overshadowing him. He managed to clear the rest of his country and take Trieste without Soviet help or interference. Though the country remained theoretically a monarchy, Tito's National Liberation Front wielded the real authority, and at the end of the war he called a constituent convention that put him officially in power.

The Yugoslav situation was unique, however, in that the country was off the main line of advance of any of the major Allies. What happened in France was more typical, and what happened in Poland more tragic, than the good fortune enjoyed by Tito.

Throughout their lifetimes there were various attempts to unite the separate French Resistance movements into one great whole. Ideological preconceptions and personal rivalries served to prevent this, as did the peculiar problem of de Gaulle, "Fighting France," and what to do about it. De Gaulle was determined to control all aspects of the French opposition to Germany, but his contacts with the Resistance inside France were tenuous. He did not appear to understand either the problems or the aims of the resisters; they wanted a new, regenerated and rejuvenated France; he seemed to them to want an older France, out of the days of Richelieu or at best Napoleon. Eventually, it was de Gaulle who won; he was the only man whose prestige was sufficient to rally all shades of Frenchmen behind him. Many times, though, it looked as if the Resistance was as preoccupied with its internal politics as it was with fighting the Germans.

Because of the Allied invasion of Normandy, the French never got the chance to try a full-scale, independent, national uprising. They did come close, however. As the Normandy invasion took place, there were general risings in Limousin, the Vercors, Auvergne, and Brittany. A massive interdiction campaign slowed the German movement of reinforcements to the battle front; German troops from eastern France, supposed to reach Normandy in three days, took more than two weeks instead. The price for this was steep; the French Forces of the Interior (FFI), as they called themselves, lacked heavy weapons and armor, and they received relatively scanty supplies from the Allies until the latter realized how widespread the rising was. There were reprisals and massacres, both of armed Frenchmen and of open towns, such as the little village of Oradour-sur-Glane, wiped out by a passing German column out of sheer bloody-mindedness.

In Paris the French rose up and liberated the city before the arrival of the Allies, thereby in some measure resurrecting the national pride after the humiliation of 1940. All over Paris even now, though reminders of the events of 1940 are noticeably lacking, there are small commemorative plaques recalling the liberation of 1944. By late in the year the French Resistance was operating formally alongside the Allies, and was given the responsibility for clearing much of southwestern France and the Biscay coast ports. On his return, de Gaulle quickly took over the leadership of the Resistance cadres, and many of the FFI soldiers were soon drafted into the regular French Army, also fighting beside the Allies. Conscription into the army was one way to deprive potential rivals of their underpinning. Ironically, former Resistance fighters tended not to make excellent regular soldiers; the necessary mental attitudes of both were too far apart.

Triumph in France was matched by tragedy in Poland. The Poles too looked forward eagerly to liberation, but their anticipation was clouded by the fact that the Russians would be their liberators. Once more geography was to prove Poland's curse. Polish-Soviet relations had been stormy at best throughout the war; the Russians insisted that the large share of Poland they had taken in 1939 would remain Russian, they constantly snubbed the Polish government in exile in London, and eventually, early in 1943, they broke off relations with the Poles, using Polish requests for an investigation of the Katyn Forest massacres as their excuse. If the Poles did not trust the Russians enough to believe the Russian denials of the massacres, the Russians would have nothing to do with them. It was hypocrisy that would have done credit to George Orwell's vision of 1984, but it served the Russian purpose. Bringing out tame Polish Communists, the Russians moved to set up a puppet prospective Polish government. The Polish underground, desperate to save their own souls rather than come under Russian domination after German, decided they must liberate themselves.

Just as the French had risen up in Paris to present the arriving Allies with a functioning France that had to be acknowledged, the Poles rose up in Warsaw as the Russian forces neared. On August 1, the Russian advance patrols were nearing the eastern suburbs of Warsaw. They had just completed an immense two-month drive that had all but wrecked German Army Group Center. In Warsaw the Polish Home Army, under the command of General Tadeusz Bor-Komorowski, and acting on orders from the London government, rose against the German garrison occupying the city.

Catching the Germans unprepared and busy with the Russians, the Poles soon had control of most of Warsaw. The idea was that when the Russians arrived, which they would do within days at most, the Poles would be able to claim equal status, as masters in their own house. To the dismay not only of the Polish government in London, but of the Western Allies as well, the Russians stopped. Stalin blandly announced—publicly—that the Russian offensive had run out of steam; it would be necessary to regroup and re-supply before resuming the offensive. This news was gratefully received and correctly interpreted by the Germans: they were free to pull units in for the suppression of the Warsaw rising. For the third time in the war the unhappy city was the scene of bitter fighting. It had been besieged and taken in 1939; in 1943 the desperate Jews in the Warsaw ghetto had risen up against their tormentors, and after a heroic resistance had been virtually wiped out by the Germans. Now the Home Army was to follow the same tragic path.

While Churchill and Roosevelt both pleaded with Stalin, the Russian dictator shrugged his shoulders; it was a shame, but the Red Army simply could not move; he was very sorry. The Polish government begged Churchill for help. The British went again to the Russians: if they would not intervene themselves, would they allow the British to fly missions to Warsaw, drop supplies, and refuel at Russian airstrips for the return trip. That seemed a small enough request, but the Russians replied that such an up-setting matter would seriously inconvenience their logistics ar-rangements; they refused permission for Allied planes to land in Russian territory.

The British tried another tack. There were several Polish bomber squadrons in the R. A. F. Now they, and other R. A. F. planes as well, loaded up with every pint of gas they could hold and flew resupply missions all the way to Warsaw and back. Un-fortunately, that was the absolute extreme limit of their range, and they could carry so little in the way of supplies that the trip was hardly worth the risk. Nonetheless they took it. Much of what they were able to drop fell into German hands as the Polish perimeter grew smaller and smaller.

In the city itself resistance lasted for more than two months. The Poles fought with Molotov cocktails, light machine-guns, and mortars. The Germans brought in armor and heavy artillery. At point-blank range they blasted their way from house to house, from room to room. The suppression was turned over to the SS, and the Germans employed specialist troops for this job, the Kaminski Brigade, ex-Russian prisoners, and the Dirlewanger Brigade of German convicts. Neither the aged, nor women, nor children were spared by the Germans. Medical supplies gave out, then food gave out, then water. The Germans were deliberately razing the city as they went along. After sixty-three days, out of ammunition and everything else, the survivors of the Home Army, perhaps half of the original 40,000 surrendered. The Germans suffered 10,000 killed, 7,000 missing and presumed killed, and 9,000 wounded. It was further estimated that nearly 250,000 civilians had died during the battle. Stalin sighed, and the Red Army sat within earshot of the small-arms fire in Warsaw until the sounds died away.

The Poles were only the most obstinate of all the Resistance movements. All of them came out into overt action as the regular armed forces of the Allies approached. Short of achieving the national uprising, what they really hoped to do was to assert their title to consideration at the end of the war. The only way they could do that was by making a valid contribution to the defeat of the Axis, and their efforts were such that they did slowly win recognition and respect. Thus Tito gained power and support from the British, and the FFI merged its efforts with the returning forces of de Gaulle. In Russia the partisans eventually controlled more than 80,000 square miles of territory behind German lines; in Norway the underground was strong enough and numerous enough to cut the railways in a thousand places in one night. In northern Italy the partisans came to control a substantial part of the country. The Danish underground mounted a rescue operation that saved large numbers of Danish Jews from the fate of their co-religionists elsewhere. The Belgians formed a secret army, the Poles stole a V-1 rocket from a development site and smuggled it out of the country to the Allies.

The questions remain: how much did the Resistance accomplish, and how much did it cost? Unfortunately, there can be a definitive answer to neither question. The underground tied down large numbers of Axis troops and it destroyed huge amounts of material. There is no doubt its contribution was a major one and a vital one, but to equate it with any given amount of conventional activity is impossible. They were different sides of the same war, and neither would have been successful, or at least as successful as soon, without the other.

Even less can be said of the costs of resistance. The final accomplishment was the culmination of untold small acts of defiance.

All that can be said with certainty is that the bill, in pain, sorrow, and loss of life, was immense. No one can say how many people were imprisoned, tortured, and killed through, by, or as a reaction against, the activities of the Resistance. The cost in human suffering was enormous, and it was some measure of the German tyranny that people were willing to pay such a price to be rid of it.

22. The Strategic Bombing Campaign

AS THE GROUND FORCES LAY locked in messy, mortal combat, as the cauldron of the Resistance simmered and bubbled up, there was a third war being fought. High in the heavens men froze and sweated, fought and died. The air forces of the warring powers waged their separate wars with each other and with their rivals ashore and afloat. Of the many controversies surrounding World War II, few are more virulent than the whole question of strategic bombing and its contribution to the war.

In the Battle of Britain the Germans had made the first attempt in history to subdue another country from the air. They had failed miserably. As an offshoot of the German attack, the British had unleashed their own strategic bombing offensive against continental Europe. They began with little. Several of the dominant personalities of the Royal Air Force were bomber advocates, but during the late thirties the government had—rightly as it turned out—upgraded the fighter defenses at the expense of the bomber force. The British effort was therefore slow to develop. Their bombers had limited range and limited payloads, and in their early strikes, they could do little more than infuriate the Germans, and that at almost prohibitively heavy cost. In one famous disaster, for example, a force of twenty-two Wellington bombers raided German shipping in the Heligoland Bight and only seven returned home; the rest were either shot down over the target or failed to make it all the way back to their bases. That was in December of 1939. Through early 1940 the bombers were busy supporting the French as best they could, though the French, intensely fearful of German retaliation, were extremely dubious allies as far as the air war went. Next it was a matter of striking at potential invasion ports, bombing barges and landing craft concentrations. Not until late

1940 had the air war settled down, with the Germans involved in the Blitz, and the British retaliating wherever they could.

The technical problems were enormous, and the results disappointingly small. Bomber and aircrew losses were so heavy that the British were soon forced to confine themselves to night bombing. While that cut their losses, it also cut their efficiency, as targets became harder to find and easier to miss. After a year they estimated that only one bomb in ten fell within five miles of its target. The bombing campaign thus had an extremely long gestation period, and it was months and even years before it reached the level of intensity where it began to pay dividends.

For the Royal Air Force the last months of 1940 and all of 1941 was a period of experimentation and improvisation. Both the techniques and the material slowly improved. It was February of 1941 before the first of the British four-engined heavy bombers, the Stirling, went on operations. The Stirling was outstanding as an example of the kind of thinking that prevented more rapid development in the closing years of peace. Its wingspan was limited to less than one hundred feet, that being the standard size for R. A. F. hangar doors at the time of its conception, and its fuselage was made a given width so it could take the regulation service packing case. Nevertheless, the Stirling proved a useful, docile aircraft, and a major addition to Bomber Command.

Initially, the British thought they could fly close formations of bombers, thus providing mutual protection, that they could fly in the daytime, and that they could attack specific targets with some degree of precision. They found they were wrong in all of these assumptions. As they moved on into this learning period and took their losses, they not only bombed by night, but they did it in a different manner. Instead of the formation, they flew in a "stream," where each plane would take off, then make its way independently along a given route to its target. Over the target they had to settle for "area bombing" instead of the precision they had at first supposed possible. Officially, they held to the dogma of precision bombing, but they gradually recognized that area bombing was in fact what they were doing, and that became the policy late in 1941.

As the British learned their lessons, so of course did the Germans. Their radar network improved and so did their control of the night fighters and the fighters themselves. On both sides radar would pick up an incoming plane and vector a patrolling night fighter on to it. When it got close enough, the night fighter would find its target on its own short-range radar, then close in for a visual sighting and the kill. The scientists and the aircrew worked hand in hand on these and similar matters. The Germans sent their bombers over England and used radio beams as navigational aids; all the pilot had to do was stay on the beam till he reached his target. The British countered this by inventing a way to warp the beam, so the German bombers gradually diverged from their targets and often bombed empty spaces. As the German radar system got better, the British countered it too. They discovered that a small piece of tinfoil dropped out of a plane caused a radar reflection. So they sent decoy planes over the enemy coast to drop tinfoil—"window," it was called—and confuse the radar operators while the real bombers flew through to their targets.

Had the bombing proponents had their way, the campaign would have escalated a great deal faster than it did, but the other services were equally adamant in their demands for resources. At the end of 1941 the British Chiefs of Staff were seriously questioning the validity of the whole bombing effort. It seemed to be absorbing an inordinate amount of matériel for the results that were being achieved, and there was discussion of abandoning the whole idea. The British desperately needed aircraft to use as convoy escorts both along the coasts and in the Western Approaches, and Coastal Command became a successful rival to Bomber Command for the allocation of material. They decided to keep on more because of what they had already invested in the project than because of any positive results so far accomplished.

If 1940 and 1941 was a period of groping in the dark, literally as well as figuratively, in 1942 the R. A. F. began at last to make a bit of headway. As the spring weather came in, the British mounted greater and greater raids. At the end of May they undertook the first thousand-plane raid, against the city of Cologne.

It was a cast of desperation, with Cologne only incidentally the target. Bomber Command and its new chief, Air Marshal Arthur Harris, were really aiming at the British government and the service chiefs of staff. When Harris took over Bomber Command late in February of 1942, he found he had just over 300 planes in his force. That was few more than Bomber Command had possessed way back in 1940. So far Bomber Command had just not shown enough results to justify a higher priority than it was getting. Harris was to change all that. He was a fervent believer in strategic bombing and he was determined to convert his bosses to his view. He immediately set about planning for an operation that would impress everyone. A thousand planes in one raid, hitting one target, in one night! It seemed magical, but Harris and his staff made it work.

To do it they had to strip Bomber Command's facilities of everything, and everyone, who could get into the air. Planes were pulled out of repair shops and reserve facilities, pilots called up from training squadrons and from leave, and robbed from Coastal Command. While the preparations went on, the British experimented with better methods; they developed improved guidance systems to bring their planes over the target in more concentrated bunches, they played about with the proper proportions of high-explosive bombs to incendiary bombs. High explosives could knock things apart, then incendiaries could set fires. Then another wave of bombers with more high explosives could knock out the fire-fighters and more incendiaries could compound the devastation. The ideal of destruction would be to create a fire-storm, a fire so hot and so intense that it would suck its own fuel into it and keep itself alive while consuming everything—human and material— around it. It was a long while before the bombers were able to achieve such paroxysms of destruction, but eventually they managed it.

The Cologne raid was a commencement exercise. The R. A. F. put 1,134 aircraft into the air, including decoys and night intruder aircraft, designed to draw off or fight German night interceptors. Something over 900 planes actually bombed Cologne. Forty-four failed to return, which was regarded by the R. A. F. as an acceptable loss rate, though unhappily, most of the losses were among new crews, with the result that premature effort would have to be paid for again farther down the line. In the city, fires raged for two days, and it was several days before the smoke cleared sufficiently for British photo-reconnaissance planes to take pictures so they could assess the damage. It turned out that about 20,000 homes were destroyed or damaged, about 1,500 commercial properties were damaged, and fifty or sixty factories were knocked out, some for short periods, some for longer. Rail and communications were interrupted for as long as two weeks, and vital services—electricity, water, sewage—were disrupted temporarily. Nearly half a million people were homeless, but only about 500 were actually killed or wounded.

The raid was not quite the success Harris had predicted; he had said it would wipe Cologne permanently off the map. He was far off in this. It turned out that to destroy even one city, it had to be raided again and again and again. The British finally realized that to wage a bombing campaign capable of winning the war all by itself, they would need perhaps 6,000 heavy bombers on operations at any given time. They and the Americans together never even came near that figure. Harris also predicted that the raid, and ones like it, would soon destroy German civilian morale. This attitude, basically a holdover from the prewar period, never proved true. Civilians showed themselves able to endure an amazing amount of punishment, and in fact rather than having their morale broken by the ruin of their homes and the deaths of their families, they became more supportive of their nation's war effort. One of the remarkable aspects of wartime planning was that governments seldom seemed to apply their own experience to their enemies' situations. The British knew *they* had not broken under the German bombing but they assumed the Germans would break under their bombing.

On the other hand, in some respects the raid was remarkable, even though it did fall short of predictions. More damage was done to Cologne in that one night than had been done there so far in the war. The British had hit Cologne more than a hundred times already, without accomplishing as much as they now had done in one big attack. The "big raid" was definitely the way to go; the real problem now would be to sustain the effort. And on that score, the raid was an unqualified success; one of the first communications Harris received after the raid was a congratulatory message from Churchill. It was immediately obvious that Bomber Command had scored a great plus with both the British public and the government. Whatever the R. A. F. did or did not achieve in the skies over Germany, they had certainly improved the situation in the rear areas.

Constrained to produce an encore, the bombers went back to hit targets in the Ruhr Valley, Germany's great industrial complex. Subsequent raids were not as productive as the one on Cologne, though; the British simply could not keep up the pace with the men and matériel then available, and the Germans rebounded more rapidly than anyone had expected they would. An inescapable difficulty was that the German economy contained a great deal of surplus fat, and the Germans could suffer a large amount of damage before it began to hurt them, or to decrease their capacity for waging war.

In fact, German production capacity never did fall off as a result of the bombing offensive. After Albert Speer took over as

Minister of Production, German factories increased their output substantially. In spite of Allied bombing and the necessity to decentralize, production figures in key industries kept going up right to the very last stages of the war. What really killed the German war machine was not loss of production, but the inability of production to accelerate as rapidly as the demands of war entailed. Even though the Germans kept improving their output, their combat wastage and loss ratio increased even faster, and it was this factor, rather than production stoppages or breakdowns, that finally made the well run dry.

An important part of that wastage, of course, came from the bombing campaign and the need to combat it. By mid-1942 the British were still at it. Their techniques were constantly refined; they had now acknowledged the need for saturation bombing. It was not enough to hit a target once, then do it again in two or three months. You had to hit, hit again, and hit yet again. Bomber Command's vision was of night skies raining devastation on every German city every night. It was still, given the limits of their aircraft, easier to hit western than eastern Germany, but fortunately for them, the heaviest industry was in the west; in the Rhineland, the Ruhr Valley, and the Saar Basin. They concentrated their efforts on Cologne, Dusseldorf, Essen, Dortmund. They also bombed the ports from which material was shipped eastward to Russia; Hamburg, Bremen, and Lubeck. They hit Berlin every time they could, just to show the Germans it could be done. As head of the Luftwaffe, Hermann Goering had once boasted, "No Allied plane will ever fly over the Reich!" Now British aircrews stenciled his words on the noses of their bombers and next to them tallied up the number of their missions over Germany.

The Americans arrived in 1942 and immediately began setting up the apparatus to undertake their own bombing campaign. They came in a trickle in the spring, and it mounted to a near-flood as the year went on. The U. S. 8th Air Force was the command made responsible for the bomber offensive, with General Ira C. Eaker as its chief. Initially, they hoped to be operating in great numbers by late 1942, but the necessary diversion of units to North Africa prevented this. It was August before the first operations began, and for the rest of the year, flying in relatively small numbers, they mounted daylight attacks against targets in France. In January of 1943 they hit north German targets, penetrating the airspace of the Reich itself, and they soon ran into trouble.

The Americans insisted on repeating most of the mistakes the British had already made. It was not, as was thought at the time, because they were either stupid or wildly overconfident, but rather because they came to the battle with different ideas based on different equipment, and had to see for themselves the error of their ways. British experts said that precision bombing was impossible, and that the necessary degree of accuracy to get results was unattainable. The American response was that they had a gadget, the Norden bombsight, which could hit the target every time. In the phrase of the day, they could "put a bomb in a pickle barrel," and do it from 30,000 feet. The British said that German fighter opposition was too strong for unescorted bombers. The Americans believed they possessed the answer to this too. British heavy bombers—the Stirling, Lancaster, and Halifax—carried lighter defensive armament than American types. The Lancaster had eight machine guns in three turrets, two in a nose turret, two in a top turret, and a four-gun turret in the tail. The last sub-type of the Flying Fortress, the B-17G, carried thirteen machine-guns—all of heavier caliber than the British—in chin, nose, dorsal, center fuselage, ventral, waist, and tail positions. There was of course a penalty for this; the maximum normal bomb load for the B-17G was lighter than that for the Lancaster, and the number of crew members was larger. The Americans had to use more planes and more men to deliver less payload than the British.

They insisted, however, that their heavily armed planes could fly successfully in the daytime and they sent them off in tight formations, stacked up "boxes" ostensibly able to give each other protection against German fighters. That too exacted its toll, for a substantial amount of the damage done to American planes was a result of the defensive fire of other American planes. The first raids over Germany went well, however, and led 8th Air Force to believe its ideas were being vindicated.

The Americans and British had agreed on a mutually supportive scheme of operations. The British would continue their night attacks and area or saturation bombing, aimed basically at the German civilian population and general disruption of the war economy; the Americans would operate by day, aiming at specific crucial targets. The R. A. F. occasionally had trouble convincing its aircrews that their raids had purely military value, and com-

manders had to insist that every general target contained a definitely military objective. New ways had to be developed to increase
accuracy; specially selected crews were drafted into "pathfinder"
squadrons whose job it was to locate a target and mark it with
flares and specially colored bombs, so that follow-up squadrons
could bomb where they were supposed to. Late in 1943 a new
type of radar that allowed them to bomb through cloud was fitted
to some Fortresses so that bad weather need not cause abortion of
missions.

As the Americans got organized, and with the R. A. F. now
fully into its stride, the tempo increased markedly in 1943. Units
based first in North Africa flew across the Mediterranean to hit
Italian factories and to strike at the Balkans. Later, heavy-bom-
bardment groups operating out of southern Italy crossed the Alps
to bomb Austria and southern German targets and flew costly
missions to eastern Europe, especially to hit the Rumanian oil
refineries around Ploesti. From Britain, both by day and by night,
the bombers regularly struck at the Rhineland, the Ruhr, and increasingly at Berlin.

The Germans responded fiercely, but Hitler insisted that the
Luftwaffe was an offensive weapon and was extremely reluctant
to designate defense of Germany as its primary task. Eventually,
he was forced to do so, but he did it with an ill grace and with
mental reservations that made it very difficult for the Germans to
operate at full effectiveness. An outstanding example of his meddling came in the famous case of the Messerschmitt ME262, the
world's first operational jet fighter.

For years experts had experimented with the possibilities of
jet propulsion as a more powerful replacement for the propeller-
driven aircraft. The British eventually produced a jet aircraft that
entered combat three weeks before the end of the war in Europe.
But the Germans beat them to the punch with a jet that became
operational in 1944. Faster than contemporary Allied fighters, it
might well have regained a degree of air superiority for Germany;
Hitler, however, infuriated by the Allied "terror bombing," ordered
that all existing jet fighters be modified as fast bombers to fly
retaliatory missions to Britain. This set the fighter program back
at least four months and ended whatever chance may have existed
for the Germans to become once more masters of their own skies.

As the scientific and developmental battle went on, so did the
search for strategic answers. The British by 1943 were resigned to
a campaign of pure straightforward pounding. The Germans were

tough, but if hit long enough and hard enough, sooner or later they would break. The Americans, committed to precision bombing, became preoccupied with a search for the magic target. Surely, they told themselves, there must be one vital, vulnerable spot in the enemy war machine. Knock out that one specific component, and the Germans would come tumbling down.

They thought they found the answer in the German city of Schweinfurt. Here was concentrated the majority of the German ball-bearing industry. Destroy the factory, the theory went, and the magic one-shot answer would have been found. On August 17, 1943, the 8th Air Force struck at Schweinfurt and at aircraft factories in Regensburg and Weiner Neustadt. Of 376 aircraft on the joint mission, sixty were shot down by the fierce German reaction. Sixteen-percent losses were prohibitive; a week of that would have wiped out 8th Air Force. Nonetheless, Schweinfurt appeared a winning target. In a second raid, in October, the Americans lost another sixty planes, this time out of fewer than three hundred. In the week of that raid their total losses were 148 planes and 1,500 airmen. It was too much, and 8th Air Force could not stand the pace; all they were really proving, at immense cost, was that the British were right—unescorted daylight bombing was impossible.

Having reached the same impasse the British had reached two or three years earlier, the Americans then went on to a different answer. U. S. planes flying deep penetration missions into Germany were escorted across France and the Low Countries by British Spitfires or American-built Mustangs and Thunderbolts. The fighters took on the German fighters of the coastal defenses and got the bombers through. Then, when they reached the limit of their range, the fighters turned back and the bombers were left to go it alone. As soon as the escorts fell away, the German home defense squadrons came up to hit the bombers. The simplest answer to the problem, therefore, was to increase the range of the fighters; provide them with extra fuel and they could cover the bombers all the way to the target and back.

This was the same problem that had beset the Germans in the Battle of Britain; their fighters had not been able to provide cover for the bombers all the way to the target. Ironically, the answer had existed long before the problem. The American Curtiss F11C-2, a short-lived fighter with the U. S. Navy in the mid-thirties, and the German Heinkel He51, a biplane fighter that served in the Spanish Civil War, had both been fitted with auxiliary gas tanks slung under the belly. All that had to be done now was to produce a droppable extra tank, let the plane use it in the early stages of the flight, then drop it when it was empty. Allied planes could thus enter German air space with full tanks, escort their bigger brothers all the way to the target, and come home safely. In December of 1943 the first P-51 Mustangs flew close escort to Kiel, and then, in March of 1944, for the first time, Mustangs flew all the way to Berlin and back.

It was quite often such simple ideas as the drop-tank that made the difference between life and death for individuals, and between mastery and defeat for air forces. The mainstay of the German defense, for example, was a beautifully streamlined fighter known as the Focke-Wulf 190. Fast, agile, and deadly, the F-W was a match for any of the Allied planes. Up against the heavier American Thunderbolts, which were the biggest single-engined fighter of the war, the Focke-Wulf could break off the combat by rapidly climbing away from the Americans. Then one day a new Thunderbolt appeared, with bigger, wider propeller blades, dubbed "paddleblades" by the pilots. Suddenly, the Thunderbolt could claw its way up into the air right after the Focke-Wulf, and German pilots had lost another advantage.

In the long run, more than any one plane, or any one operation, it was the sheer momentum of the bombing campaign that began to pay off. After five long years the bombers reached the point of destructiveness proclaimed by their champions at the start of the war. During the entire war, the Allies dropped 2,700,000 tons of bombs on Germany; nearly three quarters, 72 percent of that figure, was dropped between July 1, 1944, and the collapse of Germany. Only when the Allied bomber force could achieve that degree of concentration could they attain decisive results. The kind of results they did achieve were shown by the great raids of the war, such as those on Hamburg and Dresden.

The destruction of Hamburg took place in late July and early August of 1943, so it was a concentrated attack that served as a foretaste of what would come later, when the Allies were regularly able to mount this type of raid. Hamburg was the second largest city in Germany, and a major shipping and industrial center. It had been steadily bombed throughout the war—more than 130 times already. The Germans had learned to live with this and had created in the city a model civil defense organization, with plenty of shelters, fire fighting equipment, warning systems, and all the paraphernalia of a city under attack. With its industry, its population concentration, its wooden center dating from medieval days, it was a perfect target. The Allies decided, in an operation code-named Gomorrah, to wipe Hamburg out.

By now they had their techniques perfected. The major weapon used was the incendiary bomb, with enough high explosive mixed in to create fuel for the incendiaries. They also used delayed-action bombs, particularly useful in impeding the fire-fighters, and phosphorus bombs, perhaps the most cruel of all the different types. The first attack was on the night of July 24-25, by 740 planes from Bomber Command. The results were spectacular. Massive fires were set off, and the German civil defense mechanisms were quickly overwhelmed. The next day the Americans arrived and hit Hamburg again in a heavy raid that cost them a whole squadron wiped out by the ferocious German fighters. The second night Hamburg was left alone while the R. A. F. finished off Essen, but on the next day, the 26th, the 8th Air Force was back again. At night fast twin-engined Mosquito bombers of the R. A. F. put in nuisance raids to keep the Germans awake, then just before midnight of the 27th, the heavies came back again.

In two great waves of bombers sowing a carpet of destruction across the city, the R. A. F. created a fire-storm. Thousands of individual fires merged into one great all-consuming blaze. Buildings collapsed and their debris was sucked into the vortex of the storm. The wind drew fleeing people irresistibly into the fire. In the air raid shelters all the oxygen was sucked out and the occupants suffocated, or were baked alive by the heat of the fires raging overhead. Thousands of people simply disappeared.

The fires continued to rage unabated, but two nights later the British came back and did it again, hitting parts of the city that had so far escaped with minor damage. Finally, on the night of August 4, the British launched their last attack. They planned to hit with everything they had, but heavy weather made it impossible for anything but the Lancasters, who could get above the storm, to fly. Even so another 1,400 tons of bombs fell on the ruins of the city that night.

As the last R. A. F. bombers droned away to the westward, they left behind them a scene of awesome destruction. The fires, the rescue work, the opening of shelters full of dead, the mercy-killing of the hopelessly burned, went on for days. The worst German attack on Coventry had destroyed about a hundred acres; Operation Gomorrah wiped out 6,000 acres of Hamburg; more than half the city was destroyed, 300,000 homes were burned, three-quarters of a million were homeless, somewhere between 60,000 and 100,000 were dead. In spite of all the German efforts to keep the disaster quiet, a wave of dread swept over Germany. The Royal Air Force had finished with Hamburg; the battle of Berlin lay ahead.

For all its suffering and devastation, Hamburg was but a curtain raiser to events to come. By 1945 the wiping out of the great city was past history. The Allied bombers, escorted by their long-range fighters, ranged unceasingly over the battered Reich. Their mastery of the air was no longer a matter of dispute and the vaunted Luftwaffe, that had brought Poland, the Netherlands, and France to their knees, could rarely put planes in the air. There was little fuel for operations and less for pilot training. Still the Allied armadas droned on. By the last months of the war, they were hard put to find useful targets. Out of their search came the raid on Dresden.

The capital of the old state of Saxony, Dresden was a city of immense age and charm. Napoleon had fought a battle near there back in 1813, but the twentieth century seemed largely to have passed Dresden by. By February of 1945 the Germans were reeling, and the bomber offensive had in large measure been diverted to the disruption of German communications, as an adjunct to the ground campaign now being fought on the western borders of the Reich itself. "Bomber" Harris, however, still believed in the efficacy of strategic bombing; Dresden was to be his last "big raid," ostensibly because it was thought to be a communications center for the eastern German armies, more probably because it had not previously been hit, and it seemed about the right size for a full-scale strike.

Dresden was hit, first by the R. A. F., then by the Americans, in mid-February. The city was virtually destroyed, and upward of 60,000 people were killed. Two months later the strategic bomber campaign was called off; shortly after that the war ended.

Final judgment on the bomber offensive remains elusive. Its cost, in allocation of resources, in aircraft, and in aircrew, was heavy. The bombers never achieved what their original champions claimed they would do; German morale never cracked, and only at the very end of the war did the German ground forces suffer any real shortages of supplies that could be traced to the bombing. Yet the shortcomings of the bombers seem to stem more from the exaggerated prior claims of their supporters, rather than from their inability to achieve striking results. For certainly the results were striking; Germany lay in ruins, hundreds of thousands of her citizens were dead, further hundreds of thousands had had to be diverted into civil defense or countering the bombers by military means. No one who saw the ruins of Hamburg or Berlin would question that the bombers were effective; it was more a matter of disagreement as to whether or not they had been the one war-winning weapon, and the answer to that was that they had not. Neither had any other single item.

As the war receded into the distance, argument came to center less on the value of the bomber as a weapons system, and more on the morality of it. That particular question could be indulged only after the passions of the war had cooled. Total war followed a logical course from the killing of soldiers to the killing of those who provided weapons for the soldier, to the lessening of the efficiency of the enemy's war machine—if necessary, by the incidental killing of his women and children. Many years ago Carl von Clausewitz had written, "War is an act of force, and to the application of that force there is no limit. Each of the adversaries forces the hand of the other, and a reciprocal action results which in theory can have no limit. . . ." The first stumbling bombing of World War I led on to the more efficient bombing of World War II; Coventry and Rotterdam led inexorably to Hamburg and Dresden. From the point of view of the directing intelligence, morality did not apply.

PART IV: TOWARD THE ELUSIVE VICTORY

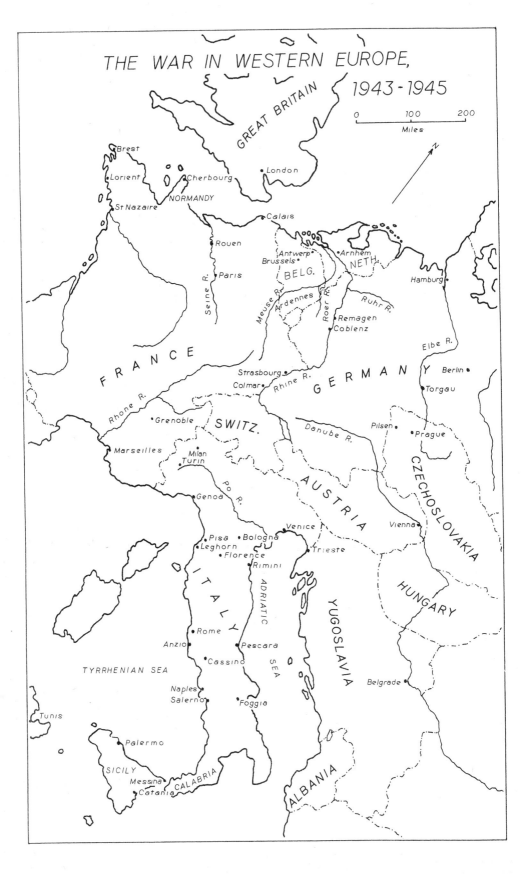

THE WAR IN WESTERN EUROPE, 1943-1945

GREAT BRITAIN

0   100   200
Miles

Brest
Lorient
St Nazaire
Cherbourg
NORMANDY
London
Calais
Rouen
Seine R.
Paris
Antwerp
Brussels
BELG.
Meuse R.
Ardennes
Arnhem
NETH.
Roer R.
Ruhr R.
Hamburg
Remagen
Coblenz
Elbe R.
FRANCE
Strasbourg
Colmar
Rhine R.
GERMANY
Berlin
Torgau
Rhone R.
Grenoble
SWITZ.
Danube R.
Pilsen
Prague
Marseilles
Milan
Turin
AUSTRIA
CZECHOSLOVAKIA
Genoa
Po R.
Venice
Vienna
Pisa
Leghorn
Florence
Bologna
Trieste
HUNGARY
Rimini
ITALY
ADRIATIC SEA
YUGOSLAVIA
Rome
Anzio
Pescara
Cassino
TYRRHENIAN SEA
Belgrade
Naples
Salerno
Foggia
Tunis
Palermo
SICILY
Messina
CALABRIA
Catania
ALBANIA

23. The Collapse and Invasion of Italy

IN THE SUMMER OF 1943 two muddied currents merged in the Mediterranean. The first was the Allied strategic problem of where to go and what to do now that the North African campaign was ending. The second was the Italian political problem of how to get out of an increasingly pointless war.

The Allies at Casablanca had decided on the taking of the island of Sicily, as a means of utilizing their strength in the theater, and of easing their shipping problems. In spite of the American desire for an invasion of the Continent, they accepted the British contention that Sicily was a valuable objective; they were also susceptible to the point that it was better to use troops in the Mediterranean to some advantage, than to withdraw them and have them cooling their heels in Britain through late 1943 and into 1944, waiting for the invasion. In this they were conscious of the immense battles being fought in Russia, and they believed rightly that the Russians would resent the downgrading of the one area where there actually was contact between Western Allied and Axis ground forces. For a variety of reasons then, most of which made good sense at the time, the Combined Chiefs of Staff agreed on Sicily as the next campaign. They did not, as they began staff planning for the invasion, consider going on to invade the Italian mainland.

Yet Italy was ripe for invasion and for collapse, because the Italians and their Fascist regime were reeling on the ropes. The war had turned increasingly sour for them and they had long since lost any real interest in it. Mussolini was bankrupt politically, with little support among his own administration, and regarded everywhere as a mere puppet whose strings were pulled by Hitler. Mussolini himself recognized this, much as he hated it, and fought against it whenever he could, which was not often. More and more the Germans took over direction of the Italian war effort. Il Duce was bullied into sending Italian troops off to fight the Communist menace in Russia; Italians were used extensively on anti-guerrilla operations in the Balkans. Everywhere they were regarded and treated as second-class citizens of the Axis alliance, and they responded by being overtly unhappy and performing poorly. They were in exactly the situation of the troops of the Kingdom of Italy in the Napoleonic Empire, and though many units and individuals fought bravely, as a people their hearts were not in Hitler's war— if they ever had been.

Hitler's response to Italian dissatisfaction and grumbling was to send more German troops south. When Mussolini wrote of the threat of Allied invasion and asked for the return of his troops fighting in Russia, Hitler sent Germans instead. There were not too many of them, but they formed part of the mobile garrison of Sicily, and they were scattered at key points throughout the Italian Peninsula as well. Field Marshal Kesselring, "Smiling Albert" as the Allied troops called him, was the German commander for the Mediterranean. Fortunately for German-Italian relations, Kesselring was something of an Italophile, which was rather rare in German military circles, and he and the Italian Comando Supremo managed to get along in what otherwise might have been a very awkward situation. As the possibility of an Allied invasion neared, Hitler ordered Erwin Rommel, back from Africa and sick leave, to command a shadow army group in the Alps, to be activated in the event of a landing. Unlike Kesselring, Hitler was aware of the possibility of Italian defection. He did not think that in such an event the Germans could hold the entire peninsula, but he issued orders that the German forces were to fall back and hold the shoulder of the northern Apennines, keeping the Allies out of the Po Valley.

Musing on his allies, Hitler once remarked disgustedly, "The Italians never lose a war; no matter what happens, they always end up on the winning side." By 1943 the Italians, or many of them in high places, recognized that they were on the losing side and that it was time to get off it. To do so, they had to achieve two things: they had to get rid of Mussolini and they had to get Allied help to protect them from the German reaction. The spur that forced them to deal with the first of these was the invasion of Sicily.

On July 10 the greatest armada of the war, more than 3,000

ships, dropped anchor off the beaches of southern Sicily. Nearly half a million Allied soldiers made up the invasion force, larger than would be put into the early stages of the Normandy landings. Overall command went to General Eisenhower, as the Mediterranean theater chief. Under him General Sir Harold Alexander led 15th Army Group made up of two armies, the British 8th commanded by the desert victor, Montgomery, and the American 7th, under General George S. Patton, who had commanded the Casablanca landings and had then moved into still greater prominence during the Tunisian campaign.

Sicily was garrisoned by about 350,000 Axis soldiers, under General Alfred Guzzoni; many of these were local coastal reserve forces, who did not care for their German allies. The main strength of the defense was six mobile divisions, two of them German. As always, for an Axis faced with the superior enemy mobility conferred by sea power, the problem was whether they should try to hold all the possible landing sites, which was beyond their strength, or whether they should concentrate in some central position, then react when the Allied moves were revealed. In that case they would be hindered by Allied air superiority. The dilemma was essentially insoluble, and in Sicily, in Italy, and in Normandy the Germans were bothered by it.

In Sicily they concentrated inland, hoping to move and seal off the beaches as rapidly as possible. The landings therefore went relatively smoothly, encountering light opposition from the Italian coastal defenders. The weather was bad, with heavy seas running, and the invasion took the Axis by surprise. The most difficult part of the operation was a series of airborne drops. On the night of the initial landing, American paratroopers and British glider-borne infantry were scattered all over southern Sicily by high winds and the inexperience of their pilots. On subsequent nights, the 11th and the 13th, large numbers of Allied airborne troops were shot down by the Allied ships, as the transport planes flew over the invasion fleet to their drop zones. The Italians and Germans had been mounting fairly heavy but ineffectual hit-and-run bombing attacks against the shipping, and the gunners shot at anything that flew.

In spite of these setbacks the airborne troops secured some major bottlenecks on the approach roads to the beaches, and their very dispersion over the countryside helped to dislocate the enemy response. The crisis of the landing came on the 11th when the Germans mounted heavy armored counterattacks in the American sector, but they were beaten off, and within the next couple of days, the Allies had a secure beachhead.

The campaign then developed into a race between the Americans and the British. The latter, on the right, had been assigned the major role of advancing northward across the Catania plain, forcing their way past the great volcanic mass of Mount Etna and taking Messina, the key point from which the enemy would either resupply Sicily or escape across the Straits to the mainland. The Americans, with whose performance in Tunisia General Alexander had not been impressed, were assigned the subordinate role of clearing the western part of the island and protecting the British flank.

But the British stalled in the Catania plain, meeting the heaviest enemy resistance so far. Guzzoni knew the vital importance of Messina as well as the Allies did and he was determined to bar the direct route as long as he could. The Allies therefore began to sideslip to the west, and first the Canadians, on the British flank in the center of the island, then Patton's troops on their left, began to pick up momentum. Within two weeks of the landing, the Allies controlled the southwestern two thirds of Sicily, and the Axis were being pushed back into the northeast corner. At the end of July, the Italians decided they would have to evacuate the island, and the German commander, General Hube, as Kesselring's deputy, agreed that he must go too.

Montgomery's troops at last thrust their way past Catania and worked around the slopes of Mount Etna. Patton's, aided by several short amphibious leaps, drove along the northern shore. Nonetheless, in spite of Allied pressure, the Axis managed to evacuate their troops pretty well on schedule. The Straits of Messina are only about three miles wide; the Germans lined them on both sides with heavy concentrations of anti-aircraft guns, and ferried their troops over even in daylight, largely unmolested by Allied aircraft. On August 17 the British and Americans entered Messina to find the enemy had gone; more than 100,000 troops with 10,000 vehicles had safely gotten away.

There were rewards to the Allies. Allied casualties of about 16,500, compared with 164,000 on the Axis side; most of those were surrendering Italians, but they caught, killed, or wounded about 32,000 Germans. They now had Sicily, and the central Mediterranean was clear for shipping. Probably most important were the side effects: the taking of Sicily brought Mussolini tumbling down; and it led the Allies into a long, weary campaign on the Italian mainland.

American troops had entered the major city of western Sicily, Palermo, on July 22. By then the town was a wreck, after heavy bombing by Allied aircraft. The fall of Palermo spurred the Italian leaders to desperation: they had to get rid of Mussolini and they had to do it fast. Their absolutely overriding desire was to avoid fighting in Italy. At whatever cost, they wished to spare their country from becoming a battleground; they had no wish now to pay for Mussolini's mistake in 1940 when he blithely assumed that Britain, like France, was finished, and leaped in to gain a share of the spoils at the last moment.

Getting rid of Il Duce turned out to be easier than might have been expected. In spite of all Mussolini's power, Italy was still a monarchy, and he still officially only the premier of the country; there was, therefore, a higher authority to whom the dissidents could appeal. Unfortunately, the king, Victor Emmanuel III, was hesitant and dilatory. He took a great deal of persuading before he finally came around to the pro-Allied camp, but eventually the anti-Germans, led by Marshal Pietro Badoglio, convinced him that he must oust Mussolini.

On the 24th there was overt opposition to Mussolini in a session of the Fascist Grand Council. Most of it was directed against the way the war effort was being handled, and Mussolini actually thought he could use it as a lever to free himself somewhat from Hitler's coils. He had no idea that it was he himself his hitherto pliant supporters were after. The next day he was summoned to an audience with the king. The plotters had convinced the Italian monarch that he should dismiss Mussolini, who would then be taken into custody and held under close arrest. The aging dictator still retained some popularity with the masses of Italians, and no one knew what he might do if given time to muster a counteroffensive.

Instead, everything went as planned. The king demanded Mussolini's resignation and told him he had already replaced him with Badoglio. They parted amicably, and the ex-dictator walked out of the palace and into the arms of the carabinieri, who put him in a police van. They took him through the streets of Rome, past squares where bands were playing their customary Sunday afternoon concerts, and by suppertime the bloodless coup was over.

The first of the Italians' two problems was now resolved. The other one, negotiating the change of sides, was trickier. Mussolini's successor Badoglio, on assuming office, immediately announced that Italy would remain in the war and would continue faithful to her alliances. He then equally immediately opened negotiations with the Allies, working through neutral territory in Portugal. The problems were immense; not only were there Italian troops over in the Balkans and out in Russia, hostages to good behavior, there were also German troops in Italy. The contacts with the Allied representatives had to be made in great secrecy, for the new Italian government was profoundly and rightly afraid of the German reaction should they discover what was happening.

Actually, in July and August, according with Hitler's earlier decision, the Germans did not plan to fight in Italy. If the country tried to defect they would garrison it and take it over. If it were invaded by the Allies, they planned to fall back northward. They were conscious of Allied air superiority and even more of Allied amphibious capability, and they believed Italy could not be held. The German contingency plan for an invasion of Italy was therefore that Kesselring should withdraw his forces from southern Italy, carrying out demolition work as they went, and that the Germans would hang on in the north, around Florence.

Meanwhile, the Allies, who originally never intended to invade Italy at all, had changed their minds. As far back as May, at the Trident Conference in Washington that was their next meeting after Casablanca, Churchill had pressed for an invasion of southern Italy as a follow-up to the Sicilian operations. He thought possession of the southern part of the peninsula would allow the Allies to threaten a landing in the Balkans; further, there were large airfields in the plain around Foggia, and Allied bombers based there could reach the Rumanian oil fields. Churchill thought the still-forthcoming invasion of Sicily would bring Mussolini down, that the Italian war effort would collapse, and that the Germans would probably not fight in southern Italy; the Allies might even get Rome for nothing, and that would be a major victory, the first Axis capital to fall.

The Americans were thoroughly upset at this. Every time they thought they had Churchill and the British pinned down to a hard date for the invasion of France, he seemed to run off in pursuit of some new will-o'-the-wisp. Yet once again they gave in; in return for an absolute promise that France would be invaded no later than May 1, 1944, they agreed that the Sicilian operation ought to be exploited, and that the Allies would go on to invade and occupy southern Italy. They planned a cautious assault across the Straits of Messina and a march up the Italian toe of Calabria. Later on, in July, when the Sicilian defense was collapsing, they became a bit bolder and planned a second landing farther up the peninsula.

Neither the German nor the Allied intentions were known to the Italians. Their efforts were concentrated on getting the Allies to protect them from the Germans as much as possible. The Italians wanted the British and Americans to land fifteen divisions in the north of Italy, around Leghorn or Genoa, and in this way deliver the whole country at one blow. Such a request was absolutely ludicrous; the Allies lacked the fifteen divisions, and even if they had had them, they did not have the shipping to carry and supply them, or the air support to cover them. They countered by offering to land in Calabria, and if the Italians rose and helped drive the Germans out, they would put four divisions ashore south of Rome. In addition, the Italians would have to surrender unconditionally to the Allies, and their postwar treatment would depend on how much help they were to the Allied war effort.

Such an offer was not very attractive; the Italians did not know the Germans planned to pull out, and an Allied landing south of Rome seemed only to guarantee the kind of fighting they were seeking to avoid in Italy. Yet as the Germans moved more troops into northern Italy—officially in response to the Sicilian situation, actually because of Mussolini's fall—the Italians felt more and more forced to accept the Allied deal.

There was confusion right up to the end. On September 3, 1943, the fourth anniversary of the declaration of war, British and Canadian troops of 8th Army made an assault crossing of the Straits of Messina and landed on the European continent, this time to stay. The same day, the Italian government signed a secret armistice with the Allies. The Germans started to pull out of Calabria; the Italian field command, still uninformed of the armistice, did not know what to do, and ended by doing nothing.

Meanwhile, the U. S. 5th Army, British and American troops under General Mark Clark, was preparing to invade south of Naples. Their choice of Salerno as a landing site was a compromise between their desire to get a major port, Naples, as soon as possible and their equally strong desire to have air cover while they made their landings. Allied naval leaders had assigned only light aircraft carriers to the Mediterranean, because of the demands of the Pacific, and therefore the planners had to rely on land-based air cover flying from Sicily. Naples was just out of reach for effective combat air patrols, so they had instead to settle for Salerno, a few miles south of it.

Only as the invasion fleet made its final run in toward the coast was the Italian armistice publicly announced. The troops were jubilant, believing this meant no opposition on the beaches. What it actually meant was that they would encounter Germans instead of Italians.

Field Marshal Kesselring seemed to be the last man in Europe who still believed in Italian protestations of good faith. He had a contingency plan to cover an Italian defection and one to cover an Allied invasion; he did not have a plan to cover both events at once. Now, stunned but quickly recovering, he ordered his units to continue falling back from Calabria, as the British advanced, and he ordered other troops to hold up the Allied landing at Salerno until the southern forces were safely by. Hastily, local German units around the Gulf of Salerno moved into position, just in time to meet the Allied troops coming ashore.

The Allies landed in the early pre-dawn hours of September 9, British on the left and Americans on the right. Both ran into sporadically heavy resistance, but by the end of the day there were several thousand troops ashore. The Allies thought they had done well to get on land in the face of heavy German defenses; the Germans thought they had done well with their scratch forces to hold the enemy to a shallow beachhead. The crisis did not come for three days; by the 12th the Germans had rushed units south from Rome and had made contact with those retreating from Calabria, and they hit the beachhead hard. For a few hours it looked as if the Americans might be pushed back into the sea, and Kesselring had hopes of staging another Dunkirk. He might well have done so, but when he had asked Rommel in northern Italy for the release of reserves, Rommel said no. The Desert Fox saw no sense in sending troops all the way down past Rome, when the Germans did not intend to stand down there anyway. So the British held, and the Americans recovered their equilibrium, and by the 15th the Allies were secure and forcing their way inland.

A week later, General Eisenhower ordered Alexander to keep on and occupy Rome. Ironically, both the Allied and the German high commands agreed that the Germans could not hold south of the capital, and that the best defensive line would be Pisa-Florence-Rimini, up in the north. But Kesselring was not so sure of this. His troops in Italy had quickly disarmed the Italians once the news of the armistice had been announced; they had seized the road, rail, and communications networks, and the situation seemed to be well under control. Kesselring was much more optimistic a personality than Rommel and he assessed the Allied moves so far as pedestrian, hesitant, and extremely cautious. He kept reporting back to Hitler that he thought he could hold south of Rome, and that there was no sense giving the Allies anything that they were not strong enough to take.

Eventually, Hitler accepted this view of things, which conformed so well to his own desires anyway. Kesselring was told to hang on between Naples and Rome as long as he could. He began building successive defensive positions across the peninsula, determined to make the Allies fight for every mile.

In the face of this stiffening opposition the weaknesses of the Allied view soon became apparent. They had expected to get something for nothing. Denied a cheap victory, the proponents of the Italian campaign, most notably Churchill, kept asking for more men and matériel with which to gain their ends. But those Allied leaders who had not been especially in favor of going to Italy in the first place now remained adamant; Italy had all the resources it was going to get. The result of this, in turn, was that Alexander, as the field commander, was continually asked to deliver victories but denied the means to win them. He launched a whole series of operations on successive shoestrings; these inevitably ran into trouble, and as they reached crisis stages, the Allies then found themselves forced to allocate the resources they had initially refused. More than any other campaign of the war, Italy was beset by divided counsels at the top, uncertain perception of what the campaign was supposed to achieve, and a sense among the troops of being a second-class operation, undertaken because the Allies did not really know what else to do at the time. Partly because of these factors, partly because of the terrible terrain, Italy became the theater of fighting that most resembled the horrible static trench warfare of World War I. Few soldiers of World War II experienced the kind of deadening, soul-destroying fighting that had characterized the earlier war, but most of those who did experience it fought in Italy.

As the Allies wheeled out of Salerno for the push up the peninsula, they linked up with 8th Army, coming up from Calabria. They ended up with 8th Army on the Adriatic coast of the peninsula and with 5th Army on the western, Tyrrhenian coast. Between the two armies lay the chain of the Apennines, forbidding, lunar, barely passable to small groups, and generally such bad country that fighting deep in the mountains was out of the question. It therefore became impossible to flank the Germans on their inland side. Unfortunately, it also proved impossible, in all but one instance, to flank them on their seaward side as well. Partly this was because of the Italian coast which, though it looks wide open, actually offers relatively few spots that are suitable for an amphibious operation. Even more it was because the theater lacked the sealift capacity to supply both the existing fronts, and new beachheads as well. The upgrading of the Pacific and the preparations for the invasion of France both robbed the Mediterranean of any potentially surplus shipping. This deficiency was further compounded by the needs of the air force. The Allies soon were in possession of the Foggia airfields and they wished to use them for bases from which to bomb the Balkans. Every shipload of material for the air forces meant one less shipload of material for the ground forces struggling their way up the peninsula. The air offensive took priority, rightly or wrongly, so the ground troops did without not only the mobility that might conceivably have sprung them out of their impasse, but even many of the essentials for sustaining their effort.

For the Germans it became the kind of war they were now used to. German writers criticize the Allied command and what they consider as its lack of initiative and daring. The more thoughtful among them, however, admit as they do so their ignorance of the vast complexities of amphibious operations. The Germans thus settled down behind the successive rivers that break out of the Apennines and run to the sea; as they held one river line, they would prepare the next behind it; when their fixed position was finally breached, they fell back, destroying everything as they went, to the next river. Then the whole deadly scenario had to be played all over again.

On the Adriatic side, 8th Army fought its way up the coast. Its ultimate target was the town of Pescara, the terminus of one of the few good roads running through the Apennines to the other side of the peninsula. If they had taken Pescara and that road, they might have been able to break across to Rome, levering the Germans on 5th Army's side of the country out of their positions, and the great prize would have fallen. But below Pescara is a series of small streams—the Biferno, the Trigno, and, most important, the Sangro—and on each of these the Germans stood fast. As summer dust turned to fall mud, as the cold winter rains came on, 8th Army made a series of head-on attacks against the German lines. There was no alternative; it was like a football game with no passes and no end runs; just put your head down and bull your way up the middle. So it was with 8th Army; British, Canadians, New Zealanders, Indians, South Africans, all wore their hearts out slogging their way across the valleys and onto the heights behind. The Germans were always dug in, they always had good maps and good fields of fire, they had thoroughly swept the country as they retreated, and they were good soldiers determined to hold on.

Finally, late in November, 8th Army produced one last drive. They got over the Sangro and pushed along the coast but they lacked the stamina to get to Pescara. Christmas found the 1st Canadian Division, the last unbroken point of the British advance, fighting desperately from house to house in Ortona. They took it, but only after Ortona became Canada's World War II equivalent of Vimy Ridge, and that was as far as they could go. When they at last ground down at the start of 1944, Pescara was still five miles away; it might as well have been five hundred.

On the other side of the peninsula, 5th Army encountered the same thing. They took Naples at the beginning of October, and thus had a port through which to supply. The Germans held on the Volturno, a rushing mountain stream. With the British component of 5th Army working along the coast, and the American inland, they broke across the river in mid-October. Rome lay a hundred miles ahead, and for the first forty of those the mountains came right down to the sea, in tangled masses crisscrossed by tumbling streams and marked by jagged outcrops of rock.

In this ideal defensive terrain the Germans constructed a series of positions. The lay of the land was such that they ran into one another, and different portions of lines were known by different names: the Winter Line, the Bernhard Line, the Barbara Line. The most famous, and the strongest, of them all was the Gustav Line. This was part of a general system that ran up along the lower reaches of the Garigliano, past the mouth of the Liri Valley and the main road leading to Rome, and into the mountains from there, up the Rapido River. The key point in the whole line, overlooking the shoulder where the Liri met the Rapido, was the town of Cassino. Above the town, on top of a mountain mass, lay the famous Benedictine Abbey, the mother house of the black monks of the Benedictine Order, one of the great religious foundations of Christendom.

By the time 5th Army reached the Gustav Line it was already worn down from the heavy fighting in the approaches. The Germans had, as Kesselring promised Hitler, fought for every yard. On mountains where supplies had to be carried by mule, and finally on the backs of infantry, the German and Allied troops had savaged each other in swirling cloud and bitter cold. At Monte Camino, Monte Maggiore, Mignano and San Pietro Infine, in company- and battalion-size actions, the British and Americans pushed forward. It was Christmas before they broke the Winter Line, and mid-January before they reached the Gustav Line. Here they stopped; this was Kesselring's main position south of Rome, and he was going to hold it to the bitter end.

The Allies battered against the Gustav Line for nearly five months. In the main line of resistance, they faced, as usual, a German defense with both lines securely anchored, the western on the sea and the eastern in impassable mountains. Alexander was left no apparent alternative but to drive straight through.

There was another possibility, however. Earlier, in November, the Allies had considered making an amphibious assault behind the German lines. This was to have been coupled with 8th Army's drive to and through Pescara. Since Montgomery did not get that far, the idea was shelved. Now it was brought out again, and as it evolved, it became part of a complex plan.

In mid-January the British corps of 5th Army would attack along the seacoast, at the end of the Gustav Line. That would dislocate the Germans; then, concurrently, the Americans would drive across the Rapido River and through Cassino, and a third Anglo-American force would land up the coast at the little port of Anzio. German reserves would not be able to counter all of these moves, and the Gustav Line would have to break.

Unfortunately, the plan did not go as it was supposed to. It was hastily prepared, because of the inevitable demands for shipping. The preparations for the Normandy invasion were well advanced by now, and as a secondary effort, the Allies were planning a landing in southern France. The Anzio operation had to be squeezed in, and shipping scraped up here and there to support it. As an example of the interlocking nature of the Allied global effort, Anzio caused the downgrading of a scheduled amphibious operation in the Bay of Bengal, and there were virtually cabinet-level meetings to decide on the disposition of as few as half a dozen landing ships, until Churchill was forced to grumble, "Sometimes

I think the whole war depends on some damned thing called an LST." He was right; the Landing Ship Tank, or "Large Slow Target" in sailors' slang, had become one of the crucial items of the war inventory.

On January 17 the British attacked across the lower Garigliano, gained a foothold, and succeeded in drawing in the local German reserves from the Gustav Line. To its right the U. S. IInd Corps put in what was supposed to be the main attack. Hurriedly, not knowing exactly what they were doing or why, the 36th Texas National Guard Division tried to cross the Rapido just below Cassino. Their attack broke down with heavy losses, and they made hardly a dent in the Gustav Line. The Texans were so upset that they demanded—and subsequently got—a Congressional investigation into what they regarded as the wanton sacrifice of their division; yet they made so little impact that the Germans in their war diaries noted nothing more than increased patrol activities.

The haste and muddle at Cassino was all undertaken so that the Anzio operation could be carried out within the necessary time constraints of the larger war. The 36th Division's attack was to draw in reserves so the landing at Anzio could proceed unopposed, and there, on January 22, 50,000 British and American troops of the U. S. VIth Corps came charging ashore against virtually no Germans at all. Having done that, and succeeded in totally surprising the German command, they stopped. The official doctrine for amphibious landings was that you got ashore, dug in and secured your beachhead against the inevitable counterattack, and then went on from there. This the American commander, General John Lucas, now did, with the blessing of General Mark Clark; no one, after all, had yet forgotten the near-run thing at Salerno.

But the Allied halt gave the Germans time to react, and they rushed reserves down from Rome; within hours they had contained the new threat. As in virtually every operation in Italy, the Allies initially caught the Germans by surprise, but then the speed of the German reaction and the slowness of the Allied exploitation negated the surprise and re-created an equilibrium. Alexander was put in a quandary: he now had two fronts in a static situation, too far apart for mutual cooperation, and his superiors were badgering him because of the shipping he was absorbing. At Anzio the whole beachhead was under fire, the Allies were in the position of a besieged garrison, and they stayed that way for four months. The Germans made vicious but unsuccessful attempts to drive them back into the sea, and the Americans and British made equally vicious and equally unsuccessful attempts to break out of the vise.

Churchill was undoubtedly the most disappointed of all. He was the great champion of the Mediterranean and the Italian campaign, and he had pressed for Anzio. Now it looked as if all his cajoling and bargaining for supplies had gone for nothing. He waxed caustic and sarcastic over Anzio: he had expected to be hurling a wildcat on shore, but instead had got a stranded whale; when told there were nearly 20,000 vehicles in the beachhead he replied, "We must have a great superiority of chauffeurs. . . ." But neither bitter remarks nor the removal of the commander at Anzio had much effect. The only comfort to be had was that Italy was serving the purpose now of drawing in German troops from as far away as the Balkans, France, and Germany itself.

That could hardly solace the infantry huddling in their holes before Cassino, staring across the rushing Rapido, or gazing up at the mist-shrouded mountains and the great Benedictine Monastery, which seemed to glower menacingly back. In the first part of February the Americans tried to break across again, above Cassino this time; with great courage and heavy casualties they managed to make a minuscule salient in the German line. Inland from them was a new element, the Free French Expeditionary Corps, mostly colonial troops from North Africa, used to mountain terrain, and they too made some limited gains, at equally heavy cost.

Alexander then brought what he considered his best troops over from 8th Army, and launched the third attempt at Cassino with the New Zealand Corps. Its commander, General Bernard Freyberg, requested an air strike against the Benedictine Monastery, which all the troops were sure the Germans used as an observation post. On March 15, heavy bombers flew over Cassino and the ancient monastery and pounded them to rubble. The results were disastrous. The monastery had been empty; with good observation all over the mountains, the Germans had had no need to occupy it, and they had scrupulously respected its territory. Now they moved into it and set up their observer posts. Cassino town itself was converted into a mass of masonry and junk, which made ideal cover for the defenders, and the Germans settled down in the choked cellars and alleyways, and fought it out with the New Zealanders and Indians who tried valiantly and unsuccessfully to force their way in. By late March they had fought each other to exhaustion. At Anzio, and at Cassino, the campaign was stalled.

It looked as if the invasion of Italy had reached a dead end.

The calendar marched inexorably on, toward spring, toward the invasion of France. If the stalemate in Italy was to be broken, if it was all to be more than a mere holding operation, things had to happen and they had to happen soon. Finally, the Allied high command agreed to allocate sufficient resources to get to Rome before the Normandy landing, seeing that as the best way to distract German attention from what was coming. At the end of March there were roughly twenty Allied combat divisions in Italy; by the first of May there were twenty-eight. Leaving only four of these to cover all of the Adriatic side of the peninsula, Alexander massed his forces before Cassino and piled them secretly into the Anzio beachhead.

He was going to smash through the Gustav Line and push his way both up the coast and up the Liri Valley. When his offensive was well and truly launched, and the Germans all pulled in to meet it, the Anzio forces would break out inland, take up a blocking position and, if all went well, virtually the entire German Army in Italy would be caught and destroyed. Rome would fall as a matter of course, there would be a rollicking dash north all the way to the Alps, and the Italian campaign would end in a justified burst of glory.

Alexander's May offensive was one of the great setpiece battles of the war, with a huge international cast: Americans, British, Canadians, Free French, Poles, Indians, New Zealanders, South Africans. After dark on the evening of May 11 more than 2,000 artillery pieces began a barrage that ran from the mouth of the Garigliano all the way up past Cassino and into the mountains. An hour before midnight the troops jumped off. The Germans were surprised, but not panicked, and there was heavy fighting and slow going. For some of the Americans along the seacoast it was their first taste of combat, and with heavy casualties and the courage of innocence they forged steadily ahead. To their right, Algerians, Moroccans, and Senegalese of the Free French Corps scaled the mountains and began filtering through the German lines; to their right again Indians and British opened the door of the Liri Valley, and before the Germans could shut it, the Canadians surged through it and up the highway toward Rome. Up in the Apennines the Polish Corps, made up of men who had survived German blitzkrieg and Russian prison camps, circled down and finally raised their eagle banner over the ruins of the monastery. It took more than a week of steady, toe-to-toe slugging, but eventually the

Germans could stand it no more. They cracked, then they broke wide open. The Americans lunged up the coast, to Formia, to Gaeta, to Terracina; the French came down off the mountains to meet the Canadians as they pushed up the Liri, and suddenly the Gustav Line was gone, and everyone was off to Rome.

It was a bad two weeks for Kesselring. He had laid out two fall-back positions: the Hitler Line, a few miles up the road to Rome in the Liri Valley, and then the Caesar Line, in the Alban Hills outside Rome. The former had possibilities, the latter was no more than staked out.

The Hitler Line lasted five days. The British and Canadians reached it on the 18th, tried to take it on the run, and did not quite have enough steam left to do so. Five days later they put in a full-scale attack and crashed through. Once more the Germans pulled out and headed north, harried by Allied fighter-bombers.

Meanwhile, up at Anzio, the American commander, General Truscott, was ready to go. The axis of his attack was to run straight out from the beachhead; a short drive of a couple of miles would take him to Cisterna and cut the coastal line of retreat. Continuing in the same direction would take him fifteen miles to Valmontone; that would cut the Liri Valley escape route and trap ten German divisions, the bulk of the available fighting forces in Italy. On the 23rd, Truscott leaped. One of the great fighting generals of the war, Truscott had his troops fired up and they made steady progress toward Valmontone.

On the 26th, as the trap was all but closed, General Clark intervened. He was unhappy with the overall plan; he feared Alexander was going to allow British 8th Army to beat American 5th to Rome. Jealous of the honor, and feeling he and his men deserved it, he ordered Truscott to change the axis of his advance; instead of continuing to Valmontone, Truscott was to go straight for Rome. Obediently, Truscott shifted around, losing enough momentum as he did so that the desperate Germans stalled him off in the Alban Hills. For a week they held on in the hills and at Valmontone, until the Gustav Line troops were safely back, then, declaring Rome an open city, they scooted north.

On June 4, 1944, the first Allied troops, Americans from 5th Army, entered Rome. Eighty years earlier, after seven tries, U. S. Grant had wired Lincoln, "Vicksburg is ours, and fairly won"; now Alexander and Clark could say, "Rome is ours, and fairly won," but they had missed the real prize of the campaign; they had failed to destroy the German Army in Italy.

*   *   *

The May offensive was still a great one. It broke the Gustav Line, smashed the Hitler Line, allowed the Anzio breakout, took Rome, and carried the Allied armies 200 miles up the peninsula in one vast swelling tide.

Then, in the midst of this gloriously exhilarating pursuit, the troops in Italy had the rug pulled out from under them. Churchill and Alexander had both overextended their credit, and just as the gamble was paying off, their bills were called in.

In November of 1943, at the Tehran Conference, Roosevelt and Churchill had agreed with Stalin that they would launch an invasion of southern France as a supplement to the Normandy operation. The Americans believed they would need the extra port facilities of Marseilles to supply their armies, and they envisaged a great pincer movement that would squeeze the Germans out of all southwestern France. Now both Alexander and Churchill pressed that this operation be abandoned. If they got into the Po Valley, and there was little doubt they would, they could exploit in either direction. They might well have enough momentum to carry them through the passes into the Danube Valley, to Austria and Vienna; the whole of southeastern Europe might be liberated in a rush. Alternatively, if they could not go in that direction, they could as well force their way westward, into France by way of the Riviera coast, and they would reach southern France without the necessity of another seaborne invasion.

The American high command stood fast. They knew Stalin did not want Western Allied troops in eastern Europe; they also used as an argument their feeling that the French would insist on an operation aimed primarily at the liberation of France, though up to this point the Americans had not been overly responsive to French views on the conduct of the war. Mostly, Roosevelt believed that since the agreement to invade southern France had been taken with Stalin's concurrence, he could not change it now. Ironically and unhappily, all of this sensibility about the Russians' feelings came a mere couple of months before the Warsaw rising. The Americans felt they had succumbed to Churchill and the Mediterranean for the last time. They now insisted that the earlier commitments be honored.

In Italy the pursuit flowed on. The long columns of infantry trailed through Rome; heavily laden G. I.'s trudged past the Colosseum, crossed the Tiber bridges, and took up the path that led to the north. The tanks, at last freed from their inglorious role as mobile artillery tied to infantry, swept up the Italian highways, hot on the heels of the Germans. Tactical aircraft strafed and bombed the retreating enemy columns. But the Germans remained tough and wily; they did not panic, they did not rush. They dropped their rear guards at every bend in the road and they blew up every culvert. Their staff work functioned smoothly as always, and finally, in late July they noticed a diminution of the Allied pursuit. For some reason the pressure was slackening, and they began to have a bit of breathing space.

The answer was simple enough: to get ready for the invasion of southern France the Allies were pulling seven divisions out of Italy, all of the Free French Expeditionary Corps, and three veteran American divisions. Not only were they moved out, but they had to travel back south to Naples, all the way against the stream of the pursuit going north. There was a significant dislocation of the Allied communications as a result of this, and the Germans began to recover once more.

The end result was that northern Italy remained under Axis control virtually to the end of the war. The Germans by early August were in their northern defense position, the one they had originally thought to hold a year earlier, and this, the Gothic Line, proved every bit as tough as the Gustav Line had last year. Behind them there was a good deal of partisan activity in the western mountains, and there was the enfeebled Mussolini. Imprisoned in isolation by the Italian government, he was rescued in a daring coup by German airborne troops; and brought back behind German lines. Now he set up a shadow Fascist government, usually called the Salo Republic, and it managed to control a small portion of German-held territory.

Neither he nor the partisans mattered a great deal, however. The Italians as a people and as a state had long lost their gamble to keep the war from their homeland. The decision on that was up to the Germans and the Allies, and now, once again, the front had stabilized. The Germans put up a strong defense around Arezzo, and it took a full-scale Allied attack to push them out of it. By late August they were on a line that ran from Pisa to Florence along the mountain peaks to the Metaurus River. Alexander still hoped, with his reduced forces, to break clear of the mountains and into the Po Valley. There was heavy fighting all through September, and the Canadians on the east coast reached Rimini, while the Americans in the center broke through the Futa Pass and got to Firenzuola. Hitler had pulled out German divisions as soon as he knew of the Allied withdrawals, and Kesselring lacked sufficient troops to man his line as completely as the fortifications demanded. The Allies were thus actually through to the rearmost portions of the original Gothic Line when the winter rains hit them, and everything ground to a halt. Ten miles short of Bologna and the breakthrough into the Po Valley, the exhausted 5th Army gave over its drive. On its right 8th Army too sank worn out into the autumn mud. Time, circumstance, and their friends as well as their enemies had robbed them of complete victory.

24. The Normandy Invasion and the Campaign of France

ROME FELL ON JUNE 4; two days later Allied troops landed on the beaches of Normandy, and the great invasion, so long awaited, so long deferred, was on at last. Preceded by years of planning and preparation, it was the dramatic high point of the war.

With their usual tenaciousness, the British had been working toward the return of the Continent ever since they had been chased off it. Even with German bombers in the air over London, with their last seventy tanks sent off to North Africa, they had calmly set about the business of organizing the invasion. They knew they must go back, and with the quiet determination so much a part of the national character, they never doubted that at some point they would do so.

When the Americans appeared on the scene, they were as determined as the British to invade France, but less patient. Only as the military might of Germany and the excellence of her armed forces became manifest to them did they accede to the British view, that the war was going to take longer than they initially hoped. From the east, of course, there was constant pressure from Stalin for the "Second Front"; by that he meant the invasion of France, as he refused to take British efforts in the Mediterranean too seriously. It is a tribute to Churchill's patience, hardly his strongest quality, that he never reminded Stalin that there had been a "second front" in 1940, but that at that time Stalin was busy befriending Hitler.

The invasion had been long delayed, from 1942, a target date that never meant anything except to the most optimistic Americans, to 1943, which might conceivably have been a reasonable proposition, and finally to 1944. The postponements arose partly from the material and manpower buildup, but by the first part of 1944 south-eastern England was packed with thousands of aircraft, tanks, trucks, jeeps, and hundreds of thousands of men, so the troops joked that if the invasion did not come soon, England would tilt and sink beneath the weight of the preparations for it.

As troublesome as the problem of providing the material were the questions of what actually should be done with it. An amphibious operation is an immensely complicated affair, when conflicting requirements have to be juggled to a successful resolution. Most difficult of all is the fact that several items of the equation are outside human control: the state of wind and tide, the phase of the moon, visibility, weather. Sailors want a moonless night for their approach to a hostile shore, airmen want moonlight so they can see to drop their paratroops. If a landing is made at low water the enemy's underwater obstacles can be seen and avoided, but the ships are constrained to beach farther out, and the troops must move over greater exposed distances.

The biggest question, though, was whether or not the Allies needed a port, and how soon. Contradictory though it may seem, getting ashore in an amphibious landing is not as hard as staying there. The real supply-and-support problem comes not with the initial landing, but with the follow-up material, the men and supplies necessary to turn a landing into an invasion. The planners did not doubt their ability to put five divisions ashore in Normandy —they had already put more than that on the beaches of Sicily— but their problem was how to build up and supply the hundred divisions they wanted to get ashore all told.

The shortest crossing of the Channel would take the Allies over to the Pas de Calais, around Boulogne, Calais, and Dunkirk, where the British had been driven off four years ago. While doing everything possible to make the Germans think this was where the assault was coming, the Allies actually decided to land farther down the coast, on the Normandy peninsula. The beaches were not bad, though they could have been better; they could hope to take Cherbourg, a major seaport, and supply through that. To solve their immediate problem, however, they decided to take their ports with them. Several great floating caissons, as well as many old ships, were to be floated across and then anchored in position and sunk off the beaches, creating artificial harbors—the "Mulberries" as they were code-named. The remains of these can still be seen off the Normandy coast, and though they were eventually badly damaged by storms, they served their purpose admirably, and relieved the

Allies of the immediate problem of getting a port. In giving the invaders more options for landing, they compounded the problems of the defenders.

For the Germans faced the same kinds of questions as did the Allies; they too knew the invasion had to come, and for them also it was a problem of where, when, and how to meet it. The Germans had officially sixty divisions in France and the Low Countries, but more than half of them were second-line formations, either training divisions or coastal defense formations with reduced establishments and mobility. One of their major problems, especially concerning mobility, was that they had now definitively lost command of the air, and this aggravated their disagreements over how to react to the expected invasion.

In the air the bomber offensive was still gaining momentum, but the attacks, moving ever farther into Germany, were forcing the Germans to concentrate, albeit unwillingly, on home defense. As the Allies waxed stronger in the air over Germany, they gained increasing tactical mastery of the air over France. By the spring of 1944 the air forces were able to promise a massive interdiction campaign that they hoped would seal off Normandy and prevent the arrival of German reserves. Anything that moved by day, and much that moved by night, would do so at its own peril. And to the efforts of the tactical air forces could be added the disruptive campaign of the French underground as well.

Some of the German commanders were aware of this, others were not. The Commander-in-Chief West was Field Marshal Gerd von Rundstedt, one of Hitler's old standbys. Several times he had been retired by Hitler for disagreements of one type or another, but he was always recalled; Hitler could not get along without his professional expertise. Under von Rundstedt, in command of Army Group B, consisting of three armies spread from Brittany north to the Zuider Zee, was Erwin Rommel, transferred out of the northern Italian imbroglio to take command of the invasion front. Rommel and von Rundstedt had different views on how to meet the invasion, and this divergence in turn was compounded by Hitler's own ideas on the matter.

Rommel, drawing on his experience in the desert, wanted to concentrate forward on the invasion beaches and defeat the British and Americans as they came ashore. He believed that it would be impossible to move reserves long distances under Allied air supremacy, and therefore, that if the Allies once did get firmly ashore, they were there to stay. It was Rommel who made the now famous remark that the first day of the invasion would be "the longest day," and he believed that if the battle were not fought and won in the first day, it would not be won at all.

The flaw in this reasoning, and it was one readily apparent to the more conventional von Rundstedt, was that you could not concentrate on the invasion beaches unless you knew which beaches were going to be invaded. Once again the Germans were up against the mobility of Allied sea power, and if they followed Rommel's reasoning about the way to meet the invasion, but met it at the wrong place, disaster would result. To further von Rundstedt in his ideas, he had never fought a campaign against an enemy possessing unchallenged air superiority, so he had little idea of what that would mean. He believed that reserves could be moved forward, and that the logical, conventional thing to do was to keep them well back and well in hand until the landing was thoroughly underway. Then when the Allies had passed their point of no return, the reserves could be committed for a climactic battle that would destroy the invaders.

This difference of opinion, fundamental as it was, was further complicated by Hitler. He insisted on final control over the release of reserves, so it was conceivable that not only would they not be located forward as Rommel wanted, but they would not even be available when von Rundstedt wanted. In fact, Hitler's intuition, cleverly aided by the Allied deception plan, told him that the landing would come in the Pas de Calais; until it did, everything else could be disregarded as a plot to lure the reserves away from that vital stretch of coastline. As the invasion neared, it was obvious to the Germans only that they were not ready for it. That, of course, was not obvious to the Allies.

To run the invasion, the Allies brought Eisenhower back from North Africa as Supreme Commander. Montgomery left 8th Army in Italy and came home as Ground Force Commander, Admiral Sir Bertram Ramsay was the naval commander, and Air Vice-Marshal Sir Trafford Leigh-Mallory led the air forces. A great deal of politics was involved in the appointment of the commanders, especially in the choice of Eisenhower as the overall leader. The American Chief of Staff, General Marshall, had hoped to lead this climactic campaign of the war; so equally had the British Chief of the Imperial General Staff, General Alan Brooke. Both were too involved in worldwide matters to be spared, however, so the burden

—and the opportunity—fell on Eisenhower, who had already demonstrated in the Mediterranean his ability as a military manager.

When Eisenhower and Montgomery arrived in Britain they were shown plans to land three divisions over the beaches, and two by air behind the enemy defenses. Both immediately said they wanted three by air, and five over the beach. The result of this upgrading, to which the Combined Chiefs of Staff agreed, was an increase of shipping and resources, and that in turn pushed the date for the southern France invasion on into the summer. Initially, southern France had been scheduled for before the Normandy landing, then pushed back to be roughly concurrent with it. Now it went back to August. The invasion of Normandy, code-named "Overlord," was to have priority over everything else.

The original "hard" date for the landing was May 1, 1944. However, Eisenhower's demand for additional forces put that also back to the first part of June, and finally the best combination of tide, moon, and light led to scheduling the landing for June 5. After the invasion armada was actually underway, the weather turned chancy, and the whole operation had to be set back one day, so that D Day became the 6th of June, 1944. It was a remarkable display of planning expertise and security that the invasion actually could be set back a day without the entire affair collapsing.

For it was a huge undertaking; all told, the Allies mustered 2,876,000 soldiers, sailors, and airmen. They had 11,000 aircraft and several thousand vessels, from great battleships to tiny landing craft that would hold a few men, from fast patrol boats to protect the flanks of the armada to the lumbering caissons of the Mulberry harbors. Most of the troops were already embarked and at sea when the news came in of the fall of Rome, a happy augury for this greatest of all undertakings in the war. The massive fleet, with unending streams of aircraft droning overhead, made its way to offshore rendezvous, formed up into task groups, and headed across the stormy Channel for the distant French shore. The ships carried soldiers of the United States, Britain, Canada, and France. In the air overhead were men from all of those nations plus Poles, Czechs, and airmen of the whole Empire-Commonwealth. General Eisenhower, who alone made the life-and-death decision to risk a break in the weather front, later called his task a "crusade in Europe," and though it might not have been immediately apparent to many of the seasick soldiers in the lurching small craft, there was much of that about it. For a few short days, this was the only place in the war to be. For a great many young men, these few short days were to be the last they would ever see.

The Allies had designated five landing beaches, plus several drop zones for their paratroops and airborne infantry. The left, east flank of their landing was the Orne River. British airborne troops would drop on the bridges over the Orne and hold them as a secure flank; their symbol was the winged horse, Pegasus, and the bridge over the Orne on the coast road is still named "Pegasus Bridge," a counterweight lift bridge with the pockmarks of small arms and field piece shells on it more than thirty years after the event. British troops would land on the east flank beach, named "Sword." Five miles west was the second beach, "Juno," at the resort town of Courcelles; this was slated for the Canadians. To the west again where the little town of Arromanches huddles between moderately high bluffs, was "Gold," the second British beach. There was then a gap of several miles, until the first American beach was reached; this was "Omaha," in front of the villages of Vierville and St. Laurent. Then, past the Carentan Estuary, was the second American beach, "Utah." Inland from it was the small town of Ste.-Mère-Église, scheduled to receive the American paratroops.

Most of the landing went right, but much went wrong. The British airborne took and held the Orne River crossings, as they were supposed to. The American 82nd Airborne Division dropped in Ste.-Mère-Église and had a hard fight to secure bridgeheads across the Merderet River on the road to Cherbourg. The 101st Airborne, dropped to secure the exits from Utah Beach, had heavy losses when its men came down in the swamps of the Douve River. Held down and dragged under by their chutes, many paratroops died alone in the dark waters of the marshes.

The British and Canadians came ashore on their three beaches against heavy opposition and many obstacles but they had prepared well. They had excellent fire support from the fleet, including veteran battleships; though they took their losses—many of their swimming tanks, equipped with flotation gear, foundered in the heavy seas—they got ashore and secured their beaches. Down the line, the Americans at Utah hit the beach with relatively little opposition, as the Germans in the area were fully occupied fighting it out with the widely scattered paratroopers of the two airborne divisions.

At Omaha it was different. The U. S. 1st Division landed here, and ran not into poorly organized coastal formations, but the German 352nd Division, a veteran formation recently moved into the area. Omaha is a beautiful beach, a long, broad stretch of clean fine sand. Above the tide line the beach comes up fairly steeply to a shingle, and behind that rise high bluffs which give a commanding view of the whole sweep of beach. Only small, easily dominated roads and tracks break through the bluffs, up and away from the beach. Just to the west of the beach was a major protrusion known as Pointe du Hoc, fitted as a battery position for heavy guns that could control the whole beach.

The Americans plastered the Pointe du Hoc with every gun they had, then sent a Ranger battalion straight up the cliffs to take it. After fierce fighting and heavy losses the Rangers secured the point, only to find the heavy guns had been moved out anyway. But the Germans above Omaha did well enough without them. The first American assault waves were deluged with fire, and many boats and amphibious vehicles were hit in the water. Those that got ashore could not climb the crumbly shingle. Soldiers huddled, disorganized and demoralized, seeking whatever shelter they could find from the all-seeing enemy. By late morning the Germans thought they had the situation under control.

Slowly, a momentum built up; here and there little groups, squads of men, individuals, scampered across the open spaces and painfully began inching up the bluff. Many were hit and killed but some got through. The American infantry began to filter through and into and behind the German positions. The engineers never gave up trying to clear lanes through the mines and wire. Ever so slowly, the tide began to turn, and by a supper hour when few could stop to eat, the Americans were on and off their beach. Omaha was far from secure, but the Germans were being pushed back; a flood of new troops and a trickle of supplies were coming in; it cost the Americans 2,000 casualties in the one day, but they held the beach.

They might not have done so had the German reaction been stronger. Omaha was not counterattacked because the higher command believed it was being wiped out anyway. That was a local matter, however, and the general German reaction was hesitant and confused. When news came in of the landings, which, given the state of the weather, caught the Germans badly off balance, Rommel sent orders for the movement forward of two good divisions from reserve. Hitler himself held these up, for he still believed Normandy was but a feint, and the real attack was coming in the Pas de Calais. Therefore the troops immediately in the area were left to deal with the landing. Under constant air attack, and with terribly confused and confusing information confronting them, they were able to mount only one counterattack during the first crucial period of the landings. This was sent against the British. Five miles past the British beaches lay the major town of Caen, communication hub and key to the area. The British hoped to get this by nightfall of the first day. As it was, both the local German troops and the first few units to arrive from reserve came in around Caen; it was not until July 8, more than a month later, that the battered city fell, at a heavy cost to the Canadians and British who took it.

Eisenhower's headquarters, SHAEF—Supreme Headquarters Allied Expeditionary Force—had a definite timetable for their operations, based on what they thought they could get ashore in the way of supplies and men, and the kind of German reaction they expected. By June 23, or D+17, they hoped to clear the Normandy Peninsula; by D+35, July 10, they expected to be at the mouth of the Seine to the eastward and to have cut off the Brittany Peninsula to the south and west. From that base they planned to drive more or less straight east.

In its initial phases this schedule went well awry. The German reaction to the invasion, once they finally decided this was actually it, was stronger than expected. In spite of the air interdiction and the efforts of the French Forces of the Interior, heavy reinforcements reached Normandy, and it soon became obvious that the Germans proposed to give battle, if not on the beaches, at least well forward, in front of Caen and along the approaches to Cherbourg. As Ground Force Commander in the immediate post-landing stage, Montgomery directed the British and Canadians to take Caen, and the Americans to take Cherbourg. The former he regarded as the communications key to the latter, and the latter was necessary because the Allies badly needed a port. The supply capacity of the Mulberry harbors was limited and was lessened even more by a series of storms that damaged them soon after they were created.

Toward both objectives the Allies made heavy going. The Germans committed most of their armored reserves around Caen, and their heavy Tiger tanks took an impressive toll of the British and Canadian Shermans. The battle for Caen degenerated into a regular slugging match. Farther to the west the Americans made relatively slow progress in the bad country of the bocage. Over the centuries the frugal Norman farmers had hedged their little fields diligently. Now each field, of a few hundred square yards, was surrounded with living banks of hedges bordering sunken dirt lanes. Each hedgerow became a minor fortress. Tanks trying to climb the banks would expose their bellies to German anti-tank weapons; soldiers attempting to worm their way through the hedges would be picked off by machine-gun nests. The Americans were forced to fight their way forward yard by yard in platoon- and company-sized catch-as-catch-can operations.

Nonetheless, they persevered and on June 18 they reached the south coast of the Normandy Peninsula at Barneville. Cherbourg was cut off, and the Germans could not reopen a way to it. Von Rundstedt massed his armor at Caen, hoping to drive toward Cherbourg, but the pressure exerted by the British kept him tied down, and by the 20th the Americans were in the outer suburbs of Cherbourg. The Germans resisted calls to surrender, and a bitter fight for the city lasted until the 27th. So thoroughly had the Germans done their demolition work that it was well into August before the port facilities were reopened at all.

But by the end of June, with Cherbourg secured, the Allies were ready to turn eastward. The Americans began to shift their forces around, away from Cherbourg toward the south, preparatory for a huge left wheel. Both Rommel and von Rundstedt could see it coming, and they pleaded with Hitler for more reserves. He still held major forces north of the Seine, waiting for the landing that never came in the Pas de Calais. Meanwhile, the usual stream of do-or-die orders issued forth from Fuehrer headquarters. These seem to have impressed the ordinary soldiers, who fought with their customary skill and tenacity, more than the generals. By the end of June both Rommel and von Rundstedt were convinced the battle was already lost and wanted to fall back toward the Seine; Hitler responded with a dose of his usual medicine; he relieved von Rundstedt and replaced him with Field Marshal Kluge, who, if he had less skill than von Rundstedt, had more faith in Hitler.

In early June the U. S. 1st Army, under General Omar Bradley, launched its main drive south from Carentan toward St.-Lô. Still trapped in the hedgerows, the infantry and armor made slow progress, leading to disparaging comments from the newspapers on the way the fighting was proceeding. St.-Lô did not fall until the 8th, after it had cost the Americans 11,000 casualties, and instead of achieving his major breakthrough, Bradley was forced to pause and pull his tired forces together. The British and Canadians, meanwhile, had finally forced their way past Caen, in a massive attack preceded by several hundred bombers laying a "carpet" of heavy bombs over which the troops were supposed to be able to advance with ease. Unfortunately, the idea looked better than it worked, and though the British and Canadians at last had achieved what the original planners had set as a D-Day objective, they too were fought to a halt by the 20th.

Nonetheless, things were not going too badly. In terms of territory occupied, the Allies were nearly a month and a half behind schedule, but in terms of troops and supplies ashore, they were doing about as planned. So far they had thirty-four divisions ashore, and they and the Germans had both suffered about the same number of casualties, around 120,000. That in itself was a tribute to the Allies' matériel superiority and their ability to wage mechanized warfare, as the attackers normally expect to suffer significantly heavier casualties than the defenders, until some major break is achieved, at which point the defenders' casualties then mount disproportionately. In spite of the disappointing advances, all was going well.

On July 20, Colonel Count Claus von Stauffenberg attended a briefing in the war room of the Fuehrer's headquarters in East Prussia. Excusing himself for a phone call during the briefing, he left his briefcase behind him under the table, right next to Hitler. One of the German officers, leaning over to look at a map, found the briefcase in the way of his foot and idly leaned down and moved it inside the solid piece of wood that formed the end legs of the table. Shortly thereafter, as von Stauffenberg was on his hurried way back to Berlin, the briefcase exploded. Several people were killed, but Hitler, protected by the solid table, escaped with minor cuts, bruises, and shock.

In Berlin, von Stauffenberg and his fellow plotters, mostly army officers with a sprinkling of distinguished civilians, made a half-hearted and hesitant attempt to seize the reins of power. As good gentlemen they made poor plotters, and the news that Hitler had survived the bomb plot quickly swept the rug out from under them. There was a welter of sudden shootings as the rebels tried to eliminate the officials still loyal to Hitler, and then more shootings as those loyal—or who had not yet tipped their hand—tried as rapidly as possible both to demonstrate their loyalty to their master, and to get rid of any surviving plotters who might implicate them in the affair. Hitler immediately ordered the unexecuted plotters saved so they could be tortured for information. All sorts of high-ranking Germans were caught up in the subsequent roundup, some who were genuinely anti-Nazi, some who just had the misfortune to have their names on lists as possible supporters of a coup d'état. Rommel's name was on one list; he was at home recuperating from a wound inflicted by a strafing Allied plane. As Germany's greatest war hero he could not be admitted a traitor, and he was allowed to commit suicide to save his family. Rommel was relatively lucky. Many of the plotters ended up hanging from meathooks by wire nooses, strangling while movie cameras recorded their death agonies for the delectation of Hitler and his chosen circle.

So ended the only real attempt ever to overthrow the Nazi regime from within Germany. After that there was nothing left but to go down with the ship.

The July Plot may have brought comfort to the Allied troops in their battles against the Wehrmacht, but it brought little tangible profit. Suspected dissidents were ruthlessly pruned and quickly replaced, and there was no break in the tempo of the war. In Normandy, General Bradley was planning an operation named "Cobra" designed finally to carry the Americans clear of the hedgerows, and to set them up for the long-awaited wheel to the eastward. The Americans heavily outnumbered the Germans in front of them, for Kluge like his predecessors was still preoccupied with the Caen area. On the morning of the 25th, Allied planes laid another bombing carpet west of St.-Lô, which practically wiped out the German Panzer division holding the sector—as well as 500 Americans hit by bombs dropped short—and in its wake 1st Army dashed forward.

The German reaction was still strong, but the Americans gambled that they were nearly through and pushed on boldly. Within five days the front had cracked; Allied armor, supported by rocket-firing tactical aircraft, began to shake loose. The Germans pulled out successfully along the coast to the west, then mistakenly turned east. Their troops ran into rampaging Allied forces and lost hundreds of vehicles, tanks, trucks, weapon carriers; virtually an entire corps was ruined.

On the British front the Canadians had put in a vicious spoiling attack past Caen that drew German reserves and cost heavy casualties. While the Canadians fought it out Montgomery slipped his British troops west to shore up his link with the now moving Americans. By the end of July, within a short week, the whole situation had changed. The Normandy invasion was over, the breakout was on, and the campaign of France about to begin.

The great Allied breakout was accompanied by a command shuffle. There were now too many troops ashore for Montgomery to command all of them effectively; he therefore became commander of 21st Army Group, with Crerar's 1st Canadian and Dempsey's 2nd British armies under him. General Bradley took over 12th Army Group with General Courtney Hodges' 1st and George Patton's 3rd U. S. armies under his direction. Patton had just come over from Britain, having spent the last two months ostentatiously parading about London and Dover as part of the plan to keep Hitler's mind on the Pas de Calais.

The big break came as Patton pushed his two corps, the westernmost of the entire Allied armies, down the bottom of the Normandy Peninsula. The Cobra operation had already cracked the front here, at Avranches, and in the first three days of August, Patton's tanks raced seventy-five miles. One corps split off to overrun the weakly held Brittany Peninsula. The whole area quickly fell, but the Germans holed up in the major ports, Brest, Lorient, and St. Nazaire, and had to be regularly besieged to get them out.

Patton's other corps began the long-awaited left wheel, and within a week it was at Le Mans. Hodges' people were extending the break eastward against much heavier resistance, and the British and Canadians were pushing due south, making much slower progress and still receiving the brunt of the German attention. Meanwhile, all along the Loire and the Seine, and the roads between Paris and the front, the Allied tactical air forces ranged at will, shooting up targets of opportunity. Medium bombers and fighter-bombers flew low-level strikes against roads, bridges, rail lines, crossroads, in an attempt to seal off the whole lodgment area.

By August 13 two American corps, one of Hodges' and one of Patton's, were pushing northward toward Argentan. The Canadians were driving south toward Falaise. West of them, inside a large pocket, were the largest part of three German armies. On the 7th they had launched a major tank attack at Mortain, designed to break through to the coast and isolate Patton's advance. For three hectic days some of the American divisions were subjected to very heavy pounding, but Bradley diverted reserves that stabilized the situation, and by the time the Germans gave it up they suddenly realized they were in danger of being cut off themselves. There then began a confused scramble to get out of the shrinking pocket through the "Falaise gap."

Hitler, still fiddling with maps in East Prussia, was days out of date and still ordering attacks here and there when Kluge finally convinced him that immediate retreat was the Germans' only salvation. In fact, the retreat had already begun, and salvation, for the moment, came more from the Allies than from the Germans' own efforts. Bradley, fearing mutual casualties if his troops from the south started shelling Canadians from the north, and thinking the trap was beginning to empty anyway, decided not to close it. As the Germans streamed eastward past Falaise, losing a great deal of equipment in the process, both jaws of the trap swung east with them. Fifty thousand German troops were caught in the pocket, and another 10,000 killed in the attacks on it. The majority of the German forces from Normandy, with the Allies flanking them on either side, now began a race for the crossings of the Seine. Hitler replaced Kluge with Field Marshal Walter Model.

The great race lasted a little more than a week. Patton's 3rd Army reached the river at Mantes-la-jolie, "pretty Mantes," thirty miles below Paris, on the 19th. That put the Germans in another pocket, and as the Americans spread both up and down stream, the British and Canadians drove steadily for the lower reaches of the river. Here the German resistance was strongest, as they sought to keep from being cut off again. Several thousand were trapped south of Evreux, several thousand more around Rouen. Most managed to get across the river, but their organization was a shambles, and their losses in men and equipment heavy.

Paris rose on the 19th. Hitler had ordered it destroyed; if he could not have it no one would. Eisenhower had planned to bypass it, not wanting to add to his supply problems the necessity of feeding several million additional civilians. He had reckoned without the French in the city, as well as the absolute determination of Charles de Gaulle that Frenchmen would liberate their own capital, and that he himself would profit by it. As long as they could, the Allies had stalled off de Gaulle's return to France, but when he finally got over the Channel, he immediately announced the establishment of a legal government, and began acting as if he were running the country. Part of Patton's army was the French 2nd Armored Division, and de Gaulle completely bypassed the chain of command and told its commander, General Leclerc, to go for Paris. Leclerc did, carrying neighboring American divisions along with him, and the race to get to Paris became a repetition of the race to get to Rome three months earlier. The Germans delayed their demolition plans, the whole matter being slightly less dramatic than it has subsequently been portrayed. There was some sporadic fighting in the city, and the next thing anyone knew, there was Charles de Gaulle, marching solemnly and triumphantly through the Arc de Triomphe, down the Champs Élysées, past the statue of Georges Clemenceau, and eventually in to hear mass in Notre Dame. While students, FFI, Communists, Leclerc's troops and the Americans took on the rapidly retreating Germans, Paris celebrated the Liberation. As a country, France has been perhaps more dominated by its capital than any other, and the arrival of the Allies in Paris was the emotional peak of the war for a nation that had already plumbed war's depths.

Meanwhile, the Allies had also landed in southern France. After a great deal of proposal and counterproposal, and requests by the British that the agreed-to southern France operation be abandoned in favor of exploitation of the success in Italy, Operation "Anvil" took place on August 15. General Truscott's VIth Corps went ashore that morning, to be followed shortly thereafter by two French corps under General de Lattre de Tassigny. The whole force made up U. S. 7th Army, led by General Alexander Patch. Resistance was occasionally heavy, but nowhere as fierce as in the north, and Patch pushed his troops forward boldly. The French took the great port of Marseilles by the 28th, and the Americans moved up the Rhone Valley and across the mountains on the Route Napoleon, the path the ex-emperor had taken on his return from Elba.

The German defense consisted mainly of second-line troops, with a stiffening of good formations. Thousands were captured but more thousands escaped northward. By the end of August the Allies had already reached Grenoble, with more French and Americans pouring ashore behind them.

The usefulness of the campaign remained arguable. Eisenhower had insisted on it as a means of relieving supply congestion and logistical strain, and also as a potential lower jaw to trap the German forces in southwestern France. But these pulled out anyway, squeezed by what was happening to the north of them, and leaving only last-ditch garrisons to hang on to the Biscay coast ports as long as possible. All of these were eventually rounded up and overrun by the French Forces of the Interior. The Mediterranean ports did prove useful, but only to the troops who landed there; they did little for the northern invaders. In fact, so fast was the northern campaign developing that the Allies decided they did not even need to supply through the Brittany harbors, but instead tried to set up their supply bases farther east along the coast, thus reducing the distance goods had to be moved up to the front. In early September the forces in southern France, now 6th Army Group under General Jacob Devers, linked up with patrols from Patton's troops and thus became the right flank of the drive to the German border. Whether they might have achieved more had they been used in Italy remains one of the great tantalizing strategic questions of the war.

By the beginning of the last week of August, the Allies were along the Seine from Troyes, a hundred miles above Paris, all the way to the sea. Four armies—Crerar, Dempsey, Hodges, and Patton—were champing at the bit. The Germans had lost more than half a million men in Normandy and they had gotten few more than a hundred tanks back over the Seine. The Allied problem was now more one of supply than of the enemy. In the great leap out of Normandy they had outrun their supply capacity. Now, all the field generals wanted to drive on into the Low Countries and even Germany, but there was not sufficient support for all of them to do it. They had originally agreed to a steady advance all along the front, the "broad front" strategy, with everyone going forward in step, and supplies keeping pace. Now, all of the generals clamored instead for a single deep drive, but Bradley wanted it done on his front by Hodges or Patton, and Montgomery wanted it done on his front by Dempsey. Crerar and the Canadians on the coast were out of the running; they were handed the unhappy task of clearing the Channel ports as the Allies pushed north, a job that cost them such high casualties as to cause a crisis at home in Canada over the issue of conscription for overseas service.

Eisenhower eventually compromised and allowed Montgomery to push Dempsey forward, with Hodges supporting on his right. Patton was told he could move as far as possible on whatever supplies were left over. The disgusted but ebullient Patton scrounged what he could, and leaped forward a hundred miles to the Meuse, where he ran out of fuel temporarily, and where the Germans, scared by the threat his advance represented, shored up their defenses to slow him down.

Dempsey and Hodges went straight up the road to Brussels, their tanks grinding over the old World War I battlefields of the

Marne and the Somme, where thousands had been slaughtered taking yards in the days before tanks and aircraft came of age. Within a week the Americans were in Mons and the British in Brussels—another capital where they were joyously welcomed back—and then by a stroke of luck Dempsey got the great port of Antwerp before the Germans could destroy the docking facilities. The Germans still held on the lower reaches of the Scheldt, the river that was Antwerp's heart, but it looked as if the whole defense were breaking down. Hitler responded by recalling von Rundstedt yet again and putting him back in command of the Western Front, with orders to stop the Allied advance, no matter how he did it.

The terrain and the lack of supplies were more successful than the Germans. The British bogged in the watery maze of the lowlands; the Americans, as they came into Luxembourg and the Ardennes and up against the outer reaches of the German "West Wall," simply lacked the material to sustain their momentum.

In the face of the growing logistical difficulties and the advent of autumn, Eisenhower gave in to Montgomery's arguments. If he were given supply priority, Montgomery said, he could mount a massive operation that would carry the British 2nd Army across the Rhine. Thus was born Operation Market-Garden, the most famous airborne assault of the war. In Market, three airborne divisions—two American and one British—would drop behind enemy lines and secure a series of river crossings all the way to the Rhine, sixty miles from the Allied front lines. Farthest out on the limb would be the British 1st Airborne Division, landing at Arnhem and taking and holding the great Rhine bridge there. In the Garden half of the operation, 2nd Army, led by the Guards Armored Division, would dash up the corridor created by the airborne troops, and the Allies would have a long narrow path that would compromise the entire German position in the Low Countries and carry them into Germany.

The daring attack opened on September 17 with the airborne divisions droning over from England and landing all over their targets. The U. S. 101st Airborne got several bridges; farther up the corridor the U. S. 82nd Airborne had a hard fight for the major crossing of the Maas at Nijmegen, and did not secure it until the 20th. The British, meanwhile, landed seven miles from Arnhem and had to fight their way into the town. By chance several good German outfits were in the area, and the enemy reaction was fierce. Nonetheless, the paratroops pushed into Arnhem, got a hold on the northern end of the bridge, and then could get no farther.

Meanwhile, the ground troops, from sixty miles away, set off on their dash to the rescue. Tanks, self-propelled guns, reconnaissance cars, all roared up the roads to Eindhoven and the 101st, Nijmegen and the 82nd, and on toward Arnhem. The farther they got, the more trouble they met. The corridor was so narrow the Germans could reach it with artillery from both sides; the roads often led straight as a die across the lowlands, and the tanks, moving single file, could be held up by one well-sited gun. The weather turned poor, air support and supply broke down, and though the British got close enough to Arnhem to allow some of their exhausted paratroops to break out of the German ring, they could not quite make it all the way.

The whole operation was a daring innovation for Montgomery, who generally preferred to have all his battles planned to a nicety, and was hardly known for the unconventional nature of his strategies. He himself later insisted that had he had all the material he wanted, he could have made it work. As it was, though, Market-Garden virtually exhausted Allied resources for the moment, and forced them to squander pilots, planes, and soldiers who were either insufficiently trained, or already nearly worn out by fighting since D Day. Montgomery thought of Market-Garden as the operation that might have led to the winning of the war in 1944. What it really showed was that the Allies were not strong enough to end it in 1944.

The campaign in France, even though it ended on the sour note of Arnhem, was one of the great campaigns of military history, certainly one of the great ones of the Second World War. The Germans had lost enormous numbers of men and even greater amounts of material. Under Eisenhower's direction the campaign had gone generally smoothly and harmoniously. France and Belgium were liberated, ports were opened, supply problems mastered. All over Europe, the Germans were in disarray; in Italy they barely hung on to the last slopes of the Apennines; in the east the Russians were banging at the frontiers of the Reich. By day and by night the bombers still dropped their deadly loads on the Fatherland. It could only be a matter of time now. Within months, at most, the Master Race would be mastered.

25. Winning in the Pacific

THE TIDE OF WAR that had turned against Japan in 1942 mounted inexorably during the next eighteen months. The long costly battles in the Solomons and along the coast of New Guinea had steadily sapped the imperial vitality. Carrier losses had been heavy, the losses in trained pilots even worse. American submarines took a deadly toll of the shipping that flowed along the arteries of the Greater East Asia Co-Prosperity Sphere. It was increasingly obvious that every basic assumption of the Japanese war plan was incorrect: the Allies had not quit, they had not suffered significant defeats on the perimeter, they had not been too busy elsewhere to bother with Japan, they were not—worst misassessment of all— effete and decadent. Now the Aleutians were gone, and the north was quiet, but in a great irregular arc from southern China all the way around to the central Pacific the battles raged; the skies filled with smoke, the jungle with the rattle and blast of explosions, and the seas with sudden death.

The Allied situation in China did not significantly improve during 1944. The Chinese were still all but exhausted, riven by internal dissensions, and prey to conflicting advice and advisors. The American Generals Stilwell and Chennault completely disagreed on how to conduct the war. Stilwell's basic idea was that with proper training, organization, and equipment the Chinese could win their own war, and he constantly pressed that they be encouraged to do so. Chennault's view was that air power was the answer, and he had progressively moved into the limelight. By late 1943 Chennault's 14th Air Force was dominating the sky over southern and central China and striking Japanese targets on Formosa. It was also eating up the major portion of the supplies reaching China.

The Japanese responded to Chennault's pressure by proving

EAST ASIA - WEST PACIFIC
1937/41 - 1945

that Stilwell was right, or at least that Chennault was wrong, and that air power alone could not win the war. Through the middle months of 1944 they launched a series of limited offensives in south and east-central China that eventually overran more than half of Chennault's air bases, and quite literally knocked the pins out from under him. Stilwell was still fully occupied trying to keep open some kind of cooperative link with the British in Burma, and for a few weeks it looked as if China might collapse at last and simply bow out of the war. Stilwell's recommendations were met with the same irascibility with which they were offered, and when Roosevelt suggested that he be put in supreme command of the entire Chinese war effort, Chiang Kai-shek responded by demanding he be recalled home. Reluctantly, Roosevelt gave in, having little real option; Stilwell left the theater and was replaced by General Albert C. Wedemeyer. Wedemeyer's tact achieved what Stilwell's brilliance and acerbity could not. Cooperation with the Burmese front was preserved, Chiang was mollified, and the Japanese were brought to a halt by the end of the year. China remained in the war, though Chennault, who had steadfastly maintained he could win the whole war with 147(!) bombers and fighters, did not do so. As the year ended, both sides were licking their wounds, and the Japanese, temporarily halted, were catching their breath before resuming the attack on the airfields.

The Chinese theater and events in Burma were closely intertwined. Indeed, much of the rationale of the Burmese campaign, aside from the natural desire of the British to regain imperial territory, was provided by the necessity of keeping supply routes open through to China. Burma, of course, was a relatively isolated country in its own right, and before the war its links with India had been almost exclusively by sea. Therefore, to reach China, or even to keep the Allied armies fighting in northern Burma, it had been necessary to construct huge and costly facilities from India to Burma. In addition to a great number of airfields, there was built the once-famous Ledo Road, from the northeastern extremity of India up at the top of the Brahmaputra Valley, across the Naga Hills and into Burma. It took several hundred thousand support troops and laborers in India to keep the soldiers fighting in Burma.

For late 1943 and 1944 the Allies decided on a four-phase operation. Wavell was relieved by Admiral Lord Louis Mountbatten, who became Supreme Allied Commander Southeast Asia Command. Under him General William Slim and his British 14th

Army planned two drives along the Burma-India frontier. To the northeast Stilwell's Northern Combat Area Command—this was Stilwell wearing one of his several different hats, before he was recalled home—also planned two offensives straddling the Burma-China frontier. If all went well, the British and the Chinese-American forces would link up somewhere in north-central Burma, the land routes to China would be reopened, and a general advance south, clearing Burma, could then take place.

To these four offensives had to be added a fifth, the Japanese. They were expecting increased Allied activity and they responded by planning a drive of their own, in the center of the front, near Imphal, designed to take the British base areas before they could get fully set for their own offensives.

Stilwell was the first to move. His initial offensive operation began in October of 1943, a conventional drive by two Chinese divisions south along the Hukawng Valley. Like most Chinese formations, these were weaker in numbers and equipment than similar formations in other armies, and they met stiff resistance from the Japanese, who were about equal in strength, though officially only one division strong. The second of Stilwell's operations was of a different sort. The earlier activity of Orde Wingate's Chindits had sufficiently impressed the Combined Chiefs of Staff that, in addition to the Chindits, they had authorized the formation of a similar American force. Officially, this was entitled the 5307th Composite Unit (Provisional), but it became better known as Merrill's Marauders, after its commanding officer. In February this unit came into action, and Stilwell used it to keep his drive going, with a series of end-run penetrations, while the Chindits were dropped deep behind Japanese lines to do their stuff again. Wingate himself was killed in an air crash in March, but the Chindits continued to perform valuable, if costly, service.

The goal of Stilwell's entire campaign was the major communications town of Myitkyina, where the Hukawng Valley met the Irrawaddy River. The Marauders took Myitkyina airfield in May, but the Japanese garrison of the town itself held on grimly. To the south the Chindits cut off enemy resupply routes but could not hang on to their isolated positions until Myitkyina was taken, and they were eventually levered out by fierce Japanese attacks. It was not until August that the town finally fell to the attacks of Stilwell's troops, and then they once again took up their drive south, down the Irrawaddy this time. By the end of the year they had reached part of the Burma Road at last, and linked up with Chinese forces attacking west along it. The land link to China was finally reopened, at immense cost in men and materials.

The first of the two British offensives was launched along the seacoast, from the frontier south to the Burmese port of Akyab. This entailed a ninety-mile drive by one corps of Slim's army, and this Second Arakan campaign, as it was known, started in November of 1943. The main Japanese defense position was along a mountain spur that ran right into the ocean near the town of Maungdaw. The mountain blocked the overland route to Akyab, and there the British stuck. For two long months they tried to take the height from the Japanese and were unable to do it. In February of 1944 the Japanese counterattacked, encircling and cutting off the forward British and Indians. It was the same old approach they had been using for two years and it had always worked before. The British were more dependent upon supplies and support than the Japanese were: cut them off and they either fell back or fell apart.

This time it was different; Slim was determined not to give in to tried and true Japanese methods. He began an emergency air lift that kept his embattled troops going, sent up reserves who took to the jungle in their turn, and by late February it was the Japanese encirclers who were encircled. For once the biter was bit, and most of the enemy troops were wiped out, mercilessly hunted down through the jungle.

With the diversion out of the way, the British then took the Maungdaw ridge in a series of heavy, hard-fought battles. They finally broke through in April, and were about to finish the drive to Akyab when they were diverted to Imphal and Kohima by the major Japanese offensive there. Before they regained their momentum the monsoon rains came in, and it was not until the beginning of the winter dry season that they finally reached Akyab.

The second British drive, a projected advance to the Chindwin River by the other flank of 14th Army, was forestalled by the Japanese drives in the Chin Hills. General Renya Mutaguchi's 15th Army, consisting of 100,000 hard veteran troops, drove across the frontier into the Manipur plain to deprive the British of bases for their own offensive. The keys to the plain were the towns of Imphal at the southern end and Kohima at the northern. The Japanese attack was expected by the British, but both its strength and its speed were a surprise. They rolled up out of the Chindwin Valley, across the Chin Hills, and moved rapidly through mountains thought all but impassable. They scooped up

British outposts and arrived in front of the two towns nearly as fast as the news of their coming. By the end of the first week of April, both towns were surrounded, and the British IVth Corps, 50,000 strong, was cut off, most of it in Imphal and a small garrison in Kohima.

Once again, as he had on the seacoast, Slim ordered the garrisons to hold on. The air forces flew round-the-clock resupply missions, and fighters and medium bombers mounted tactical air-support operations, serving in effect as the artillery the troops on the ground lacked. For a few days it looked as if Kohima would go under, and it probably would have, had it not been for the strafing and bombing by the planes that broke up or weakened the heavy Japanese attacks. But after two weeks relieving forces broke through, and the siege of Kohima was lifted.

Imphal took much longer; the Japanese kept the town under constant pressure, and at the same time dug in and resisted fiercely the attempts of relieving forces to advance to the south. The British numbers mounted to 100,000 men as reinforcements were flown into the beleaguered city, but still the Japanese lines around it held fast. They were encountering increasing difficulties; they had expected to capture large amounts of supplies—indeed, they had based their whole logistical schedule for the operation on the risky presumption that they could live off British goods, and now the fallacy was shown to be disastrous. The monsoon rains began; sickness growing to epidemic and hunger growing to starvation took their toll, and at last, in mid-June, they began to fall apart. After eighty-eight days the British finally broke through, and their units in Imphal linked up with the relieving forces fighting their way into the town. Wearily, Mataguchi's army, what was left of it, took up its retreat.

The result of the Kohima-Imphal battles was that the Japanese mobile resources in Burma were all but used up. Late in the year, after the monsoon had ended, Slim was able to take up his advance, not only to the Chindwin but well beyond it. Early in December his troops linked up with the Chinese, now commanded by the American General Daniel Sultan, who had taken over Stilwell's Burmese responsibilities. The year ended on a rising note, with the Japanese falling back all along the line in central Burma, and the united Allies approaching Mandalay and Lashio, the Burmese terminus of the Burma Road.

On the American side of the Japanese Empire, progress was

no less hard won, and even more dramatic in its results. The 1943 decisions on relative priorities of Germany and Japan had resulted in increased allocations of resources to the Pacific war, and by 1944 their weight was definitely beginning to tell. Under MacArthur's leadership in the Southwest Pacific Area, the Allies undertook a 2,000-mile drive that carried them back to the Philippines. In the central Pacific the navy and Marines under Admiral Nimitz continued due west, so that they ended up meeting MacArthur's forces as the latter swung north. The vast distances covered and the territory taken made it look easy; in fact it was anything but that.

For General Douglas MacArthur, in spite of the brilliance of the campaign he waged in New Guinea and the East Indies, late 1943 and much of 1944 was a period of frustration. His ideas on the retaking of the western Pacific had been rejected by the American Joint Chiefs of Staff and subsequently by the Allied Combined Chiefs. MacArthur wanted to utilize land-based air power and leap-frog along the coast of New Guinea, through the Philippines, to the China coast, where a lodgment could be secured as a base for air attack and eventual invasion of the Japanese home islands. The China coast was accepted as the penultimate objective, but the Joint Chiefs also accepted the navy's contention that it was cheaper, and a better return for resources, to go straight west through the islands to the Philippines. The prospect that someone else might fulfill his pledge, "I shall return," was anathema to MacArthur, and so, through 1944, there was a race for the Philippines.

In that race were two major hurdles. The great port of Rabaul at the eastern tip of New Britain Island blocked MacArthur's advance; the huge naval base in Truk Lagoon, in the eastern Carolines, blocked Nimitz'. Both of these sites were major bastions of the Japanese defense perimeter, and no one, especially after the experience of prying Japanese troops out of prepared positions on Tarawa, looked forward to taking them. But as the year turned, and as the Americans slowly began to attain command of the sea and the air, they decided not to do so. The great bases could be isolated by air strikes, submarines could deny them the supplies needed for viability, and they could be bypassed. Lesser islands all around and beyond them could be taken, and as the tide of war rolled westward, both Truk and Rabaul were left withering in isolation.

The Japanese too had revised their plans and estimates. Hurt by their losses, recognizing their inability to recoup as rapidly as the enemy, they decided on a contraction of their defense lines. They had to hold on to the Indies, the major point of the whole exercise, but they could pull back in the central Pacific. The new line ran Kuriles-Bonins-Marianas-Carolines—western New Guinea. Troops still to the east of that were left to trade their lives for time while the new defenses were prepared. The Japanese told themselves that eventually the Americans would overreach themselves; with their charts and dividers and parallel rulers they plotted courses and distances. They were going to fight Tsushima all over again; they were going to trap and destroy the United States fleet.

MacArthur and Admiral Halsey, commanding the naval forces in the Southwest Pacific Area, spent the first third of 1944 isolating Rabaul. After very hard fighting around Madang and Saidor, the Americans and Australians pushed up along the coast of New Guinea. In April they leaped beyond their land-based air cover and landed major forces at Hollandia, cutting off the Japanese 18th Army. Meanwhile, attacks on New Britain, the upper Solomons, and another long jump to the Admiralty Islands completed Rabaul's encirclement. The whole campaign was a masterful illustration of the possibilities of combined operations, with naval, air, and ground forces successfully and amicably cooperating and supporting each other. The Hollandia operation especially achieved that unusual but most desirable of military aims, the destruction of a major enemy force with relatively little fighting.

The American forces swept on to the westward, leaving the rear areas to be mopped up by Australian ground forces, which had some heavy fighting for the rest of the year before the Japanese ultimately disintegrated. In May, MacArthur's troops landed in western—Netherlands—New Guinea. One of their problems was to find and take islands or localities where the terrain was suitable for heavy-bomber bases. Late in May they landed on the island of Biak, in the Schouten Islands, a group north of western New Guinea. The Japanese had an airfield here, as well as a garrison of 10,000 troops, which they managed to reinforce by another thousand during the fighting. The U. S. 41st Infantry Division made its landing against determined opposition, and while American fleet units isolated the island, the infantrymen fought it out. A second American division was landed, and slowly the Japanese were worn down. It took four weeks to make Biak secure, and isolated resistance lasted yet another month. The Americans suffered 2,800 casualties, including nearly 500 killed, while the Japanese lost more than 6,000 killed, and only about 500 captured.

From Biak the Americans went on to Sansapor on the western end of New Guinea. The Japanese had also garrisoned and fortified the large island of Halmahera as a communications link to the west of New Guinea. This too the Americans bypassed, landing on Morotai to the north of it in September. With the taking of Morotai, New Guinea was isolated and left over to mopping up. The two-year battle along the coast was essentially over, and the Japanese had everywhere met defeat. Superior American techniques, equipment, and strategy had won the day, and the lengthy campaign, an exhausting ordeal in which climate, terrain, and disease were almost as vicious as the enemy, reached a triumphant conclusion. Even without his great coup at Inchon in the Korean War the New Guinea campaign marked MacArthur as one of the great captains of military history, and it is regrettable that it is not better known. MacArthur's forces were now ready for the northern swing.

In the central Pacific theater Nimitz' sailors and Marines had digested the painful lessons of Tarawa. Communications, fire-control, and air support techniques were all refined and perfected, and the navy moved on with its task of isolating Truk. The first jump after Tarawa was into the central Marshall Islands, to the beautiful Kwajalein Lagoon.

The navy had now developed a new weapons combination, the fast carrier task force. Gone were the days when a patched-up battleship rescued from the mud of Pearl Harbor, one weak aircraft carrier, and a couple of battered cruisers represented the U. S. Navy's striking force. Now as a preliminary to the assault on Kwajalein, Admiral Mark Mitscher swept through the island group with Task Force 58: twelve carriers, six new fast battleships, a dozen cruisers, and even more destroyers. Divided into four groups around the carriers, the Americans struck at will, looking for trouble, pounding the islands and their airstrips, daring the Japanese fleet to come out. A thousand miles west, Admiral Koga's Combined Fleet, for the moment without any operating aircraft carriers, sat and waited for its opportunity.

After three days of heavy bombardment the soldiers and Marines went ashore, the former on Kwajalein itself, the latter on smaller islands around the lagoon. The Japanese fought as fiercely as they had on Tarawa, but the improved techniques employed by the Americans made a significant difference to the casualty ratios. Out of 8,000 Japanese, 130 survived; the Americans landed 41,000 troops, of whom fewer than 400 were killed and about a thousand wounded. The atoll was secured in a week.

Two weeks later the Americans leaped 400 miles to the western Marshalls and landed on Eniwetok, another tropic lagoon. Again the Japanese fought to the death, losing their entire 2,200-man garrison for American losses of about four hundred. While the amphibious forces fought their way across Eniwetok, Mitscher staged a raid on Truk. Warned of the approach of the American carriers, the Combined Fleet scooted out to the west and safety, but the Americans found fifty merchant ships and more than 350 planes at Truk. With little loss to themselves they sank thousands of tons of shipping and wiped out 275 aircraft. Truk Lagoon became a vast underwater repository of the refuse of war, where sunken ships and their cargoes of tanks, shells, and guns, and their drowned crews, are now sights for underwater tourists. The Japanese, recognizing the growing isolation and vulnerability of Truk, pulled the fleet back behind the Marianas, still biding their time, waiting for the chance to strike back.

The long-awaited opportunity came in June, when the Americans leaped another thousand miles, from Eniwetok to the Marianas. Admiral Spruance's 5th Fleet concentrated against the two islands of Saipan and Tinian; while they did so, Task Force 58 ranged ahead of them, pounding bases as far as the Palaus to the southwest, and Iwo Jima and Chichi Jima to the north, in the Bonin group. Cut off on all sides from air and sea reinforcement, the Japanese garrison of Saipan prepared to die for the Emperor as their predecessors had done.

Two U. S. Marine divisions landed on Saipan on June 15. In spite of a heavy bombardment they met staunch resistance from the Japanese, who included both soldiers of the regular garrison, plus about 6,000 sailors from the Imperial Fleet, commanded by Admiral Nagumo, who had led the Pearl Harbor striking force. The Marines made heavy going; they were reinforced by an army infantry division which made even slower going. The army and Marine commanders fell to squabbling over essentially doctrinal differences—the army believed in a cautious, methodical approach; the Marines, imbued with the vulnerability of the offshore fleet behind them, had been taught to take ground in a hurry and never mind the casualties—and Marine General Holland Smith ended up relieving the army divisional commander. It was not until July 9 that resistance finally ended, with the standard suicide charge by the surviving Japanese. More than 3,000 Americans were killed and more than 13,000 wounded. The Japanese losses were as usual much heavier. Of perhaps 30,000 people on the island—soldiers, sailors, and Japanese civilians—about 27,000 died, including thousands of civilians who committed suicide along with the last soldiers; the commanding general and Admiral Nagumo both committed ritual suicide as well. Napoleon once remarked that a victory was no victory without prisoners—but he never fought the Japanese.

So fierce was the fight for Saipan that Spruance delayed his assault on nearby Tinian, and also on Guam. Meanwhile, the enormous fleet off Saipan, more than 500 vessels, provided the ideal target for the Japanese. Admiral Koga had been killed in an air crash, and to his successor as commander of the Combined Fleet, Admiral Soemu Toyoda, it appeared as if the time had come at last to give battle. His fleet was now based at Tawitawi in the Sulu Islands, just north of Borneo. He had expected to hit the American ships supporting MacArthur, but Mitscher's attacks on the Palaus led him into the central Pacific instead.

Toyoda skimmed the cream off the Combined Fleet to make a Mobile Fleet, the best Japan had, under Admiral Jisaburo Ozawa. Ozawa mustered nine aircraft carriers, five battleships, thirteen cruisers, twenty-eight destroyers, and a total of 473 aircraft. His planes had longer range than the Americans', though they achieved it by lacking such refinements as armor plating for the cockpits or self-sealing gasoline tanks. He also expected to be supported by the remaining land-based aircraft from the Marianas. Dividing their fleet into five groups built around the carriers, the Imperial Japanese Navy sallied forth to annihilate the enemy.

The Americans were split into several groups, busily pounding Saipan and the assorted islands which might otherwise have provided support. Task Force 58 itself was split in two, with Mitscher and Spruance together west of Saipan, and the other half of it off bombarding Iwo Jima, several hundred miles away. Yet the Americans knew precisely what they were doing. Submarines had watched the Japanese in Tawitawi—indeed, had made such a nuisance of themselves that the Japanese had not dared put to sea for training of their new carrier pilots. Coastwatchers and submarines reported the progress of the Mobile Fleet and its dispositions as it threaded its way through the Philippines. By the time the Japanese entered the open waters of the Philippine Sea, Spruance knew almost as much about them as they did themselves. Calmly he pulled in his scattered task groups, so that when the Japanese came within extreme range on the early morning of June 19, Task Force 58 was ready for them: fifteen carriers, seven new fast battleships, twenty-one cruisers, sixty-nine destroyers, 956 planes. The Japanese were headed for a battle of annihilation all right, but it was not what they expected: in American folklore the great Battle of the Philippine Sea is known as "the Marianas Turkey Shoot."

The Japanese first strike was supposed to be a massive attack by land-based planes from Guam. Unfortunately for them, there were only about fifty planes left on Guam, and even more unfortunate, the Americans showed up over the island just as they were taking off. The Japanese lost thirty planes and never got out of sight of Guam.

Back in Task Force 58, the air group commanders were champing at the bit, but Mitscher, uncertain exactly where the enemy was, held them in check. About mid-morning, radar picked up a wave of incoming enemy planes, sixty-nine of them, 150 miles out. American dive-bombers and torpedo-bombers took off and orbited to the eastward, out of the way of trouble, and able to attack Guam and deny it to the enemy as a landing strip for planes in difficulty. And there were soon plenty of them. Four hundred fifty Hellcat fighters met the Japanese; the Americans had the advantage of height; the heavy Hellcats could blast the lighter Zeros out of the sky with one good burst, and by this stage of the war, American pilots were far more experienced than their opponents. The Americans lost one plane, the Japanese lost forty-two; they scored one hit on the battleship *South Dakota*.

Ozawa's second wave of carrier planes was 128 strong. The Hellcats met them sixty miles out and killed half before they reached the fleet. They scored a hit on the small carrier *Bunker Hill*. Ninety-eight Japanese were shot down. A third wave failed to find Task Force 58 and therefore lost only seven planes. The last raid, eighty-two strong, got scattered. Those who reached the fleet were all but wiped out. Some fled for Guam, where Hellcats caught them as they tried to land. Only eleven of the whole raid survived. By the time the sun set on the 19th, Japanese carrier air strength was a thing of the past.

It was not only the American fliers who had a field day. The submarine *Albacore* sneaked past the Japanese screen and put a single torpedo into the brand-new carrier *Taiho*, Ozawa's flagship.

Down she went, and Ozawa had to move to another carrier. Three hours later the submarine *Cavalla* hit *Shokaku* with a three-torpedo spread, and she blew up and sank a couple of hours later, after valiant but unsuccessful efforts by her crew to fight the spreading gas and oil fires.

In the darkness Ozawa headed off to the northwest. He had but a hundred planes left; he believed, mistakenly, that he had inflicted heavy damage on the enemy and he planned to reopen his attack as soon as he could refuel and rearm. The American reconnaissance planes did not spot the still-retiring Mobile Fleet until late the next afternoon, at the extreme end of their search patterns. Mitscher consulted with his air group commanders and asked if they could reach the enemy. It would be chancy, and the pilots would have to fly back in the dark, almost out of fuel; it would be a very close affair, but they decided it was worth it.

Just as the sun set, the American dive-bombers, torpedo planes, and fighters appeared over the Mobile Fleet. They set two carriers on fire and sank a third, the *Hiyo*. Between the sinking, the damage, and dogfights in the air, they destroyed another sixty-five aircraft. Then they headed for home.

Home was a long way off, and one by one the planes went down. The fuel gauges flickered toward empty, then settled firmly on the red line, and the planes gently dipped toward the sea. It was full dark now. The Americans sent destroyers racing ahead to pick up aircrew; risking submarine retaliation, the carriers turned on their lights as beacons for the returning planes. With no margin for maneuver, the fortunate planes crash-landed on flight decks; the slightly less lucky went into the water near the carriers and were picked up by the escorts. Destroyers rescued 150 of the somewhat less lucky who ditched en route back. About fifty had no luck at all.

Yet the deed was done; the great battle fought and won—or lost. In Tokyo the Tojo cabinet resigned. At sea, the empty Japanese carriers fleeing northward would never be a threat again. From now on, they came out to sea at their own risk, to serve as decoys and targets. The Imperial Fleet would definitely try again, for the Japanese preferred death to ignominious surrender. But after the Marianas Turkey Shoot it would never again be a major threat.

The Pacific is the greatest ocean in the world, and the flow of ships, men, and matériel was ever westward: 2,500 miles from San

Francisco to Pearl, 2,000 miles from Pearl to Tarawa, 500 from there to Kwajalein, 1,200 more to Saipan. From there, 1,200 to the Philippines, or 1,200 to Tokyo. The endless Pacific rollers washed the beaches clean of the debris of death and battle. As the Marines and infantry flowed on to another island and yet another, the great supply depots built up behind them. For every man who was shot at in this war dozens toiled behind the front, hauling crates, shuffling papers, drinking beer, fighting boredom. Foolish mistakes cost millions of dollars. The earliest shipments of sugar to the southwest Pacific went out in paper bags. They rotted and disintegrated in the first tropic rainstorm; bulldozers created islands in the swamps made of huge mounds of sugar, and on top of those islands later, better-packaged stores were piled. Still the goods and the men spewed out of the American West Coast ports; it was a war in which technical expertise counted for much, and where the Japanese labored for months with picks and shovels and wheelbarrows, the Americans made airstrips in hours and days with bulldozers, steam shovels, and huge earth-movers. The material flood reached out to the islands, to New Zealand, to Australia. And at the business end of the machine, old men of eighteen and nineteen turned their faces to the north, to the Philippines, to Japan, to the only way home again.

From Saipan the Marines went to Tinian, within artillery range. Every gun on Saipan was lined up hub to hub, and together with the fleet, pounded away at the Japanese garrison. Yet still they fought. The Americans declared the island secured on August 1; it took three more months of deadly hide and seek to ferret out and kill the last of the defenders from the caves on the southern end of the island.

Guam was next—American before the war, now held and fortified by 19,000 Japanese. It took three weeks of heavy fighting by army and Marines to secure the island, but some of the garrison got into the hills and did not surrender until long after the war officially ended. With the capture of Guam the Marianas were secure, and the Carolines and Truk, well bypassed. The American high command was definitely looking forward to the Philippines now, and Admiral Nimitz decided the next move was to be to the western Carolines and to the Palau Islands. Spruance and the rest of the central Pacific leaders went off to new commands, and Halsey took over 5th Fleet, which became 3rd Fleet in the transformation. Task Force 58 therefore became Task Force 38, with Mitscher still running it. The next target was Peleliu.

Peleliu is a small island two miles wide and six long. Its highest point is a hill officially named Urumbrogol Mountain, later changed by the troops to Bloody Nose Ridge. It was garrisoned by 10,000 Japanese dug into a honeycomb web of connecting caves and bunkers. The conquest of the island followed the same pattern as all the others, with one notable exception. Marines followed by army infantry landed on the southwest corner, fought their way onto and across the local airstrip, and then had to dig the Japanese out of the caves squad by squad, or one by one. It took seven weeks to secure Peleliu and the surrounding islands of the group. The Japanese, who managed to reinforce with another 4,000 during the fighting, had 13,600 killed, and 400 were taken prisoners. The Americans had 7,900 casualties, including 1,750 dead. Those figures provided the notable factor about Peleliu: it cost the highest casualty rate—nearly 40 percent—of any amphibious assault in American history.

While the assault troops fought it out, changes were in the making. At the Quadrant Conference in Quebec the timetable of advance was quickened. MacArthur and Nimitz had expected to take one more set of intermediate islands before reaching the Philippines. Now it looked as if there were a possibility that they could move straight to the heart of the Philippines instead. Japanese naval power and air strength were obviously weakening— though that was more obvious in headquarters than it was on Peleliu—and it was a time for daring initiatives. Asked if they could advance their timetables, MacArthur and Nimitz both said they could. After feverish staff work and exceptional interservice cooperation, the target date for the invasion of Leyte in the central Philippines was moved up from mid-December to October 20. While army and Marine officers moved frantically to rearrange troop allocations and reinforcement schedules, the navy roamed the Philippine Sea, striking heavily at targets on Formosa and other islands which might be used as supporting bases for the 350,000 Japanese in the Philippines themselves. The end result of these strikes was minor damage to American units, and the destruction of another 650 Japanese aircraft, just as they were attempting to rebuild their shattered squadrons after the beating in June.

In the Philippines, the Japanese were well aware that the Americans were coming. Their troops were commanded by the conqueror of Malaya, General Yamashita. The islands were doomed to succumb to any enemy possessing naval and air control, as the Japanese knew from their own experience in 1941-42. But the archipelago was central to the entire empire; if it fell, all communications with the East Indies and much of Southeast Asia would go with it. The Japanese Army determined to put up a fierce fight for the Philippines, and the navy decided, once again, that while the Americans were tied to the amphibious landing forces, there might just be a chance to wipe them out. If all went well, and if they were lucky, the whole tide of the war might be turned. They set in train what was to become the greatest naval battle in history, the Battle of Leyte Gulf.

The invasion of the Philippines began on October 20, right on schedule, when units of the U. S. 6th Army, under General Walter Krueger, landed in Leyte, a large island in the center of the archipelago. Yamashita poured in reinforcements, and while the ground troops fought it out, the Japanese Navy moved to implement its immensely complicated plan for the annihilation of the U. S. Fleet.

The Sho Plan, or Victory Plan, called for a complex converging operation by initially widely separated units of the Japanese Navy. The Main Body, under Admiral Ozawa, was to sortie from the home islands, move south, and act as a decoy to draw off Halsey's 3rd Fleet. The Second Striking Force, Admiral Shima, was also to sail from the home islands, south through the Formosa Strait, west of the Philippines, to the Sulu Sea. There it would fall in with part of the First Striking Force, under Admiral Nishimura, coming north from Singapore and Borneo. This so-called Third Section of the First Striking Force, plus Shima's Second Striking Force, were to turn northeast and sail into Leyte Gulf via Surigao Strait, where they would pounce on the amphibious assault ships under Admiral Kincaid. Meanwhile, the rest of the ships from the south, redesignated Central Force, were to make their way under the command of Admiral Kurita through the Sibuyan Sea and San Bernardino Strait, down past the island of Samar, to Leyte Gulf from the north, where they were to hit the aircraft carrier groups supporting Kincaid's landing forces.

All of these plans resulted in a series of interconnected but separate engagements that combined to form the Battle of Leyte Gulf. There were six encounters in sequence.

In the earliest of them, and well ahead of the Japanese schedule, two American submarines, *Darter* and *Dace,* intercepted Kurita's Central Force while it was still west of the island of Palawan in the South China Sea. Pressing home their torpedo attacks, they sank two cruisers, including Kurita's flagship, the *Atago*, and crippled a third. Still possessing five battleships, including the superbattleship *Musashi* (the largest in the world), nine undamaged cruisers, and fifteen destroyers, Kurita pressed on. The second attack came next day, the 24th, when planes from the 3rd Fleet caught Kurita in the Sibuyan Sea. The Japanese had no air cover; their weakened carriers were all up north, so the Americans attacked at will; in five strikes they hit all the battleships and disabled the *Musashi*, so that she began to flee back westward. The Americans then came back for one last time and finished her off; flooded bow and stern, she went down with 1,100 of her crew still aboard. Kurita, complaining he was doing all the work and suffering all the consequences, turned back during the night, but then he subsequently changed his mind and resumed his track toward San Bernardino Strait.

Meanwhile, in the third preliminary bout, planes from Ozawa's Main Body attacked units of Halsey's 3rd Fleet, sinking the small carrier *Princeton* for a loss of two thirds their own number. Halsey now knew there were Japanese carrier units to the north of him, and he also had the reports of his own returning pilots that Kurita was stopped and retreating. He therefore led 3rd Fleet off northward after the Japanese Main Body, unaware that Kurita had now had third thoughts and had once again turned back to fight. By dark on the night of the 24th, the stage was set for the three main battles.

Shima's Second Striking Force, plus Nishimura's Third Section had made their way through the Sulu and the Mindanao Sea, and entered the confined waters of Surigao Strait. Nishimura led, with two battleships, a cruiser, and four destroyers. Shima, two hours behind him, had three cruisers and four destroyers. They hoped to surprise the soft-skinned American transport vessels, and if they were lucky, wipe them out. Once more, however, the Americans were ready for them. Kincaid had given Admiral Jesse Oldendorf the bulk of his shore bombardment vessels; these were ranged across the top of Surigao Strait, and the Japanese were sailing right into a trap. Emotionally, it could hardly have been a more satisfying trap, manned as it was by the ghosts of Pearl Harbor, the old prewar battleships raised from the mud and rebuilt. As the war went on and newer ships came into service, these slower vessels had been relegated to supporting amphibious landings. Now they, plus their attendant cruisers, destroyers, and torpedo boats, were to get their innings at last.

Nishimura, in the lead, was attacked first by the torpedo boats, and he ran a gauntlet of them for twenty-five miles; at the end, waiting front and flank, were the bigger ships. The destroyers darted out and launched their own torpedo attacks, then the cruisers and battleships spoke up. The old battleships paraded back and forth across the mouth of the strait at a stately five knots, firing full broadsides as they went. The Japanese forces, already in confusion, were deluged by hits and the splashes of near misses. In a hectic hour's action, Nishimura, his two battleships, his cruisers, and three of his four destroyers all went down. In the midst of the gunflashes, the splashes, the cries of thousands of men drowning for their Emperor, one destroyer survived and turned back down the strait. Meeting Shima's force coming north this survivor sent one of the least revealing messages in naval history—"I am having steering trouble"—and kept on her way Shima soon realized what had happened and turned back too. The Americans pursued far enough to sink one of his cruisers, then Oldendorf, conscious of his responsibility to protect the transports, in his turn went back to his station.

With the Battle of Surigao Strait fought and won, it was Halsey's turn. Dawn of the 25th found him to the north, east of the island of Luzon, and his search planes picked up the Japanese Main Body. In what became known as the Battle of Cape Engano, the nearest point on Luzon, Halsey's planes caught and sank four Japanese carriers—all but planeless and able to serve only as sacrificial decoys—and a destroyer. Halsey was on the verge of making surface contact and closing in for the kill when he received a chilling message. With Kincaid busy in the south, and Halsey busy in the north, Kurita had suddenly appeared out of the mouth of San Bernardino Strait and was striking at the light carriers and their escorts supporting the landing; the wolf was in among the fold at last.

It was a David and Goliath fight; the Japanese still had their four surviving battleships plus several cruisers and destroyers, while the American admiral Clifton Sprague had only six escort carriers and half a dozen destroyers and destroyer-escorts. His whole force mounted nothing heavier than a five-inch gun. The Americans raced off to the southward, while the destroyers popped away at the giants, and the fighter-bombers leaped off the little carriers to plaster the battleships with the light fragmentation bombs they had been using against shore targets—roughly equivalent to throwing pebbles at a charging rhinoceros. Sprague yelled for help;

planes came screaming in from all points of the compass. Halsey turned back from his near-triumph, Kincaid came dashing back from Surigao Strait. Still it was only a matter of time before the "jeep" carriers would be overwhelmed. *Gambier Bay* went down; so did three of the gallant little escorts. What probably saved the rest of them was the fact that the Japanese were firing heavy armor-piercing shells, and the carriers were so lightly built that many shells went right through them without encountering enough resistance to make them explode. After two hours it looked as if the Americans were on the point of annihilation, when suddenly Kurita turned away, back where he had come from. On the verge of contact with the amphibious ships that were the target of the whole endeavor, Kurita became convinced he was sailing into a trap and broke off the action, reputedly prompting the oft-quoted remark from a sailor on one of the escort carriers, "Hell, they got away. . . ."

In fact they did not quite get away. As they fled, carrier planes caught them in the Sulu Sea and sank another cruiser. The end result of the battle was the destruction of the Imperial Japanese Navy as a fighting force. They lost three battleships, four carriers, ten cruisers, and nine destroyers—more than 300,000 tons of combat ships, as against 37,000 tons for the Americans. Only one recourse lay open to them now. During the battle several Japanese pilots deliberately crashed their planes into American ships: the time of the suicide plane—the kamikaze—had arrived.

Concentrated naval battles tend to be relatively short, compared with land campaigns. The Battle of Leyte Gulf lasted in its entirety but a few days. The land campaign to secure the Philippines went on until the end of the war and really involved three interrelated operations: the drive to secure Leyte itself, the northern advance into Luzon and the fight for that main island, and the southern advance to clear the islands south of Leyte.

MacArthur and his planners had regarded the taking of Leyte as largely a preliminary operation, designed to gain them bases for their air power, which they would then use in the main battle for Luzon. Initially, Yamashita agreed with them: the island was lightly garrisoned, and the Japanese commander did not intend to fight a major battle there. However, he became caught up in the momentum generated by the battle itself and began shipping reinforcements into the island. Most of the new troops had to be brought in by fast transports running the gauntlet of American air strength. The Japanese had weak air units in the Philippines and they largely destroyed themselves in fierce attacks on the Americans that in the end achieved no real effect.

On Leyte the campaign ground slowly ahead. The Japanese had good defensive positions, the weather was bad with heavy rains turning the roads to mud, and the supply buildup went more slowly than planned. The Japanese managed to put together a defensive line running along the mountainous spine of the island and there they held on. Once Yamashita had a chance to assess the full impact of the loss of the naval battle, he recommended that Leyte be abandoned. His superiors turned him down, however, so he continued to filter troops into the island and determined to make a fight for it as long as he could.

Exerting gradually increasing pressure, the American vise slowly closed around the Japanese. By the first week of December the western Leyte ports through which the Japanese reinforced were taken by amphibious assault, and they were cut off. They launched one last offensive, designed to seize American airfields, an offensive notable for one of the rare appearances of Japanese parachute troops, but they lacked the resources to hold on to their gains. By mid-December the defense was collapsing, and by the end of the year the Americans had entered the mopping-up phase, which in fact lasted for another four months, while isolated and roving bands of Japanese were rounded up. In the end the Leyte campaign had destroyed the Japanese Navy, exhausted most of their Philippine air strength, and cost them 70,000 ground force casualties, seriously weakening their ability to hold the rest of the islands.

In mid-December, while the fight for Leyte still went on, units from the U. S. 8th Army, the follow-up force to 6th Army, landed on Mindoro, a smaller island just off Luzon, and rapidly set up airstrips. MacArthur planned to invade Luzon by way of Lingayen Gulf, the same route used by the Japanese in 1941, and drive down the central plain to Manila. Krueger's forces landed on January 9 after heavy suicide attacks on the invasion fleet by Japanese planes that sank twenty ships and damaged another two dozen. Yamashita had 250,000 troops still on the island, but shortage of equipment and transport plus the superior mobility of the Americans had forced him into a static defensive role. He had organized his forces into three main groups, each assigned a sector of the island, and told them to fight to the end.

Therefore, as the Americans drove south from Lingayen, in

some places they met relatively light opposition, and the chief problem of their advance was logistical; but in other places they came up against the Japanese in prepared positions and had to fight hard for every yard. One of their major concerns was the rescue of American prisoners of war and civilian internees. These victims of 1942 had suffered tremendous deprivations at Japanese hands; several thousand had been shipped off to Japan itself, but other thousands still remained in camps on the island, and the Americans were afraid the Japanese might well massacre them as the battle went against them. One of the determinants of the progress of operations thus became the quick capture of prison camps before the guards could kill the inmates.

As Krueger's soldiers fought their way south from Lingayen, MacArthur utilized to the full the amphibious and airborne capability he now possessed. Landings at unexpected points along the coast kept the Japanese off balance, and they were further dislocated by airborne drops, including one on the island of Corregidor in February, and a later one in the suburbs of Manila itself. In 1942 MacArthur, uncertain of his exact relation with the Filipinos, had declared Manila an open city. Yamashita was constrained by no such diplomatic problems and the Japanese fought hard to hold on; most of the city was in ruins by the time it was cleared. The last fighting was around the University of the Philippines and the old walled city called the Intramuros; it was necessary to breach the ancient Spanish walls with point-blank artillery fire, and then the infantry went in and rooted the Japanese out one by one. By mid-March central Luzon was under American control, and Yamashita's forces pushed back into the extremities and the mountains of northern Luzon. Krueger's 6th Army handed over to 8th Army, and went off to train for the invasion of Japan. Eighth Army spent the rest of the war whittling down the enemy, but by the time the Japanese surrendered in August, there were still 50,000 troops at large in Luzon, so to the very end they were doing their best to tie down and kill Americans, a thankless, unrewarding battle for both sides.

The same kind of deadly game went on in the southern Philippines. The 100,000 ill-equipped Japanese troops there had hoped to be left alone, but MacArthur needed the southern islands for air bases to support the projected Australian invasion of Borneo, and to operate against the East Indies shipping lanes. He therefore directed 8th Army to send some of its units from Luzon south. Only on the large island of Mindanao were the Japanese able to put up an effective resistance. In the other islands they faded into the backlands as the American forces landed, and hung on until mobile columns of Americans and Filipino guerrillas finally ran them down, or starvation reduced them to collapse. In Mindanao they were strong enough to retain the eastern part of the island until the general Japanese surrender, by which time, subjected to constant ground pressure and relentless air attack, they were here too in a state of near-starvation and semi-collapse.

In all, the Philippine campaign cost the Japanese the entire 350,000 men they had garrisoning the islands. The Americans themselves suffered 62,000 casualties, including almost 14,000 killed. As the war flowed by to the northward several things were obvious. The Japanese Empire was doomed; by the end of 1944 their fleet and air forces were both mere shadows of what they had been. But it was equally apparent that they were not yet ready to admit defeat. If victory consists, as Clausewitz said, of making the enemy accept your will rather than his own, the Allies had not yet achieved victory. The home islands of the empire lay ahead, and no one in his right mind could possibly relish the task of taking on the Japanese on their own territory. But the prison camps on Luzon had hardened any Allied hearts that yet needed to be hardened. It might be that the Japanese would insist on dying as a people before they would concede defeat. If that was what they wanted, so be it. The Americans had the matériel, the manpower, and the expertise to do it, and by 1945, after the long road from Pearl Harbor to Manila, they were as determined as their enemies on a fight to the finish.

26. The Collapse of Germany

THERE HAD BEEN THOSE who hoped the war with Germany would be over by the end of 1944. They were doomed to disappointment. *Festung Europa*, Fortress Europe, had been cracked wide open, but the German war machine was still not destroyed; there seemed no real diminution of German fighting spirit. Though the air forces of the Western Allies ranged at will over the skies of the Reich, the supplies still poured forth; the guns still fired, the troops were still clothed, fed, and armed. Victory for the Allies lay at the end of the road, but it was farther off than they hoped. Goaded by Hitler's will and the great momentum of the Nazi state, the beast fought blindly on.

Mid-December saw the Russians cross for the first time onto native German territory. In the south they and the Yugoslavs had cleared Belgrade, half of Hungary was theirs, and they were into eastern Czechoslovakia. In unhappy Poland they had closed up to the Vistula, and in the north, parts of East Prussia itself were already under Red control. There began a great flight out of the eastlands; for centuries the Germans had moved east, by sword, by religious conversion, by purchase—the ideas of the Master Race were far older than Adolf Hitler. Now the tide flowed in the other direction, and once-complacent German overlords fled in terror for their lives. In the northern winter women, children, and old men trudged west, or fought for places on the Baltic ships. The millions who had been enslaved and transported as workers for the greater glory of Germany watched them go and hardened their hearts. There was little mercy now for those who in the hour of their triumph had shown none at all.

In Italy the Germans held on the last slopes of the northern Apennines; the Italian theater was definitely second-class now, and everyone there knew it. General Alexander and his army commanders looked at their maps and speculated on what might have been, but they knew that their fleeting moment of glory had passed them by; those hectic, heady weeks in midsummer when Rome had fallen at last and the Allies had streamed northward in pursuit of the battered Germans, only to have their momentum broken by the Allied high command, were the closest the hard-fighting troops in Italy ever came to winning a war. Now they were doomed to fight out the rest of it, and many to give their lives, for mountain peaks that no one but they would ever remember. As the year changed, Alexander went up to command the Mediterranean theater, and Mark Clark took over as the army group commander in Italy; Kesselring too went home, replaced by a subordinate, General Heinrich von Veitinghoff. In the kind of ultimate irony that dogged the whole adventure in Italy, Clark and von Veitinghoff both believed they were fighting to achieve the same objective: Clark said the Allied armies must get to Austria to forestall the Russians; von Veitinghoff said his men must hold at all costs, because only that sort of sacrifice would prevent a Russian takeover of south-central Europe.

In western Europe the great offensive had finally slowed at last. The Allies had not made it across the Rhine. They had cleared France and Belgium, they had taken Antwerp, they had finally managed after costly fighting to clear the seaward approaches to Antwerp, and their supply situation was now satisfactory at least, but they had essentially achieved the Franco-German frontier rather than the Rhine, or the winning of the war, by the advent of winter. Eisenhower's Supreme Headquarters Allied Expeditionary Force had now moved to Paris, and from there he planned his coming moves. He had three army groups under him: Montgomery's in the north and along the coast; Bradley's from Luxembourg all the way down to Nancy; and Devers', up from the southern France invasion, on the upper Rhine to the Swiss frontier. With plenty of air support above them and good supply lines behind them, all the field commanders were keen to press forward. The only thin spot was in the center of Bradley's 12th Army Group, where General Troy Middleton's VIIIth Corps of Hodges' 1st Army was battle-weary and weak; fortunately, it was in a relatively quiet area, around the Ardennes Forest, and there could be no heavy fighting in the Ardennes in the middle of winter.

Elsewhere the situation looked good. Eisenhower decided on a three-phase operation: the Allies would close up to the Rhine, they would then seize bridgeheads across it, and finally, they would drive into Germany. Though they would proceed forward together on a "broad front," priority for material went to Montgomery in the north, headed for the industries of the Ruhr. Bradley and Devers would get along as best they could. This was more or less acceptable to all but Bradley's 3rd Army commander, George S. Patton. A complex, driven man, Patton was senior on the army list to his superiors, and difficult to handle. Much of his personality he suppressed in favor of the harder, flamboyant side he thought troops needed in a leader. He and Montgomery had become virtually personal rivals and he resented what he regarded as Eisenhower's truckling to the British. The Supreme Commander might defer to his allies, but Patton and 3rd Army were going to go as far as they could as fast as they could. Patton was a great soldier, but he was not an easy subordinate.

For the Germans the situation looked unrelievedly grim. The satellites were gone, the Reich itself was being systematically bombarded from the air, the manpower pool was failing; boys of fourteen and men of sixty were appearing in the ranks of the Volkssturm, the so-called People's Army that was supposed to defend the homeland in its extremity. Hitler put his hope in new weapons, and such was the magic of his repetitive oratory that some Germans still believed him. Yet the V-1 flying bomb, and even the V-2, first of the true missiles, did not deter the Allies from their course. Other magic answers failed to materialize, or fell short of their promises when they did. The new jet fighters were sidetracked into useless bombing roles; newer rocket fighters proved as dangerous to their pilots as to the enemy. The race to complete an atomic bomb was long lost in shortsightedness and internecine rivalries and bickerings.

With the failure of the miracle weapons to achieve miracles Hitler fell increasingly back on illusion. He was sure the Allies would fall out. As the war progressed downhill for Germany, he put more and more emphasis on the anti-Bolshevik nature of his Russian war. The Germans had not invaded Russia because they wanted to wipe out the Slavs and take their territory for the Germans, but because Germany had recognized her duty to save western civilization from the Red menace. Surely the Western Powers would wake up to their danger, would realize the true nature of their ally, and would change sides. Ideologically, Hitler was probably right; though they were all basically antithetical, fascism and capitalism perhaps had more points of contact than capitalism and communism. Emotionally, he could not have been more completely wrong. To assume that the Allies would fall out and that the West would side with Germany against the East was to ignore the mountain of hatred the Germans had created for themselves. In the context of 1944-45, it was utterly inconceivable to anyone outside Germany that the Germans were preferable to the Russians. Hitler, however, clung to that fiction, and more and more his thoughts turned to the closing days of the Seven Years' War, when Frederick the Great had managed to stave off disaster and survive because his enemies fell to quarreling with each other.

Meanwhile, there was work to be done. Already some of his generals were hinting that the Western Front should be allowed to collapse, and that all of Germany's efforts should be bent to holding back the Russians. Better that Germany be overrun by the Western Allies than the Reds, and the farther east the British and Americans got, the more desirable at the ultimate end of the war. This was anathema to Hitler; if he were to be defeated, it would be because the Germans were unworthy of his genius. That being the case, there was no reason why Germany and Germans should survive him. He was not concerned with easing the postwar situation for the cowardly remnant who lacked his courage or his convictions. He insisted that all was not lost anyway. If Germany could gain time, much might happen: the Allies might break up, the new weapons might become available, miracles might still happen. Deep in his lair he looked at his maps, he mused, he plotted, he raved, he saw an opportunity.

That weak Allied sector in Luxembourg; the Ardennes again. Suppose the Germans were to fight—and win—the campaign of 1940 all over again! Using its incredible improvisatory and organizational skills, the high command scraped up a strategic reserve of twenty-five divisions and two Panzer armies. Hitler planned to break the Allied line in the Ardennes, race through and wheel northwest to Antwerp; all the northern Allied armies would be cut off and destroyed. They were too strong to be driven out of France, but they could be badly knocked about, their timetables seriously disrupted. While they reeled back, the Germans could race back across Germany and defeat the Russian offensive that must be coming early in 1945. After that, who knew what might happen. It was a great mishmash—part Frederick the Great at Rossbach-Leuthen, part Schlieffen Plan, part Sichelschnitt.

The generals demurred. Von Rundstedt, cautious and professional, said it would not work; even Model agreed with him: the Germans simply did not have the men and material to do the job.

Hitler overrode them; it could work, it *must* work. Out of his illusions coupled with the Wehrmacht's recuperative powers was launched the last great German offensive of the Second World War.

The Allies knew something was in the wind. As professional intelligence evaluators, however, they believed correctly that the Germans did not have the matériel for a major counteroffensive, and that therefore they would have sense enough not to launch one. It was Hitler rather than the German Army that surprised them.

In Bradley's Army Group, Patton to the south of the Ardennes was preparing a drive eastward toward the Rhine. General William Simpson's 9th Army, north of the Ardennes, was preparing to move in support of Montgomery on their left when he got past the Roer River dams. In the middle, Hodges was left weak, his 1st Army assigned an essentially subordinate role. Having had heavy fighting all the way from Normandy, it now contained tired units low on manpower, or new ones just getting their feet wet.

The Germans had prepared as carefully as they could. They had created two new Panzer armies, 6th under General Sepp Dietrich, and 5th under General Otto Manteuffel. Advance units included a commando group under Colonel Otto Skorzeny, the man who had rescued Mussolini from his mountain prison in Italy. Since then Skorzeny had become Hitler's jack of all trades. Now his commandos included a group of English-speaking Germans dressed in captured American uniforms and equipment. Their task was to confuse the enemy and to take and hold the bridges over the Meuse, the river whose successful crossing would shake the Germans loose on the road to Antwerp. After waiting for a period of bad weather to come in and ground the Allied air forces, the Germans struck early on the morning of December 16.

The immediate success was impressive. The opening drive shattered two American divisions spread along the Schnee Eifel ridge in the north and along the Our River in the south. Routed and overwhelmed, both divisions broke up into component parts, with battalions, companies, and even platoons wandering about the wintry forests, fighting Germans when they bumped into them, or looking desperately for friends. The Germans capitalized on the confusion, which Skorzeny's commandos compounded. As soon as the news got out that there were enemy soldiers abroad in American uniforms, informal but strict security measures sprang into being; the soldier who faced a squad of grim-looking infantrymen and could not immediately tell who played first base for the Brooklyn

Dodgers, or who was Betty Grable's husband, was in serious trouble.

Pushing on through the hills and forests, the Germans made for the road junction at Bastogne. Here they encountered and surrounded the U. S. 101st Airborne Division, which had been ordered up and told to hold on at all costs. Summoned to surrender, the American commander, General MacAuliffe, replied with one word "Nuts!" which then had to be interpreted as well as translated for a German emissary unfamiliar with American slang.

Bastogne not only slowed the German 5th Army down, it stopped them, for they expected to capture American fuel dumps, which were now denied them. On the northern side of the drive Dietrich was making even less headway. Mishandling his armor, he had passed the Schnee Eifel but he could not lever the Americans off the shoulder of the Eisenborn Ridge. With a narrow front he pushed west; at one point his troops began to break northward, west of Malmédy, but were thrown back after a hard fight. As they retreated, the Germans massacred a hundred American prisoners they could not take with them.

The Allied response was far swifter than the Germans had hoped it would be. Eisenhower canceled all his prospective drives and concentrated every effort on pinching out the German attack. The German irruption was such that Bradley's communications were cut with his northern troops, so Eisenhower gave temporary command in the north to Montgomery; in the south Patton's 3rd Army did a ninety-degree turn to the north and drove toward Bastogne, a feat of sudden improvisation to match anything in the war. Montgomery arrived in the north, "tidied up the front" as he termed it, and ordered the Americans to do what they were doing anyway, hold hard and counterattack as soon as possible. By Christmas Day—not the Christmas many had hoped to spend—the Germans had gone as far as they were going. They had created a long narrow salient, forty miles wide at its base, and about sixty miles deep. The very point of their advance was five miles short of the Meuse, so they never even really achieved their first objective, let alone distant Antwerp. The next day several Allied armored divisions crashed into their northern flank, and Patton's tankers fought their way through to the surrounded troops at Bastogne. Even more portentous, the sky cleared.

The minute the bad weather front moved off, the air was full of Allied planes. The fighter-bombers ranged everywhere over the battlefield, and nothing that moved and looked German escaped their attention. Hitler refused to be deterred by the pleas of his generals and frantically shuffled pins about on the battle map, as if that would relieve the plight of his soldiers, now fighting desperately to escape the trap their initial success had created for them. More than twenty Allied divisions pounded at the eleven German ones inside the salient, and slowly, the Bulge disappeared. The Germans fought hard and tenaciously, but by mid-January, though they were not cut off and trapped, they were back where they had started from. When the Battle of the Bulge ended, six weeks after it began, Hitler had succeeded only in delaying the Allies by that much time. He had lost 200,000 men and 600 tanks and most of his remaining aircraft. He had used up his last disposable strategic reserve, nothing remained to use against the Western Allies, and nothing against the Russians. As the front subsided into temporary quiet, and the dead were gathered off the blackened snow of the Ardennes, the Russians opened their main drive into Germany.

The great Russian summer offensive of 1944 had halted at the gates of Warsaw. Through the fall and into the winter there was savage fighting for the city of Budapest, but the northern front remained relatively quiescent. In this lull Hitler transferred substantial units westward to take part in the Ardennes offensive. He tried to fortify the Eastern Front but lacked matériel to create any real depth in his defensive positions.

The Red Army was now a fighting machine with few equals either for numbers or proficiency. German intelligence gave them numerical superiority of eleven to one in men, seven to one in tanks, and twenty to one in artillery and aircraft. Hitler refused to believe such figures, but he was not in the front line facing the ominous masses of Soviet soldiers. For the Reds the long hard road was nearly at an end. They were about to enter German territory, had already done so in East Prussia, and the Germans were now to be repaid in their own kind for their Russian policies. Where American and British tanks sported names like "Daisy Mae" and "Donald Duck," the Russians carried slogans "For the Motherland!" and "Death to the Germans!" The long harvest of bitterness was ripe for reaping.

The Russian offensive started January 12 when General Ivan Konev's First Ukrainian Front—a "front" being the equivalent of a Western Army Group—launched its attack just north of the Carpathian Mountains. Two days later General Zhukov picked up the gauge north of him, and the next day the entire front was aflame.

The Germans cracked before the onslaught, and within ten days the Russians had leaped forward nearly 200 miles, from Warsaw almost to Poznan, from the Vistula River to the Oder River. They were only fifty miles from Berlin.

Late February was spent in the clearing of the remainder of Prussia, the taking of Danzig, and the occupying of parts of Pomerania. The Germans fought hard to hold on to these ancient Germanic lands, but there was nothing more they could hope to achieve than a temporary stemming of the tide. Behind the thin line of fighting troops was a gigantic *sauve qui peut*, as more hundreds of thousands of refugees fled in terror to the westward. To the south, in the Danube Valley, the Soviets at last broke past ruined Budapest; Vienna fell in April and by the middle of that month, Nazi Germany consisted of a long narrow strip, roughly fifty miles to a hundred miles wide, running from the Baltic coast down into Yugoslavia and northern Italy. Once more the Russians paused momentarily for breath, brought up their supplies, and gathered for the final leap that would carry them into Berlin.

In the west the fighting went on through the early months of 1945. Hitler still refused to believe that the Allies were as strong as they were, or the Germans as weak as they were. He now directed that there be a second offensive, this time farther south in Alsace-Lorraine against General Devers' 6th Army Group. Launched on New Year's Day, it made steady if slow going. The Americans were prepared to sacrifice territory for time, and the gravest problem presented by the whole offensive was political. American troops of General Patch's 7th Army, and French of General Jean de Lattre de Tassigny's 1st French Army, had occupied the great city of Strassbourg. In Paris, de Gaulle feared Eisenhower was willing to give it up if tactically desirable and he absolutely refused to countenance the surrendering of a major French city to the Germans again, no matter how temporarily, or however sound the reason. The Americans held on the Moder River, and the Germans ran out of steam before the month was out. Once more they had frittered away badly needed troops; indeed, one of the reasons for the abortion of their offensive was the overriding necessity of drafting units off to the Eastern Front to try to stem the rampaging Russians.

Eisenhower then turned his attention to a large body of Germans still west of the upper Rhine around Colmar. Hitler refused to let them retreat in time, so American and French units surrounded them, and the "Colmar pocket" was effectively wiped out

by the first week of February. It was some measure of the serious-
ness of Hitler's Alsace offensive, and how much damage he could
really do now, that the one Allied army group involved could both
withstand the attack and undertake offensive operations of its
own at the same time. The Germans had bought time, but to what
purpose? so that more thousands of Jews and Slavs could be sent to
the gas chambers and ovens? Now, in mid-February, their time was
gone, and the Western Allies were ready for their drive into and
over the Rhine.

In the second week of February the Western Allied armies fell
on the Germans like an avalanche. It started in the north, where the
British and Canadian troops of Crerar's 1st Canadian Army drove
into the heavily fortified and forested area of the Reichswald. Germans, including new SS units that seemed to the Canadians to con-
sist largely of young fanatics, fought for every inch, and died in
their holes as the tanks and infantry ground steadily forward. On
Crerar's right Dempsey launched a pincer movement, and to the
right again Hodges' Americans, after more than a week of fierce
bludgeoning, fought their way past the Roer River dams, only to
find that the Germans had wrecked them at the last minute, creating floods to the northward that temporarily slowed the British
troops. But now the tempo increased on down the line, until battle
raged from Nijmegen all the way up the Rhine to the Moselle.
Twist, turn, and writhe as they might, there was no way the Germans could withstand the weight and ferocity of the Allied attack.
Eisenhower's "broad front" plan did not have initially a great deal
of strategic finesse, but at the tactical level, the Allies were now far
superior to their enemies. The stereotyped gum-chewing American
or Canadian farmboy had become a careful, cool professional
aware of his matériel predominance, calculating in his use of it.
Not since the days of Napoleon and Robert E. Lee, not even in
1940, had there been such sophisticated and successful application
of all arms of war. Tanks, artillery, air support, the indispensable
infantry, the endless logistical train—all combined harmoniously.
The Allied war machine worked like a great orchestra under the
hands of a master conductor, playing a majestic and terrible symphony of war. By the first week of March they were closed up to
the Rhine as far south as Coblenz.

The main axis of the advance was to have been north of the
Ruhr, into Germany across the Hanoverian Plain. On March 7,
however, after heavy fighting in the Heurtgen Forest, tanks of the
9th Armored Division in Hodges' 1st Army dashed forward to the

Rhine and took the great bridge at Remagen before the Germans could blow it up. Suddenly, the Allies were over the Rhine, and the great river barrier was breached. As American units poured across, the Germans mounted shaky and piecemeal counterattacks. Meanwhile, all the way back to Eisenhower in Paris the cry went out that the Allies had a bridge, then a bridgehead. Plans and movement orders were quickly shuffled about, and the long columns of trucks and tanks turned in their tracks and headed for Remagen. By the time the Germans did succeed in blowing the bridge the Allies were on the other side to stay. At the same time, Patton's infantry fought its way across the Moselle, working hand in hand with Devers' troops on the right. Within a couple of days Patton shook loose his armor, which tore great swaths through the disintegrating Germans facing them, and on the 21st, 3rd Army too was over the great river, at Oppenheim. By the time the smoke cleared west of the Rhine, more than a quarter of a million Germans had been taken prisoner, and another 50,000 to 60,000 killed, for about 10,000 Allied casualties. The German Army in the west had ceased to exist; the heart of Hitler's Germany lay open before the Allied armies.

Now at last the long trail that had begun years ago, when many of the British or American soldiers were still playing rugger or football in school, neared its end. In places the Germans held hard; but they could muster only about twenty-five real divisions against more than eighty Allied. As in 1918, more and more Americans were arriving, and behind them was an immense and ever-growing weight of armor and air power. The air forces were finally running out of targets, as Germany lay in ruins beneath the black wings of the Lancasters and the silver B-17s. Hitler issued the usual standfast orders, but there were fewer and fewer troops to obey him. Again he played musical generals, recalling Kesselring from Italy to take over the west; even Smiling Albert could find little to lift his spirits as the Allied advance picked up momentum. Within a week of its crossing, Patton's armor was seventy-five miles into Germany and Hodges had come the same distance from Remagen. Now Montgomery leaped the wider lower Rhine, and his troops too took off to the east. Within another week they had closed up to the Weser; even more important, they and the Americans to the south had closed a great ring around Model's Army Group B, trapped in the industrial area between the Rhine and the Ruhr. Model kept on fighting long after any hope of relief or breakout was gone. Not until the middle of April was the Ruhr

Pocket finally overrun, after Model had committed suicide; more than 300,000 German troops surrendered, the largest single surrender in the war.

By then the Canadians had cleared Holland, where they were so enthusiastically welcomed by the population that Canada and Holland still retain fond memories of each other more than thirty years later. The British were driving for Hamburg and the Elbe. Hodges was surrounding thousands more Germans in the Harz Mountains, and Patton, Patch, and de Lattre were heading toward the upper Elbe, the Danube Valley from the north, and the borders of Czechoslovakia. The great German highways, the *Autobahnen*, provided arteries for the endless columns of tanks roaring into the heart of the Reich. Stunned civilians, fed on the lies of unending victories, came out of their ruined homes to watch unbelievingly as the conquerors swept by.

The whole edifice was collapsing now. Down in northern Italy the U. S. 5th and British 8th armies, who had painfully inched their way forward to the last positions of the Gothic Line all winter, gathered their strength for the last battle. The Germans had, as usual, methodically strengthened their position; it seemed to matter little to them that they were fighting a hopeless war as the Russians were but forty miles from Berlin. On April 2 the Allied drive began, 8th Army leading off on the Adriatic coast. Twelve days later, with German reserves fully committed in the east, 5th Army began its attack. The Germans held hard for a week, then could stand the pressure no longer, and rolled back into the Po Valley. As they rushed northward in a desperate attempt to salvage what they might out of the wreckage, the 5th Army at last entered Bologna and Modena, then flowed out into the plain after them. For the next two weeks there was once more, as the summer before, a pursuit in open country, with the Allies fanning out over the flat river valley, heading for the distant mountains, Alps this time, no longer Apennines. The British pushed into and past Venice, heading toward Trieste. Americans reached the French frontier along the Riviera, then Turin, and drove toward the Brenner Pass and Austria.

In the midst of the confusion and the surrenders and the fighting, the Italian partisans, who had controlled considerable stretches of territory behind German lines for the winter, came out in the open at last. Mussolini's Salo Republic collapsed like the house of cards it was, and the ex-dictator thought now only of how to get away. He did not succeed. On April 28 he, some last supporters, and his mistress, Clara Petacci, were caught by the partisans near Lake Como. They were quickly tried and as quickly shot, and Benito Mussolini, once Il Duce, ended up hanging by his heels from a lamppost in front of a Milan gas station.

The next day the remnants of the Italian Fascist Army surrendered, and General von Veitinghoff negotiated a complete surrender of all the German forces in Italy, to take effect at noon on May 2. The long thankless task was over at last, and the Allies had finally won their victory, one that tied down countless German troops, but one that fell far short of Churchill's initial hopes and expectations.

As the Allied armies raced across western Germany several things preoccupied their attention. One was the rumor of a mountain fastness, the National Redoubt, deep in the heart of the Bavarian Alps. There were dark, troll-like yearnings in the mythology of nazism, and out of them Goebbels had created the idea of a stronghold where the last and greatest of the Nazis would gather, in the event of the *Götterdämmerung*, and fight on forever. The Allies knew only enough of this to worry about it and to orient some of their advance toward southern Germany in an effort to forestall it.

A second problem was Berlin itself. The Russians were now driving hard for it and were determined that they and not the Western Allies would conquer the enemy's capital. The Allied leaders had already agreed on the postwar disposition of Germany: it was to be divided into zones of occupation; Berlin was to be well inside the Russian zone but was to be garrisoned by all the Allies jointly. Churchill began to have second thoughts on this matter and privately wanted the Western Allies to get to Berlin first if at all possible. He was ultimately upstaged both by the speed of the Russian advance and by a decision made apparently unknowingly by Eisenhower. Aware that the Russian occupation zone would extend west to the Elbe, that anything taken east of the Elbe would cost American or British casualties and then have to be turned over to the Russians, Eisenhower agreed in an exchange of telegrams with Stalin that Berlin was not an objective of the Western Allies, and that his troops would make no attempt to take it. Out of the exigencies of this military decision was born the series of "Berlin crises" that has been a marked feature of the postwar world.

It was a time when decisions made in an ostensibly purely military context were foreshadowing the shape of the postwar political settlement. Thwarted in his intuition about Berlin, Churchill directed Montgomery to make sure that British forces crossed the Elbe and got as far as the Baltic coast. They eventually reached Lubeck on May 2, thus effectively sealing off the Danish Peninsula from the Russian advance. Meanwhile, as the American armies dashed on into south-central Germany, their political leadership was thrown into disarray by the death of President Roosevelt on April 12. He left the presidency and its problems to his vice-president, an all but unknown named Harry S Truman, a man whom Roosevelt had taken as vice-president purely for domestic political reasons, and who came to high office deliberately kept ignorant of most of Roosevelt's plans and problems. Truman was required to learn fast.

Roosevelt's death was perhaps Hitler's last surge of joy. In 1762 it had been Elizabeth of Russia's death that had saved Frederick the Great from being overrun, and by now Hitler, living out his life in a huge underground bunker in the center of Berlin, was convinced of the reality of historical parallels. After the news of the President's death Hitler and his entourage waited for the immediate change of sides they confidently expected.

Of course none came. The United States was not Germany, where one man's will could turn the world upside down. By now, too, the Allies were fully aware of the true nature of the Greater Reich. They had started to liberate the first of the concentration camps. They had come across the gas chambers, the crematoriums, the piles of shoes, of extracted gold fillings, the evidence of "scientific" experiments, the trenches filled with starved bodies, the barracks still filled with starvelings who could barely lift their hands to beg for water. The liberators were horrified, sickened—and hardened—by what they encountered. The first soldiers into German concentration camps would never think the bombing of Hamburg or Dresden to be morally reprehensible.

The final Russian drive of the war began on April 16. They reached Berlin on the 22nd and surrounded it on the 25th. The Germans continued to fight, with no hope of ultimate victory or rescue. Hitler remained in his underground bunker, summoning vast armies that lay face down on the Russian steppes, or dead on the slopes of the Apennines. Above ground the Russian artillery blasted away, building by building. The machine guns chattered in the night, and soldiers who had come all the way from Siberia worked their way into the ruined halls from which so much sorrow had emanated. One by one the blocks fell. Civilians huddled in cellars and shrank from the invaders; in the midst of the chaos life went on: the postal service continued to function, and while there was fighting on one side of a block, the mail was still being delivered on the other side. But the end could only be put off, not changed. On May 2 resistance collapsed, and the Russians began mopping up the die-hard survivors.

By then Americans and Russians had met at Torgau on the Elbe, and the Red armies had closed up to Wismar on the Baltic, where the British had just arrived. Germany no longer existed. The meetings that both sides had come so far to achieve went off amicably, even triumphantly, with toasts of vodka and wine, impromptu music, and a great deal of backslapping and fumbling phrases in foreign languages. There were some embarrassments. Eisenhower had agreed that Patton would not advance beyond Pilsen in Czechoslovakia. The Russians were slow; the Czech underground rose in Prague and then found the Americans for reasons unknown would not advance to their aid. The Czechs felt it was only a marginal improvement on their situation to be liberated by the Russians, but once again they had become pawns in the affairs of the greater powers.

Strange things happened in the confusion of the end of the war. Years ago Hitler had designated Hermann Goering as his successor; Goering had faded badly through the war, but now he came out of his sybaritic near-retirement; he sent Hitler a telegram, pointing out that Hitler could no longer direct events and asking if he were now free to take over. Hitler reacted with rage, sacked him, for whatever that was worth, and appointed Admiral Karl Doenitz as his successor instead. On May 1, as the resistance in Berlin was falling apart at last, Hitler married his mistress of many years, Eva Braun, and the two of them, followed by the Goebbels family—children and all, faithful sycophants to the end —committed suicide. Retainers burned and buried the bodies of the Fuehrer and his bride outside the bunker, disguising them successfully enough that for years there were rumors of Hitler being alive somewhere, usually in South America. The survivors of the bunker filtered away, some to be caught and shot by the Russians, some to make good their escape, to disappear into the shadows along with the Thousand-Year Reich. The next day Russian soldiers hoisted the red flag with the hammer and sickle on the landmarks of devastated Berlin.

Grand Admiral Doenitz, the second leader of Nazi Germany,

did not last long. The only possible task for him was to end it all as quickly as possible. The Germans still hoped that somehow they could play one side off against the other. In the last week of the regime there was a great effort to hold on the eastern side, and to encourage the Western Allies to come as far as they could. It came to nothing, since the Germans no longer had the power to hold anywhere. They then tried to surrender only to the Western Allies; this too was refused, and finally, on May 7, "V-E Day" for victory in Europe, German representatives signed the act of unconditional surrender. The European phase of World War II was over.

27. The Collapse of Japan

IN 1281 THE MONGOL EMPEROR Kublai Khan sent a great invasion fleet to conquer Japan. Instead of reaching the islands, the fleet was destroyed by a providential typhoon. The Japanese thought this was sent by the Sun Goddess to protect the Son of Heaven and the Land of the Rising Sun. Now the sons of the Son of Heaven were left to their own devices and, anxious to avoid the humiliation of living through defeat, a disgrace unthinkable, they flocked to form the suicide corps that became the twentieth-century version of the Divine Wind, the *kamikaze*. The young Japanese, sufficiently trained to get their planes airborne and guide them to a target, attended their own funerals, wrote letters home filled with touching passages of poetry, and climbed into their planes. Locked into the cockpits, loaded with bombs, carrying enough fuel to get to the American fleet but not back again, they took off to seek death for their Emperor.

Nearly all found what they sought, for the Americans were moving steadily closer. In the air long-range bombers from the Marianas and from bases in China were pounding the cities to ash and rubble; the island-hopping campaign was now reaching native Japanese territory, with the landings on Okinawa and Iwo Jima in the Bonins; and all the time, the submarines of the U. S. Fleet were strangling the Japanese.

At the start of the war the Allies and the Japanese both had about the same number of submarines in the Pacific: sixty-three Japanese, sixty-nine Allied, of which thirteen were Dutch, and the rest American. The Dutch were soon removed from the board, and the American submarine fleet was left to fight it out with the Japanese. Each had advantages and disadvantages, but as the war went on, the Americans, with a greatly increasing number of boats and with their more-sophisticated equipment (radar as it became available), and better sound gear than the Japanese, gradually gained the upper hand.

It was not that way in the beginning. The Japanese were the equals of the Americans and in one important way their superiors. They possessed an infinitely better torpedo, the famous "Long Lance"—bigger, faster, farther ranging than anything the Americans had. For the first two years of the war the Americans were plagued by faulty torpedoes that more often than not failed to detonate when they hit a target. Submarine captains would sail thousands of dangerous miles, fire their torpedoes at sure targets, and watch in frustration as the torpedoes either exploded prematurely or did not explode at all. It was late in 1943 before the faults were finally remedied and after that the American score mounted rapidly.

One of the ironies of the submarine war in the Pacific was that while the Japanese concentrated their submarines as adjuncts to their surface fleet and made relatively few attacks against the great support train or the amphibious fleets, the Americans almost immediately went after Japanese merchant shipping. The United States had entered World War I largely in protest over German unrestricted submarine warfare and she had approached war in the Atlantic over the same problem; but after Pearl Harbor, Americans immediately discovered the vital nature—and the vulnerability—of the Japanese merchant fleet.

At that time the Japanese possessed about eight million tons of merchant shipping. They had not organized their navy for a convoy system or provided escort vessels as the British had; they anticipated no need for them in east Asian waters. The result was a sinking rate that grew slowly but steadily until late 1943, and then dramatically after that. American submarines sank more than a thousand vessels—nearly five million tons of shipping. Air and surface action disposed of more than another thousand vessels—usually smaller coasters and trawlers—for another three million tons. New construction could not hope to replace the losses. By 1944 the Japanese Empire was starving for imports. The most significant losses were in oil tankers; ships could not put to sea for lack of fuel, planes could not fly, pilots could not be trained. The Americans, and the British submarines that operated out of Ceylon around the East Indies, were doing to Japan what the Germans had failed to do to Britain: they were strangling her. By the start of 1945 there were less than two million tons of merchant shipping left, far less than Japan required for the most minimal peacetime uses. Her distant garrisons in China and the north withered, and could not even be transported home. Paralysis gripped the empire.

Death came from the air as well as the water. By late 1944 the Americans were able to begin bombing the home islands. Their new long-range bomber, the B-29 Superfortress, son of the B-17, was designed specifically for the distances of the Pacific. Based on Saipan and Guam and in southern China, the Army Air Force reached out to hit Japan itself. This led to considerable strategic argument among the Joint Chiefs of Staff. The U. S. Navy had all but destroyed the Japanese fleet, and its job was virtually done. The navy ranged at will in the waters off Japan, searching vainly for further targets. The army believed that to defeat Japan it would be necessary to mount an invasion and overrun the entire country. The air force leaders, however—though officially they were still part of the army, they were acknowledged as all but independent—maintained that Japan could be defeated by bombing alone.

After the problems encountered over Germany, such a view might have seemed illusory. There were, however, significant differences in the Japanese situation: Japan's cities were much more vulnerable than Germany's, being largely built of highly flammable materials; her industry was more concentrated than the German and therefore made a better target; and equally important, the Japanese economy was far weaker than Germany's had been, so that the effects of a heavy bombing campaign would make themselves felt much earlier. Telling against these points were the meager successes to date. The early bombing results were not all that impressive. The bombers had a sixteen-hour round-trip from the Marianas; no fighters could fly that far as escorts, and the B-29s therefore had either to take heavy punishment from the Japanese home defense squadrons, or they had to bomb from prohibitively high levels with corresponding loss of accuracy. The real answer to these problems was to move in closer, to get nearer islands for the bomber bases and nearer ones still for fighter escorts. The Joint Chiefs of Staff therefore decided to take the island of Okinawa, the largest island in the Ryukyu chain and the first island that would be ancient Japanese territory, and Iwo Jima, a small island in the Bonin or Volcanic Islands due south of Japan, which could be used as an emergency field for the B-29s, and a base for fighter escort to Japan.

The Japanese too were revising their plans and ideas. General Tojo and his entire cabinet had resigned after the Battle of the Philippine Sea, to be replaced by another general, Kuinaki Koiso, but they were still far from ready to concede defeat. They had decided to create an inner, last-ditch defense line running from Iwo Jima to Okinawa, to Formosa, Shanghai, and southern Korea. Here they would hold on to the end. They would use suicide pilots as much as possible to destroy the American fleet. Then, if necessary, they would fight the last battle in the home islands. The Japanese believed that this would give the enemy only two alternatives: either negotiate peace, or pay a prohibitively high price to achieve unconditional surrender. In the event, the Americans found a third alternative.

Iwo Jima is an eight square-mile island of sulfuric sand and volcanic ash. It lies about 700 miles south of Tokyo. The Japanese had put radar stations on it to warn of the approach of the American Superfortresses, which regularly flew right over it on their way to and from Japan. They had also stationed fighters on its two airstrips, and these were a thorn in the side of the 20th Air Force as it sought to destroy Japanese cities. Knowing it was a desirable target, they also garrisoned it with 21,000 troops under General Tadamichi Kuribayashi, and these troops built some of the strongest defense works of the entire war—1,500 pillboxes and blockhouses, miles of trenches, hundreds of connecting tunnels. The highest point of the island, Mount Suribachi at its southern end, was thoroughly honeycombed. From this inner defense line there could be no turning back; no soldier could hope any longer for rescue from the Imperial Fleet. For its entire garrison, Iwo Jima was the end of the line.

The task of taking it was given to the U. S. Marine Vth Amphibious Corps, consisting of the 4th and 5th Marine divisions under General Harry Schmidt. The air force and the navy provided weeks of aerial bombardment, then heavy naval units closed in for three days of unrelenting pounding by battleships, cruisers, and carrier aircraft. On February 19 the Marines landed on a long black-sand beach, the southeastern side of the island. Under full observation from Mount Suribachi the 5th Marines fought their way across to the other shore, isolating the mountain from the rest of the island. To their right the 4th Marines reached the edge of Airfield No. 1, slowly began a right wheel, and stuck. The whole area was swept by small-arms and medium artillery fire. By night the Marines were firmly ashore, but at heavy cost; they had already suffered 2,400 casualties, including 600 killed.

It took four more days to secure Mount Suribachi. The Japanese stayed in their holes and caves, and the Marines went after them with grenades, large satchel charges that blew in the mouths of the caves, and flame-throwers. The mountain—it was little more than a bare hill—had to be taken yard by yard, and then, with the Japanese popping back up out of holes or shamming dead, retaken yard by yard again. On the 23rd the Americans finally reached the summit; the photo of a squad raising the American flag on the mountaintop became a symbol of the entire war for the United States.

On the flat the Marines ground forward, the 5th on the left, 4th on the right, and later the 3rd Division in the center. The Japanese resistance centered on a feature called the Motoyama Plateau, where their defense lines were particularly concentrated. Marine and naval air groups from the carriers flew close support missions: strafing, bombing, and dropping napalm—a jellied gasoline that clung to everything while it burned—within yards of the forward infantrymen. The second airfield was overrun and slowly the Japanese were confined to the northern end of the island. But just as the Americans had perfected their techniques of air and ground and naval coordination, so too the Japanese had worked on their defensive tactics. There were no more wasteful banzai charges that left the ground littered with Japanese dead and achieved little. Every soldier in every squad fought cannily and tried to take his enemy with him when he died. The Americans had estimated five days as necessary to secure the island; instead it took a month. During that time suicide planes hit the carrier *Saratoga,* putting her out of action for the rest of the war, and sank the escort carrier *Bismarck Sea* with a loss of 350 of her crew.

It was the end of March before the last opposition was finally hunted down. Of the 21,000 Japanese, about 200 were taken prisoner; the rest all died. The Marines and navy suffered 6,800 men killed and more than 18,000 wounded, the first island battle in which American casualties outnumbered those of the enemy. Twenty-six Medals of Honor were awarded, twelve of them posthumously. The island proved worth its cost. Even before the fighting stopped, crippled B-29s were sliding onto the landing strip, and by the end of the war more than 2,200 of them had landed there, carrying more than 24,000 crew members who had cause to bless the sailors and Marines who had taken Iwo. Yet in terms of the numbers involved, Iwo Jima was still the single bloodiest battle of the Pacific war; it was a grim portent of what lay ahead.

Some 850 miles west of the Bonins lies the beautiful island of Okinawa; the most important of the Ryukyus, it is almost exactly equidistant from Manila and Tokyo. It was the next American target, a narrow, irregularly shaped island about seventy miles long. Its position presented the Americans with considerable problems, but its taking was thought worth the effort. The chief difficulty lay in the fact that it was within reach of land-based aircraft from southern Japan, but beyond the range of similar American planes from the Philippines. Most of the air cover would have to be provided by carrier-borne planes, and that meant the carriers themselves must stay on station, especially vulnerable to suicide attacks. Intelligence reports estimated that there were about 75,000 Japanese troops on the island, so in that sense it was going to be a major fight; actually, counting impressed laborers and local defense forces, there were more than 100,000, so the Americans significantly underestimated what they were up against.

The advantages were that Okinawa was strategically located; it lay athwart all the lanes to the south. With its taking, Formosa would be isolated, and just as Japanese medium bombers could reach Okinawa from southern Japan, so American medium bombers could reach southern Japan from Okinawa. It was large enough to have several airfields and it had a number of good anchorages in its heavily indented coastline. Admiral Nimitz decided to sacrifice strategic surprise in favor of a campaign of isolating the island: the Japanese might know the Americans were coming; they would not be able to do anything about it.

The isolation of the components of the empire was already proceeding apace anyway. Late in 1944 and into 1945 units of the U. S. Fleet had scoured the waters north of the Philippines, striking at targets on Formosa and anyplace else that seemed worthwhile. As the spring of 1945 came on, the navy spread northward. Carrier aircraft hit islands throughout the Ryukyus, the B-29s struck increasingly at Japan itself, the submarines became bolder and bolder, ranging even in the Inland Sea between the home islands, searching for targets that became fewer and fewer as the war waned.

The landings on Okinawa went well; the fighting less so. At the end of March, the U. S. 10th Army, under General Simon Bolivar Buckner, seized several islands offshore to serve as close support bases. They then landed early in April on the southwest-central part of Okinawa. The landings were not heavily resisted by the Japanese, and the Americans had soon cut the island in half. Marine units then swung left, to the north, and moved up the island, while army units wheeled south and right. The Marines met little more than token opposition until they got as far north as the Motobu Peninsula, which they secured by mid-April after a hard fight.

In the south, however, the Japanese put up their battle. General Mitsuru Ushijima had been ordered to hold on until the kamikaze planes had driven off or sunk the American amphibious support ships; when that had been accomplished, he was to counterattack and drive the invaders back into the sea. To help himself hold out, he had built three successive fortified lines across the bottom of the island. The first of these was called the Machinato Line; then came the main Shuri Line, its high point around the old Shuri Castle which dominated the whole area; and finally there was a last-ditch position at the bottom of the island, across the Naha Plain, around the Yaeju Dake Escarpment.

The Americans were totally ignorant of these before they reached them, and they got a nasty surprise when they hit the Machinato Line on April 7. It took six days of very hard fighting, with heavy casualties on both sides, before Ushijima abandoned the first line and fell back to the second. His losses had been worse than he had anticipated, and the American fleet was still obviously offshore. But the Shuri Line was even stronger than its predecessor; once more the order was to hold on at all costs.

This the Japanese did. The Americans butted against the line, the strongest they had yet encountered in the Pacific war, time and time again, but could make little headway. Some of Buckner's subordinates asked to be employed on an amphibious end-run, but any possible landing places were open to Japanese artillery fire, and in the end there was nothing to do but fight it out. Ushijima had trouble with his juniors, too, and early in May he succumbed to their desire for an offensive. It was a costly mistake, to the matter of about 5,000 casualties, and its result was to exhaust the last Japanese reserve. Both sides were left pounding each other, like two tired fighters, and it took another two weeks for the American to pound the harder. On the 21st, Ushijima gave up the Shuri Line and carefully pulled his troops back to their last position. He tried to hold the Okinawan capital city of Naha, and it took two Marine divisions fighting house by house to clear it.

Not until mid-June did the army units break the position on the escarpment, after which it was a matter of time. Split up into segments, the Japanese were overrun in another week. Buckner was killed by an artillery shell three days before the battle ended; the Japanese commander committed suicide, and so did thousands of his soldiers and the civilians of the island. A decade after the war ended, huge piles of bleached bones could still be seen at the bottom of the cliffs in the southern part of the island.

The main object of the Japanese defense, of course, had been less the destruction of the American soldiers than their ships. While Ushijima's men bought time with their lives, the American fleet was tied to the island. They had expected this and had made precautions for it. The main combat element, Task Force 58—it was back to "Fifth" Fleet again—cruised eastward of the island. The amphibious forces were necessarily right offshore, with the carrier support groups beyond them. To seaward of everything was a screen of radar picket ships, destroyers, and escorts to give early warning of approaching kamikazes—and to be themselves targets for the suicide planes.

At the same time that the suicide attacks were launched, the Imperial Navy made its last challenge. Admiral Seiichi Ito gathered up what fuel he could find in the home islands—enough for a one-way trip—and sailed from the Inland Sea. He flew his flag in the great superbattleship *Yamato*—80,000 tons and armed with eighteen-inch guns—but all he could bring with him besides her was a cruiser and eight destroyers. There were no illusions about chances for survival as they put to sea. American submarines reported their presence before they were out of sight of land. At noon on April 7, carrier planes caught them halfway to Okinawa, hitting them so fiercely that the great *Yamato* soon went down. The cruiser and three destroyers went with her, and there was nothing left for the remainder to do but head back to Japan. They had just enough fuel to get there.

The kamikazes fared better. In the two months that the fleet stood off Okinawa they flew 1,900 missions, in addition to about 3,700 conventional aircraft sorties. They hit the radar pickets especially hard, and altogether they sank thirty-six American vessels, most of them smaller types. Four American carriers were damaged; so were three British, for with the tailing off of the naval war against Germany, a British Far Eastern Fleet had ap-

peared under the command of Admiral Sir Bruce Fraser. Ten battleships were hit, as well as thirteen other smaller carriers, five
cruisers, sixty-seven destroyers, and a large number of amphibious
vessels. About 5,000 sailors were killed. Yet the Japanese did not
dislodge "the fleet that came to stay," and in the end, both Okinawa
and the waters around it were secure.

The cost was high: nearly 50,000 American and Allied casualties, more than 12,000 of them killed. Japanese casualties were
even higher: 117,000, of whom 110,000 were killed. Nearly 8,000
aircraft were lost. If they still wanted to fight, the Japanese were
going to be hard pressed to find much material with which to do it.

By summer of 1945 the entire ramshackle empire was coming
apart at the seams. In the eastern part of the East Indies, Australian
troops under General Sir Thomas Blamey were operating in
Borneo, pushing the dispirited Japanese garrisons back into the
middle of the island. In the western Indies, British units were striking at will against oil refineries and other enemy-held targets. Troops
of the Netherlands East Indies Army were once more appearing
on the scene. In Burma the British were pushing steadily south.
Mandalay had fallen in March, and early in June an amphibious
landing retook the capital of Rangoon. Those forces that were not
isolated by the speed of the British advance were falling back toward the Thai border in disarray, and the long painful war in
Burma was all but over.

In China too the tide had turned at last. The Japanese were
still able to mount offensives early in 1945, and they also seized
full control of Indochina from the residual French garrisons that
had lived a shadow life for all these long years. But by early May
their last offensives had petered out. Their troops were low on
both morale and matériel—their best troops either used up or
long ago drafted off to more-active theaters—before the submarines
isolated them. By mid-May, they were pulling out of southern China
and seeking to reinforce Manchuria, conscious that the Russians
had won their war and were now hungrily eyeing territory in Mongolia and Manchuria. There were still hundreds of thousands—
millions—of Japanese soldiers under arms, but with the heart of
the empire being steadily gnawed away, the limbs were increasingly
powerless to affect its fate.

The heart was indeed being gnawed—by fire. It was not only
that the Americans were getting close enough to do real damage,
they had also changed their ideas of how to do it. The man chiefly

responsible for this was an irascible cigar-chewing flier named Curtis LeMay. Taking over the bombing effort against Japan early in 1945, he decided on major shifts of tactics. The B-29s would bomb at night, they would come down to 7,000 feet to do it, and they would use incendiary bombs in far greater proportions than had been done previously. The results were spectacular—and terrible. On the night of March 9 more than 200 Superfortresses dropped 1,600 tons of incendiaries and burned out the center of Tokyo; by the next dawn sixteen square miles of the city were gone. The bombers moved on to other cities: Yokohama, Nagoya, Kobe, Osaka. They bombed by night and by day. They brought their fighter escorts with them from Iwo Jima, and they took on the Japanese home defense squadrons and chased them out of their own sky. In two months they had virtually destroyed the five major cities of Japan; more than three million were homeless in Tokyo alone. Like the navy, the bombers now began to search for targets and they started hitting the smaller cities as well. Already suffering severe shortages, their sons and husbands gone to distant battles from which they never returned, the Japanese were slowly beginning to weaken. By late July and early August the Americans were sending over 800 bombers at a time, and army and navy planners were working up for the invasion of the home islands.

Initial planning called for an invasion of the southern islands in the fall, perhaps about the first of November. Then the Joint Chiefs of Staff estimated that in early 1946 they could invade the main island of Honshu, probably near Tokyo itself. There were major problems to all of this. Both the British and the Russians wanted to be involved. The Americans reluctantly conceded to British requests; the British had worked amicably with the U. S. Fleet in the Okinawa campaign, but there were occasional problems. The attitudes and usages were different, and the whole British Far Eastern Fleet was only large enough to serve as a task group in the 5th Fleet. To a certain extent the Americans did not want to be bothered with the British; to a rather larger extent than has generally been realized, they were hesitant about doing anything that would give the British a greater claim on the postwar settlement of affairs of east Asia. Few Americans were deeply aware of what the British had done in Burma but they were highly aware of what they, the Americans, had done in the western Pacific.

The Russians presented an even thornier problem. As early as 1943 the Joint Chiefs had insisted that a Russian declaration of war, and active participation in Manchuria at the very least, was a prerequisite for full victory against Japan. They still held this view in the early months of 1945, and it was largely American desire for Russian assistance against Japan that led them to make major concessions to Russian territorial ambitions in Europe as the war was ending there. By the beginning of the summer, however, things looked different; the bombing campaign was now achieving satisfactory results, and the earlier desire to base B-29s in Siberia was given up. Russian behavior in Germany had not made them appear unqualifiedly desirable as allies. Still, the general estimate was that it would cost the invaders one million casualties to overrun the home islands. It was obviously highly desirable that at least some of those casualties should be incurred by Russia rather than the United States. As August began, the matter of Russian intervention was still undecided.

When Harry S Truman became President of the United States, he inherited something of which he had so far been totally ignorant: one of the first things he was told was that the United States possessed a new weapon that was almost ready for action. It was a new type of bomb, whose power was created by the splitting of the atom. American and British scientists had been working for years on the problem of nuclear fission, engaged in a quiet but deadly laboratory race with the Germans. The race really began in August of 1939 when Albert Einstein wrote President Roosevelt a letter in which he announced the possibility of creating a controlled nuclear reaction. He pointed out that such a reaction might be used to create a powerful bomb. Almost six years and two and a half billion dollars later, the first atomic bomb in history, a test bomb, was detonated at Los Alamos, New Mexico. That was on July 16, 1945. Ten days later, at the Potsdam Conference in the ruins of Berlin, Truman and the other Allied leaders issued an ultimatum to Japan, calling on her to surrender immediately or suffer the consequences of new and terrible weapons. The ultimatum did not clearly spell out what the Americans possessed, and the Japanese, thinking they were already being hit with as terrible weapons as could be devised, announced that they would fight on. Truman authorized the dropping of the new bomb anytime after August 3.

This decision was not the result of agonizing thought. There had been discussion among military and political leaders and a committee made up of the scientists who had developed the bomb. There were a few half-hearted suggestions that the Japanese might be invited to a demonstration of the bomb, but these received little support. Bombs are made to be used, and the scientific committee concluded by recommending that a Japanese city be struck in such a way that it would provide a clear idea of the power now possessed by Japan's enemies. There were only four cities left in Japan that had not already suffered major damage. At first the Americans thought to bomb Kyoto, but it was a religious and cultural shrine, the traditional home of the Emperors in the time of the Shogunate. They decided instead to go for Hiroshima, a manufacturing city of about seven square miles and 350,000 population.

The great bomb was dropped from a B-29, jauntily named *Enola Gay*; an aerial bomb, it exploded above the center of the town at nine-fifteen on the morning of August 6. There was a blinding flash and a great boiling gust of flame, smoke, and dust rising to a mushroom-shaped cloud that towered over the city. Within a second, four square miles of the city vanished, nearly 80,000 people died, and Hiroshima was destroyed. In the midst of terror and devastation, the atomic era was born.

There was great rejoicing in the Allied world. The enemy had been smitten. It was not known at the time that the enemy was already trying to surrender. A new government, under Premier Suzuki, had approached Soviet Russia as early as May with a request that Russia mediate the conflict. However, the Japanese insisted upon surrendering on terms, and the Russians had their own designs for eastern Asia, which did not include a premature end to the war before the Russians got what they wanted, so the hesitant attempts came to nothing. Now, on August 8, the Russians declared war on Japan and Red Army troops poured over the Manchurian border and began a rapid occupation of territory. The next day the Americans dropped a second atomic bomb, on the city of Nagasaki. Again the giant fireball and the mushroom cloud appeared in the sky, and again thousands disappeared in a sudden flash, leaving other thousands behind to suffer the maiming and radiation poisons.

That was enough. The Japanese government, at the urging of the Emperor—the army was determined to fight on—offered on the 10th to surrender, its only condition being that the person of the Emperor and the imperial throne remain inviolate; the Allies responded positively, and on August 14 the Japanese accepted the terms and surrendered. The Russians raced troops into the Korean Peninsula and southern part of the island of Sakhalin, and the first American units arrived in Japan on August 26. At the end of the month the U. S. Fleet anchored at last in Tokyo Bay, under that most magnificent of mountains, Fujiyama, whose white peak hung like a cloud in the western sky. General MacArthur and representatives of all the Allied nations were aboard the flagship, the new battleship *Missouri,* and on Sunday, September 2, the Japanese delegation, a small, rather innocuous-looking group whose leaders wore formal morning dress, signed the official surrender documents. The war was over. Its legacy and its suffering remained.

28. Winning and Losing

THE YEARS FROM 1939 to 1945 may well have seen the most profound and concentrated upheaval of humanity since the Black Death. Not since the fourteenth century had so many people been killed or displaced, disturbed, uprooted, or had their lives completely transformed in such a short space of time. The years at the very end of the war, and immediately following it, once more illustrated the old adage that it is quite possible to win the war and lose the peace.

The areas where the war was actually fought lay in ruins. Northern France, the Low Countries, the great sweep of the North German Plain, and a wide swath running all the way to Moscow and Stalingrad lay devastated. In the countryside it was not so bad; targets had been fewer, and there were substantial areas that had been bypassed by the fighting. The farther back in the country one lived, and the more basic one's life, the less likelihood there was of its being disrupted. But the cities were heaps of rubble, railways were lines of craters and twisted rails, bridges were down, canals and rivers blocked, dams blown, and electric power grids destroyed. Most of the paraphernalia of modern society was damaged to greater or lesser degree.

Across the world in the Pacific and east Asia it was the same. Inestimable amounts of property damage had been done, huge nations—China and Japan—and the great empires of the colonial powers were all brought low. Millions of starvelings shambled among the ruins, seeking some way to put their lives back in order.

Yet the damage was by no means universal. Those countries of the industrialized world that had fought in the war, but had not experienced any fighting on their own soil, had prospered almost in direct proportion as the combat zones had suffered. If in Europe and Asia it might be hard to tell the winners from the losers, there was absolutely no question that the North Americans were winners.

*   *   *

Some of the tale, if by no means all, is told by the casualty figures. About seventy million men, at one point or another throughout the war, had borne arms. Roughly seventeen million of them were killed by the war, along with at least another twenty million or more civilians who had the misfortune to live in the wrong place at the wrong time.

These casualties were extremely unevenly divided. On the Axis side Germany mustered nearly twenty million soldiers, though her peak strength at any one time was just over ten million. Three and a quarter million died in battle, slightly more than that from nonbattle causes, and seven and a quarter million were wounded. Over another million were "missing"; they simply disappeared. The Homeland was utterly devastated, unlike in World War I when the Germans had fought the war on other people's soil. The Italians had put just over three million men in the field and suffered casualties of just over 10 percent, about half of which were deaths. The navy and merchant marine were gone, and the country from Salerno to the Po Valley had been fought over. Italian figures ironically had to be entered on both sides of the ledger. By far the greatest portion of her losses were incurred in the Axis' interests, but she also had 20,000 deaths while fighting on the Allied side after 1943.

Japan had put nearly ten million men in service; her peak strength at any one time was just over six million. Her casualty figures were incredibly distorted by western standards. In European armies it was normal to suffer two or three wounded for every death, especially in this war where battlefield medicine and new drugs came into prominence. But Japan had almost two million military deaths, and only 140,000 wounded. About half a million civilians were killed in the bombing campaign, and more than 600,000 wounded. Additionally, well over a quarter of a million Japanese taken prisoner at the end of the war by the Russians as they moved into Manchuria were not returned to Japan.

In human terms, the price of victory for the winners was as high as that of defeat for the losers. China had lacked the industrial potential to mobilize as many men as her population would otherwise have supported. The greatest number reached by the Chinese armies never exceeded much over five million. Yet her war had gone on ever since 1937, and she had more than two million deaths in battle. With primitive medicine and conditions, many of her soldiers who died would have lived had they been in a European army. Her civilian deaths from bombing and military action, or from the indirect consequences of war and its upheaval such as starvation, were never counted, but must have numbered well over five million and may have been ten million.

Of the European allies, Poland had merely exchanged two conquerors for one of them; in a sense the entire population of Poland could be numbered among the casualty figures. France did better. The French collapse had been mercifully quick, though "merciful" was hardly the term one would have applied at the time. At their peak the French mustered five million men under arms. Roughly a quarter of a million were killed in battle or died from other causes; another half million were wounded or missing. Nearly half a million civilians were either killed or deported to Germany for shorter or longer periods. Thirty thousand French men and women were shot by firing squads. The northern part of the country had been fought over twice, the second time especially destructively as a result of the Allied air interdiction campaign. Industrial France was nearly as devastated as Germany. In spite of the physical destruction though, France was not as badly off after World War II as she had been after the first war. She was not entirely a country of old men and widows. Yet the second battle had sapped her vitality almost more than the first one, and the postwar governments found themselves forced into strenuous efforts just to get Frenchmen to reproduce. Building up families hardly seemed worthwhile to many if they were to be cannon-fodder every generation.

Britain had had her finest hour, and she had paid grievously for it. Her merchant fleet was cut nearly in half in spite of wartime building, many of her cities were extensively damaged, her national debt had risen to the stratosphere, her great financial holdings had disappeared. She had mobilized nearly six million men, and a quarter million of them had died in Europe, in North Africa, and in Burma. Another 400,000 were wounded or missing. As with France, the bill had been far short of that for World War I, but in 1918 the British had at least possessed the satisfaction of being sure they were the winners. In 1945 it looked instead as if they had exhausted themselves only to give way to the United States and Russia.

Of the two new superpowers, Russia had had the deeper wounds. Stalin said that Britain paid for the war in time, the United States in materials, and the Russians in blood. More than six million Soviet soldiers died and more than fourteen million were wounded. Well over ten million, perhaps as many as twenty million, civilians were killed by the war and the callous policies of both their own and their enemy's governments. Nearly a million square miles of Russian territory lay devastated. More Russian soldiers died in the one great battle for Stalingrad than Americans did in all the battles in the entire war.

The United States too had paid heavily for her part in the war. Her great advantage lay in the two huge oceans that protected her. Except for an attempt by one submarine-launched Japanese seaplane, notable only for its uniqueness, and the ill-fated Aleutian campaign, no bombs had fallen on the American continent. The only enemy soldiers to set foot in the United States were prisoners of war, delighted to be there. More than sixteen million Americans served in the armed forces; 400,000 of them died, and more than half a million were wounded. It was the most costly war in American history up to that point, far more so than World War I, and nearly equaling in deaths the losses on both sides of the American Civil War. For a people who, as late as December 6, 1941, had thought it was not their war, the Americans had made a major contribution to the Allied victory.

They had also made an immense profit from it. One of the great ironies of the American war effort was the way it was borne disproportionately by a relatively few people. In spite of the huge numbers of men in service, second only to Russia among the Allies, only a limited number of them saw combat. Those who did saw probably far too much of it. Infantrymen grumbled about the air force policy of rotating men home after fifty combat missions, but that was much fairer than leaving soldiers in combat units until the war either killed them or ended. For the vast majority of Americans it was a good war, if there can be such a thing. People were more mobile and more prosperous than ever before. The demands of the war brought the United States out of a deep depression, created new cities, new industries, new fortunes, a new way of life. Families and friendships were strained by the disparities of fate, and after the war the government passed a wide range of legislation in what was really an attempt to allow those who had fought for twenty-one dollars a month to catch up with those who had stayed home and made ten times that much.

With the end of the war there began a vast folk wandering. At its most organized it consisted of such incredible organizational feats as "Operation Magic Carpet," by which the United States brought huge numbers of soldiers back home from the distant battle fronts. Day after day the ships steamed into New York, or Hampton Roads, or San Francisco, and disgorged their hordes of khaki and olive-drab cargoes. The immense processing machine that had turned them into soldiers, sailors, and Marines a world ago now turned them back into civilians, gave them their back pay, papers that said they were entitled to the small bits of ribbon that meant so much to them and so little to others, other papers that said they had served their country honorably and well, and turned them loose to pick up the threads—if they could find them—of their former lives. Most of them made the transition easily; the "trained killers" prophesied by some psychologists quickly turned out to be normal young men, though they told some bizarre stories and were apt to be impatient when reminded by salesmen that prices had risen "because there's been a war on, y'know." The demobilization of the Allied armed forces was by no means the least spectacular of operations carried out in the course of the war, and in most places it was carried out with impressive smoothness. In the United States alone, nine million men were back in civilian life in less than a year.

At the other end of the scale this migration consisted of millions of uprooted Europeans and Asians, trying desperately to get to homes and families that in many cases no longer existed. Long columns of people—ex-prisoners, freed slave laborers, orphans, widows, old people—straggled along the roads of Europe, fleeing the Russians still or trying to get back to Poland or Rumania. In the cities the survivors poked aimlessly among the rubble. The German governmental organization had stood up under the Allied attacks until the very end of the war, but with the collapse of the regime everything else seemed to collapse as well. The conquerors soon found themselves, with good or ill will, organizing a new life for the conquered. "Displaced Person" camps were established, the enemy peoples were screened as to their roles under the former governments, public services were reestablished, war trials were initiated, and the victors, with the help of the vanquished, were soon busily engaged in sorting out the spoils and the debris.

Just as individuals benefited or suffered disproportionately from the war, so did nations. As the European war neared its end, the Allied leaders had turned their attention to postwar problems. There had been assorted ideas of what to do with Germany, the most famous of them probably being the plan by the American Secretary of the Treasury, Henry Morgenthau, that Germany ought to be stripped completely of her industrial capacity and turned into a pastoral country, transformed from industrial giant into operetta-sized states. Such an attempt to turn the clock back a hundred years was doomed to failure, but was typical of at least one end of the spectrum of ideas about the Germans.

Throughout the war substantial numbers of Allied officials had tried to deal with the problems foreseen for the postwar situation; to some extent they succeeded, but to a larger extent, they were outpaced by events. As early as December of 1941 Joseph Stalin had tried to get the British to agree that at the final reckoning, Russia would be left in possession of everything she had held at the start of hostilities—her start of hostilities, which would have given her all the Baltic states and most of eastern Poland—plus major acquisitions at the mouth of the Danube. At that time and through most of 1942, Russia was carrying the major burden of the conflict, and it was obviously in her interest to settle the future while that was still the case. With German soldiers but a few miles from Moscow, Stalin could point to the immense sacrifices his country was making, and demand equally immense rewards. For that very reason the British and the United States preferred to wait before settling anything definitively.

In May of 1943 the Soviet Union dissolved the Comintern, or "Communist International" office, the organization responsible for encouraging the spread of communism abroad. This was designed to reassure Russia's partners of her increasing respectability, and in October, when the Allied Foreign Ministers met at Moscow, the Americans, British, Chinese, and Russians—the wartime "Big Four"—announced they would not resort to military force in other states for selfish purposes after the end of the war. This Moscow meeting was a preliminary for the Tehran Conference, and at Tehran Stalin agreed he would take part in the United Nations. Problems over who would be admitted and what kind of powers each state should have plagued the early discussions on the organization; at one point the Russians wanted a seat in the assembly for every "republic" of the Union of Soviet Socialist Republics, whereupon the United States replied that then the Americans must have a seat for every state of the union. This kind of difficulty, and especially the veto question, haunted both the Tehran meeting, and even more the Yalta Conference held in February of 1945. By that time it was obvious that there were to be four major trouble spots.

The most distant of these was Japan. The Americans expected to have to invade Japan and wanted Russian help to do so. The

Russian price was higher than the Americans wished to pay—southern Sakhalin, the Kurile Islands, and concessions in Manchuria. The dilemma they faced over Japan made the Americans much more susceptible to Russian demands in Europe than they might otherwise have been. They did not at this time have the atomic bomb. In February they had instead the fanatical resistance on Iwo Jima to deal with.

A second thorny question was the perpetual one of the Balkans. The Western Allies had no wish to see the Russians on the shore of the Mediterranean, but their view was compromised by the fact that the Communists had been the most effective anti-German fighters in the Balkan states. In December of 1943 Stalin had agreed that the Russians would not dominate Czechoslovakia. In October of 1944 he and Churchill met at Moscow and Churchill slipped him the famous piece of scratch paper which said that Russia could dominate Rumania and Bulgaria, Britain would dominate Greece, and they would split the difference in Yugoslavia and Hungary. Actually, the Russians got all but Greece, where the British landed troops in the middle of an incredibly chaotic turmoil, and Yugoslavia, where Tito's brand of native communism was strong enough for him to stay clear of the Russians' embrace. The final determinant on the Balkans, as elsewhere, was who had troops on the ground and was strong enough to keep them there.

The major impediment to Allied harmony continued to be Poland. Relations between Stalin and the legitimate Polish government-in-exile in London had gone from bad to worse. From demanding that Russia's western border be the Nazi-Soviet demarcation line of late 1939, Stalin went to setting up a rival Polish Communist government, to letting the Warsaw Poles destroy themselves in the premature rising against the Germans. There was absolutely nothing the British could do about it. Poland was as far beyond their reach in 1944 and 1945 as it had been in 1939. At Yalta the Big Three—Stalin, Roosevelt, and Churchill—the latter two reluctantly, agreed that Poland was a Russian sphere of influence. In terms of the reasons for which she had declared hostilities in 1939, at Yalta Britain conceded that she had lost the war. The Western Allies then compounded their defeat over Poland: they agreed to repatriate, often against their will, Poles and other east Europeans who had fought on the Allied side. Many of those who had given so much for Allied victory got their rewards in Russian labor camps.

By the time the loss of Poland was accepted, Germany was

collapsing. The Allies had reached some common agreement on the postwar policy to follow: denazification, disarmament, demilitarization, punishment of war criminals, reparations, and dismantling of war industries. Britain had suggested in 1943 that Germany should be occupied this time, and the idea had been refined through 1944. The occupation zones were formalized at Yalta, with the British and Americans taking a lesser zone to give the French a share. Both Berlin and Vienna were to be administered by a quadripartite agreement. The divisions were as much in response to the existing situation as anything; for example, the United States took the southwestern zone because American troops were on the Allies' right flank. The question of access to Berlin did not seem especially troublesome; they agreed that Russia and the government of the Polish state—whoever should form it—would divide Prussia between them. Since it was their Poland, the Russians got the frontier between Poland and Russia that they wanted, and then obligingly moved Poland's western frontier that much farther into Germany. The Allies never got to a definitive agreement on reparations or deindustrialization, in spite of having initially agreed they wanted both. In all four of the major areas, as soon as the euphoria of victory wore off, the basic rifts in the Allied views were bound to emerge, and they did so.

Nor were these by any means the only problem areas. Of almost equal complexity were the questions of what to do with the former colonial empires. The British, the French, and the Dutch might all think that they were going to move back into Southeast Asia and the islands and go on as they had before the war. The local inhabitants felt differently. One of the reasons the United States had been reluctant to have British units operating with it in the Pacific was that Americans tended not, even after their wartime cooperation, to be overly sympathetic to British ideas of empire. The Americans had promised independence to the Philippines, and after the war they granted it. The British did not want to see their empire go.

They recognized it could never be quite the same again, but it was one thing to recognize that rationally, and another to slide back into a peace of exhaustion and a third-power status, as if Great Britain were Switzerland or Sweden. They knew the inhabitants of the empire were profoundly stirred by the war. On the one hand there had been the immense contributions of Indian and colonial troops, the great strides made in the modernization of

Indian industry. On the other there had been the destruction of the great myth, that some men are inherently superior to others because their skin is white. Without the acceptance by both parties of that myth, colonialism was no longer possible, and Burmese or Indians who had watched long pathetic columns of British and Australian prisoners being prodded along by stolid Japanese could never accept the myth again. There had been great unrest in India during the war; Churchill's government had sent out Sir Stafford Cripps to talk to the Indian leader, Mohandas Gandhi. Cripps was hardly the man for the mission—Churchill once remarked of him, "There but for the grace of God goes God"—and when he promised Gandhi independence after the war if India helped win it, Gandhi castigated the offer as "a post-dated check on a crashing bank." India wanted out of the empire, and Britain would no longer be able to hold her in. Burma went too, and eventually so did most of the rest of the nonwhite areas.

If the British ultimately faced colonial realities, the French and Dutch resolutely refused to. Even more than the British, they needed their empires to bolster their sagging self-esteem. The Dutch came back to the Indies to find the British engaged in desultory operations against the Indonesian nationalists. The Dutch took over the fight, which lasted in an on-again off-again fashion until 1950. The French finally got forces back into Indochina to find near-chaos. The old prewar garrisons had held on, under Japanese domination, until 1945. The Japanese had then imprisoned and massacred most of them. The few survivors and escapees made their way to Chinese Nationalist lines, where they were received as allies. Then they were turned over to the arriving Gaullist French, who imprisoned and tried them as Vichyites. Meanwhile, at the Japanese surrender the British moved forces into southern Indochina, and they eventually handed over power to the French. Northern Indochina was occupied by the Nationalist Chinese, and they, instead of waiting for the French, gave over the reins to the Indochinese nationalists, led by a local guerrilla named Ho Chi Minh. Negotiations between the Indochinese and the French broke down, and late in 1946 they started shooting at each other, in a war that went on until 1954. The residual legatees of the fighting were the Americans, and they in turn got involved in a war that in many ways would scar the United States more than World War II had done.

Nor was fighting and confusion confined to Southeast Asia. The Japanese collapse in China was nearly matched by the exι of Chiang Kai-shek and the Nationalists. As the Russians ꞈared war on Japan and flooded down into Manchuria, the Chinese Communists, who had virtually sat the war out in northeast China, now emerged once again. They and the Nationalists were soon locked in a battle which ended only in 1949, when the remnants of the Nationalists fled to Formosa, and the Communists definitively took over mainland China. By then, the Cold War had already begun; in both Europe and Asia the powers of the West appeared in disarray and on the defensive. How, men asked, could so much have gone wrong so quickly?

For many Europeans or Asians, the answer to that question was simple: it was all the fault of the Americans. They were big, brash, bumbling innocents in the international jungle. All they wanted to do after the war was go home and forget about it. Few of the writers who took this line seemed to carry it to the logical conclusion. It was more soul-satisfying to berate the Americans for being excessively well-behaved internationally than to castigate the Russians for being extremely ill-behaved internationally.

In fact, the United States and its leaders did make a whole series of mistakes and misassessments. The basic one was in assuming that Soviet Russia was very much like themselves. They thoroughly underestimated the paranoia that resulted from a combination of the traditional Russian fear of invasion from Europe and the outcast nature of communism itself. They equally underestimated the degree to which all their other allies were exhausted. They believed that Great Britain and France and Italy all ought to be able to fend for themselves now that the crisis was over. They cut off Lend-Lease to Britain, bringing about a near-collapse of the island's economy; they turned over a large part of their occupation zone in Germany to the French. President Truman was unpopular, and the American public wanted an immediate end to wartime measures. Few people realized how close to complete collapse western Europe was. The same thing happened in China, where it looked as if the Chinese Nationalists and Chiang Kai-shek ought to be able to put their own house in order at last. In fact they failed miserably, due more to their own inherent weaknesses and shortcomings than anything else, and China went Communist by the end of the decade.

If the Americans made mistakes in their response to the immediate postwar situation—and assuredly they did—they were largely tactical mistakes. On a longer view the picture looked different. The brilliant foreign servant George F. Kennan pointed out in one of his books that much that happened at the end of the war was the result of the line-up of participants during it. The fact was that all the democracies, if they had hung together, were still not strong enough to defeat all the totalitarian states, if *they* had hung together. In a long fight, and barring the sudden advent of nuclear power on only one side, the United States, Britain, France, and China, could probably not have defeated Germany, Italy, Russia, and Japan. It was Hitler's falling out with Stalin, and the great Russo-German war, that upset this equation, and only with the aid of one of the two major totalitarian states could the democracies defeat the others. That being the case, and the Stalinist dictatorship remaining the Stalinist dictatorship, the same country that had purged its hundreds of thousands before the war, it was inevitable that at the end of hostilities the Russians would seek to gain as much as they could in as many places as they could. Churchill, who had some growing awareness of the problem, fell from power at the end of the war, and Britain no longer had the strength to stop the Russians even had she possessed the will to do so. Churchill had spoken perhaps more presciently than he realized when he said that if Hitler invaded Hell, Churchill would make favorable reference to the devil. At the end of the war the Soviet "devil" simply called in his bills. Between an exhausted east Asia and west Europe, and a United States which did not realize the true nature of its ally—any more than anyone else had really done—the Communists got a great deal of what they wanted.

One more of the reasons they did so was that the war had created two huge power vacuums. In Europe the always-delicate equilibrium between France, Britain, Germany, and Russia had now been destroyed. This was hardly realized by the Americans, and the result was a flow of the remaining power, Russia, into the vacuum. Only when the Americans recognized that western Europe itself might well be overrun did they reverse their immediate postwar policies and start their own return into that vacuum, by means of increased troop commitments, through NATO and various other regional pacts, and through the Marshall Plan, which helped Europe immeasurably toward recovery. Finally, they found it necessary to rebuild what is now the major power of western Europe, West Germany, and the irony of history and geography came full circle.

Traditional power structures were disrupted in Asia as well. Japan and China had balanced each other off throughout the last century. Now Japan was utterly defeated, occupied by the United

States, and China was in a state of near-collapse. The Communists moved into China, with some Russian support, but soon developed an independent Chinese line. And the United States suddenly found itself the heir of Japan's defense problems. Before 1941 the United States' military frontier had been somewhere in mid-Pacific. Now it had moved forward to the Asian rim—to Korea, the Formosa Strait, and ultimately, as the colonial powers receded from the area, to Vietnam.

In both Europe and Asia, it would only be as the local powers slowly regained strength that the two superpowers would be able to disengage, the Americans more or less willingly, as they tried to get NATO to take more care of itself, or as they attempted hesitantly and not entirely successfully to withdraw from East Asian adventures, and the Russians unwillingly. In fact, the Russians tried to ease off in the mid-fifties, but found that it was impossible to lessen the pressure a little bit, for fear the whole system would blow up on them. Hence the repression of Hungary in 1956, where they slammed the lid back down, and the later repeat performance in Czechoslovakia in 1968. After such a major dislocation as that of 1939-45, it was inevitable that there should be a long and complicated working out of the new power realities, a working out that has taken much longer than the fighting of the war itself.

What, then, was it all for? Were the old diplomatic deals merely to be repeated with new participants? Were so much suffering and sorrow, so much sacrifice and bravery only of concern to the unwitting pawns in the game? Was the cynicism of the definition of a war crime—that it was something committed by members of the Axis—to triumph after all? Was there in the last analysis no difference between the one side and the other?

In 1784 an innocuous-appearing German professor in Konigsberg published a short article. The professor's name was Immanuel Kant, and the article had the tortuous and eminently German title of "Idea for a Universal History with a Cosmopolitan Intent." In it Professor Kant took issue with the current Enlightenment fiction that if society could only get rid of a few more evils, utopia was just around the corner. Utopia, he said, will never arrive. Progress there is and undeniably so. But every step forward to a new level of progress, every solution to one generation's difficulties, brings with it a new set. Each era has to solve its own problems, and in doing so it uncovers or even creates problems for its successors.

World War II certainly created as many problems as it solved; in fact, as most wars seem to do, it may have created more. That does not mean it was not worth fighting, or need not have been fought. Evil does exist in the world—it undeniably existed in Hitler's world of death camps and extermination groups—but without the possibility of evil, there is no true choice and no true freedom. In its basic definition, "Freedom" means the right to choose one's own way to die. The servants of the dictators left that choice to their masters and fought and died for causes that even they themselves often found odious. The men and women of the free nations who fought World War II chose their own doom. If they could not destroy every evil, they destroyed the most vicious of their day. If it is part of the sadness of the human condition that they could not solve the problems of their children's generation, it is part of the glory of it that they so resolutely faced their own.

Bibliographical Note

BOOKS ON WORLD WAR II, or specific aspects of it, are almost legion. They range from the official histories, to memoirs by virtually all the important participants, to specific histories of certain aspects of the struggle. The following list makes no attempt to be all-inclusive. The titles contained in it are bound together by nothing more philosophical than the fact that I have found them useful or interesting over the course of several years of reading and teaching about the Second World War.

To have listed works as they refer to each chapter would have entailed a substantial amount of repetition. They are placed here, therefore, more or less by theater or by general topic, and the reader wishing to obtain more material on a certain campaign or aspect of the war ought to have little difficulty in finding a title.

GENERAL. Those who want a fairly complete list of works available on the war, at least until the time of publication, might look at J. Zeigler's *World War II: Books in English, 1945-65* (Hoover Institution Bibliographical Series: 45, Stanford, 1971). A smaller work is L. Morton's *Writings on World War II* (Washington, 1967). The official histories vary in length, quality, and readability; one cannot get very deeply into World War II without them, but it is more convenient to list the series here than to try to refer to individual volumes. Most complete is the series entitled *The United States Army in World War II* (Washington) which runs to well over a hundred volumes, with some still appearing, and covers all aspects of the army's activities during the war. Rather more concise, and the most popularly written of all of them, is S. E. Morison's *History of United States Naval Operations in World War II* (Boston, 1947-62, 15 vols.). W. F. Craven and J. L. Cate edited *The Army Air Forces in World War II* (Chicago, 1948-58, 7 vols.). The British have also put out an extensive series of official histories, in a somewhat convoluted sequence of titles. The most important are the several volumes in the *Grand Strategy* series, by different authors, and the most useful in a purely military way is probably C. Webster and N. Frankland's *The Strategic Air Offensive Against Germany* (London, 4 vols., 1961). There are also histories of the different campaigns, and then a second group that are written in a more popular style, and some of these will be referred to below.

In a war as wide-ranging as World War II an atlas is indispensable, and the best is volume II of V. J. Esposito's *West Point Atlas of American Wars* (New York, 1958). This will be a useful place to mention general treatments of the war. There are several of these, and among the best are V. J. Esposito's *A Concise History of World War II* (New York, 1964); L. L. Synder's *The War: A Concise History, 1939-45* (New York, 1965); and B. H. Liddell Hart's *History of the Second World War* (New York, 1972). The approaches taken in these vary from the strictly factual, as in Esposito, to the highly interpretive, as in Liddell Hart.

THE PREWAR PERIOD. For general surveys of this period there are H. S. Hughes' *Contemporary Europe* (Englewood Cliffs, 1961), D. Thomson's *Europe Since Napoleon* (New York, 1958), and R. A. C. Parker's *Europe, 1919-1945* (New York, 1969). On naval disarmament, E. B. Potter's *The United States and World Sea Power* (Englewood Cliffs, 1955) is useful. Later revisions of this standard work have appeared under the authorship of E. B. Potter and Admiral C. Nimitz entitled *Sea Power*.

France and its weaknesses in the interwar period have been dealt with at length by a large number of writers. A useful survey is P. Ouston's *France in the Twentieth Century* (New York, 1972). Books that deal both with the fall of France in 1940 and as well extensively with the background to that event are Alastair Horne's *To Lose a Battle: France, 1940* (London, 1969), and William L. Shirer's *The Collapse of the Third Republic* (New York, 1969). The best-known book on the French Army between the wars is Paul Marie de la Gorce's *The French Army* (New York, 1963). Aidan Crawley's *De Gaulle* (Indianapolis, 1959) is a readable account of this towering French leader. Many works aside from Shirer and Horne deal specifically with the collapse of 1940, and those will be mentioned later.

On Great Britain between the wars the latest volume in the Oxford History of England, A. J. P. Taylor's *English History*

1914-1945, came out in 1965. It is Professor Taylor who takes the line that World War I was good for Great Britain. General studies of the period are A. F. Havinghurst's *Twentieth Century Britain* (London, 1962), and C. L. Mowat's *Britain between the Wars, 1918-1940* (London, 1955). This is as good a place as any to mention Winston Churchill's monumental and indispensable six-volume *History of the Second World War* (Boston, 1948-53), the first part of the first volume of which deals with the background to the war. Though the work is indeed indispensable, one is constrained to recall Churchill's remark to his officers when they disagreed with him, "Mind you, gentlemen, history will support my view—at least the way I write it, it will." Some of the seminal figures in the R. A. F.—Dowding, Harris, and Tedder—are treated briefly in Sir Michael Carver, ed., *The War Lords: Military Commanders of the Twentieth Century* (Boston, 1976), which has short biographies of most of the major commanders of World War II.

As to the revisionist states, the most readable biographies of Mussolini are Sir Ivone Kirkpatrick's *Mussolini: A Study in Power* (New York, 1968) and Christopher Hibbert's *Benito Mussolini* (London, 1962). A general history is Dennis Mack-Smith's *Italy: A Modern History* (Ann Arbor, 1959). Ciano's various *Diaries* (London, 1947-52), gives general insight to the later Fascist period. The standard work on the Spanish affair is Hugh Thomas' *The Spanish Civil War* (London, 1961), in which the author deals with the fact of German intervention on the Republican as well as the Nationalist side. Italy's increasing ties with Germany are covered in F. W. Deakin's *The Brutal Friendship* (London, 1962) and Elizabeth Wiskemann's *The Rome-Berlin Axis* (London, rev. ed., 1966).

The reader can drown in works on Nazi Germany. For general background there is G. Mann's *The History of Germany since 1789* (New York, 1968). More specifically on the Hitler era is T. L. Jarman's *The Rise and Fall of Nazi Germany* (London, 1955). On Hitler himself there is W. L. Shirer's *The Rise and Fall of the Third Reich* (New York, 1960), which is as much a biography of Hitler as it is a general history of his era, and Alan Bullock's *Hitler: A Study in Tyranny* (London, rev. ed., 1974). *Mein Kampf* appeared in an unexpurgated English edition (Boston, 1943). There have been collections of Hitler's speeches, his table talk, his war conferences. The army's role in the New Order has been extensively examined. Probably best known are Walter Goerlitz' *History of the German General Staff* (New York, 1954); J. W. Wheeler-Bennett's *The Nemesis of Power: The German Army in Politics, 1918-1945* (London, 1961); Gordon Craig's *The Politics of the Prussian Army, 1640-1945* (New York, 1964); and Telford Taylor's *Sword and Swastika: Generals and Nazis in the Third Reich* (Chicago, 1969).

There has been less written on Japan. For a general survey there is P. H. Clyde and B. F. Beers' *The Far East: A History of the Western Impact and the Eastern Response (1830-1965)* (Englewood Cliffs, 4th ed., 1966). For the thirties there is Richard Storry's *The Double Patriots: A Study in Japanese Nationalism* (Boston, 1957). F. F. Liu's *A Military History of Modern China* (Princeton, 1956) treats the period of undeclared war, as the name implies, largely from the Chinese side.

R. D. Charques' *A Short History of Russia* (New York, 1956) and F. L. Schuman's *Russia since 1917* (New York, 1957) are general histories of Russia covering this period. On foreign policy there are the brilliant works of George F. Kennan: *Soviet Foreign Policy, 1917-1941* (New York, 1960), and *Russia and the West under Lenin and Stalin* (New York, 1961). The standard biography is I. Deutscher's *Stalin: A Political Biography* (London, 1967). Albert Seaton's *Stalin as Military Commander* (New York, 1976) in the first chapters contains material on the interwar years.

As might well be expected, there is a large amount of material on the United States, though the majority of it is domestic in orientation. A good general survey is G. H. Knoles' *The United States: A History since 1896* (New York, 1960); also A. S. Link's *The American Epoch* (New York, 1959). The classic biography of Roosevelt is Arthur Schlesinger's multi-volume *The Age of Roosevelt* (Boston, 1959). On diplomacy, isolationism, and neutrality there are F. R. Dulles' *America's Rise to World Power, 1898-1954* (New York, 1955); Selig Adler's *The Isolationist Impulse* (New York, 1957); George F. Kennan's *American Diplomacy, 1900-1950* (Chicago, 1951), which touched off the argument about the relativity of diplomacy; and B. Rausch's *Roosevelt: From Munich to Pearl Harbor* (New York, 1950). On American naval and military posture there are R. F. Weigley's *History of the United States Army* (New York, 1967) and his *The American Way of War: A History of United States Military Strategy and Policy* (New York, 1973), both volumes in the series of the Macmillan Wars of the United States; and for the navy there is Thaddeus V. Tuleja's *Statesmen and Admirals: Quest for a Far Eastern Naval*

Policy (New York, 1963). The definitive study of Japanese-American prewar relations is H. Feis' *The Road to Pearl Harbor* (Princeton, 1950). Needless to say, Pearl Harbor has received extensive examination. The most popular accounts are W. Lord's *Day of Infamy* (New York, 1957) and J. Toland's *But Not in Shame* (New York, 1961), which takes the story from Pearl Harbor to Midway. Probably the best specific study to date is Roberta Wohlstetter's *Pearl Harbor: Warning and Decision* (Stanford, 1962).

Many of the works listed above, especially those dealing with Germany and with Britain during the period 1937-39, have sections on the prewar crises. As mentioned in the text, A. J. P. Taylor's *The Origins of the Second World War* (New York, 1962) is crucial, whether or not one agrees with it. Particularly condemnatory of Chamberlain is Leonard Mosley's *On Borrowed Time* (New York, 1971). The standard biography is by K. Feiling, *The Life of Neville Chamberlain* (New York, 1946). For the Czech crisis there is K. Eubank's *Munich* (Norman, Okla., 1963). Laurence Thompson's *The Greatest Treason: The Untold Story of Munich* (New York, 1968) is a very readable account that emphasizes both the banality of the participants and the divisions among them.

THE EUROPEAN WAR: EARLY PHASE. For all the campaigns there are the standard histories of the war referred to earlier. Probably the two best surveys of the Polish campaign are R. M. Kennedy's *The German Campaign in Poland, 1939* (Washington, 1956) and a French work, R. Jars' *La Campagne de Pologne* (Paris, 1949). An interesting personal memoir is Gen. K. S. Rudnicki's *The Last of the War Horses* (London, 1974). The question of western inactivity is dealt with in J. Kimche's *The Unfought Battle* (New York, 1968).

For the Russo-Finnish War there is V. A. Tanner, *The Winter War: Finland Against Russia, 1939-1940* (London, 1961). Marshal Mannerheim wrote his *Memoirs* (New York, 1954), dealing extensively with relations between his unfortunate country and Soviet Russia.

On the Norwegian campaign B. Ash wrote *Norway* (London, 1964), and K. Derry's *The Campaign in Norway* (London, 1952) is a useful volume of the United Kingdom Military Series. The British naval officer Captain D. G. F. W. MacIntyre wrote a study specifically on *Narvik* (New York, 1960). A more recent study of the whole war in Norway is R. Petrow's *The Bitter Years: The*

Invasion and Occupation of Denmark and Norway, April, 1940-May, 1945 (New York, 1974).

As might well be expected, the greatest military collapse of the twentieth century, the fall of France, has inspired an enormous amount of investigation. The general studies by W. L. Shirer and Alastair Horne have already been referred to. Gamelin wrote his memoirs, and Reynaud wrote his twice, the first under the title, in French, *France Has Saved Europe* (Paris, 2 vols., 1947), and again under the title, in its English translation, *In the Thick of the Fight* (New York, 1955). It is safe to say that memoirs of French generals and politicians have been somewhat critically received in the English-speaking world. This is equally true of de Gaulle's *War Memoirs* (London, 3 vols., 1955-60). Probably the most balanced account of events by a close observer is General Sir E. Spears' *Assignment to Catastrophe* (New York, 2 vols., 1954). Marc Bloch's *Strange Defeat* (New York, 1949) has also been highly regarded. For the actual military operations, there are several works available. T. Draper's *The Six Weeks' War* (New York, 1944) is old but surprisingly good, considering it was published while the war was still on. *The Battle of France, 1940,* by Colonel A. Goutard (New York, 1959) takes the view that France's defeat was pure military stupidity and cuts the ground from under all the generals who claimed they were outnumbered, or undermined by their politicians. The most thorough examination of the whole matter is J. Benoist-Mechin's *Sixty Days that Shook the West* (London, 1963). The British part in the campaign is covered by L. F. Ellis' *The War in France and Flanders, 1939-1940* (London, 1953), another volume of the U. K. Military Series. Dunkirk has been extensively dealt with. A recent treatment is R. Collier's *The Sands of Dunkirk* (London, 1961). Airey Neave in *The Flames of Calais* (London, 1972) discussed the question of the utility of the heroic defense of the old town by the British. The latest treatment of Mers-el-Kebir is Warren Tute's *The Deadly Stroke* (New York, 1973).

The Battle of Britain has received nearly as much attention as the Battle of France. Any of the following are useful: E. Bishop's *The Battle of Britain* (London, 1960); Basil Collier's *The Battle of Britain* (New York, 1962); A. McKee's *Strike from the Sky: The Story of the Battle of Britain* (London, 1960); and Drew Middleton's *The Sky Suspended: The Battle of Britain* (London, 1960). A slightly different tack is taken in Constantine Fitzgibbon's *The Blitz* (London, 1957). Perhaps the best single short work is Len

Deighton's *Fighter: The True Story of the Battle of Britain* (London, 1977), written recently enough to dispose of many of the common myths, and also concentrating heavily on the matériel and equipment problems of both sides. Several works have appeared on the question of the German invasion. P. Fleming's *Operation Sea Lion* (New York, 1957) is a good general coverage. R. Wheatley's *Operation Sea Lion: German Plans for the Invasion of England, 1939-42* (Oxford, 1958) is the most detailed study.

The Battle of the Atlantic has also received extensive coverage. General works on the naval war are S. W. Roskill's *White Ensign: The British Navy at War, 1939-1945* (Annapolis, 1960); P. K. Kemp's *Key to Victory: The Triumph of British Sea Power in World War II* (Boston, 1957); F. Ruge's *Der Seekrieg: The German Navy's Story, 1939-1945* (Annapolis, 1957); T. V. Tuleja's *Twilight of the Sea Gods* (New York, 1958). More specifically there is D. G. F. W. MacIntyre's *The Battle of the Atlantic* (London, 1961). One of many books on the U-boats is Heinz Schaeffer's *U-Boat 977* (London, 1952). The classic technical study on the big ships is S. Breyer's *Battleships and Battlecruisers, 1905-1970* (New York, 1973), and the best account of the convoys is in M. Middlebrook's *Convoy* (London, 1976). Almost all of the big-ship episodes have received treatment by one or more writers. A. McKee's *Black Saturday* (New York, 1959) is about the sinking of *Royal Oak;* Dudley Pope wrote *Graf Spee: Life and Death of a Raider* (New York, 1956). On the *Bismarck* there are R. Grenfell's *The Bismarck Episode* (London, 1948), and W. Berthold's *The Sinking of the Bismarck* (London, 1958). D. Woodward dealt with *The Tirpitz and the Battle for the North Atlantic* (New York, 1953), and F.-O. Busch with *The Sinking of the Scharnhorst* (London, 1974), on which there is also M. Ogden's *The Battle of the North Cape* (London, 1962).

THE WAR IN THE MEDITERRANEAN. For the naval aspects of the struggle in the Mediterranean there are the general naval histories referred to above; there is also D. G. F. W. MacIntyre's *The Battle for the Mediterranean* (London, 1964). S. W. C. Pack covered *The Battle of Matapan* (London, 1961). A view from the other side is M. A. Bragadin's *The Italian Navy in World War II* (Annapolis, 1957).

On Greece and Crete there is C. Buckley's *Greece and Crete, 1941* (London, 1952); A. Heckstall-Smith and H. T. Baillie-Grohman's *Greek Tragedy, 1941* (New York, 1961); and R.

Crisp's *The Gods Were Neutral* (London, 1960). More especially on Crete there is A. Clark's *The Fall of Crete* (New York, 1962), and J. H. Spencer's *The Battle for Crete* (London, 1962).

For the desert campaign in Libya and Egypt there are D. W. Braddock's *The Campaigns in Egypt and Libya, 1940-1942* (Aldershot, 1964), and A. Moorehead's *The Desert War* (London, 1965): Correlli Barnett wrote a critique in *The Desert Generals* (London, 1960); Sir John Smyth's *Leadership in War, 1939-1945* (New York, 1974) is also mostly on North Africa, and R. Crisp's *Brazen Chariots* (London, 1959) is an evocative memoir of tank-fighting in the desert. Rommel has attracted a good deal of attention, as in P. Carell's *The Foxes of the Desert* (London, 1960), H. W. Schmidt's *With Rommel in the Desert* (London, 1951), and D. Young's *Rommel* (London, 1950). A more recent assessment is D. Irving's *On the Trail of the Fox* (London, 1977). J. H. Robertson's *Auchinleck: A Biography of Field Marshal Sir Claude Auchinleck* (London, 1959) is the standard work on this ill-used general. Alan Moorehead's *African Trilogy* (London, 1959) is an evocative view by one of the leading correspondents of the war. A. Heckstall-Smith, in *Tobruk* (London, 1959), dealt with the sieges of that small but once-famous port. Much British attention has focused on the great battle of El Alamein, but a lot of what was written on it can now be disregarded. Field Marshal Sir Michael Carver wrote a straightforward military account, *El Alamein* (London), in 1962; F. Majdalany did the same in *The Battle of El Alamein: Fortress in the Sand* (London, 1965), and so did Brigadier C. E. L. Phillips, *Alamein* (London, 1962). Carver mused on how strange it was that it all seemed so easy after Montgomery arrived, and wondered why it had been so hard before that. Montgomery in his *Memoirs* (London, 1958) rather implied that the answer to that lay in his own brilliance, and it was not until the publication of F. W. Winterbotham's *The Ultra Secret* (New York, 1974) that the real answer—the British reading of the Germans' codes—came out. A far-from-flattering view of the man some regarded as Britain's greatest soldier of the war is in Alun Chalfont's *Montgomery of Alamein* (New York, 1976).

Canadians retain strong views on the Dieppe raid, and the best single volume on that unhappy incident is T. Robertson's *The Shame and the Glory: Dieppe* (Toronto, 1962).

The invasion of French North Africa and the campaign there has attracted relatively less attention than many areas of the war. Auphan and Mordal's *The French Navy in World War II* (Annapolis, 1959) has chapters on it. Some of the agonies of divided French loyalties are dealt with in M. Blumenson and J. L. Stokesbury's *Masters of the Art of Command* (Boston, 1975). The Darlan episode has many of the earmarks of a modern spy story, and P. Tompkins in *The Murder of Admiral Darlan* (New York, 1965) attempted to unravel the threads of it all. Martin Blumenson's *Kasserine Pass* (Boston, 1967) thoroughly covered that traumatic event, and his *The Patton Papers* (Boston, 2 vols., 1972-74) deals with Patton's role in North Africa, as well as the rest of the career of that enigmatic soldier. A biographical treatment is L. Farago's *Patton: Ordeal and Triumph* (New York, 1964).

THE RUSSO-GERMAN WAR. There are several good general histories of this titanic conflict. Alexander Werth's *Russia at War* (New York, 1964) is especially good on the domestic Russian attitudes and Alan Clark's *Barbarossa: The Russian-German Conflict, 1941-1945* (New York, 1965) is a standard account. A popular German treatment is P. Carell's *Hitler Moves East, 1941-1943* (Boston, 1965). H. Guderian's *Panzer Leader* (New York, 1965) has a good deal to say on the use of armor in Russia. The Red Air Force is treated in R. Wagner's *The Soviet Air Force in World War II* (New York, 1973). A more personal account is H.-U. Rudel, *Stuka Pilot* (New York, 1958). A. Dallin's *German Rule in Russia, 1941-1945: A Study in Occupation Policies* (New York, 1957) in a dispassionate way does much to explain the passion of the Russian reaction to the German invasions. An excellent long-range military-historical study which compares Hitler's invasion with previous western ones is W. G. F. Jackson's *Seven Roads to Moscow* (New York, 1958). As the great turning point of the war, Stalingrad has received much attention. J. E. Vetter edited *Last Letters from Stalingrad* (MacLean, Va., 1955). General studies are V. I. Chiukov's *The Battle for Stalingrad* (New York, 1964), H. Schroter's *Stalingrad* (London, 1960), and R. Seth's *Stalingrad—Point of Return* (London, 1959). The French Guy Sajer wrote a moving memoir in *The Forgotten Soldier* (New York, 1971). On the siege of Leningrad the best-known work is Harrison Salisbury's *The Nine Hundred Days* (New York, 1969). Also good is L. Gouré's *The Siege of Leningrad* (Stanford, 1962). The post-crisis period has been relatively less well covered, and for that the general histories of the Russo-German war are most helpful.

OCCUPATION, RESISTANCE, BOMBING, AND ALLIED PLANS AND PROBLEMS. Much is available on the German occupation of Europe and the resistance to it. The best general survey is Henri Michel's *The Shadow War: European Resistance, 1939-45* (New York, 1952). Eugene Davidson in *The Trial of the Germans* (New York, 1966) deals with some of the key German figures and their policy roles. A short treatment is in G. Wright's *The Ordeal of Total War* (New York, 1968), and Kenneth Macksey wrote generally on *The Partisans of Europe in the Second World War* (New York, 1975). On the Vichy question there are R. O. Paxton's *Parades and Politics at Vichy: The French Officer Corps under Marshal Petain* (Princeton, 1966) and *Vichy France: Old Guard and New Order, 1940-1944* (New York, 1972). Many British writers have covered the connections between the indigenous Resistance operations and the Allied attempts to channel and control them. There are also works on specific countries. P. Howarth edited a work on *Special Operations* (London, 1955); R. Collier's *Ten Thousand Eyes* (London, 1958), B. Marshall's *The White Rabbit* (Boston, 1953), and D. Howarth's *We Die Alone* (New York, 1955) are all worth reading. D. Lampe covered the Danish Underground in *The Savage Canary* (London, 1957), and T. Bor-Komorowski, commander of the Polish Home Army, wrote *The Secret Army* (London, 1950). A great deal has appeared on the French Resistance, perhaps in some respects as an antidote to France's military collapse. A general review is P. de Vomecourt's *Who Lived to See the Day: France in Arms, 1940-45* (London, 1961); an intriguing personal memoir, which also tells much of both the strengths and weaknesses of the Resistance movement, is Henri Frenay's *The Night Will End: Memoirs of a Revolutionary* (New York, 1976). The beginning of the Resistance is covered in Martin Blumenson's moving *The Vilde Affair* (Boston, 1977), from which the story of listening to the BBC is taken.

The effectiveness of strategic bombing remains a subject of contention, and there is a vast number of books on the subject generally, and on specific aspects of it. For the technical side of what the bombers could do, and how they were developed, William Green's *Famous Bombers of the Second World War* (New York, 2 vols., 1959-60) is the work to start with. There have been many German works on the air war; notable were C. Bekker's *The Luftwaffe War Diaries* (New York, 1972), which is regarded as a semi-official history; W. Baumbach's *The Life and Death of the Luftwaffe*

(New York, 1960); and K. Bartz' *Swastika in the Air: The Struggle and Defeat of the German Air Force, 1939-1945* (London, 1956). Adolf Galland, the famous German fighter pilot chief, wrote *The First and the Last: The Rise and Fall of the German Fighter Forces, 1938-1945* (New York, 1957). Specific raids or periods of the campaign have been covered by many writers. Martin Caidin wrote *The Night Hamburg Died* (New York, 1960), and also *Black Thursday* (New York, 1960), about the first American daylight raid, against Schweinfurt. D. J. C. Irving wrote *The Thousand Plane Raid* (New York, 1966), which describes the first of Harris' "big raids." Martin Middlebrook's *The Nuremberg Raid* (New York, 1974) is an engrossing examination of the technical and human problems of the air war.

The Cold War prompted extensive discussion of how the wartime allies got along, and why they fell out. The newest book to review the problem, and what is likely to be the last memoir by one of the participants, is W. Averell Harriman's *Special Envoy to Churchill and Stalin, 1941-1946* (New York, 1975). An exhaustive study of the three great powers and their leaders is H. Feis' *Churchill, Roosevelt, Stalin: The War They Waged and the Peace They Sought* (Princeton, 1967). The Australian war correspondent Chester Wilmot touched off the great debate about American naivete in *The Struggle for Europe* (London, 1952); though his conclusions have often been challenged, the work remains fascinating reading. Even earlier than that, W. L. Neuman wrote *Making the Peace, 1941-1945: The Diplomacy of the Wartime Conferences* (Washington, 1950). The enduring question of what to do with Germany is treated in J. L. Snell's *Wartime Origins of the East-West Dilemma over Germany* (New Orleans, 1962). Slightly more specific were A. Armstrong's *Unconditional Surrender: The Impact of the Casablanca Policy upon World War II* (New Brunswick, N. J., 1961) and M. Viorst's *Hostile Allies, FDR and Charles de Gaulle* (London, 1965); Roosevelt's treatment of de Gaulle during the war does a great deal to explain de Gaulle's treatment of the United States in the sixties.

THE EUROPEAN WAR: LATER PHASE. The general problem of continuing in the Mediterranean and invading Italy, as opposed to going directly into France, is discussed in M. Howard's *The Mediterranean Strategy in the Second World War* (New York, 1968), and in Trumbull Higgins' *Soft Underbelly: The Anglo-*

American Controversy over the Italian Campaign, 1939-1945 (New York, 1968). An overview of the entire Italian campaign is in E. R. R. Linklater's *The Campaign in Italy* (London, HMSO., 1951). Separate episodes have been covered in detail by several writers. Hugh Pond wrote *Sicily* (London, 1962) and *Salerno* (London, 1961). Cassino as the crisis of the campaign has had a number of chroniclers; an interesting German view is R. Bohmler's *Monte Cassino* (London, 1964). British accounts are C. Connell's *Monte Cassino, The Historic Battle* (London, 1963), and F. Majdalany's *The Battle of Cassino* (Boston, 1957). Martin Blumenson wrote on the Rapido incident in *Bloody River* (Boston, 1970), and H. L. Bond in *Return to Cassino: A Memoir of the Fight for Rome* (London, 1964) provided an infantry officer's moving recollection of the fight. R. Trevelyan did a similar memoir in *The Fortress: A Diary of Anzio and After* (London, 1956), while L. J. W. Vaughan-Thomas in *Anzio* (London, 1961) wrote a general British account, and Martin Blumenson in *Anzio: The Gamble That Failed* (London, 1963) did a general American account. An overall critique of the great May offensive is W. G. F. Jackson's *The Battle for Rome* (New York, 1969). Concerning the attempt to crack *The Gothic Line* there is the work by D. Orgill (New York, 1967).

For a general account of the German failures in France there is M. Shulman's *Defeat in the West* (New York, 1948). Sir Frederick Morgan filled in the pre-invasion period in *Overture to Overlord* (New York, 1950). The great invasion itself has been thoroughly covered. Paul Carrell produced the most popular German account, *Invasion—They're Coming!* (London, 1962). On the Allied side is David Howarth's *D-Day, the Sixth of June, 1944* (New York, 1959). S. L. A. Marshall did another of his classic studies of men under fire in *Night Drop: The American Airborne Invasion of Normandy* (Boston, 1962), and Cornelius Ryan popularized a phrase with *The Longest Day: June 6, 1944* (New York, 1959). For the post-D-Day period there is E. M. G. Belfield and H. Essame's *The Battle for Normandy* (London, 1965), Alexander McKee's *Caen: Anvil of Victory* (London, 1964), and E. Florentin's *The Battle of the Falaise Gap* (London, 1965). A general account of the campaign of France after it opened up is Martin Blumenson's *The Duel for France, 1944* (Boston, 1963). General Montgomery also covered the whole campaign in *Normandy to the Baltic* (London, 1947). A French view is R. Aron's *De Gaulle*

Triumphant: The Liberation of France, August, 1944-May, 1945 (London, 1964). Southern France has not been as thoroughly covered as northern France, but Marshal de Lattre de Tassigny's memoir, *The History of the First French Army* (London, 1952), is basically on that campaign. The July Plot is covered in virtually all the books on Hitler and his Germany, and specifically in Constantine Fitzgibbon's *20 July* (New York, 1956), and R. Manvell and H. Fraenkel's *The July Plot: The Attempt in 1944 on Hitler's Life and the Men Behind It* (London, 1964). Arnhem has had many recorders. C. Hibbert's *The Battle of Arnhem* (London, 1962) is a general account. Cornelius Ryan in *A Bridge Too Far* (New York, 1974) tried to repeat for Arnhem what he had done with D Day.

A general treatment of the campaign of Germany is G. Blond's *The Death of Hitler's Germany* (New York, 1954). All of the innumerable works on Hitler deal with his last days, often at stultifying length. The German missile campaign is the subject of Basil Collier's *The Battle of the V-Weapons* (London, 1964). As might be expected, the Battle of the Bulge has been thoroughly examined. Specific aspects of it were covered by S. L. A. Marshall in *Bastogne* (Washington, 1964), and R. Gallagher in *The Malmedy Massacre* (New York, 1964). The most popular general treatment was John Toland's *Battle: The Story of the Bulge* (New York, 1959). Most of the material on the Russian advances comes from German works, but there is available Maria Galantai's *The Changing of the Guard, The Siege of Budapest, 1944-1945* (London, 1961). A classic popular general account of the closing days of the war in Europe is John Toland's *The Last 100 Days* (New York, 1956). On the western breakthrough into Germany there is C. B. MacDonald's *The Battle of Heurtgen Forest* (Philadelphia, 1963); MacDonald's *Company Commander* (Washington, 1947) has become a classic memoir. R. A. Briggs did *The Battle for the Ruhr Pocket* (West Point, Ky., 1957), R. W. Thompson wrote *The Battle for the Rhineland* (London, 1958) and *The Eighty-Five Days: The Story of the Battle for the Scheldt* (London, 1975), and K. W. Hechler did *The Bridge at Remagen* (New York, 1957). On the Bavarian Redoubt there is R. G. Minott's *The Fortress that Never Was: The Myth of the Nazi Alpine Redoubt* (London, 1965), and finally, on Berlin itself, S. E. Ambrose's *Eisenhower and Berlin, 1945: The Decision to Stop at the Elbe* (New York, 1967), and A. Tully's *Berlin, the Story of a Battle*

(New York, 1963), as well as the many works on Hitler suggested above.

THE WAR IN EAST ASIA AND THE PACIFIC. Far Eastern geography is so complicated that an atlas such as Esposito's excellent *West Point Atlas of American Wars* referred to earlier is indispensable for dealing with the war in that area. Potter's *U. S. and World Sea Power* and John Toland's *But Not in Shame* have excellent coverage of the whole war and of the period up to Midway respectively. The fall of Singapore, as a major disaster, has attracted many British writers. A most interesting general account is Noel Barber's *A Sinister Twilight: The Fall of Singapore, 1942* (Boston, 1958). The outstanding single event of the Malayan campaign was the sinking of the *Repulse* and the *Prince of Wales;* on this there are R. Grenfell's *Main Fleet to Singapore* (London, 1951) and B. Ash's *Someone Had Blundered: The Story of the Repulse and the Prince of Wales* (London, 1960). The collapse of the Malay Barrier is treated in R. C. H. McKie's *The Survivors* (Indianapolis, 1953), and the horrible conditions of fighting in New Guinea will be found discussed in R. Paull's *Retreat from Kokoda* (London, 1960). The extremely complex battle at Midway is made clear for the reader in Thaddeus V. Tuleja's *Climax at Midway* (New York, 1960) and Walter Lord's *Incredible Victory* (New York, 1967); it was Professor Tuleja who made sense out of contradictory movement charts by discovering that some Japanese carriers had their island structures on the port side, whereas most carriers carry them to starboard. The view from the other side is in M. Fuchida and M. Okumiya's *Midway: The Battle that Doomed Japan* (Annapolis, 1955).

China continues to be the poor relation in writing on the war. General Stilwell published his view of affairs in *The Stilwell Papers* (New York, 1948), and so did his successor in *Wedemeyer Reports!* (New York, 1958). Barbara Tuchman took a longer view in *Stilwell and the American Experience in China, 1911-1945* (New York, 1970). A more specialized study is L. Anders' *The Ledo Road: General Joseph W. Stilwell's Highway to China* (Norman, Okla., 1965).

For the British campaign in Burma there is a short military critique, G. F. Matthews' *The Re-Conquest of Burma, 1943-1945* (Aldershot, 1966), and J. Bagaley's *The Chindit Story* (London, 1954). A. F. Campbell wrote *The Siege* (London, 1956) on

Kohima, and on the companion battle, Sir G. C. Evans and Anthony Brett-James covered *Imphal* (London, 1962). The classic memoir of the campaign is Field Marshal Sir William Slim's *Defeat into Victory* (London, 1956).

Virtually all of the island operations have been covered by official histories or monographs, either by the U. S. Army or the Marine Corps. For the general course of these and the development of the operational methods, there are F. O. Hough's *The Island War: The United States Marine Corps in the Pacific* (Philadelphia, 1947), and J. A. Isley and P. A. Crowl's *The U. S. Marines and Amphibious War: Its Theory and Practice in the Pacific* (Princeton, 1951), the standard study of the Marines' war. There are also Robert Leckie's *Strong Men Armed: The United States Marines Against Japan* (New York, 1967), E. B. Potter and Admiral C. W. Nimitz' *Triumph in the Pacific* (Englewood Cliffs, 1963), and H. M. Smith and P. Finch's *Coral and Brass* (New York, 1949).

More specific works are Brian Garfield's *The Thousand Mile War* (New York, 1969) on the Aleutians; also R. L. Sherrod's *Tarawa: The Story of a Battle* (New York, 1954). On Guadalcanal and the naval battles around it there are S. B. Griffith's *The Battle for Guadalcanal* (Philadelphia, 1963), and R. Leckie, *Challenge for the Pacific: Guadalcanal, the Turning Point of the War* (New York, 1965). Even with a good general coverage, some events have received much more treatment than others. R. L. Eichelberger wrote *Our Jungle Road to Tokyo* (New York, 1950), but there has been a great deal more on the central Pacific than on the southwest fighting. Clark Reynolds traced the development of the new naval combination in *The Fast Carriers* (New York, 1968), while J. J. Fahey's *Pacific War Diary, 1942-1945* (Boston, 1963), provides the memoir of a young participant in the war. Japanese views are in T. Hara, F. Saito, and R. Pineau's *Japanese Destroyer Captain* (New York, 1961), and S. Hayashi and A. D. Coox' *Kogun: The Japanese Army in the Pacific War* (Quantico, Va., 1959). F. O. Hough chronicled *The Assault on Peleliu* (Washington, 1950). Leyte Gulf has received a great deal of attention, beginning with J. A. Field's *The Japanese at Leyte Gulf: The Sho Operation* (Princeton, 1947), and G. V. Woodward's *The Battle for Leyte Gulf* (New York, 1947). A later study is S. E. Smith's *The Battle of Leyte Gulf* (New York, 1961).

For the submarine campaign against Japan there is E. L. Beach's *Submarine!* (New York, 1951), and for the Japanese side,

M. Hashimoto's *Sunk: The Story of the Japanese Submarine Fleet, 1941-1945* (New York, 1954). A thorough general treatment is T. Roscoe's *United States Submarine Operations in World War II* (Annapolis, 1949). For the strategic bombing campaign there are W. H. Morrison's *Hellbirds: The Story of the B-29s in Combat* (New York, 1960), and Martin Caidin's *A Torch to the Enemy: The Fire Raid on Tokyo* (New York, 1960). Stories of Japan's air forces are M. Okumiya, J. Horikoshi, with Martin Caidin, *Zero!* (New York, 1956), and S. Sakai with Martin Caidin and F. Saito, *Samurai!* (New York, 1957).

R. Henri wrote *The U. S. Marines on Iwo Jima* (Washington, 1945), and a later treatment is R. Wheeler's *The Bloody Battle for Suribachi* (New York, 1965). For Okinawa and the kamikaze campaign there are R. E. Appleman's *Okinawa: The Last Battle* (Washington, 1948), and M. Ito and R. Pineau's *The End of the Imperial Japanese Navy* (New York, 1962). R. Inoguchi, T. Nakajima, and R. Pineau wrote *The Divine Wind: Japan's Kamikaze Force in World War II* (London, 1959), and the French novelist Jean Larteguy edited *The Sun Goes Down: Last Letters from Japanese Suicide Pilots and Soldiers* (London, 1956).

A great deal has been written on the atomic bombs. The classic account of the bombing itself is John Hersey's *Hiroshima* (New York, 1946). The director of the bomb development project, Leslie R. Groves, wrote *Now It Can Be Told: The Story of the Manhattan Project* (New York, 1962). M. Amrine did *The Great Decision: The Secret History of the Atomic Bomb* (New York, 1959), and W. L. Lawrence wrote *Dawn over Zero: The Story of the Atomic Bomb* (New York, 1947). From the Japanese point of view, which as might be expected is markedly different from the American, there are M. Hachiya's *Hiroshima Diary: The Journal of a Japanese Physician, August 6-September 30, 1945* (Chapel Hill, N. C., 1955), and T. Nagai's *We of Nagasaki: The Story of Survivors in an Atomic Wasteland* (New York, 1951). Herbert Feis ties the bombings and the surrender together in *Japan Subdued: The Atomic Bombs and the End of the War in the Pacific* (Princeton, 1961).

Finally, problems of the end of the war have tended to shade rapidly into problems of the Cold War, and there is a considerable literature on many of the matters merely touched in passing at the close of the war. On Nuremberg and the War Crimes trials a most interesting work is Bradley F. Smith's *Reaching Judgment at Nuremberg* (New York, 1977). J. M. Blum presented a liberal view of what the war did to and for, and what it did not do to and for, the United States in *V was for Victory: Politics and American Culture During World War II* (New York, 1976). For longer views, Andre Fontaine's *History of the Cold War* (New York, 2 vols., 1970) began with the Russian Revolution, and L. J. Halle's *The Cold War as History* (New York, 1967) does an excellent job of putting the postwar upheaval in perspective, as does the previously mentioned G. F. Kennan's *Russia and the West Under Lenin and Stalin* (Boston, 1960).

Index

ABDACOM, East Indies defense and, 204–207
Abyssinia. *See* Ethiopia
Adam, Wilhelm, 61
Air warfare: in Battle of the Atlantic, 128; in Battle of the Bulge, 354–355; in China, 327, 329; and invasion of Norway, 87; and Japanese Pacific offensives, 201, 202–203, 204, 205; at Midway, 215–216. *See also* Battle of Britain; Bombing; *Kamikaze*; Strategic bombing of Europe
Aircraft: German, 351; and interwar military theory, 28; number of German vs. Allied in 1940, 93; sent from Allies to Russia, 234–235. *See also* Air warfare
Aircraft carriers: and Battle of Midway, 215–216; and bombing of Tokyo, 214
Alam el Halfa, Battle of, 220–221
Alamein, El, Battle of, 219, 220, 223
Albania, Italian takeover of, 37
Aleutians, 214, 247, 248
Alexander, Bernard, 176–177, 220
Alexander, Sir Harold, 293, 294, 298, 304, 305–306, 307, 308, 350
Algeria, 224, 226–227
Aliakmon Line, 143–144
Allied conferences: Arcadia, 184; Bolero, 184; Casablanca, 184–185; concerns of, 183–184; and decision to invade France, 223–224; Potsdam, 186, 187; Quadrant, 186; results of, 187; Tehran, 186, 307; Trident, 185–186; Yalta, 186–187
Allied Foreign Ministers, Moscow meeting of, 382
Allies (World War I). *See* World War I
Allies (World War II): and aims of individual states, 175–177; nature of coalition of, 175–183; solidarity against Axis, 351–352; tactical decisions by, 245–247; war aims of, 185; war machine of, 357. *See also* Allied conferences; *and under individual names of*
Alsace-Lorraine, France, 356
American-British-Dutch-Australian Command. *See* ABDACOM
American Nazi Party, 117
Amphibious landings: at Anzio, 303; at Iwo Jima, 367; at Peleliu, 340–341; techniques of, 259–260. *See also* Normandy invasion
Anglo-French relations: and Dunkirk evacuation, 98–99; and fall of France, 101; interwar, 29–32
Anglo-German Naval Agreement (1935), 30, 43
Anti-Communist Pact (1937), 37. *See also* Axis Pact
Anti-Semitism. *See* Jews
Anzio, Italy, landing at, 302, 303

Appeasement policies, 56–57; at Munich, 61, 62
Arcadia Conference (1941), 184, 223
Ardennes Forest, Belgium, 26, 94, 96. *See also* Battle of the Bulge
Arnhem, Battle of, 325–326
Arnim, Jurgen von, 230
Aryan types, in Nazi ideology, 191–192
Atlantic Charter, 120–121
Atomic bomb, American use of, 374–375
Attlee, Clement, 187
Auchinleck, Sir Claude ("Auk, the"), 148, 219, 220
Auschwitz, 198
Australia: Japanese threat to, 213–214; in offensive in Pacific, 255, 334; and South African theater, 222
Austria, 35, 37, 55–57. *See also* Austro-Hungarian Empire
Austro-Hungarian Empire, 21, 33, 55
Axis, 45, 219–220, 292. *See also* Italy; Japan; Nazi Germany; World War II

B-25 bombers, 213
B-29 Superfortress, 366
Badoglio, 295, 296
Bali, Japanese conquest of, 205
Balkans, 140–141, 247, 383; *See also* Greece; Yugoslavia
Baltic republics. *See* Estonia; Latvia; Lithuania
Bataan, 209–211
"Bataan Death March," 211
Battle of the Atlantic, 123–126; British ships lost during, 128; famous battles of, 131–136; U-boats sunk in, 126–127; and U. S. entry into war, 130
Battle of Britain, 105–114, 275; and aircraft production, 110; impact on U. S., 118–119; military effects, 115; Soviet attitude toward, 150
Battle of the Bulge, 352–355
Bavaria: Beer-Hall Putsch, 40; Soviet Government in, 39
Beaverbrook, Lord, 110
Beck, Ludwig, 61
Beer-Hall Putsch, 40
Belgium: German invasion of, 43, 91–98; liberation of, 324–326; and Maginot Line, 25–26; Resistance in, 273
Belgrade, Yugoslavia, bombing of, 143
Belsen, 198
Benedictine Abbey, Cassino, Italy, 301; bombing of, 304
Berlin, Germany: Allied-Soviet race toward, 356, 360–362; bombing of, 112, 113, 280, 282; Russian invasion of, 361–363
Biak (Schouten Islands), 334–335
"Big Four," 382
Big Three. *See* Allied conferences; Churchill; Roosevelt; Stalin

407